Modernisation of the Criminal Justice Chain and the Judicial System

IUS GENTIUM
COMPARATIVE PERSPECTIVES ON LAW AND JUSTICE

VOLUME 50

More information about this series at http://www.springer.com/series/7888

Annie Hondeghem · Xavier Rousseaux
Frédéric Schoenaers
Editors

Modernisation of the Criminal Justice Chain and the Judicial System

New Insights on Trust, Cooperation and Human Capital

This book has been published with the support of the Interuniversity Attraction Poles

Programme initiated by the Belgian Science Policy Office

Springer

Editors
Annie Hondeghem
Public Governance Institute
KU Leuven
Leuven,
Belgium

Frédéric Schoenaers
Centre de Recherche et d'Interventions Sociologiques (CRIS),
University of Liège Liège,
Belgium

Xavier Rousseaux
Centre d'histoire du droit et de la justice (CHDJ)
Université catholique de Louvain (UCL)
Louvain-la-Neuve
Belgium

ISSN 1534-6781 ISSN 2214-9902 (electronic)
Ius Gentium: Comparative Perspectives on Law and Justice
ISBN 978-3-319-25800-3 ISBN 978-3-319-25802-7 (eBook)
DOI 10.1007/978-3-319-25802-7

Library of Congress Control Number: 2015954618

Springer Cham Heidelberg New York Dordrecht London

Printed on acid-free paper

Springer International Publishing AG Switzerland is part of Springer Science+Business Media (www.springer.com)

Foreword

Le magistrat doit être plus qu'un juriste; il doit être capable de se livrer à une approche sociale, humaine et psychologique du judiciaire.

During my career working in the Belgian and international justice systems, a lot of changes have occurred at local, national and European level. While these changes were initially more demand-driven, a slide has taken place towards a more event-driven way of change. It is hard not to speak about a "before Dutroux" and "after Dutroux" era. The same can be said about the "before 9/11" and "after 9/11" period.

As shown by my own experience as a magistrate in the fight against organised crime and terrorism, the three concepts of trust, cooperation and human capital, which are the subjects of this foreword, are unfortunately not always straightforward.

In Belgium, the Dutroux case turned the entire judicial landscape upside down: a new board of Prosecutors General was introduced to deal with national criminal policy; three national prosecutors were tasked with ensuring coordination between the 27 (later 12[1]) judicial districts; and the Federal Prosecutor's Office was established to increase the efficiency of investigations and prosecutions that supersede the authority of local prosecution offices.

Starting in 2001, a fundamental reform of the Belgian police took place whereby the three services (municipal police, gendarmerie and the judicial police) were merged into an integrated police service structured on two levels, federal and local.

Within fifteen years, the entire judicial and police landscape has been reshaped.

At the European level, discussions on the creation of an area of freedom, security and justice in the European Union took off with the European Council in Tampere in 1999. The need to establish a judicial cooperation unit led to the establishment of Eurojust, but the area of freedom, security and justice continues to develop and adapt every day. Old phenomena such as fraud and new phenomena

[1]http://justice.belgium.be/fr/ordre_judiciaire/reforme_justice/arrondissements/ (last visited 27.05.2015).

such as foreign fighters demand an ever-evolving approach from all actors involved in the criminal justice chain. The Internal Security Strategy identifies the main threats the EU is facing and sets out the political implications for Europe.

The role of prosecutor requires us to cooperate with and trust the information we receive from the police, almost blindly. There is a requirement to have accurate information and a need to have the right legal weapons and necessary legal framework in place to bring criminals to justice.

In 1995, I was involved in the first-ever Islamist terrorism trial in Belgium; there was trust and good cooperation between the prosecutors and the police, but the lack of a legal framework on terrorist organisations and the informal cooperation between the intelligence services and the justice department led to rather limited successes. There was trust, cooperation and human capital, but it was not a true success.

Five years later, in 2000, I was involved as a national prosecutor in terrorism and organised crime cases. Things proved to be not yet ideal; in a case against the Animal Liberation Front, suspects were caught in the act, but it still took two weeks to organise coordination between the different police departments.

Nevertheless, there is a simple solution: sit together, ensure common objectives and maintain a multidisciplinary approach. Everyone should be part of these common objectives. This line of thought led to the establishment of Pro-Eurojust in March 2001 with 15 Member States. On 13 June 2001, prosecutors from seven EU countries sat together in the context of Pro-Eurojust and discussed an Al-Qaida network operational in the EU. Reluctance to share information and a lack of trust between the Member States remained and uncooperative behaviour prevailed. However, they did become acquainted with each other, which led to systematically more bilateral exchanges and some tangible results.

During the first six months of Pro-Eurojust and in the aftermath of the Dutroux case, Pro-Eurojust's focus was on trafficking in human beings, illegal immigration and the sexual abuse of children. However, 9/11 happened and the focus shifted towards terrorism.

After 9/11, the added value of having trust, cooperation, coordination, good communication and a good exchange of information was clear. Eurojust saw the light, and everyone agreed on the need for cooperation at European level.

In 2004, the bombings in Madrid reaffirmed the need for coordination and cooperation, and reactivated a new set of changes. One year later, the EU network of counter-terrorism prosecutors was established; today, these prosecutors are obliged to inform Eurojust of all counter-terrorism measures, as stated in Article 12 of the Council Decision on the strengthening of Eurojust (2009/426/JHA)[2] and Article 2 of the Council Decision on the exchange of information and cooperation concerning terrorist offences (2005/671/JHA).[3]

---

[2]Council Decision on the strengthening of Eurojust and amending Council Decision 2002/187/JHA setting up Eurojust with a view to reinforcing the fight against serious crime, OJ 2009 L 138 of 04.06.2009, pp. 14–32.

[3]Council Decision 2005/671/JHA of 20 September 2005 on the exchange of information and cooperation concerning terrorist offences, OJ L 253 of 29.09.2005, pp. 22–24.

To provide an answer for the specific needs in the field of counter-terrorism, I chair the Counter-Terrorism Team (CTT) within Eurojust. The CTT is composed of magistrates, analysts and legal officers who specialise in the topic. The main objectives of the CTT are to establish a centre of expertise on terrorism, to provide support for the annual strategic and tactical meetings of the National Correspondents on Terrorism matters, and to support the publication of several reports on the topic, such as the Terrorism Convictions Monitor, which provides analytical and statistical information and a regular overview of terrorism-related convictions and acquittals throughout the European Union.

Eurojust's goal is to stimulate and improve the coordination of investigations, prosecutions and cooperation between the competent authorities in the Member States in relation to serious cross-border crime. It provides support for the establishment and maintenance of mutual trust and cooperation by enabling interpersonal links between the judicial and the investigative authorities of Member States—and third States—through the use of several coordination tools, such as coordination meetings, coordination centres and joint investigation teams. By doing so, Eurojust assists the development and maintenance of mutual trust, cooperation and human capital.

Several of the authors in this book will discuss the issues related to the situation of the Belgian judicial landscape. Despite the many improvements made during the last twenty years, the underlying system has not always adapted.

How can we ensure trust, cooperation and human capital is in place when dealing with these kinds of events? It is our experience that a multidisciplinary approach is needed to stay on top of things. And more than ever there is a need for the criminal justice approach to be modernised. A proactive and preventative criminal policy is necessary, and that is exactly what Eurojust offers. Criminal justice can only operate when it is built on mutual trust, cooperation and human capital.

June 2015

Michèle Coninsx
President of Eurojust

Contents

Contributors

Joséphine Bastard Centre de Recherche et d'Interventions Sociologiques (CRIS), University of Liège, Liège, Belgium

Emmanuel Berger University of Namur, Namur, Belgium

Mélanie Bost Cegesoma and Royal Military Academy, Brussels, Belgium

Geert Bouckaert Public Governance Institute, KU Leuven, Leuven, Belgium

Bruno Broucker Public Governance Institute, KU Leuven, Leuven, Belgium

Marloes Callens Public Governance Institute, KU Leuven, Leuven, Belgium

Alice Croquet Centre de Recherche et d'Interventions Sociologiques (CRIS), University of Liège, Liège, Belgium

Anne-Cécile Douillet Ceraps, University of Lille 2, Lille, France

Christophe Dubois Centre de Recherche et d'Interventions Sociologiques (CRIS), University of Liège, Liège, Belgium

Jean-Claude Farcy CNRS Retired Researcher, Grenoble, France

Aurore François Laboratoire de recherches historiques, UCL, Louvain-la-Neuve, Belgium

Virginie Gautron Law and Social Change Laboratory, University of Nantes, Nantes, France

Annie Hondeghem Public Governance Institute, KU Leuven, Leuven, Belgium

Neil Hutton Law School, University of Strathclyde, Glasgow, UK

Daniel Kettiger Center of Competence for Public Management, University of Bern, Bern, Switzerland

Andreas Lienhard Center of Competence for Public Management, University of Bern, Bern, Switzerland

Jacques de Maillard Institut Universitaire de France, University of Versailles CESDIP, Versailles, France

Laurence Montel University of Caen, Caen, France

Christian Mouhanna National Center for Scientific Research, Centre de recherches sociologiques sur le droit et les institutions pénales (CESDIP), Paris, France

Françoise Muller Centre d'histoire du droit et de la justice, UCL, Louvain-la-Neuve, Belgium

Enika Ngongo Centre de Recherches en Histoire du Droit et des Institutions, Saint-Louis University, Brussels, Belgium

Stephan Parmentier Leuven Institute of Criminology, KU Leuven, Leuven, Belgium

Kirsten Peters Saint-Louis University, Brussels, Belgium

Bérengère Piret Centre de Recherches en Histoire du Droit et des Institutions, Saint-Louis University, Brussels, Belgium

Xavier Rousseaux Centre d'histoire du droit et de la justice, UCL, Louvain-la-Neuve, Belgium

Frédéric Schoenaers Centre de Recherche et d'Interventions Sociologiques (CRIS), University of Liège, Liège, Belgium

Jolien Vanschoenwinkel Public Governance Institute, KU Leuven, Leuven, Belgium

Derk Venema Radboud University, Nijmegen, The Netherlands

Frédéric Vesentini Institute for Statistics, Evaluation and Foresight, Wallonia, Belgium

Pascaline le Polain de Waroux Centre de Recherches en Histoire du Droit et des Institutions, Saint-Louis University, Brussels, Belgium

Mathieu Zagrodzki UVSQ-CESDIP, Versailles, France

Stavros Zouridis Tilburg University, Tilburg, The Netherlands

Introduction

Research on "Justice in Relation to Society" is an expanding domain but is generally lacking a multidimensional approach in the social sciences. The IUAP (Interuniversity Attraction Poles) project 7/22 "Justice and Populations: The Belgian Experience in International Perspective, 1795–2015" is a multidisciplinary programme funded by BELSPO (Belgian Science Policy Office), studying the relationships between justice and populations. The Belgian experience is systematically examined in its international context, that of an increasingly globalised world. For the domain of justice, especially for the twentieth and twenty-first centuries, this necessitates an innovative approach to demonstrate how "justice" is historically and geographically located in terms of the global/local context, and how the "local" can be expanded to look at inter-, trans- and supranational aspects of justice. This is of particular relevance in Belgium because in several aspects and at different times in its history it has functioned as a "laboratory of Western Culture" (e.g. penal policies; experiences of wartime occupation; and the Belgian colonies).

The originality of this project is to shift from a top-down to an almost bottom-up perspective, which implies a focus on "populations": both judicial actors and social groups, and communities and individuals, in their dealings with justice. From a social science perspective, this means that class, age, gender and ethnic or national differences are taken into account in all research projects. Other central scientific objectives are put forward. Firstly, a shift from more "justice-centred" approaches to the study of interactions between judicial institutions, social groups and individuals. Secondly, a will to deepen diachronic knowledge, comparing past and present societies: identifying both long-term continuities and evolutions and moments of crisis and transformation. Thirdly, an international perspective, discussing issues of justice in a comparative and critical way, comparing national experiences, but also examining transnational transfers and the circulation of concepts, knowledge and practices within the framework of global processes. And fourthly, an interdisciplinary approach as the above objectives imply the involvement of various disciplines: history, legal studies, sociology, criminology, political science, management studies and archival science.

This book is the result of the first international conference of the programme organised on 30–31 October 2014 by the WP1b. in Brussels[4]. The rationale of the conference was to present the first results of a research work package dedicated to analysing the impacts of changes in justice since the 1990s.

Over the past twenty years, the environment of judicial organisations has changed considerably. Justice and trials are the centre of attention in the media, a phenomenon of "judicialisation" of society has appeared and the European States and political spheres have extended their interventions towards the general working of justice. These elements are also reinforced by a general crisis of legitimacy endured by the Belgian judiciary following, among others, the Dutroux affair. More generally, since the 1990s this crisis was also noticeable in most other continental countries in which a deep questioning of the judicial administration model, considered to be too slow, too expensive and blind, appeared. All these elements have contributed to the emergence of new requirements and expectations that are, directly or indirectly, addressed to justice and its actors. We now expect and require that the various courts improve their performance with regard to their efficacy and efficiency, the quality of their decision-making process, their accessibility and their capacity to function with "external" partners (networking). In addition, justice also has to face another requirement: the obligation to justify its capability to improve its performances. Justice is now placed under a stronger control (official and unofficial) from different spheres (media, politics and society).

These elements constituted and demanded a fundamental change process. Indeed, the literature agrees that, historically, these specific public institutions have always been protected against management or organisational concerns. Justice has always been able to preserve an autonomous and independent organisational model that almost no one dared to question. What is the situation today? Now the central question concerns the impacts of the new requirements on the everyday lives of the jurisdictions. As a starting hypothesis, we can assume that expected changes and their implementation among the judiciary have deep impacts with regard to the structures of the jurisdictions, the organisation of the professions, the nature of the link with stakeholders and the trust present among them.

From the Middle Ages to the 1990s, judges and public prosecutors were confined to two main organisational and management models. We can identify the first organisational period which extends from the Middle Ages until approximately the end of the eighteenth century. During these years, judges were the "instruments" of the aristocracy and/or monarchy and were required to serve them. The second period starts at the beginning of the nineteenth century with the diffusion of Montesquieu's work about the separation of powers. In its pure configuration, the

[4]This conference concerned more specifically work package 1b "The State Justice System: Functioning, Reform, Actors" and had been organised by five partners (KU Leuven, Université catholique de Louvain, Université de Liège, Université de Namur, Centre de recherches sociologiques sur le droit et les institutions pénales (Cesdip-CNRS). All the contributions to this book were written in the context of the Interuniversity Attraction Pole P7/22 "Justice & Populations: The Belgian Experience in International Perspective, 1795–2015" (BeJust 2.0).

second period ended in the middle of the 1990s. Nevertheless, during this long period, the judiciary has been progressively organised, won autonomy from the State and the general organisation of the legal institutions gradually adopted an "individualising autonomous bureaucracy". Globally, the same observations can be made regarding the other actors of the penal chain: police departments and jails.

In our opinion, the end of the twentieth century marks an essential turning point for courts and other judicial bodies. They entered a new organisational era in which the new dominating paradigm offers characteristics not observed until now. Now placed under pressure, the judicial institutions are changing and it seems that the new paradigm has specificities such as the generalisation of collegiality between magistrates (collectivisation of the working relationships), the development of partnerships with external actors (redefinition of the place of jurisdictions in the public space) and the search for high organisational performances.

The book has three parts, which all deal with the modernisation of the judicial system in general and the criminal justice chain in detail.

Part I gives a reflection on the reforms which have been introduced in four countries: Belgium, the Netherlands, France and Switzerland.

Annie Hondeghem and Bruno Broucker give an overview of the reforms in Belgium which have been proposed from the nineties until today (Chap. 1). Their conclusion is that most of the reforms deal with the same topics: scale enlargement, more management autonomy and digitalisation. All the reforms aim to increase the efficiency of the judicial system. However, implementation of the reforms takes a long time and results are limited so far.

Increasing productivity was also the purpose of the reform in France as described by Christian Mouhanna and Frédéric Vesentini (Chap. 2). The introduction of the penal response rate as a central measurement of the activity of the Public Prosecutor's Office aimed to reduce the number of cases dropped. A historical analysis of the data (1999–2010) revealed however that the number of cases dropped did not really decrease, but that new labels were introduced in order to improve the results of the Public Prosecutor's Office activities.

A historical approach is also taken in the chapter by Virginie Gautron, who analysed the handling of misdemeanours in five French courts since the 2000s (Chap. 3). She found that judges reacted to the directives to speed up the resolution of criminal cases in different ways. An obsession with quantity however tended to become more important than finding the most appropriate punishment, and while the new practices might have increased productivity, they have not increased the speed of justice.

Daniel Kettinger and Andreas Lienhard deal with the new position of the Public Prosecution Service in the Swiss criminal justice chain since 2011 (Chap. 4). By abolishing the position of the examining magistrates, public prosecutors are now in charge of the entire preliminary proceedings process. This made an important change in the cooperation between the Public Prosecution Services and the police necessary. According to the authors, it seems that the reform has so far been a success.

Anne-Cécile Douillet, Jacques de Maillard and Mathieu Zagrodzki examine the effect of the increasing use of quantitative indicators on the national police in France (Chap. 5). On the one hand, they find an increased centralisation at all levels of the police. On the other hand, they also find adjustment, avoidance and even cheating strategies used to provide the figures, because staff do not always see the purpose of producing copious amounts of data. This implies that the effects of centralisation are counterbalanced by centrifugal practices.

Stavros Zouridis analyses the evolution of the criminal justice system in the Netherlands from a strategy–organisation configuration perspective (Chap. 6). As a response to a changing environment, the criminal justice system has adopted its organisational strategy. Zouridis distinguishes four strategies: incident-driven legalism, policy-driven managerialism, information-driven risk management and collaborative law enforcement. These strategies are illustrated by specific reforms in the management of the judicial organisations.

Part II deals with trust and cooperation in the criminal justice chain and the judicial system. Both have a huge impact on the performance of the judicial organisations.

Jolien Vanschoenwinkel and Annie Hondeghem start with an analysis of the concepts of trust and distrust, with an application to the criminal justice chain (Chap. 7). Based on a literature review, they consider both as separate concepts. In the empirical research, based on interviews with public prosecutors, examining magistrates and police staff in one judicial district in Belgium, they check the concepts of trust and distrust. They develop their own definition, which is adapted to the environment of the criminal justice organisations.

Marloes Callens, Geert Bouckaert and Stephan Parmentier explore the organisational trust phenomenon in a specific case study of the Flemish juvenile Public Prosecutor's Office and the juvenile court (Chap. 8). They find that flexibility, loyalty, openness and workload serve as important bases to determine trustworthiness. They also find evidence for an ingroup/outgroup culture between the juvenile Prosecutor's Office and the juvenile court.

Alice Croquet and Frédéric Schoenaers analyse the decision-making process around the Area Security Plans in Belgium from a sociology of organised action perspective (Chap. 9). This decision-making process takes the form of successive informal dialogue steps, culminating in the ratification of the plan in the Area Security Council. Based on the concept of "apparent consensus", they find evidence of the plural nature of the collective decision-making. The local police however seem to have a determining role in the final version of the plan.

Neil Hutton analyses the sentencing decision-making process (Chap. 10). He states that this decision-making should not be understood simply as decisions by individual judges, but as a form of collective action involving the work of other human and non-human actors. While some of the sentencing work is visible through documents produced by the different actors involved in the case, much sentencing work remains invisible, and is based on the judgement of professionals. Trust plays an important role here.

Joséphine Bastard and Christophe Dubois analyse the decision-making process of the Belgian Sentence Implementation Courts which are responsible for the decisions about early release from prisons (Chap. 11). Different actors play a role in this process, which makes it a collective action. The authors underline the role of documents and "sense-making" in the decision-making process. In making sense of various documents, the actors are progressively framing the decision of the court.

Part III deals with the human capital of the judiciary from a historical perspective. The Belgian magistrates as socio-professional group are studied in different periods. Xavier Rousseaux gives an introduction to this part in Chap. 12.

The following chapters introduce a few in-depth analyses of exploitable periods or topics through sources and software gathered. Three investigations of international periods of Belgian magistracy were made possible by integration of the research data into the software.

The tool's future possibilities and developments are detailed in Chap. 13. Aurore François and Françoise Muller introduce the research axes that have been selected for this project. On the one hand, the advantage of Web-based database technologies is to facilitate access to existing public data, still long and difficult to manipulate. Magistrates' identity data such as age, gender, place and date of birth and death enable one to reconstruct close groups and generations. The reconstruction of magistrates' careers goes hand in hand with the reconstruction of the institutions in which they served. This sheds light on individual paths and changing institutions. Lastly, intellectual works are another type of public data, which can be easily accessed and put in context by linking with the database. On the other hand, the multiplication of digital information systems has bolstered privacy protection and even created a digital "right to oblivion". Therefore, the database designers have established a distinction between the data necessary for free and consistent research and the data available to the "general public". As required by research and laid down by the Commission for the Protection of Privacy, the most sensitive personal data are collected and structured, but will not be published on paper or through digital channels. This information will only be used as quantitative or anonymised data.

In Chap. 14, Emmanuel Berger's attention has been drawn to Belgian magistracy's training. In a period when Belgian judicial authorities made a break with the jurisdiction map drawn up at the time of the annexation to revolutionary France, the study of the relations between "Belgian" and French magistrates holding positions as prosecutors or judges highlights the tensions that emerged in judicial districts, which were a new concept in the early nineteenth century.

King Leopold II's colonisation undertaking in Africa was a second factor for the development of a "Belgian" magistracy, which was often left in the background, as described by Laurence Montel, Enika Ngongo, Bérengère Piret and Pascaline Le Polain in Chap. 15. Alongside other European magistrates, Belgian magistrates established a colonial judicial system that was based on the metropolitan judicial system and developed a specific culture that—in turn—influenced metropolitan magistracy.

The tensions magistracy experienced over the course of an unprecedented military and civil occupation in the First World War (1914–1918) enable a study of the relations between law and power. This is done by Mélanie Bost and Kirsten Peters in Chap. 16. The first occupation, which was the first of its kind in twentieth-century Europe, laid the basis for a *modus vivendi* between the occupied magistrates and the occupying authorities. The occupation is a laboratory of the relations between law and force. By contrast, the second occupation (1940–1944), which was also experienced by several European magistracies, confronted magistrates with a dictatorial regime. Yet, the corporative cohesion of Belgian magistracy globally enabled it to better resist the occupant's will to interfere in its way of working.

The last chapter (Chap. 17) presents reflexions about the database and the prosopographical enterprise through foreign eyes: those of a French social historian of justice (Jean-Claude Farcy) and of a Dutch legal philosopher (Derk Venema).

In a context of structural constraints and human agency, the modernisation of the criminal justice chain is a complex result of past choices and present political decisions. What the book will demonstrate is that an interdisciplinary social science approach helps to understand, and maybe to adjust, any attempt to produce an efficient modernisation of the criminal justice chain in a complex democratic society.

Annie Hondeghem
Xavier Rousseaux
Frédéric Schoenaers

Part I
Justice Reforms in Continental Europe

Chapter 1
From Octopus to the Reorganisation of the Judicial Landscape in Belgium

Annie Hondeghem and Bruno Broucker

1.1 Introduction

On 9th August 1996, a fourteen year old girl was kidnapped in Bertrix, Belgium. Following testimonies, Marc Dutroux, his wife and a collaborator were arrested. On 15th August 1996, the police found two girls alive in a cage in Dutroux's house (Fijnaut 2001; Gelders and Van de Walle 2003). A few weeks later, four other girls, kidnapped in the years before, were found buried at Dutroux's house. This shocked the country enormously, especially when it became clear that Dutroux had been convicted before as a sexual offender and that the police had suspected him in this case but failed to find the girls in an earlier search (Gelders and Van de Walle 2003). The conviction grew that some of the girls could have been rescued if the police and the magistrates would have collaborated properly. On 22nd April 1998, the unimaginable happened when Dutroux escaped from the courthouse in Neufchâteau due to the inattentiveness of a local police officer. Dutroux was captured that same day, but both the Minister of Justice and the Minister of Internal Affairs had no other option but to hand in their letters of resignation to the King. A few days later, the Chief Commander of the State Police was forced to resign as well (Hondeghem et al. 2010; Fijnaut 2001).

It is this 'Dutroux-case' that triggered political debates regarding failures in the Belgian criminal justice system. Since then, the Belgian Justice System has gone through an intense period of reforms (Daems et al. 2013). In this chapter, we give an overview of the main reform efforts and discuss at length the current reform which was started by the former government. For every reform, we discuss objectives, general principles and results. We end with some concluding remarks, and a vision for the future.

A. Hondeghem (✉) · B. Broucker
Public Governance Institute, KU Leuven, Leuven, Belgium
e-mail: annie.hondeghem@soc.kuleuven.be

A. Hondeghem et al. (eds.), *Modernisation of the Criminal Justice Chain and the Judicial System*, Ius Gentium: Comparative Perspectives on Law and Justice 50, DOI 10.1007/978-3-319-25802-7_1

1.2 Historical Overview of Reforms in the Belgian Judicial System

In this overview, three main reforms are discussed: the Octopus reform, the Themis plan and the New judicial landscape. Despite the fact that only the first resulted in concrete actions, all three were valuable for agenda-setting and attitude building in favour of reforms.

1.2.1 Octopus Reform

1.2.1.1 Objectives

Urged by the Dutroux-case, eight major political parties started in May 1998 the process of negotiating a grand reform plan aimed at radically reforming the Belgian criminal justice system (Daems et al. 2013). By the end of that year they achieved a consensus regarding what was called the 'Octopus reform' (Van Daele 2010), introduced to tackle the discontent towards the judicial system and to increase its efficiency (Gelders and Van de Walle 2003).

1.2.1.2 General Principles

The Octopus Reform had two major reform packages: one for the police system and one for the judicial system. Regarding the former, the integration of three police forces (the gendarmerie, the judicial police and the local police) into two aimed to achieve a police force at the local level and one at the federal level (Fijnaut 2001; Daems et al. 2013).

Within the judiciary, three general lines of reform were introduced (Hondeghem et al. 2010): (1) the Public Prosecution; (2) the judicial organisation; (3) the Higher Council for Justice. Regarding the reform of the Public Prosecution, the following principles were proposed (Depré et al. 2010; Fijnaut 2001; Parmentier et al. 2000):

- The creation of a federal Public Prosecutor's Office for cases that are better dealt with at a central level (for issues of international interests);
- The further development of the Board of Prosecutors-General and redefinition of its role;
- The reinforcement of the prosecution offices at district level, following the principles of horizontal integration: the integration of the local Prosecution Offices in Social and Labour matters with the Public Prosecutor's Office;
- The integral treatment of files at courts of First and Second Instance (principle of vertical integration).

Regarding the judicial organisation, 'horizontal mobility' would be introduced; local magistrates, including labour auditors, would gain competencies in order to exercise the criminal procedure before courts in all judicial districts within the jurisdiction of the Court of Appeal (Parmentier et al. 2000). The Octopus agreement also questioned the actual size of the judicial districts, and suggested that the number of districts should decrease by scale enlargement (Depré et al. 2010). Other elements of reforms were the reinforcement of the legal position of victims in criminal procedures and the introduction of hearing and information rights for certain types of victims in the post-sentencing phase (Daems et al. 2013).

Finally, the Higher Council for Justice was created in 1999, to play a key role in the appointment of judges and public prosecutors and to deal with complaints against the judiciary.

1.2.1.3 Results

Despite criticism on the police reform in terms of a lack of clarity in task division, the multiplication and complexity of advisory boards, and the way the reform has been evaluated, it seems that it has, in general terms, been quite successful (Daems et al. 2013). Regarding the judicial system, mixed results can be presented: the Higher Council for Justice has been installed, the Public Prosecution to some extent has been reformed (with the creation of the Board of Prosecutors-General), but the judicial system in itself remained quite similar. The scale of the judicial districts was untouched and the mobility of magistrates was absent, although this proved crucial for the system's efficiency. Moreover, the Octopus reform had been developed top down, with uncertainty regarding the availability of necessary budgets and capacities to allow such reform (Depré et al. 2010).

1.2.2 *Themis Plan*

1.2.2.1 Objectives

In 2005, the Minister of Justice introduced a new reform plan. This 'Themis'-plan aimed to reform the functioning of the judicial power (Depré et al. 2010). Its main objective was to reduce the inefficiency, caused by the centralisation of resources at the Department of Justice and a too large fragmentation of judicial entities. Concretely, the Themis-plan wanted to establish the decentralisation of management to the level of the districts and of the Courts of Appeal (Depré et al. 2010).

1.2.2.2 General Principles

It was suggested to consign the management of the resources of the Courts and Public Prosecutor's Offices to a 'judicial administrator', who would support the magistrates with the management of the resources (personnel and others) (Plessers et al. 2008). More concretely, the plan advocated installing a management committee *at the level of the Court of Appeal* ('*ressort*') to take all strategic and operational decisions. That structure would be an integrated one, containing both the public prosecution and the courts. Every '*ressort*' would also contain a 'management bureau' consisting of two managers and a director (Depré et al. 2010). The director would be present at both the management bureau and the management committee to enhance communication between both, to ensure the realisation of the strategic goals decided by the committee, and to take care of daily management.

At the level of the districts, a 'district-level board' would be installed. That board would contain the different heads of the Courts, representatives of Police Courts and Peace Courts, and the heads of Public Prosecution Offices. It would decide upon strategic and operational goals and would generate a district level management committee, consisting of a member of the courts, a member of the Public Prosecution and a manager. The latter would be the director of the management bureau of the ressort (Depré et al. 2010).

When ready, the plan was presented to the different judicial organisations for advice, but was partly rejected: especially the dyad structure of Courts and Public Prosecution Office was found problematic and the fact that the director of the management bureau did not have to be a magistrate was also found unacceptable. Therefore, the Themis-plan was adjusted in March 2006 (the so-called Themis II): the division of management at the level of Courts of Appeal and at the level of districts remained. The dyad system was abolished resulting in a separate management for Courts and Public Prosecution, with their respective management committee (Depré et al. 2010).

1.2.2.3 Results

Themis was the first reform project to introduce explicitly autonomy and responsibilities within the judicial system, together with the idea of introducing external managers into the system. The plan also wanted to create a "Modernisation Unit" at the Federal Administration to support the implementation of the plan. In Themis II this unit was replaced by the "Commission of Modernisation". Themis did not succeed in abolishing the number of entities. In the reform plans the entities remained underneath a new umbrella layer covering the district level, with limited responsibilities. The real managerial power was given to the level of the Courts of Appeal, while the managers weren't really made accountable for their efforts. Though Themis II tried to create a consensus by addressing the criticism on Themis I, it was never introduced within the Belgian Justice System (Depré et al. 2009).

1.2.3 A New Judicial Landscape

1.2.3.1 Objectives

In 2009, given the unrealised objectives of the former reform projects, the Minister of Justice, Stefaan De Clerck,[1] took the initiative for a new plan. The newly installed government wanted to build a judicial system that would be easily accessible, affordable and feasible (De Clerck and Dupré 2010). Therefore, the government started to discuss how the available resources could be invested more efficiently. This resulted in a plan wherein the creation of a 'new judicial landscape' was at the centre. The objectives can be summarised as follows:

- More efficiency and effectiveness by district scale enlargement: resources would be decentralised to provide lower entities with more managerial autonomy.
- Specialisation: bigger geographical entities to create, where necessary, specialised entities.
- Increased mobility for magistrates and judges, and improved management to tackle the slowness of judicial procedures.
- Better service delivery and increased proximity for citizens through ameliorated communication whilst maintaining the locality of Courts of First Instance.
- Increasing the divide of powers: by decentralising resources, the influence of the Minister of Justice on the judicial power is reduced to the negotiation of management contracts.

1.2.3.2 General Principles

The 2010 reform as initiated by the Minister of Justice contained four major principles (De Clerck and Dupré 2010). First, an integration of the jurisdiction of first instance: the Courts of First Instance, of Commerce, of Labour, of Police and the Peace Courts would be integrated into one court, internally divided into different sections with its own specificity. Rare cases would be integrated into specialised courts responsible for several districts or at the level of the Court of Appeal. Similarly, the same integration was proposed for the public prosecution at the level of the Public Prosecutor's Office and the Labour Prosecution. This integration would result in 16 districts instead of 27, combined with the internal and external mobility of magistrates, lawyers and personnel. The managerial power of the Court and Public Prosecution Office would remain in the hands of a '*corps chief*',[2] a magistrate, who, over time, would become a real manager. This manager would be supported by a managerial committee under the charge of a 'management director' (De Clerck and Dupré 2010).

[1]De Clerck came into office after the resignation of minister Vandeurzen who had started the reform project.

[2]This is the translation of 'korpschef'.

Second, the creation of a “Board for the Courts”, alike to the Board for the Public Prosecution which already exists since the nineties, representing the Public Prosecution as a whole and developing a coherent policy for the Public Prosecution. The reform plan included a similar Board for the Courts, though it was recognised that the specificities of the courts should be taken into account. General principles for its installation would be: a general assembly with the Presidents of the Courts of Appeal and five members of the Courts of First Instance (De Clerck and Dupré 2010).

Third, the reform plan sought a way to enable more managerial autonomy at the decentralised level. More resources would be provided to the individual entities and their managerial board and to a new central institution: ‘the Shared Board of Management’, constituted of the Minister of Justice, representatives of the Department of Justice, the Board for the Public Prosecution and the Board for the Courts. This Shared Board would have the responsibilities for the tasks which have to be taken care of on a common ground, such as financial resources, personnel, and so on. The general idea was that the Minister of Justice would negotiate the budget for the Shared Board, for the Board of the Public Prosecution and for the Board of the Magistrates. In a second stage, the lower entities would receive a budget in accordance to their managerial contract (De Clerck and Dupré 2010).

Fourth, the judicial institutions would be rationalised. During the last decades several new institutions had been introduced, such as the Higher Council for Justice, the Commission of Modernisation, the Advice board for Magistrates, … but some of them have comparable responsibilities. Therefore, their position, role and competences would be reviewed (De Clerck and Dupré 2010).

1.2.3.3 Results

The ‘New Judicial Landscape’ was not implemented as such. A discussion took place in a parliamentary commission (called Atomium because of the involvement of 9 political parties, both from the majority and from the opposition) in the fall of 2009, but it was clear that there was significant opposition against the plan. The main critique dealt with the integration of the Labour Courts and the Peace Courts into an integrated Court of First Instance. Politicians had been approached by those working in these courts to plead against the integration.

The discussion was removed from the parliament and taken over by the government. In April 2010, a compromise was approved by the government, but as the government fell in the same month, it was never implemented.

1.3 The Judicial Reform (2014-)

It is clear that the reform of the judiciary has been on the agenda for a long time, but so far implementation has been lacking, not because of an unclear problem analysis or bad proposals, but because of the complex political decision making in the area of justice and the lack of continuity in reform plans due to the frequent succession of ministers

On December 6th 2011, after 540 days of negotiations, the new Di Rupo government was installed, with Annemie Turtelboom as Minister of Justice. The government declaration contained the following paragraph: "The number of judicial districts will be reduced to half of them at least, however with respect of the institutional agreement on the judicial district of Brussels and with respect of the current number of local courtrooms[3]" (Government declaration, December 1st 2011, p. 138). The time had come for reform.

In April 2012 the main headlines of the reform were approved by the government, which resulted in three legislative proposals: one for the scale enlargement, one for the mobility of magistrates, and one for the managerial autonomy. The first two proposals resulted in the Law of December 1st 2013: "Law with regard to the reform of the judicial districts and changes in the judicial procedure law with a view on improving the mobility of the members of the judiciary". On February 18th 2014, the second law was approved: "Law with regard to the implementation of managerial autonomy in the judiciary".[4]

The judicial reform specifically aimed at efficiency increase, specialisation improvement and the enhancement of autonomy of the judiciary. This should lead to better service delivery, by reducing backlog and accelerating judicial decisions (Turtelboom 2012). The proximity of justice for citizens was also an explicit objective, confirmed by respecting the current number of local courtrooms in combination with scale enlargement.

Hereunder the objectives, the content and the challenges for the three main aspects of the reform are discussed.

1.3.1 Scale Enlargement

The division in 27 judicial districts, that dated from the French period, was the basic structure for the Public Prosecutor's Office and for the Courts of First Instance. However, other divisions were in existence for the Police Courts (34), the Labour Courts (21), the Courts of Commerce (23), and the Courts of Assise (11). The appeal processes (Court of Appeal, Labour Tribunal) were organised at the ressort level (5 in total), while the Court of Cassation is the sole organisation responsible for the whole country. Finally, the Peace Courts are organised at the canton level, and are 187 in total. The huge fragmentation of the judicial

[3]This is the translation for zittingsplaats.

[4]These are translations from Dutch: "Wet tot hervorming van de gerechtelijke arrondissementen en tot wijziging van het gerechtelijk wetboek met het oog op een grotere mobiliteit van de leden van de rechterlijke orde" (1 december 2013) (BS. 10.12.2013) and "Wet betreffende de invoering van een verzelfstandigd beheer voor de rechterlijke organisatie" (18 februari 2014) (BS. 04.03.2014).

Fig. 1.1 New judicial map. *Source* http://justitie.belgium.be/nl/rechterlijke_orde/hervormingjustitie/

organisation is obvious: over 300 judicial organisations are responsible for justice. In comparison, the Netherlands contain around 50 courthouses (Depré et al. 2010).

As a result of the Law of 1st December 2013 the number of judicial districts is reduced from 27 to 12. Eight of them cover the provinces. Because of the language issue, the judicial district of Brussels is reserved (with separate courts for the two language groups and a separate Public Prosecutor's Office for Halle-Vilvoorde) (Turtelboom 2012). This also implies that the Leuven judicial district remains separate. Because of the German community, a separate judicial district is created for Eupen, resulting in the fact that the province of Luik is not totally covering its judicial district. Above a picture of the new judicial map is provided (Fig. 1.1).

At first sight, there is fragmentation reduction within the judicial landscape, which should lead to more efficiency in resource management (HR and other).

However, some remarks have to be made:

- Henegouwen is one judicial district at the level of the court, but two at the level of the Public Prosecutor's Office, because otherwise, the judicial district would be the same as the ressort, which could lead to insufficient checks and balances[5];

[5]There is also an argument that this decision is due to political matters.

Table 1.1 New judicial landscape, number of organisations

	Courts	Public prosecution
Federal	Court of Cassation (1)	Prosecutor-general at the Court of Cassation (1) Federal Prosecutor (1)
Ressort	Court of Appeal (5) Labour Tribunal (5) Labour Court (9) Court of Commerce (9)	Prosecution-general (5) Prosecution-general for Labour Legislation (8)
District	Courts of First Instance (13) Police Courts (15)	Public Prosecutor's Office (14) Public Prosecutor for Labour (9)
Canton	Peace Courts (187)	

Source http://justitie.belgium.be/nl/rechterlijke_orde/hervorming_justitie/nieuws/news_pers_2014-04-01.jsp
PS. The Court of Assise is organised at the provincial level; there are 11 of them

- The division in 12 judicial districts is true for the Courts of First Instance, the Police Courts and the Public Prosecutor's Offices, but for the Labour Courts and the Courts of Commerce the division in ressorts (level of Courts of Appeal) is used, with again a separate regulation for Brussels/Leuven and Luik/Eupen;
- The Peace Courts are still organised at the level of the canton; which leads to 187 entities;
- The former courts are still in existence, but as divisions of the new courts; a separate Royal Decree[6] has been approved for this; 118 divisions were created in total: 7 for the Labour Tribunals, 31 for the Labour Courts, 24 for the Courts of Commerce, 23 for the Courts of First Instance, and 33 for the Police Courts.

In sum, the complexity of the judicial landscape remains, leading to the question whether the scale enlargement will have the expected effects such as efficiency increase and the improvement of specialisation?

In Table 1.1 we give an overview of the new judicial landscape.

It is clear that in the implementation of the judicial landscape, some choices have been made.

First, the scale of the Courts of First Instance differs from that of the Labour Courts and the Courts of Commerce as they are organised respectively on the district and on the ressort level. As a result, the idea of an integrated court, central in former reform ideas, has been left out. This is due to the resistance among the Labour Courts to be integrated into the Courts of First Instance. The argument put forward is specialisation, but it cannot be denied that the Labour Courts have more personnel, which means that an integration would lead to personnel reduction.

Second, the principle of territoriality has been maintained. Courts have judicial power over a specific territory. In the future this could be nuanced since the

[6]Royal Decree of March 14th 2014 regarding the division of the Labour tribunals, the Courts of first instance, the Labour courts, the Courts of commerce, and the Police courts.

principle of case division[7] has also been approved, implying that cases could be spread among the courts based on their specialisation opposed to territory. One could for example decide to handle all environment cases in a specialised court. This has to be approved in a regulation regarding case division.

Third, the courts as they existed before the reform, are kept as a division of the new court. For reasons of proximity for citizens, the distance to the court may not to be too big. Probably, this choice can also be explained as a strategy to diminish resistance against the reform as people can more or less continue to work at the same location.

Whether the new structure will be successful, is, at this stage, difficult to determine, as it will depend on some crucial factors, such as leadership where the new 'corps chiefs' have been appointed and are responsible to build this new organisational landscape. They will have to be able to steer at a distance because certain divisions will have a degree of autonomy. The divisions are led by the former 'corps chiefs', who now have the statute of division head. A good understanding between the new 'corps chief' and the division heads will thus be an important factor of success.

1.3.2 Mobility

Since many courts have a small number of staff, frequently resulting into staff problems, increasing staff mobility has been introduced as a solution. By enhancing mobility of judicial staff and magistrates the efficiency of personnel planning can be increased. Indeed, mobility can be a solution in cases of long term absence due to illness, pregnancy, or in case of structural staff problems (Turtelboom 2012).

Mobility will be organised as follows (Turtelboom 2012): Peace Judges will be appointed at the district level instead of the canton level. The same goes for judicial staff (clerks, administrative staff, secretaries of the Public Prosecutor's Offices, …), while magistrates will be appointed at the ressort level instead of having a permanent appointment in a district, which previously had meant the need for a vacancy in another district before mobility could take place. Finally, the supplementary magistrates[8] will be integrated in the formal personnel plan.

The enhancement of mobility is an important leverage for a more flexible personnel planning. Again, the future will demonstrate whether this will be realised: in the Law of 18th February 2014, a rule is included that magistrates can appeal against their nomination in another than their current district. The same holds for judicial staff. This seems to be a weakening of the mobility principle already. In other words: change in attitude and culture will be a crucial condition for success.

---

[7]This is the translation of zaakverdeling.

[8]This is the translation of 'toegevoegde rechters'.

As a result of ageing, Justice will need a more flexible personnel planning. Figures show that 50 % of the 2500 magistrates are older than 50 years, 36 % is older than 55 years and 18 % is older than 60 years (Geens 2015). This will lead to a huge loss of expertise. In addition, due to savings only a limited number of magistrates will be replaced. A possible solution is the prolongation of the retirement age, but although some magistrates might welcome this, others will still prefer to retire earlier.

1.3.3 Management

The call for more management autonomy in the judiciary system is not new. The first ideas were formulated in the Themis-plan (Plessers et al. 2008), but lacked implementation (cf. supra). It was the Octopus agreement that made it possible to appoint the 'corps chiefs' in a mandate system, thereby recognising their managerial responsibility, apart from their judicial duty (Depré and Hondeghem 2011, p. 24).

Important is that, with regard to autonomisation, a macro-, meso- and micro-level must be distinguished (Depré and Hondeghem 2011, p. 17–23). At the macro-level, autonomy deals with the relationship between the executive and the judicial powers. In most countries, the Ministries of Justice, headed by the Minister of Justice, are responsible for management in the judiciary. In such a structure, resources are managed centrally and little autonomy is given to the judicial organisations. This results in efficiency loss, bureaucratic heaviness and buck passing. In a system of autonomisation, the judicial branch itself is responsible for resource management. At the micro-level, autonomisation delegates management responsibility to the lowest level of the judiciary. The 'corps chief', or in the case of collegial governance, a committee is responsible for management. At the meso-level, an intermediate structure is created shifting some management responsibilities to a higher level (e.g. the ressort level) because of scale or specialisation advantages.

The current reform primarily deals with autonomisation at the macro-level. A College was installed for the courts as well as for the public prosecution, with the following competences[9]:

- To obtain accessible, independent, timely and quality justice through the organisation of communication, knowledge management, quality management, work processes, informatisation, strategic personnel policy, statistics, workload measurement and workload division;
- To support the management of the judicial organisations.

The Colleges have the power to give guidelines and advice to the management committees of the judicial organisations (cf. infra), which implies that they can abolish decisions of the judicial organisations, with respect of appeal procedures.

[9]Law of February 18th 2014: "Law with regard to the implementation of management autonomy in the judiciary".
For the public prosecution another competence was added: to give support to the implementation of the criminal justice policy determined by the College of Prosecutors-General.

The Colleges contain 10 members, partly designated, partly elected; there is language parity, and the members have a mandate of 5 years. The president's term is 2.5 years. The Colleges are supported by an administration, responsible for the support of the College, but also of the management committees in the judicial organisations. Also, they can organise internal audits. The administration is led by a director with a 5-year mandate.

The objective of the autonomisation at the macro-level is to transfer management competences from the Federal Justice Department to the judicial branch. A dual structure has been chosen, meaning that there are separate Colleges for the courts and for the public prosecution. The lack of duality was an important critique of the Themis project (cf. supra). Management issues which are common to the courts and to the public prosecution, will be dealt with by both Colleges in common, or by the Colleges in common with the Federal Public Service Justice.

A three years management agreement on objectives and resources will be made between the Minister of Justice and the Colleges. The Minister can provide a financial envelope for the expenses of the Colleges, or the needs of the judicial organisations. The new system of management agreements is not operational yet as a Royal Decree has to be approved first.

This implies that in a transition phase the Federal Department of Justice remains responsible for management in the judiciary service. The management committee of the Federal Department has been extended to two magistrates, who will assist the Director-General of the judiciary system. We can expect that in the near future an important discussion will take place on when and which competences will be transferred to the Colleges.

With regard to the autonomisation at the micro-level, less evolution has taken place. The law defines the structures which will be responsible for management; these are the management committees presided by the 'corps chief'. The management committee of the courts consist of: the president, the division heads and the chief clerk; in case there are no divisions, two judges are added. In the Public Prosecution Offices, the management committee consists of the Public Prosecutor, the division Public Prosecutors and the chief secretary. It is striking that no specialist in management is part of the management committees, as it is, for example, the case in the Netherlands with the management director.[10] This was the case in former reform proposals (see Sect. 1.2). The chief clerk and chief secretary lack, on average, a background in management as they are mostly oriented towards judicial issues. The non-integration of a specialist in management in the management committee can be considered a missed opportunity since the burden will rest with the 'corps chief'.

In order to manage the judicial organisation, the management committee has to make up a management plan.[11] Details are given in the law of 18th February 2014:

[10]This is the translation of 'directeur bedrijfsvoering'.

[11]This is the translation of 'beheersplan'.

"The management plan includes the description of the planned activities of the judicial organisation in the next three years and the resources which are necessary for these activities. Personnel resources are determined based on the results of a regularly and uniformly performed workload measurement based on national norms (…), eventually complemented with other objective criteria" (BS 04.03.2014, p 18206). However this workload measurement is still not finalised, although it was started a long time ago (Depré et al. 2007). As a result the personnel resources for the judicial organisations, as determined in the law of 1st December 2013, are based on the old system of personnel planning.[12]

The autonomisation at the micro-level thus starts with some difficulties. First, there is little local management capacity. Second, the instruments to manage an efficient and effective system are still missing. It is clear that priority has been given to the autonomisation at the macro-level by installing the Colleges and transferring competences from the Federal Public Service of Justice to the Colleges. However, for the last aspect, there is still a long way to go. In a transition phase, the management committee of the Federal Public Service Justice has been extended with two magistrates, but most of the management is still performed by the executive branch. Only after a transition phase will the articles in the law which refer to the real management competences of the Colleges, come into effect. When this will be the case, is still an open question. The new management model will have to prove its strengths. Therefore, it is positive that the new law includes an evaluation of the model every two years.

1.4 What Will the Future Bring?

Reforms have a long history in Belgium, but under the former government implementation has started. Some issues that would cause too much resistance have been postponed or removed. First, the integrated court has been replaced by three separate courts (First Instance, Labour, Commerce). Second, the Peace Courts stayed untouched so far as they are organised at the canton level.

In the meantime a new government (Michel) has been installed since 11 October 2014. The Minister of Justice is Koen Geens, who was the Minister of Finance in the former government. He launched a new 'plan for justice' in the spring of 2015. This plan is very wide and consists of 4 main chapters (Geens 2015). The first chapter summarises some important data, such as output, personnel, infrastructure and finance. The second chapter deals with the improvement of procedures in the judiciary. Proposals are made to reduce the number of procedures, to make them more efficient and to promote alternatives for conflict resolution. The third chapter deals with criminality and insecurity. A vision is developed on the handling of crimes, criminal procedures, security and penitentiary policies.

[12]In Dutch the word is 'personeelsformatie'.

The fourth chapter is focused on the efficiency of the judiciary. Measures are proposed to increase the revenues, reduce the costs and optimise investments in infrastructure and information technology. This chapter also deals with the management of the judiciary.

The autonomisation of the judiciary which started under the former government will be continued. As explained, some crucial management instruments still need to be finalised in order to make the autonomisation process successful. First, the workload measurement should be finalised by the end of 2015, resulting in national norm figures for each type of court and each type of public prosecution office. Whether this will be the case is uncertain since the process of workload measurement has been going for some time and has resulted in much resistance, certainly amongst those organisations that fear personnel reduction. Nevertheless, proper workload measurement is crucial to replace the old fashioned system of personnel planning. The second important instrument is the management agreements and the management plans. The management agreement must be negotiated between the Minister of Justice and the Colleges. This should be finalised by 2017. The same goes for the management plans which have to define the expected performances of the judicial organisations.

Apart from a continuation of the reforms of the former government, some new initiatives are launched. It is announced that the number of Peace courts will be reduced. Similarly, a pilot project for an integrated Court of First Instance, Labour Court and Court of Commerce will be created. It seems that some of the issues postponed by the former government will now be relaunched. The idea is also formulated to create an intermediate structure at the ressort level for the management committees of the local judicial organisations in order for them to collaborate on specific topics, such as HRM and ICT. Experts could then be attributed to this intermediate structure instead of providing management expertise for each judicial organisation separately. We can interpret this as a kind of autonomisation at the meso-level.

This new justice plan still has to be negotiated with the different stakeholders. It is unclear whether these proposals will be approved or not. However, because of the fiscal crisis, justice is confronted with severe savings. It was agreed that justice should undergo deep savings in the period 2015–2019. According to the budget of 2015, 124 million euro have to be saved, of which 53 million in the personnel budget (Geens 2015). The Minister of Justice seeks to postpone some of the savings to later years to safeguard the reforms in the judiciary. The reforms demand indeed for important investments in the field of digitalisation and the renewal of the buildings, including safety.

The new College of the Courts has started fierce protest against the savings. In a recent press announcement it was said: "The linear savings on the courts risk to cause a judicial infarct. A minimal acceptable functioning of the courts, which make up the judicial power of the state of law, is in danger. The legislative and executive power remain passive" (Press announcement 2015, p. 3).

It looks as if the judiciary has entered a catch 22: on the one hand they receive more management autonomy to organise the judicial organisations; on the other hand there is a severe reduction of the resources needed as a result of the savings.

Ironically, one is able to decide autonomously but on their own savings. In these circumstances, the enthusiasm to implement the reforms, and to evolve towards more management autonomy, will not be high. There is a realistic danger that in this case the responsible magistrates will abdicate this 'gift' of increased power.

1.5 Conclusion

Reforms in the Belgian judiciary are a combination of continuity and change. It is striking that some 'solutions' have been formulated for a long time: scale enlargement, more management autonomy and digitalisation are all aimed at increasing efficiency. Reforms in general take a long time. It is already since the nineties that reforms have been proposed, while results seem to be limited. The reforms are also fragmented and insufficiently implemented. We refer to the workload measurement, the management contracts and plans, the transfer of competences. There is still some discussion amongst the stakeholders on the desirability of specific reforms, such as the integration of the Labour Courts and the Public Prosecutor for labour. A permanent concern is also the proximity for citizens, which has some (negative) consequences for scale enlargement and efficiency gains.

The question remains whether the reforms will provide a real solution for the daily problems in justice. These are mainly due to an old fashioned work organisation, a lack of IT-infrastructure, an outdated legislation, and a lack of objective data and evidence. It is hopeful that the justice plan of the new Minister has a wide scope and announces reforms in different fields, including the re-writing of the criminal law. However, it remains to be seen whether the stakeholders will support this plan.

References

Daems, T., Maes, E. & Robert, L. (2013). Crime, criminal justice and criminology in Belgium. *European Journal of Criminology*, 10(2) 237–254

De Clerck, S. & Dupré, I. (2010). Het gerechtelijk landschap : naar een nieuwe architectuur voor Justitie. In Hondeghem A., Van Daele D., Maesschalck J., Broucker B. (Eds.), *Een decennium justitiële hervormingen in België. Octopus revisited*. Brugge: Vanden Broele

Depré, R., Conings, V., Delvaux, D., Hondeghem, A., Schoenaerts, F., Maesschalck, J. (2007). *Haalbaarheidsstudie naar een werklastmeetinstrument voor de zetel*, 185 pp. Brussel: Federaal Wetenschapsbeleid, FOD Justitie.

Depré, R. & Hondeghem, A. (2011). Hervormingsvoorstellen voor justitie: verleden, heden en toekomst. *Ius & actores* – No 3/2011

Depré, R., Hondeghem, A., Broucker, B., Vervaet, C., Schoenaers, F., Ficet, J., Mattijs, J., Bernard, B. (2009). *Wetenschappelijke studie naar de voorstellen van een hertekening van het gerechtelijk landschap en de methodologie om het gerechtelijk landschap structureel aan te passen*. Leuven: Instituut voor de overheid. 361p.

Depré, R., Hondeghem, A., Vervaet, C., Broucker, B. (2010). De hertekening van het gerechtelijk landschap. In: Hondeghem A., Van Daele D., Maesschalck J., Broucker B. (Eds.), *Een decennium justitiële hervormingen in België. Octopus revisited.* Brugge: Vanden Broele, 131-191.

Fijnaut, C. (2001). Crisis and Reform in Belgium: The Dutroux Affair and the Criminal Justice System. In Rosenthal, U., Boin, R.A., & Comfort, L. (Eds.), Managing Crises; Threats, Dilemmas, Opportunities. Springfield, Ill.: Charles C. Thomas. P 235-250.

Geens, K. (2015) Het justitieplan. Een efficiëntere justitie voor meer rechtvaardigheid. 119p.

Gelders, D. & Van de Walle, S. (2003). *Marketing government reforms.* Paper prepared for the Annual Conference of the European Group of Public Administration, Study Group 2: Productivity and Quality in the Public Sector, Oeiras (Lisbon), 3-6 September 2003

Hondeghem, A., Van Daele, D., Maesschalck, J., Broucker, B. (2010). Algemene inleiding. In: Hondeghem A., Van Daele D., Maesschalck J., Broucker B. (Eds.), *Een decennium justitiële hervormingen in België. Octopus revisited.* Brugge: Vanden Broele, 1-7.

Parmentier, S., Fijnaut, C. & Van Daele, D. (2000). From Sisyphus to Octopus: Towards a Modern Public Prosecutor's Office in Belgium. *European Journal of Crime, Criminal Law and Criminal Justice*, Vol. 8/3, 154-186, 2000.

Plessers, J., Depré, R. & Hondeghem, A. (2008). *Profiel van de Administratieve Manager in de context van verzelfstandiging binnen justitie.* Eindrapport. Een studie in opdracht van Federaal Wetenschapsbeleid.

Press announcement (persbericht Naar aanleiding van de begrotingscontrole van de federale regering). College van de hoven en rechtbanken, 17 februari 2015.

Regering Di Rupo, Ontwerpverklaring over het algemeen beleid, 1 december 2011, 180 p. (government declaration)

Turtelboom, A. (2012). *Hervorming van de rechterlijke orde.* Retrieved from: http://justitie.belgium.be/nl/rechterlijke_orde/hervorming_justitie/documentatie/syllabus/

Van Daele, D. (2010). De organisatie en werking van het Openbaar Ministerie in België: een status queaestionis na een decennium van hervorming (splannen). In: Hondeghem A., Van Daele D., Maesschalck J., Broucker B. (Eds.), *Een decennium justitiële hervormingen in België. Octopus revisited.* Brugge: Vanden Broele, 11-73.

Chapter 2
Indicators or Incentives? Some Thoughts on the Use of the Penal Response Rate for Measuring the Activity of Public Prosecutors' Offices in France (1999–2010)

Christian Mouhanna and Frédéric Vesentini

2.1 Introduction

Starting from the 1990s, the French judicial system has been undergoing revolutionary internal changes that thoroughly altered its organisational structure, its way of processing penal cases, and even the occupational culture of the magistrates themselves. A number of court presidents and public prosecutors, growing acutely aware of the public's discontent towards what was perceived to be a sluggish, unresponsive judicial system, started experimenting with novel methods and tools meant to deliver improved judicial services to the public (Ackermann and Bastard 1998). "Houses of Justice" (*Maisons de la justice*) were created, ombudsmen were appointed, new organisational structures were designed to enhance process flows… In the early 2000s, the Ministry of Justice took over and selected what were felt to be the most interesting innovations, integrating them into nationwide policies aimed at modernising the judicial apparatus, and inviting all courts to make actual use of them. One notable example is the TTR scheme (*Traitement en Temps Réel* or Real-Time Processing), designed to bring an immediate response to an increasing number of crimes (Bastard and Mouhanna 2007). The goal was actually two-fold: avoiding dropped cases—of which there were many—, and processing police-initiated cases more quickly. Within this framework, "hotlines" were set up by courts, allowing the police to report "in real time", directly to the prosecution

C. Mouhanna (✉)
National Center for Scientific Research, Centre de recherches sociologiques sur le droit et les institutions pénales (CESDIP), Paris, France
e-mail: mouhanna@cesdip.fr

F. Vesentini
Institute for Statistics, Evaluation and Foresight, Wallonia, Belgium
e-mail: f.vesentini@iweps.be

A. Hondeghem et al. (eds.), *Modernisation of the Criminal Justice Chain and the Judicial System*, Ius Gentium: Comparative Perspectives on Law and Justice 50, DOI 10.1007/978-3-319-25802-7_2

staff, i.e. usually right after an arrest had been made. After a phone call that typically lasted no more than ten minutes, the prosecution staff had to make a decision regarding which direction to take with the case: serving a summons, dropping the case, or looking for an alternative measure.

At about the same time, the Ministry of Justice established management programs whose basic principles were shared across all local jurisdictions (Jean 2008; Vigour 2006; Gautron 2014b). The idea was to benchmark the "performances" of the various courts and require that the least effective become more productive, and to make sure that penal cases received systematic responses. Hence, instead of unique cases individually entrusted to the shrewdness of prosecuting magistrates emerged a "mass" to be processed as quickly as possible, and the activities of prosecutors' offices were monitored through various quantitative indicators designed to "supervise" the work of prosecution staff: penal response rates per court, average processing time of cases, number of cases processed by a given prosecutor over a given time period… All of a sudden, at the onset of the 2000s, magistrates—who rather used to keep their distance from the quantitative evaluation of their activities—developed an increasing awareness of those figures that mattered so much in the eyes of both Prosecutor Generals and the Ministry. Since their operating funds—equipment, staff—depended on increased productivity, prosecutors had to document and justify their penal response rates with the Ministry. The underlying objective was clear enough: reducing the number of dropped cases, which are detrimental to the credibility of the response and the judicial system in general.

Faced with the double requirement of improving response times and measuring their own activities, prosecutors' offices started optimising their decision-making processes by designing a variety of "productivity-boosting" technical and legal tools. Many alternative measures—such as mediations and cautionings (*rappel à la loi*), usually performed by ad hoc prosecution staff—were pushed forward, and scoring scales were developed to support prosecutors' decision-making. For a given offence such as a specific blood alcohol level or a precise amount of prohibited substance, the prosecutor immediately knew which procedure to apply (Perrocheau 2014; Gautron 2014a). In addition, new methods were designed for dealing with proceedings, half-way between court hearings and alternative measures. Towards the end of the 1990s, the "*composition pénale*"[1] was introduced as a way of reaching a settlement, whereby the prosecutor proposes a penalty that can be accepted by the perpetrator. The role of the judge is extremely limited here, and reduced to validating—or possibly, but rarely, rejecting—the settlement. Since such offences do show up on criminal records, the idea is to increase the speed of sentencing—after all, as some prosecutors put it, "it gains time on hearings" (Milburn et al. 2005).

2004 saw the introduction of CRPC[2] (*Comparution sur Reconnaissance Préalable de Culpabilité*), basically a guilty plea based on the same principles as

[1]Act of 23 June 1999 reinforcing the efficiency of penal procedure.

[2]PERBEN II Act, 9 March 2004 (article 137).

the *composition pénale*, except that potential sentences are heavier and include non-suspended prison terms. Another option is the *Ordonnance pénale délictuelle*, a simplified ruling procedure that allows the prosecutor to notify penal "sentences" by post. Those measures are interesting in that they make it possible to inflict a penalty—called "*sanction*", as opposed to "*peine*", in the absence of any court judgement—while saving time on hearings.

A further step was taken when mandatory sentencing was introduced in 2007,[3] clearly indicating that those in charge at the Ministry of Justice would not be content with managing penal response rates, but wanted harsher—and still measurable—penalties as well. Prosecutors' offices were henceforth appraised in terms of their performance regarding mandatory sentences, i.e. minimal penalties imposed by lawmakers for given offences—particularly reoffences, under certain conditions.

Upon examining those measures and their implementation, one is struck by the feeling of self-satisfaction that can be perceived among the prosecutors who did deploy these systems and subsequently saw their response rates improve, peaking at 89.6 % in 2013[4]—89.2 % in 2012. To them, what happened was nothing short of the long-overdue mutation of an obsolete judicial system that, instead of regulating its level of activity solely by deciding on whether or not to prosecute (the principle of opportunity), had finally found a way to operate optimally by measuring its own effectiveness and putting prosecutors' offices under external management pressure. From then on, instead of using the principle of opportunity to conceal the lack of resources and investment that typically makes it impossible for the judicial system to respond to all requests, prosecutors would implement decision-making streamlining policies that would enable them to process almost all—i.e. 89 %, officially—of said requests. In 2013, 1,303,469 "prosecutable"—more on this concept later—cases were processed by prosecutors' offices in France.

What is this supposed to mean in practice? A couple of studies with a fundamentally qualitative and microsociological approach (Bastard and Mouhanna 2007; Danet 2013) have shed some light on local transformations—both individual and organisational—experienced by prosecutors' offices. This research has highlighted the negative effects induced by such a focus on the quantitative aspects of public prosecutors' productivity. *In concreto* analysis highlights the necessary conditions of what appears to be an acceleration of judiciary time: scoring scales that merge individual cases into a shapeless mass to be processed indiscriminately; shorter hearings, hence less time devoted to listening to both pursuants/victims and defendants; burn-outs among prosecution staff, who incidentally feel that penal policies are eluding them entirely. One aspect that hasn't been studied so far is the productivity of prosecutors' offices itself. All of the issues discussed above are regular guests in the discourse of the promoters of this "fast" brand of justice, as a price to pay for a more efficient penal justice system. A closer look at the

[3]Act of 10 August 2007.

[4]From: Les chiffres clés de la Justice 2014—Ministère de la Justice-SDSE.

actual figures, however, leaves quite a few questions unanswered: are we really seeing an increase in the number of cases processed over the past 15 or 20 years, and if so, how substantial is it? To what degree are the "new" processing methods accountable for such an increase? How did the real-time processing culture spread over the years? Some of these questions can indeed be answered by examining the figures supplied by the Ministry of Justice, as well as local statistics.

2.2 Statistical Tools for Measuring Judicial Activity

While judiciary activity can be measured locally, the Ministry also provides numbers that help outline the changes occurring across all French jurisdictions. The French Ministry of Justice has a statistical division (the *Sous-direction de la statistique et des études*—SDSE) that produces annual reports and tables describing the activities of the judiciary. The publications colloquially known as "*cadres du parquet*" (public prosecutor's data) give a rather traditional picture of the activity of the various public prosecutors' offices, in terms of flows and inventories. Devoted to outgoing cases, they are very similar to the tables published in the *Compte général de l'administration de la justice criminelle* from 1825 until the late 1970s.

Over the years, some of the categories have remained absolutely unchanged. Conversely, other categories were created or modified as criminal proceedings evolved. Examples include the aforementioned *compositions pénales* (settlements)—73,700 in 2013—, *ordonnances pénales* (simplified rulings)—150,300—, and CRPC (guilty plea)—69,627—, all of which were introduced fairly recently, considering the time scale. These variations notwithstanding (more on them later), one major change occurred regarding dropped cases.

One of the points of those rating charts was to assess cases in terms of the principle of opportunity. Over the years, prosecutors ended up simply relying on them to regulate the flow of criminal cases that they were unable to process (Bruschi and Nadal 2002), which was in fact one of the main arguments pushed forward by the advocates of organisational changes in the judiciary (Brunet 1998) to justify real-time processing methods. As soon as performance indicators were introduced in public policy management in France in the early 2000s (Marshall 2008), the Ministry of Justice felt a need for greater accuracy, in order both to understand precisely what was being measured and to encourage prosecutors to improve judicial response rates.

In this context, a major innovation occurred in 1999 when a detailed table of reasons for dropped cases—which used to be bundled up into one single line—was included for publication in public prosecutor's data. To be precise, the *compte général* did use to include such a table, until it disappeared in 1932. In the 1999 table, reasons for dropped cases were categorised on two levels. First, prosecutable versus non-prosecutable—either for legal or investigative reasons (problematic elucidation). In 2013, out of 4.35 million cases "processed" by public prosecutors, 3.5 million were considered non-prosecutable, either because of incomplete/

erroneous characterisation of the facts or insufficient evidence (492,267) or because the perpetrator was unknown, which falls into the cold case (*défaut d'élucidation*) category (2,560,222). Generally speaking, for a prosecutor to classify a case as "non prosecutable" means that the magistrate objectively or subjectively considers police work to be under par—the whys and wherefores of which, although interesting, are beyond the scope of the present chapter. Suffice it to say that a significant portion of the cases that reach prosecutors' offices thus promptly exit official productivity statistics. Hence, out of 4.35 million "processed" cases, only 1.3 million are deemed "prosecutable". This is the figure used to compute the prosecution rate, i.e. the number of cases in which public prosecutors do respond (89 % in 2013).

The second level of categorisation applies to prosecutable cases only. Many of them are dropped for various reasons: inconclusive investigations, discontinuance from the plaintiff (withdrawal of default), perpetrator suffering from mental deficiency, victim considered to bear some responsibility or not to have any interest in prosecuting, damage caused considered to be slight or already compensated. About 10 % of prosecutable cases are thus dropped because they are considered—by public prosecutors—to lack legal relevance. A further 38.7 % are then processed by "alternative" means such as cautionings, mediations, and conditional discharge—no prosecution if the perpetrator compensates the damages or accepts medical treatment. 5.7 % of prosecutable cases reach a settlement (*Composition Pénale*), which is considered as an alternative measure even though such offenses do appear on criminal records. Hence, the remaining cases yielded a 46.1 % prosecution rate in 2013, i.e. 600,000 cases that actually ended up in front of a criminal, police, or juvenile court, or on the desk of an investigative judge.

2.3 Changes: Real or Cosmetic?

Examination of long term trends, though, makes it apparent that from 1992 to 2009, statistics for dropped cases (and/or prosecution rates, which are complementary) stabilised (Chart 2.1). The prosecution rate, defined as the number of prosecuted cases divided by the number of processed cases, follows the pattern below and always stays at a more or less constant level of 11–15 % (Chart 2.2).

These graphs show that, in spite of the reorganisations that have affected prosecutors' offices, in spite of the productivist, performance indicator-based policies that have been implemented throughout the 1990s, in spite of the pressure applied on prosecutors to improve prosecution rates, the number of processed cases has not changed significantly from the early 1990s through 2010. The prosecution rate itself hasn't changed either. Real-time processing has failed to induce the "productivity revolution" that some observers had been anticipating from the early field results (Brunet 1998). This *stability* of the prosecution rate is all the more remarkable that from 2002 onwards, it occurred in the context of a tense debate on security, with huge pressure towards prosecution from politicians, the media, and upstream policing actors (Danet 2008).

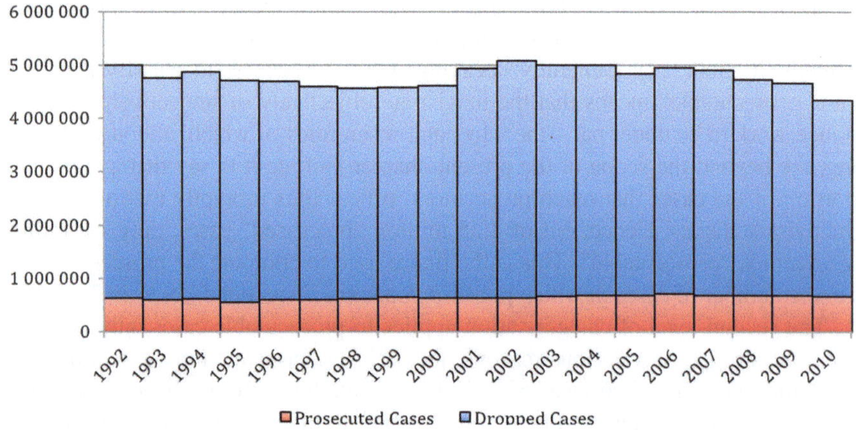

Chart 2.1 Number of dropped cases and prosecuted cases (from: Cadres du parquet)

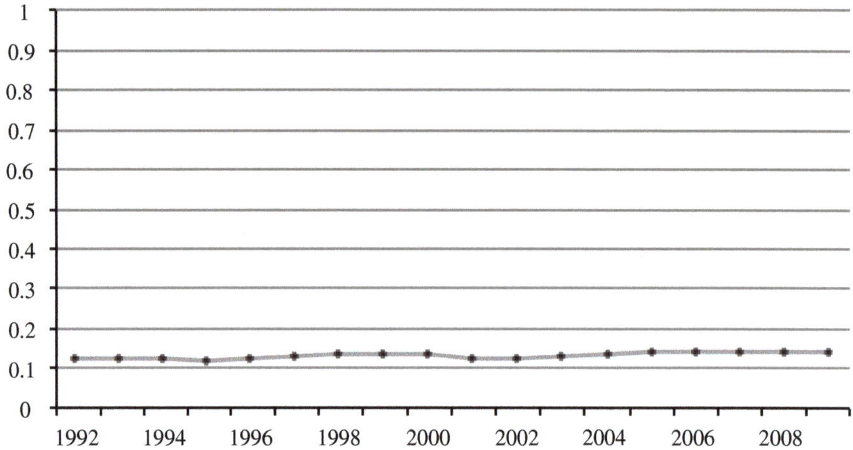

Chart 2.2 Prosecution rates (from: Cadres du parquet)

As mentioned before, though, the 1990s are precisely when the judicial world collectively realised and asserted that a 10 % prosecution rate or so—i.e. a 90 % dropped cases rate—is not something authorities (especially public prosecutors, whose activities are increasingly being monitored statistically) can easily put forward and defend. Such is the context in which statistics were reformed and a detailed table of motivated dropped cases appeared, broken down into several categories, as shown in the table below. Some of the categories have already been discussed: unknown perpetrator; incomplete or erroneous characterisation of the facts; breach of the principle of opportunity; settlements and alternatives, as well as prosecuted cases.

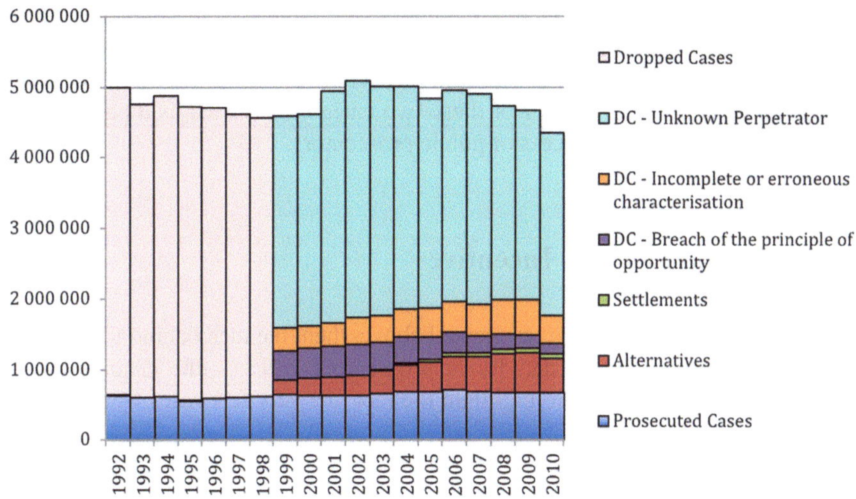

Chart 2.3 Evolution of processed cases: absolute numbers (from: Cadres du parquet)

This table (Chart 2.3) makes it easier to understand the point of this change. First of all, the magnitude of the dropped cases phenomenon, as it was interpreted prior to 1999, is put into perspective. This "overall" rate actually conceals a variety of situations. A closer look at the table shows that, starting 1999—i.e. the earliest available data—*cases dropped on grounds of inopportunity*, those that could be considered proof of either the permissiveness or the harshness of prosecutors, actually make up a very small portion of overall cases. The judiciary, prosecutors in particular, can simply claim that alternative treatments—the "third approach" (*troisième voie*), as they used to be called in France—, later followed by other measures such as settlements, somehow encroach on dropped cases as defined prior to 1999. Further research would be needed to decide whether people at the Ministry of Justice changed their accounting methods at the time precisely because they realised that the growth of alternative treatments at least partly answered criticism regarding these figures, or whether the change itself encouraged prosecutors' offices to increase their reliance on alternatives. Whatever the case may be, the ensuing years saw a reinforcement of the combined effects of "alternatives" and "settlements"—see the red and green areas in the above table.

In addition, the advent of many differentiated categories made it possible to justify high rates of dropped cases without blaming the judiciary, since after all, "unknown perpetrator" was the largest category. Coming from prosecutors, this is a more or less implicit way of blaming those who are tasked with identifying perpetrators, i.e. the police. While this "Dropped Cases—Unknown Perpetrator" category has seldom been explicitly used as an argument by prosecutors against police forces, it is in fact a way for the judiciary to defend their own efficiency and shift the blame on the police. "Incomplete or erroneous characterisation of the facts" is another and rather similar category. The whole thing is almost funny, especially if one remembers that the police—with the active support of the President of the Republic from 2007 to 2012—have consistently been criticising magistrates for their permissiveness and lack of repressive effectiveness. Still, inside the judiciary, the argument was heard: neither of these two categories is used as a performance indicator in the appraisal process of public prosecutors.

2.4 From Indicative to Incentive

According to the available data presented above, then, the idea behind the creation of the new indicator of the activity of prosecutors' offices—the *penal response rate*, examined below—was to highlight the fact that very few cases were dropped "for no reason at all".

Instead of dividing the number of prosecuted cases by the total number of processed cases, as is the case for computing the prosecution rate, the idea is to use as a numerator not just prosecuted cases, but all cases that have received some penal response, i.e. including those that were processed using alternative treatments such as cautionings, or that were rerouted towards the healthcare system, for instance. Similarly, in the same perspective, measuring the responsiveness of public prosecutors by including in the denominator cases that were actually unprosecutable because there was simply no legal case to speak of, for instance, or even no defendant, was somewhat nonsensical... As a result, the penal response rate is computed by removing from the denominator cases whose perpetrators are unknown or whose facts are improperly characterised. At the end of the day, the *penal response rate* can be defined as the number of cases that did trigger a penal response over the number of cases that could have triggered a penal response. Understandably, a penal response rate that can reach as high as 90 % is a lot more palatable than the usual prosecution rate, with its 12 % average.

This modification of the leading indicator of public prosecutors' activity quickly gained ground in the public discourse, and it did so in a two-pronged way. First, as a good management practice indicator: the French judicial system is an extremely centralised one, which is further reinforced by the fact that the Ministry of Justice must comply with recent legislation that requires quantitative reporting of activities to be included in the budget presentations of all government entities. In this respect, the penal response rate is the key indicator indeed. Both at the national scale—France has 173 regional courts (*TGI—Tribunal de Grande Instance*) that are classified into 4 different types, depending on their size—and at a local administrative level—the courts of appeal—, prosecutors' offices engage in a subtle but real competition for the best response rates.

Everyone involved in this rat race at the time used every available means to improve the indicator, "creatively" relying on various alternative treatments in a more or less organised way (Aubert 2010), highly favouring settlements (Milburn 2005), and sometimes creatively interpreting such concepts as "incomplete or erroneous characterisation of the facts". The initial reaction of magistrates and public opinion alike was to praise the stimulus effect induced by this "magical" number, as evidenced by the following extract from *Figaro Magazine,* 26 March 2005, a rather faithful reflection of the general atmosphere:

> Let us start by noting that, according to unpublished figures obtained by Le Figaro Magazine, the penal response rate has grown 2.2 % from early October 2003 to late September 2004. One of the best performances has to be credited to the Lyons area courts of appeal (see p. 51): according to Prosecutor General Jean-Olivier Viout, their 2004 response rate stands at 77 %, against 65 % a year before. In 2002, it stood at… 57.6 %, the worst score in France… To be sure, significant resources have been mobilised in the Lyons jurisdiction, which is so dear to the Minister's heart. Other courts, however, also boast remarkable performances, such as the Riom (86.4 %), Limoges (85.9 %) and Pau (83.2 %) courts of appeal. Aix-en-Provence, on the other hand, is below par with 69.5 %. Generally speaking, the south does not fare as well as northern or central France. The penal response rate only stands at 60.9 % in Toulon and 59.1 % in Nice, against 97.7 % (!) in Péronne and 94.4 % in Saumur.

This ever-improving (at least in the early 2000s) penal response rate is also used by some prosecutors in an attempt to let public opinion know how efficient they are. Every new year is another opportunity to get the following message across: "The penal response rate is on the rise", with such results as 98.7 % in Bastia in 2011,[5] 97 % in Le Puy en Velay in 2013,[6] 84 % in Every that same year.[7] Prosecutors make a reputation, both internally and externally, based on these numbers, as evidenced by the following article, from *La Dépêche du Midi* in 2007, paying homage to the Toulouse prosecutor, who had just been promoted to Prosecutor General: "*He managed his team of prosecutors like a real business 'boss'. Priorities, objectives, roadmaps,… Paul Michel took charge, and he took charge energetically. Within two years, the penal response rate (number of cases that are prosecuted)* (sic) *has literally surged…*".[8] In 2013, the Nadal committee,[9] tasked with pondering the role and future of prosecutors' offices, noted that "the 'penal response rate' now plays a key role in their operations."

In the minds of successive Ministers of Justice during the first decade of the millennium, the pressure exerted via the penal response rate was not limited to increasing the productivity of the judiciary. As shown by the advent of mandatory sentencing in 2007 and the inflationary legislation passed at the time to amend the Criminal Code and Criminal Procedure Code, the objective was clearly to bolster the sanctions pronounced by criminal justice (Salas 2010). Prosecutors were urged to seek harsher sentences and think in terms of punishment, using all available

[5]*Corse Matin,* 13/01/2012 «La parquet a donné une réponse pénale à 98.7 % des affaires».

[6]http://www.zoomdici.fr/actualite/Haute-Loire-il-faudra-attendre-(au-moins)-huit-mois-pour-etre-juge-id141566.html.

[7]"*In 2013, 90,000 case were processed by the TGI, 22,700 of which were "prosecutable", and the penal response rate went from 78 to 84 %.*" Le Parisien, 14/01/2014.

[8]*La Dépêche du Midi,* 15 November 2007.

[9]Committee chaired by Jean-Louis Nadal, *Refonder le Ministère public,* Report delivered to the Minister of Justice on the 29 November 2013.

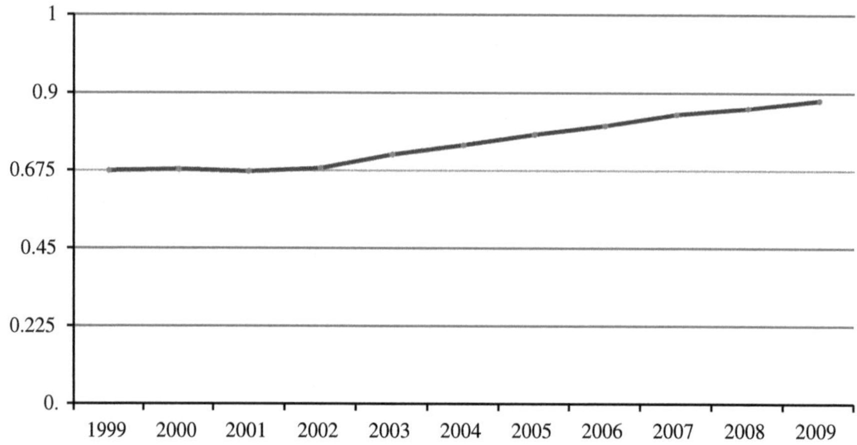

Chart 2.4 Progression of the penal response rate (from: Cadres du parquet)

responses, including those that do not qualify as "prosecution" proper, such as settlements. The response rate thus became an indicator of this harshness as well, which was one more reason for the Ministry to scrutinise it. As an example, here is how the *Dernières nouvelles d'Alsace* newspaper, in an article entitled "*Exceptional penal response*", reported the words pronounced by Saverne's public prosecutor Jean Dissler in his inaugural address at the start of the 2007 judicial year: "*Once again this year, considering in particular our fellow citizens' demand for safety and the mobilisation of gendarmerie forces, the prosecutor's office did its best to respond as systematically as possible to solved cases…*".[10]

In such a context, the penal response rate, which started to be computable as early as 1999, took over the public discourse and grew considerably over the course of a decade, from 68 % on average in 1999 to 90 % in 2010, while the prosecution rate actually remained stable (Chart 2.4).

Can this growth be attributed to better practices from prosecutors—improved supervision, increased firmness? Again, this can be established statistically, with the eye of the accountant. There are two ways of raising the penal response rate in a given jurisdiction: either by reducing the number of cases dropped because of the principle of opportunity, or by increasing the number of prosecutions or alternative treatments. However, the following graph shows that prosecutions remained more or less stable over the given time period, while alternative treatments grew and cases dropped on the basis of inopportunity decreased. This national-scale snapshot confirms what local research had diagnosed: the decision to drop a case by appealing to the principle of opportunity is often based not just on strictly judicial considerations, but on such environmental aspects as the "general

[10] *Les Dernières Nouvelles d'Alsace*, 20 January 2007.

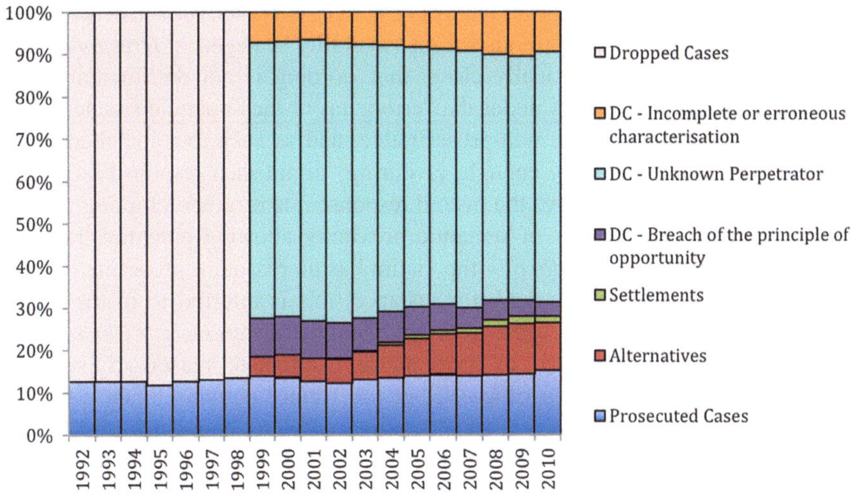

Chart 2.5 Processed cases: prosecuted versus dropped (from: Cadres du parquet)

atmosphere", as well as productivity. Settlement procedures and alternative treatments are innovations that thus encroach upon those ratings, extending the reach of the judicial fishing net (Chart 2.5).

2.5 Are Prosecutors Altering Their Interpretation?

Other variables are revealing of how cases can be "played with", classified, and oriented, i.e. dropped, conditionally dropped, prosecuted but unreferenced, or simply prosecuted. A closer look at even more detailed accounts of dropped cases, 1999–2008, confirms the idea that some "shifting" occurred among the various categories. The principle of opportunity, in particular, was less and less invoked, while alternative treatments were almost exclusively on the rise. Specifically, for instance, within just one decade, a fivefold increase of cases referred to "health, social, or vocational institutions" can be observed. How can we explain these shifts from cases being dropped for unspecified reasons ("*classement sans suite sec*") or because of the principle of opportunity ("*classement pour inopportunité*") to cases being essentially dropped, yet "referred to" other institutions ("*classement avec orientation*"), i.e. triggering some form of penal response after all?

Upon close examination, some of the reasons, although pertaining to different categories, are actually quite similar and likely to favour shifts from one to the other. One interesting example is mental deficiency ("*Etat mental déficient*"). Such cases could be dropped under the principle of inopportunity, except that the penal response rate would be adversely affected, since there is no actual penal response. Hence, they would be accounted for as not processed, and as such, included in the denominator when calculating the response rate. However, there exists another, closely related reason: the "diminished responsibility" category ("*Irresponsabilité de l'auteur*"). While semantically close, this wording is not detrimental to the response rate, because it falls under the "erroneous or incomplete characterisation of the facts" category, hence non-prosecutable, and as such, not included in the denominator. Understandably enough, favouring "diminished responsibility" over "mental deficiency" to improve the overall response rate is rather tempting.

There are other examples of semantic proximity allowing potential transfers. A "*victime désintéressée d'office*"—the victim has no reason to prosecute because a stolen good has been recovered, for instance; this is referred to in the graphs below as—is just about the same as a "*plaignant désintéressé sur demande du parquet*"—plaintiff considered to have no or insufficient reason to prosecute according to the prosecutor's office—, yet the former pertains to the principle of opportunity, while the latter is an alternative measure, hence a form of penal response. In this particular case, the statistical impact is huge, because the data point actually moves from the denominator to the numerator—i.e. not only is the penal response rate not diminished, but it is inflated to boot.

Equally questionable are some cautionings ("*rappel à la loi*") for minor offenses. Cautioning is an alternative measure that somehow "competes" with the option of simply dropping the case on the grounds that the damage caused was small—"*préjudice peu important*". Arguably, the judicial system does indeed respond here, by inviting perpetrators to recognise the illegal nature of their act. Yet, while proper cautioning, under proper conditions, may provoke an awakening and thus concur to prevention, considering the lack of proper research on the efficiency of cautionings, and given the avowed scepticism of some magistrates, one might be forgiven for suggesting that statistical pressure is a better explanation for the (excessive?) use of this alternative than the quest for a perfect penal response.

Well, did prosecutors make actual use of this porosity between the reasons for simply dropping a case and those that allow them to improve the all-important penal response rate? Several clues clearly seem to point towards a positive answer. Graphs reveal the existence of scissors effects that unambiguously point to transfers from one category to another, always in a way that makes prosecutors' offices' data look better. The example below shows the evolution—in opposite directions—of "Victime désintéressée d'office"—versus "Plaignant désintéressé sur demande du parquet", two very close categories, the first one being a dropped cases category versus the second an alternative response. The reversal sparked by statistical demands is clearly visible (Chart 2.6).

The same happens when plotting the other pair we examined above: Dropped Cases "Préjudice peu important" versus "Rappels à la loi", two reasons that have close effects for the perpetrator, yet have antithetical bearing on statistics. Again, "Préjudice peu important" refers to a dropped case while "Rappels à la loi" is an alternative response, and the transfer phenomenon could hardly be more conspicuous (Chart 2.7).

Examples of such one-sided shifts abound: statistically unfavourable reasons are transformed into other, closely-related reasons that enhance the penal response

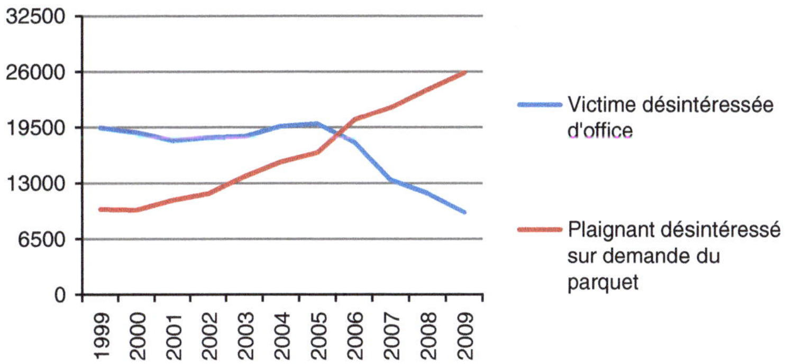

Chart 2.6 Dropped cases: case 1 (from: Cadres du parquet)

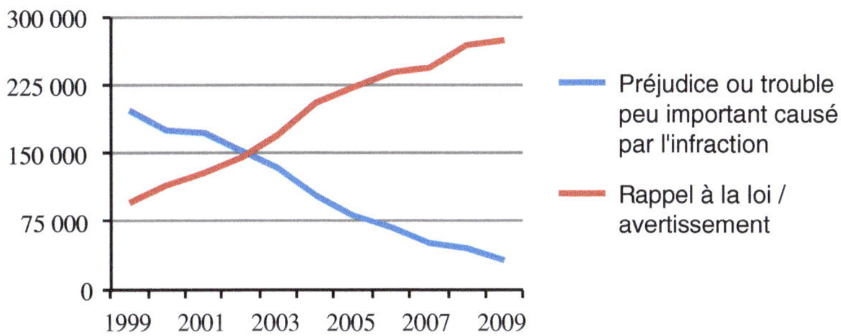

Chart 2.7 Dropped cases: case 2 (from: Cadres du parquet)

rate. In the first decade of the millennium, the concomitant statistical pressure has encouraged prosecutors to resort to these calculation methods in order to "prove" their efficiency, but the practical impact of this change raises multiple questions.

2.6 A Spreading Phenomenon

As shown by Werner Ackermann and Benoit Bastard in their research on the diffusion of innovation in French regional courts (TGI) in the years immediately preceding our studied period (Ackerman and Bastard 1998), changes in the judiciary do not occur simultaneously on the whole territory. Typically, innovations are born in specific places and only start spreading, little by little, once considered relevant by magistrates. This applies to organisational changes such as Real-time processing, and new structures, such as the Houses of Justice and Law (*Maisons de la Justice et du Droit—MJD*), but also to the diffusion of knowledge, including quantitative data and satisfying penal response rates. The map of jurisdictions is a useful tool to determine how this indicator—a major component of their appraisal process—has spread throughout the country. Exactly how this is achieved should be examined in much more detail. However, at least three mechanisms are highly likely to be at work here. First, in line with the Ackermann-Bastard model, the professional transfer of a prosecutor from one jurisdiction to the other is part of this movement, since he will be taking his knowledge and innovative data-processing skills with him. The second major explanation is that prosecutors are networked: they attend formal and informal meetings where recipes get passed on. Third, the various ratings and models used for benchmarking the courts against each other are a strong incentive for promptly finding ways to improve the figures submitted to supervisory authorities—this has been perceptible to us in many interviews conducted along years of field work, and many prosecutors confessed that this was a serious concern indeed.

Space does not permit us to include comprehensive data extensively covering the year-by-year evolution and expansion of penal response rates, whose ever-improving nature obviously raises the issue of how significant, relevant, and even sincere such a tool might prove to be. In 1999, when relevant data was first made available, response rates were quite differentiated throughout the country. Each jurisdiction having its own organisation and environment, there were many idiosyncratic reasons for this, from the nature of the legal action to the activities of the police and gendarmerie forces, through the level of staffing of prosecutors' offices, availability of legal aid, etc. The multicoloured aspect of the map clearly illustrates the disparities to be found in mainland France, disparities that cannot be linked to the size of jurisdictions since similar regional courts display very dissimilar rates (Chart 2.8).

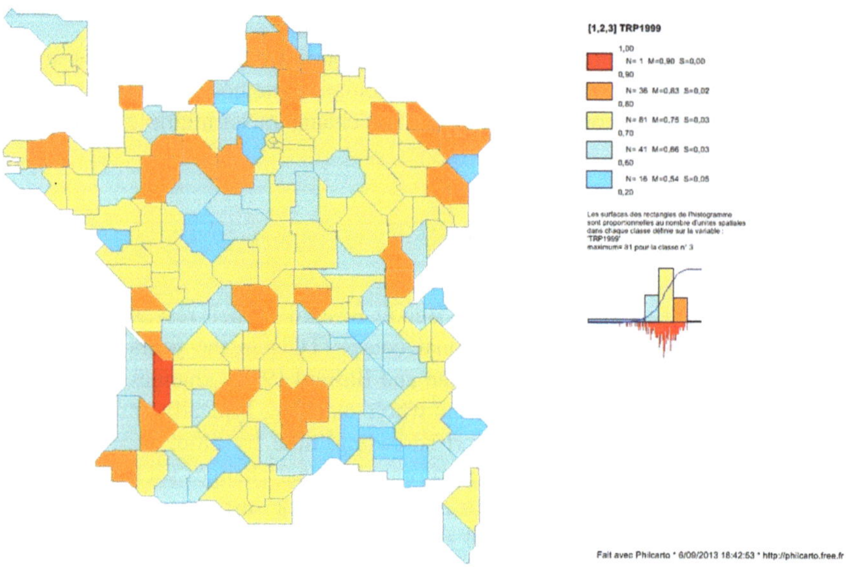

Chart 2.8 Penal response rates in France in 1999 (from: Cadres du parquet)

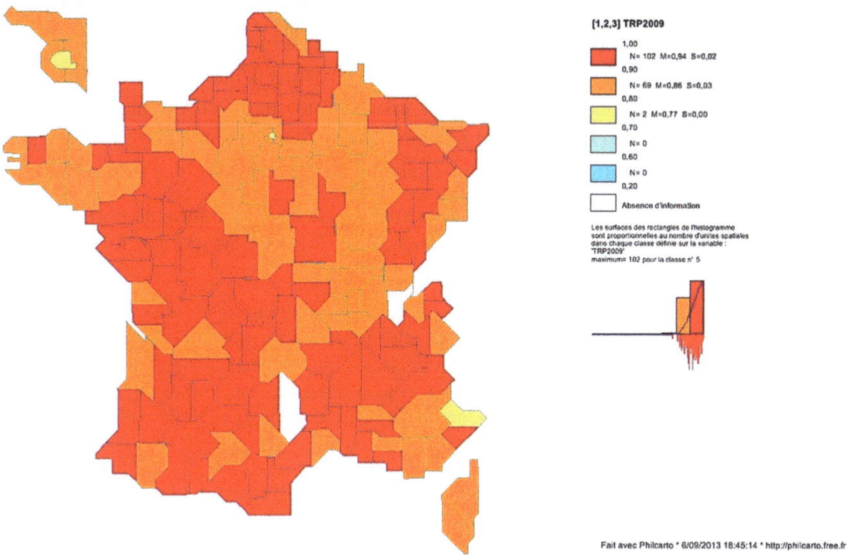

Chart 2.9 Penal response rates in France in 2009 (from: Cadres du parquet)

Ten years later, the penal response rate had become mainstream, the standard metric for measuring the performance of prosecutors' offices, and the map looked starkly different—absolutely homogeneous. All regional courts, regardless of the strong discrepancies characterising their respective environments, were aligned on similar rates, all of which exceeded 80 %, with only two exceptions—including Paris, a very specific case (Chart 2.9).

As is the case for other activities (Matelly and Mouhanna 2007), using a quantitative, activity-based performance indicator modifies the activity itself, as well as the associated statistical process. The Nadal committee (Nadal 2013), tasked with pondering the future of prosecutors' offices in France, had not failed to identify the associated effects of the primacy of the penal response rate in their operations:

> Given that the efficiency of prosecutors' offices and, as a consequence, the associated jobs, partly depend on the importance of this rate, public prosecutors have implemented procedural patterns destined to reduce the number of dropped cases as much as possible, even if that means re-characterising – hence, dressing up – as 'cautionings' many decisions that were purely based on the principle of opportunity.(…)
>
> In addition, ever-increasing penal response rates may give reason to believe that the judiciary might be able to bring a useful answer to any act of delinquency, regardless of its gravity or pettiness, which is not the case.

The inherent benchmarking logic of any performance evaluation measure thus somehow implies and ultimately brings about the fall of the metric itself, insofar as it no longer discriminates anything. In the meantime, however, practices will have been transformed and/or activities adjusted, as shown above, to meet the quantitative objective rather than to elaborate locally adapted policies. In our case, the use of this rate is part of and reinforces a larger trend called *nouveau management judiciaire* (new judicial management), which reduces the autonomy of magistrates as well as the likelihood that cases might be treated as individual occurrences, bringing about a standardisation of prosecution via scoring scales. Indeed, magistrates are becoming more and more vocal against a trend that undermines the very foundations of their profession:

> So, here is the sacro-sanct figure, which was for a while the magic formula of the good prosecutor: the penal response rate. Let us rejoice, dear colleagues, for it stands at 84.99 %. Now, is that good, or what?
>
> Let this rate reassure whoever needs reassurance, giving us reasons to think that we have done our job… But what job, and for what result? There lies the difficulty of the job of the prosecutor, who is asked to make hurried decisions on criminal matters at the risk of becoming some kind of answering machine, with no time to contextualise his actions in the larger picture and look at broader considerations about what our fellow citizens may rightfully expect from us.[11]

Then again, all criticisms and resistances to this managerialisation trend run into a massive argument: that of urgency and processing time, which absolutely and indefinitely needs to be shortened, for it is a fact that citizens expect their judicial system to be quicker.[12] The limits of penal response at all costs having been reached, those of the ever-shrinking processing time need to be accepted so that proper modes of evaluation of judiciary action—not reducible to fundamentally unreliable rates—may be thought out at last.

References

Ackermann, W., Bastard, B. (1998), *Innovation et gestion dans l'institution judiciaire*, coll Droit et société, Paris.

Aubert L. (2010), Systématisme pénal et alternatives aux poursuites en France : une politique pénale en trompe-l'œil, *Droit et société* (n° 74) , 17-33.

Bastard, B., Mouhanna, C. (2007), *Une justice dans l'urgence : le traitement en temps réel des affaires pénales,* Paris, PUF.

Bruschi, C., Nadal, J.-L. (2002) Parquet et politiques pénales depuis le XIX siècle, Paris, PUF.

Brunet, B. (1998), Le traitement en temps réel: la justice confrontée à l'urgence comme moyen habituel de résolution de la crise sociale, *Droit et société*, *38*, 91-107.

Danet, J. (2008). 1. Cinq ans de frénésie pénale, in Mucchielli, L. (2008), *La frénésie sécuritaire*, Sur le vif, 19-29.

Danet, J, dir. (2013), *La réponse pénale: dix ans de traitement des délit,* Presses universitaires de Rennes.

Jean, J.-P. (2008) «Le chantier ouvert des réformes de la justice» , *Revue française d'administration publique* (n° 125) , 7-19

[11]Address by Mme Jaillon-Bru, procureur de la République près le TGI de Nevers (public prosecutor). Solemn sitting marking the beginning of the judicial year, Tuesday 4 January 2014.

[12]*L'esprit du temps: L'accélération dans l'institution judiciaire en France et en Belgique,* B. BASTARD, D. DELVAUX, C MOUHANNA, F SCHOENAERS, GIP-CESDIP-ISP Cachan, July 2012.

Gautron, V. (2014a). La «barémisation» et la standardisation des réponses pénales saisies au travers d'une étude quantitative et qualitative de l'administration de la justice pénale. in Sayn I. (dir.), Le droit mis en barèmes, Paris, Dalloz, 2014, p. 85-97.

Gautron, V. (2014b). L'impact des préoccupations managériales sur l'administration locale de la justice pénale française. *Champ pénal/Penal field*, vol *11*.

Marshall, D. (2008), L'impact de la loi organique relative aux lois de finances (LOLF) sur les juridictions. *Revue française d'administration publique*, *125*(1), 121-131.

Matelly, J.-H., Mouhanna, C. (2007), *Police :des chiffres et des doutes*, Paris, Michalon.

Milburn, P., Mouhanna, C., & Perrocheau, V. (2005). Controverses et compromis dans la mise en place de la composition pénale. *Archives de politique criminelle*, *27*(1), 151-165.

Nadal, J.-L. (2013). Refonder le ministère public, Rapport à Mme la garde des sceaux, ministre de la justice.

Perrocheau, V. (2014). Une illustration du développement des barèmes dans la justice pénale. *Le droit mis en barèmes?*

Salas, D. (2010), La volonté de punir, essai sur le nouveau populisme pénal, Fayard, Pluriel.

Vigour, C. (2006), «Justice : l'introduction d'une rationalité managériale comme euphémisation des enjeux politiques» , *Droit et société* 2/2006 (n°63-64) , 425-455 *mis en barèmes, Dalloz.*

Chapter 3
Different Methods, Same Results as French Criminal Courts Try to Meet Contradictory Policy Demands

Virginie Gautron

3.1 Introduction

The criminal justice system has continually been a subject of reform, as justice has always been considered to be too slow, unfathomable, opaque, and even unfair. Such criticism became harsher in the late 1970s, when the number of criminal complaints increased exponentially while the number of judges held steady, such that cases took longer to resolve and those involving petty offenses were generally dropped. In 1980, Pierre Arpaillange was quick to write that "in the current state of things, all the half-measures and half-achieved reforms give the justice system nothing more than a brief respite from mediocrity" (1980, 261). Structural and procedural reforms were hastened in an attempt to modernise the judicial system, especially after the entry into force of the organic law on financing laws (OLFL), which gave "new public management" precepts greater influence. To increase judicial reactivity, systematise punishment and manage an increasing caseload, new organisational structures and processing methods were designed (Mouhanna and

English translation by Naomi Norberg.

V. Gautron (✉)
Law and Social Change Laboratory, University of Nantes, Nantes, France
e-mail: virginie.gautron@univ-nantes.fr

A. Hondeghem et al. (eds.), *Modernisation of the Criminal Justice Chain and the Judicial System*, Ius Gentium: Comparative Perspectives on Law and Justice 50, DOI 10.1007/978-3-319-25802-7_3

Vesentini, Chap. 2). Lawmakers had instituted various alternative measures,[1] including guilty pleas,[2] and simplified judgment procedures (*ordonnances pénales délictuelles*: misdemeanour orders[3]; *comparution sur reconnaissance préalable de culpabilité*: sentencing without trial after an admission of guilt (Danet 2013; Gautron 2014a).[4] Although long averse to a managerial approach, the courts and prosecutors' offices have now instituted cost controls, streamlined use of human, material and financial means, and output and quality requirements (Vigour 2006). But in addition to improving efficiency, prosecutors are now supposed to systematically—and more quickly—handle all the cases referred to them (rather than exercising their discretion to drop or close those they deem not worth prosecuting) while deciding on individualised sentencing alternatives in cases they do not send on for trial. To meet these demands, prosecutors and presiding judges are being forced to become "justice entrepreneurs" (Vigour 2006, p. 434). These changes are causing tension in the courts, as some of them are contrary to the professional ethos and traditional practices.

To explain how judges perceive and have appropriated this new managerial approach, as well as its impact on the administration of justice and on punishment (Gautron 2014a), this article goes beyond legal texts and ministerial recommendations, drawing on the results of collective, interdisciplinary, quantitative, and qualitative research into how the handling of misdemeanours[5] has evolved over a ten-year period in five courts in the western area of France called the *Grand Ouest*

[1]Alternatives to prosecution exist for cases in which prosecution seems inappropriate or too harsh. Rather than send the defendant to trial, the prosecutor's office may order a so-called "third-way" measure (warning, mediation, etc.), which is sometimes carried out with the help of external partners (associations, city officials/employees, etc.), when it deems such a measure sufficient to put an end to the disturbance caused by the offense, ensure compensation of the victim's harm, and contribute to the perpetrator's rehabilitation (French Code of Criminal Procedure (CPP) Art. 41-1). Legally however, this constitutes dropping the case.

[2]Instituted in 1999 pursuant to French Code of Criminal Procedure (CPP) Art. 41-2, guilty pleas is the harshest alternative to prosecution. Unlike the other alternatives, it must therefore be approved by a judge. The penalties that may be ordered in this context are highly similar to criminal penalties in the strict sense (fines, surrender of one's driver's license, unpaid labor, etc.). Pleading guilty is therefore an intermediate solution between simple alternatives and trial.

[3]These were initially issued only for misdemeanour vehicle-code violations, but lawmakers extended their scope in 2007 and 2011 such that they may now be issued for narcotics use, theft, receiving stolen goods, destruction, deterioration, carrying a knife or blade, etc. (CPP Art. 495 et seq.).

[4]Sentencing without trial enables the public prosecutor to propose punishment, including prison, to a person who has confessed to committing the acts of which s/he is accused. Such punishment must then be approved by a judge (CPP Art. 495-7 et seq.).

[5]Misdemeanours (*délits*) are offenses of medium seriousness, that can be punished with a prison sentence of a few months to ten years (narcotics use, theft, etc.).

(Danet 2013).[6] This approach enabled the research group, of which this author was a part, to conduct "intensive" studies while controlling as much as possible for the contextual particularities that can weigh heavily in the "balance" between the players, the courts, and the local scene on which the legal fate of the cases is played out. Conducted by legal academics, sociologists, and psychosociologists, our study is based not only on the statistical analysis of excerpts from the forms that provide the basis for crime-related statistics in France,[7] but more particularly (given the shortcomings of this quantitative instrument) on a representative sample of 7562 misdemeanour cases involving adult offenders that were handled during the first two weeks of October 2000, 2003, 2006, and 2009. The roughly 100 variables (related to the facts, procedure, penalties, perpetrator and victim profiles, length of time to reach judgment, etc.) made for an objective study of the legal fate of cases, the changes over time in how misdemeanours are handled by the criminal courts, and the similarities and differences in procedural orientation and penalty practices. While statistical analysis of the case files enabled us to objectively determine the cases' actual (rather than theoretical) itineraries through the courts, understanding the thinking behind and justifications for these itineraries required an ethnographic inquiry. We made various direct observations (in the courts, police stations, local security and crime-prevention councils (CLSPDs, Conseils locaux de sécurité et de prévention de la délinquance), etc.) and conducted sixty semi-directed interviews with professionals in these institutions (police officers, judges and prosecutors, individuals in associations that work with offenders, etc.). By using both quantitative and qualitative methods, we were able to distinguish the various ways in which judges react to their superiors' directives and expectations, in particular in terms of speeding up the resolution of criminal cases. Despite their differences, they all give priority to procedural efficiency and effectiveness of punishment, even if the punishment is less-well tailored and it takes longer to get from arrest to judgment.

[6]The research group produced five, comparative monographs to describe the changes in each court as accurately as possible. The five courts are under the jurisdiction of three different appellate courts. The group was therefore able to analyse the differences between three of the lower courts and their corresponding appellate courts. The five courts have specific morphological features and differ in size, socio-demographic environment, and the volume and type of criminal cases. Two courts (labeled DIVE and BARI) are located in rural environments and have a fairly low volume of criminal cases (between 15,000 and 20,000 per year). Two others (ARNO and ETUC) handle between 30,000 and 45,000 criminal cases per year. The fifth court (CARD) is located in an urban center (more than 500,000 inhabitants) and handles more than 60,000 criminal cases per year. DIVE, ETUC and CARD are all under the jurisdiction of the same appellate court.

[7]Called "*cadres du parquet*," these forms are sent once a year by the prosecutors' offices to the Ministry of Justice.

3.2 How Criminal-Justice Policies Have Changed in Response to Managerial Requirements: Diverse Local Practices

In the attempt to achieve the three objectives of productivity, efficiency, and "*customer*" service (Kaminski 2009, p. 87), "*managerial justice*" (Garapon 2010a, b, p. 46) has not been imposed suddenly through spectacular, controversial reforms, but through quiet, "*seemingly peripheral*" changes (Garapon 2010a, b, p. 13) that are frequently procedural and/or result from non-binding sources of law and are appreciated for their "*reactivity*" and "*technicality*" (Commaille, *in* Kaminski 2013, p. 28). They all add to the streamlining of human and financial means, greater responsibilities for judges, quickly determined individualised punishments, and various "quality-related approaches" to producing criminal judgments and receiving the public (Vigour 2006). Every court in our study had adopted the requirements of their ministry, and the government more generally, as their own (Gautron 2014a). However, they chose slightly different methods to increase judicial reactivity (3.2.1), systematise punishment at the lowest possible cost (3.2.2) without sacrificing the individualised quality of the punishment (3.2.3), and manage an increasing caseload (3.2.4).

3.2.1 Greater Judicial Reactivity

Methods borrowing from Taylorism (Rothmayr Allison 2013) were introduced in an effort to streamline the judicial system's activities. Tested by prosecutors seeking to innovate in the Paris area in the early 1990s, telephone hotlines to prosecutors' offices provided real gains in productivity and a symbolic indication of prosecutorial reactivity (Bastard and Mouhanna 2007). To answer calls quickly, take immediate action, and avoid widely diverging decisions, the prosecutors' offices also rendered their decisions automatic and uniform by drawing up "summaries" or "indexes" that, by detailing the procedural orientation and penalties/requests applicable to each offense (Gautron 2014b), tell prosecutors how to handle cases in an entire range of situations and/or determine the penalty scale, mainly for "common" offenses. Now that the police communicate by mail with prosecutors in fewer than 5 % of misdemeanour cases, the "real-time-processing" departments[8] are frequently backlogged, which causes some prosecutors to suffer genuinely at work and above all has elicited numerous recriminations from the police (Roussel, Gautron, and Pouget, *in* Danet 2013). Without ruing the earlier handling of cases by mail, prosecutors admit that they are under constant pressure and forced to shorten their discussions with detectives (*officiers de police judiciaire*) to keep up with phone calls. On the other end of the line, the wait has grown

[8]Previously, the police held suspects in custody after arrest and conducted their investigation without contacting the prosecutor (except in the case of felonies and the most serious misdemeanours), then sent their file by mail. Real-time processing means they must call the prosecutor at the end of custody to obtain his or her instructions as to the next steps to take: continue the investigation, question witnesses, transfer the suspect to the prosecutor's office, issue a warning, etc.

longer and detectives are becoming exasperated. To correct this situation, and with encouragement from the Ministry of Justice, prosecutors' offices now give precedence to contact by email, such that email exchanges constitute close to 75 % of the interactions in certain jurisdictions. They have also drawn up directives for the police (thereby eliminating all interaction with investigators) that, like the indexes for the prosecutors, indicate the procedural orientations and even the penalties the police themselves should impose according to criteria such as blood-alcohol rate, type and quantity of narcotics, value of stolen property, type of weapons, and prior offenses according to police records which, however, are full of errors (Gautron 2014b). This system was long used only for misdemeanour vehicle-code violations, but is now used for many other petty offenses in overloaded courts.

3.2.2 Systematising Punishment at the Lowest Possible Cost

Every year the draft finance law includes the objective of systematising punishment at the lowest possible cost. Doing so is considered to be an indicator of how well the judicial system is accomplishing its mission, the ultimate goal being to improve that system's performance and translate a criminal-justice philosophy based on Anglo-American "zero tolerance" into concrete results. Every prosecutor's office has complied with the ministerial order to drastically reduce the number of cases they drop, such that the average crime-response rate rose from 67.9 % in 2000 to 88.4 % in 2010 (Lenoir and Gautron 2014). There are, however, significant variations in the percentage of prosecutable cases that were dropped in the jurisdictions we studied that are not related to the size of these jurisdictions (from 2.4 % in BARI's jurisdiction to 16.9 % in ETUC's jurisdiction in 2009, while the overall average in metropolitan France was 12.3).

To compensate for this fall in the number of dropped cases, there was an explosion in alternative measures throughout France. Such measures were ordered in 37.5 % of prosecutable cases in 2009 (excluding guilty pleas), with considerable differences among jurisdictions (between 25.6 % in BARI's jurisdiction and more than 40 % in CARD's and ARNO's jurisdictions). In 2009, 15.8 % of all prosecutable cases were resolved through guilty pleas in BARI's jurisdiction, versus fewer than 5 % in CARD's and DIVE's jurisdictions (4.9 % on average in France). The expansion of alternatives has not reduced the number of prosecutions before the misdemeanour court (*tribunal correctionnel*), which increased by 44 % between 2000 and 2009 (all jurisdictions in the study taken together), in proportions that vary per specific territory (from 34 % in DIVE to 104 % in ETUC). At the end of the study period, the share of all prosecutable cases actually prosecuted reached 34.7 % in CARD, 32.9 % in ARNO, 44.7 % in ETUC, 46.5 % in BARI, and 49.5 % in DIVE (36.3 % on average in metropolitan France).

To avoid further encumbering the courts, which were generally saturated, prosecutors began using the various simplified judgment procedures lawmakers had instituted over time: misdemeanour orders (*ordonnances pénale délictuelle*) and, to a lesser extent, sentencing without trial after an admission of guilt (*comparution sur reconnaissance préalable de culpabilité*). Misdemeanour orders, which are judgments without a hearing, notice of which may be given by mail, did not meet with the same success in all five courts: BARI, ETUC, and DIVE heartily embraced this procedure, such that it constituted 59.6, 51, and 38 %, respectively, of all prosecutions in 2009, whereas ARNO only began using it in 2008 (9.7 % of prosecutions in 2009). The ARNO prosecutor's office preferred sentencing without trial (32 % of prosecutions in 2009, 10 % of prosecutable cases), while the other jurisdictions employed this alternative at a much lower rate than the national average (14.3 % of prosecutions in 2009, 5.2 % of prosecutable offenses). These two procedures changed the way the courts operated, since they transferred the handling of the majority of cases to the prosecutor's office. In almost four of ten cases, prosecutors alone have been the "first responders," without the slightest judicial intervention. If we add guilty pleas, misdemeanour orders, and sentencing without trial, in which judges intervene only when it is time to approve the requested penalties (and only rarely deny them), the prosecutors' offices themselves mete out punishment in 60–70 % of cases.

3.2.3 Quality-Related Approaches Focused on a New Strategy of Graduated Penalties

To prescribe adequate penalties for offenses that are not very serious without sacrificing quality despite their heavy caseloads, some prosecutors have developed alternatives to prosecution (mediation, referral to a medical, social or professional facility, training courses, etc.) that are derived from case law and aim to make offenders aware of their obligations (Gautron and Raphalen 2013). Prosecutors have also started to graduate punishment, such that they have real power to individualise procedures, if not penalties. Between the warnings[9] given to first-time offenders who have committed minor offenses and trials, which are reserved for the most serious offenses and/or those committed by multirecidivists, there is a whole panoply of intermediate, more or less qualitative procedures and penalties. After a warning has been given, minor offenses are usually followed by a guilty plea, then a misdemeanour order or sentencing without trial, and ultimately a classic trial. In this way, prosecutors are quite often the first to punish any repeat violations, at least as regards common, minor offenses (vehicle-code violations, use of narcotics, etc.). Since each court has its own procedural "map" indicating case itineraries according to the features of each case and the defendant's profile, the

[9]A warning consists of "indicating to the perpetrator, in the context of a serious discussion, the rule of law, the punishment provided for by the law, and the risk of punihment s/he runs if s/he repeats the offense. The objective is for the perpetrator to realise the consequences of her/his actions for society, for the victim, and for her/himself, without these being reduced to mere moral considerations." Circular of March 16, 2004 on the criminal justice policy regarding alternatives to prosecution and use of deputy prosecutors, NOR: JUSD0430045C, *BOMJ*, no. 93, 2004.

Table 3.1 Distribution of procedural alternatives in 2008 (cases involving adults only)

	National average	CARD	ARNO	ETUC	BARI	DIVE
Mediation (%)	5.0	3.6	4.0	8.8	3.2	2.1
Order to obtain care (%)	0.9	0.0	0.1	1.3	0.0	0.0
Withdrawal of the complaint (%)	4.5	5.2	12.6	11.0	4.3	1.6
Regularisation (%)	13.9	6.4	24.6	9.1	15.8	7.0
Warning (%)	46.5	59.8	32.8	42.7	47.3	74.7
Referral to a medical or social facility (%)	3.1	1.6	13.9	4.2	0.0	0.4
Other sentencing alternatives (%)	26.2	23.4	11.9	22.9	29.4	14.2

Source Ministry of justice statistics
Due to the progressive installation of court-management software starting in the mid-2000s, the data for 2009 regarding adults only are not available for BARI or DIVE

"graduated-response strategy" (prosecutor, BARI) varies from court to court, including within each appellate jurisdiction. The types of alternatives used differ markedly. For example, the percentage of warnings (excluding guilty pleas and only for adults) reached 74.7 % in 2008 in DIVE, versus 32.8 % in ARNO (46.5 % on average in metropolitan France). ARNO uses more of the available alternatives, especially having the complaint withdrawn,[10] regularising at the prosecutor's request,[11] and referring the offender to a medical or social facility (Table 3.1).[12]

In the prosecution phase, the various procedural channels are not used for the same types of conduct and/or the same defendants. Some prosecutors' offices refuse to use, or on the contrary prefer to use, certain ways of handling particular offenses when committed by first-time offenders versus recidivists. For example, misdemeanour orders are used in the majority of cases involving defendants with no priors at CARD (77.2 % of such orders in our sample) and DIVE (88.3 %), whereas only about 40 % of such orders were issued with regard to individuals who had at least one prior conviction at ETUC and BARI.

[10]This alternative constitutes conditional closure of the case: the prosecutor conditions dropping the case on the victim's being compensated (restitution of the item taken fraudulently or monetary compensation).

[11]The prosecutor may condition dropping the case on the regularisation of the situation constituting the offense. In other words, s/he can require the offender to comply with the law after s/he has been found to be in violation of the law (e.g., by purchasing auto insurance in the case of an uninsured driver). Since the circular of April 88, 2005 on the struggle against drug addiction and dependencies went into effect, prosecutors may require drug users to take medical tests designed to prove that they have stopped using drugs.

[12]Although such referrals generally concern drug users, there is no requirement to obtain care. This form of conditional case closure consists of asking the offender to make an appointment with a medical-social facility and transmit proof that s/he did so (certificate provided by the structure).

3.2.4 Caseload Management: A Constant Struggle

To manage the increasing number of prosecutable cases, judges and prosecutors have thought about how to optimise their management of cases (including the backlog), especially since their superiors' evaluations of their performance largely depend on it. To process the numerous cases without inordinately lengthening the time it takes to do so and avoid creating new backlogs, prosecutors frequently change their procedural-orientation guidelines. Using a table that is, according to the judges and prosecutors themselves, sometimes based on arguable or not very reliable indicators, prosecutors and judges try to pinpoint where the bottlenecks occur in each procedural channel and, if necessary, replace one procedure with another. These orientation guidelines thus constitute essential tools for managing and reducing the time spent on cases.

Legally speaking, the lack of strict limits on the various procedures' scope of application is a clear advantage. Lawmakers were careful not to link the procedures exclusively to certain types of offenses or offenders. The procedures for handling misdemeanours are therefore competing "processes" that prosecutors must use as best they can depending on the needs and resources of their court (organisation of cases, human and material resources, case backlog, etc.). Ministerial attempts to take control of the prosecutors' offices since the mid-2000s coexist easily with their increased margin of maneuver with regard to common offenses of low to medium seriousness. New public management promotes less hierarchical organisational structures, substantial autonomy so that depending on local particularities and constraints, public officials may attain the expected results in terms of effectiveness and efficiency (Rothmayr Allison 2013). The changes proceeding from the "*judicial policy-making model*" (Commaille, *in* Kaminski 2013, p. 28) described above have changed the very status of law as we have moved from an "*essentialist conception to a flexible, negotiated, relativistic, pluralist, pragmatic conception of the legal standard*" (Commaille 2007, p. 303). But the increasing independence of French prosecutors' offices from the Ministry of Justice hides the fact that more subtle forms of control are developing, such as the "accountability" movement that effects more than just defendants. Accountability demands that prosecutors provide regular performance reports, at least on performance that can be measured directly.

In fact, our empirical research reveals that the three objectives of efficiency, effectiveness, and efficaciousness receive significantly different treatment from the courts in the study. Of course, various contextual particularities influence the ultimate fate of cases, such as the volume of prosecutable cases and the specifics of cases. But management constraints affect the procedural options chosen: case backlog, number of misdemeanour trials that may be envisioned in light of available personnel, time to trial, number of deputy prosecutors, etc.). The variety of practices is inextricably linked to the local institutional context. In particular, prosecutors' actions depend on local resources and the number of available associations or external partners, which are key to qualitatively diversifying the alternatives to prosecution or imprisonment.

Factors related to the court's configuration, in particular the position of judges on the diversification of procedural avenues, also affect the choice of procedural options. The most recently instituted procedures (guilty plea, sentencing without trial, misdemeanour order) must be approved by a judge. Efficient caseload management therefore requires obtaining approval of such measures as frequently as possible by reaching agreement with judges on the scope of the procedures and the penalties in light of criteria such as the nature of the offense, the perpetrator's criminal record, the harm suffered by the victim, etc. While procedural diversification tends to turn prosecutors into quasi-trial judges, judges find the prerogatives they have lost in the approval phase in earlier phases. The results of local arrangements vary since no two judges or prosecutors associate the same advantages and/or disadvantages with the various procedures, for reasons related to personal values and beliefs, habits, and careers. In the process of implementing new ways of handling misdemeanours, their positions vacillate from accommodating them to more or less openly resisting them. For both judges and prosecutors, the changes in how misdemeanours are handled, especially the rarefaction of trials and the accompanying loss of ritual, are often seen as an attack on the ideal of justice as they learned it and incorporated it into their professional ethos (Gautron 2014a; Danet 2013). They all mentioned the ritual of the trial and how its disappearance has meant a loss of meaning for defendants. Unlike the administrative, standardised treatment of cases, only the judicial ritual, the trial and the fact that it is public, makes it possible to individualise the penalty, be educational, and make sure defendants gain genuine awareness of the seriousness of their actions. For a while, prosecutors and/or their substituted therefore resisted instituting the guilty plea and sentencing without trial at DIVE and misdemeanour orders at ARNO. And very few at CARD have a positive opinion of sentencing without trial.

3.3 Counterproductive Effects in Terms of Individualised Punishments

Managerial concerns have upturned the meaning and nature of punishment as well as judicial practices, at least as far as misdemeanours are concerned. An obsession with quantity tends to take precedence over finding the most appropriate punishment, such that the mere fact of providing some kind of penal response seems to count more than the punishment itself in some cases (3.3.1). In addition, the increasing independence of prosecutors' offices is increasing the risk of inequality between defenders in different jurisdictions (3.3.2), and while the practices discussed above might have increased productivity, they have not made for speedier justice (3.3.3).

3.3.1 A Marginal Qualitative Adaptation

The preoccupation with preserving, if not improving, the individualised quality of punishment has taken a backseat to caseload management constraints, first of all because procedural choices are made in a rush: whereas many alternatives require prior evaluation of the perpetrator's profile (mediations, training courses, referrals to medical or social facilities, etc.), real-time orientation practices seek to provide an immediate response and therefore do not leave prosecutors time to check the background of the person whose case they are handling. In addition, increasing the use of email has led to exchanging less information, as detectives generally provide only the offender's identity, which is necessary to determine their prior convictions, the date of the offense, and where it took place. Prosecutors do not have time to ask for further information or ask investigators what they think about the perpetrator's personality. Given the limited, essentially factual information provided and the inability of prosecutors to engage in more extensive discussions with detectives regarding offenders' profiles, prosecutors make their decisions on the basis of the seriousness of the offense and the offender's prior convictions.

Similarly, creating "indexes" tends to make personalising punishment secondary. The only item taken into account in an offender's profile is usually their criminal record (known or not to the police in the context of permanent directives, repeat offenses or recidivism for prior convictions). The effect of indexes must be qualified, however, as they are not entirely binding. Several prosecutors we spoke to considered them simply guides or aids to decision making. Items that do not appear in the indices are taken into account: how old the prior convictions or arrests were, the quantity of drugs used or possessed, the suspect's behaviour when being arrested, their income, etc. (Gautron 2014b). The effect of such indices must also be compared to that of the "implicit indices" that have long been used by some judges, in particular when there is only one trial judge, and the "*unspoken criminal judgment culture*" (Beyens and Vanhamme 2007, p. 210) that unites all judges and prosecutors, as evidenced by the strong agreement between what prosecutors request and judges grant or in terms of penalties (Gautron 2014b).

Qualitative adaptation of sanctions is only relative, if not entirely fictional. Continued diversification of procedures and sanctions is in fact guided by accounting rather than axiological concerns. For common offenses that are not very serious, warnings are the primary alternative to prosecution (46.7 % of all alternatives, except guilty pleas, involving adults in 2009, and more than 70 % in some courts). Orders to obtain care (0.8 % of alternatives involving adults in 2009, 0.3 % of prosecutable cases) and referrals to medical or social facilities (3 % of alternatives involving adults in 2009, 1 % of prosecutable cases) are rare, however. Mediation involving adult offenders decreased by 24.1 % between 2000 and 2009 to reach 1.5 % of prosecutable cases at the end of the study period. Warnings are thus an adjustment variable that reflects fluctuations in the number of prosecutable cases from year to year, as well as a sure way to increase prosecutors' response rate for a modest price that might even be lower than the price of simply dropping a case because the cost is transferred to the police (Lenoir and Gautron 2014).

Some prosecutors do of course try to develop alternatives of greater quality, in particular conditional case closures which, unlike warnings, require greater involvement on the part of the defendants (withdrawal of the complaint by the victim, mandatory regularisation, referral to medical or social facilities, etc.). In the past decade, the ARNO prosecutors' offices, and to a lesser extent those of ETUC, have chosen from a broader range of alternatives to offer, with the help of various partners (Gautron and Rétière, *in* Danet 2013), "real content, something that means something" (ARNO prosecutor). Some courts are therefore trying to add an educational component to the simplified procedures, or inventing new judicial rituals in the form of effective signs rather than symbols (Danet, Grunvald and Saas, *in* Danet 2013). For example, without the slightest legal obligation to do so, some prosecutors' offices have chosen to have misdemeanour orders given orally by a deputy prosecutor who receives the offenders individually or together and sometimes gives them road-safety documentation. Although the new judicial practices alter their view of the justice system as being exceptional and "*productive of values and symbols*" (Vigour 2006, p. 55) and disturb their professional ethos, most judges and prosecutors have accepted them. Some even view them very positively, convinced that these new ways of responding to crime have educational advantages. They have doubts about the real impact of the traditional ritual and relativise the extent to which penalties are personalised as the result of a trial, seeing trials as largely the subject of myth, and instead praise the positive aspects of guilty pleas and sentencing without trial. Most of the judges and prosecutors we interviewed doubt that the new procedures are effective in preventing recidivism, however. Both pragmatic and resigned, they see these new tools as an unavoidable way to absorb their numerous cases without clogging up the courts any further. As they all attempt to meet this goal, their agreements largely outweigh their disagreements. And it behooves judges to accept the diversification of procedures, since it helps avoid excessive delays in hearing cases and limits trials to serious and/or complex cases requiring lengthy questioning and more thorough knowledge of the defendant's profile.

Imposing managerial concerns on the justice system has thus given a stronger hold to a "*new, neoliberal way of governing people and institutions*" (Garapon 2010a, b, p. 14). Under the influence of neoliberal precepts, the rhetoric of modernisation offers only a "*promise of progress, without a direction*" (Kaminski 2009, p. 40). Neoliberalism "*dismisses all external perspectives, all comprehensive reasoning, all global views ([which it]considers to be ideological)*" (Garapon 2010a, b, p. 24). "*Crime management masks the objectives in favor of the means, creates procedures to the detriment of the substantive standards of justice, and transforms a system's social performance into internal performance by virtue of which the important thing is to do things well, not to do good things*" (Kaminski 2009, p. 40).

3.3.2 *Increasing Inequality Between Defendants in Different Jurisdictions*

Having similar orientation and punishment practices causes, or rather increases, the risk that defendants will be treated unequally. Beyond the type and quantum of punishments that may be ordered, the procedural choices also have consequences for defendants. A prior guilty plea, even if it is recorded on Bulletin 1 of the defendant's criminal record, cannot be retained later as an aggravating circumstance (recidivism). However, sentencing without trial and misdemeanour orders constitute the first term of a repeat offense, with clear effects on the severity of the punishment ordered. Prison sentences, whether suspended or not, cannot be ordered following a guilty plea or a misdemeanour order, but can be ordered in the context of sentencing without trial. While judges claim that this is due to each court's specific constraints, they also recognise that it creates a risk of unequal treatment, which is not new and is not limited to "indexed" procedures. Both the Ministry of Justice, through circulars, and prosecutors at the regional level try to avoid excessive disparities. Although they do not distribute precise directives, prosecutors general (*procureurs généraux*) hold meetings with the prosecutors in their respective jurisdictions to harmonise their criminal justice policies, sometimes also taking into account the practices of the customs administration in drug cases and those of prefectures with regard to how long drivers' licenses should be suspended. These efforts fall far short of creating uniform local criminal justice policies, instituting only a minimum level of harmonisation that takes into account local particularities over which the ministry and the prosecutors have little control. Since practices are not consistent throughout France, prosecutors present their orientation charts and indices as means to harmonise their court's responses to crime. Such practices might make it possible to overcome the inequality of the sanctions ordered by judges in classic trials, which some of them admit to.

3.3.3 *Limited Effect on Speed*

Although all the reforms discussed here have led to real gains in productivity, there has been hardly any improvement in the speed with which adults come to trial for misdemeanours (Danet, Brizais and Lorvellec, *in* Danet 2013). Diversifying procedures has not saved any time, merely made it easier to absorb the rising number of cases without a marked increase in the time it takes to reach a verdict: the courts have managed to contain the number of cases tried more than nine months after the offense was committed (28.9 % of cases in 2000 to 28.4 % in 2009), but have been unable to avoid a decrease in the number of cases tried within less than three months (36.9–24.7 %) and a concomitant rise in the number of cases taking three to nine months to be tried (34.2–46.9 %). A look at the speed with which "justice" is delivered, that is, the time between the prosecutor's

Table 3.2 Time between the real-time processing date and misdemeanour-court judgment

	25 %	25 %	Median	25 %	25 %	Average
2000	From 0 to 57 days	From 57 to 93 days	93	From 93 to 104 days	More than 104 days	118
	The quickest 10 % were processed in under 38 days			The slowest 10 % took 236 days to be processed		
2003	From 0 to 53 days	From 53 to 88 days	88	From 88 to 116 days	>116 days	131
	The quickest 10 % were processed in under 27 days			The slowest 10 % took more than 196 days to be processed		
2006	From 0 to 107 days	From 107 to 134 days	134	From 134 to 193 days	>193 days	165
	The quickest 10 % were processed in under 31 days			The slowest 10 % took more than 214 days to be processed		
2009	From 0 to 96 days	From 96 to 143 days	143	From 143 to 225 days	>225 days	188
	The quickest 10 % were processed in under 51 days			The slowest 10 % took more than 350 days to be processed		

Based on a sample of prosecuted cases (N = 3537)

office taking charge of the case and the court's reaching a verdict shows a decrease in speed. The median time to trial increased by 60 days between 2003 and 2006, going from 88 to 134 days, then to 143 days in 2009. In ten years, the average time to trial increased by 70 days. The first decile increased from less than 38 days to more than 51 days, while the last decile increased from more than 236 days to more than 350 days. Between 2004 and 2009, diversifying prosecution methods, combined with the rise of sentencing alternatives, was not enough to maintain the same time to trial as in the preceding period (2000–2004) (Table 3.2).

3.4 Conclusion

While prosecutors and judges all recognise that their new work methods, the generalisation of alternatives, and simplified procedures have made it possible to improve productivity and avoid inordinately increasing the time to trial, some fear the criminal justice system will again reach saturation. Systematisation responses to crime has led to casting a wider criminal net and progressively increasing the harshness of sanctions. Alternative procedures are rarely used for conduct that previously would have led to prosecution. They do not replace heavier convictions, but reveal a process of insidious overcriminalisation targeting populations that had heretofore avoided control through the criminal justice system or situations that previously fell within the scope of societal regulations (see, in particular, Gautron and Raphalen 2013). In addition, the progression in the rate of response to crime (more than twenty points in fifteen years) is causing an artificial increase in the number of repeat offenders and recidivists within the legal meaning of the term, who are convicted essentially for offenses of low to medium seriousness. Those who, due to the number of dropped cases, were previously found to be recidivists only after a long criminal history, are now presented as having a prior as of the second offense. Taking up to the three first offenses committed by the first defendants in our sample of prosecutions, the share of recidivism (in the legal meaning of the term and noted in the conviction) was 5.7 % in 2000, 10.9 % in 2006, and 14.5 % in 2009. In the long run, and even though the volume and/or structure of offenses will not change, these changes will probably result in harsher sentences and a new trial backlog, because trials generally involve recidivists or repeat offenders (who do not meet the legal definition of recidivist). If the criminal justice system continues to artificially produce recidivism, more and more misdemeanour trials will be required, but there is little likelihood of this given budget constraints. And if it is not possible to hold a trial for every case that requires one, our procedural model will undergo a genuine crisis. Managerial methods are apparently not enough to stem the tide and avoid the saturation of the judicial system in the near future.

References

Bastard B., Mouhanna C. 2007, *Une justice dans l'urgence. Le traitement en temps réel des affaires pénales*, Paris, PUF.

Beyens K., Vanhamme F. 2007, La recherche en sentencing: un survol contextualisé, *Déviance et Société*, 31, 199-228.

Commaille J. 2007, La justice entre détraditionnalisation, néolibéralisation et démocratisation: vers une théorie de sociologie politique de la justice, *in* Commaille J., Kaluszynski M. (ed.), *La fonction politique de la justice*, Paris, La Découverte, 293-321.

Danet J. (coord.) 2013, *La réponse pénale. Dix ans de traitement des délits*, Rennes, PUR.

Garapon A. 2010, *La raison du moindre État. Le néolibéralisme et la justice*, Paris, Odile Jacob.

Gautron V., Raphalen P. 2013, Les stages: une nouvelle forme de pénalité ?, *Déviance et Société*, 37, 1, 27-50.

Gautron V. 2014a, L'impact des préoccupations managériales sur l'administration locale de la justice pénale française, Champ pénal/Penal field [En ligne], Vol. XI, URL: http://champpenal.revues.org/8715; DOI: 10.4000/champpenal.8715.

Gautron V. 2014b, La "barémisation" et la standardisation des réponses pénales saisies au travers d'une étude quantitative et qualitative de l'administration de la justice pénale, *in* Sayn I. (ed.), *Le droit mis en barèmes*, Paris, Dalloz, 85-97.

Garapon A. 2010, *La raison du moindre État. Le néolibéralisme et la justice*, Paris, Odile Jacob.

Kaminski D. 2009, *Pénalité, management, innovation*, Namur, Presses Universitaires de Namur.

Kaminski D. (ed.) 2013, *La flexibilité des sanctions*, Bruxelles, Bruylant.

Lenoir A., Gautron V. 2014, Les pratiques des parquets face à l'injonction politique de réduire le taux de classement sans suite, *Droit et Société*, 88, 591-606.

Rothmayr Allison C. 2013, Le droit et l'administration de la justice face aux instruments managériaux, *Droit et Société*, 84, 277-288.

Vigour C. 2006, Justice: l'introduction d'une rationalité managériale comme euphémisation des enjeux politiques, *Droit et société*, 63-64, 425-455.

Chapter 4
The Position of the Public Prosecution Service in the New Swiss Criminal Justice Chain

Daniel Kettiger and Andreas Lienhard

4.1 Introduction

4.1.1 Preliminary Remarks

On 1 January 2011, the system of prosecution in Switzerland underwent a considerable and historic change: with the entry into force of the *Swiss Criminal Procedure Code* (CrimPC),[1] Switzerland's law on criminal procedure was standardised and at the same time the various prosecution systems were harmonised. The following article aims to highlight the position of the public prosecution service (PPS)[2] in the new system from a constitutional and administrative law angle as well as from the point of view of administrative theory. Special attention is given to cooperation with the police in the prosecution process. In addition, based on current research results obtained by the authors—initial experiences with the new prosecution model from the point of view of the public prosecution services are examined. In relation to this, the article restricts itself to *prosecution by the cantons* and has made a conscious decision to exclude prosecutions by federal authorities.

[1]Swiss Criminal Procedure Code (Criminal Procedure Code, CrimPC) of 5 October 2007, SR 312.0; also referred to as CCrP (Gilliéron 2014) or CPC.

[2]In Switzerland, a variety of terms are used for the prosecution authorities; for the sake of simplicity, we have generally used the term public prosecution service (PPC) for the organisation, and prosecutor for the individuals.

D. Kettiger (✉) · A. Lienhard
Center of Competence for Public Management, University of Bern, Bern, Switzerland
e-mail: daniel.kettiger@kpm.unibe.ch

A. Lienhard
e-mail: andreas.lienhard@kpm.unibe.ch

A. Hondeghem et al. (eds.), *Modernisation of the Criminal Justice Chain and the Judicial System*, Ius Gentium: Comparative Perspectives on Law and Justice 50, DOI 10.1007/978-3-319-25802-7_4

4.1.2 The Situation Before 2011

For several hundred years and until the end of 2010—due to federalism—every Swiss canton had its own system of criminal prosecution based on its own cantonal criminal procedure legislation. There were four different models of criminal prosecution (Bundesrat 2006, p. 1104f; Gilliéron and Killias 2008, p. 334; Gilliéron 2014, p. 57ff).

Examining magistrate model I[3]: The investigation was led by an independent examining magistrate.[4] The police were under his control so there was no separation between the investigation and the examining of suspects and witnesses. The examining magistrate started proceedings on his own initiative. The PPS was not permitted to issue instructions to the examining magistrate, although it was a party to the preliminary proceedings. After the preliminary proceedings were completed, the PPS was responsible for bringing charges and prosecuting the case in court.

Examining magistrate model II[5]: The examining magistrate and the PPS acted together during the preliminary proceedings. The examining magistrate was bound by the PPS' instructions. The extent of this subordination differed depending on the law and practice in the canton concerned. While some cantons granted the power to drop proceedings and to bring charges, others only allowed the examining magistrate to conduct examinations or drop the proceedings. In a majority of cantons, bringing charges and prosecuting in court are the exclusive responsibility of the PPS.

PPS model I[6]: Before involving the examining magistrate, the police—under the direction of the PPS—carried out investigations. Thereafter, the PPS ordered an independent examining magistrate to conduct examinations of suspects and witnesses. The PPS was a party to the examinations, but it was not entitled to issue instructions. After the examinations, the examining magistrate forwarded the files to the PPS which decided whether to bring charges or drop the proceedings.

PPS Model II[7]: This model was characterised by the absence of an examining magistrate. The PPS was "master" of the preliminary proceedings, carrying out examinations, bringing charges and conducting the prosecution in court. The PPS directed the police or was entitled to issue them with instructions. The advantage of this model was that it obviated the need to change the official in charge, from the examining magistrate to PPS.

---

[3]Cantons Fribourg, Glarus, Solothurn (until 2004), Vaud, Valais and Zug (until 2007).

[4]Also called examining judges or investigative judges; in Belgium "juge d'instruction/onder zoeksrechter"; in Switzerland before 2011 "juge d'instruction" in the French speaking part, "Instruktionsrichter", "Untersuchungsrichter" or "Verhörrichter" in the German speaking part.

[5]Cantons Appenzell A.Rh., Bern, Basel-Landschaft, Grisons, Lucerne, Nidwalden, Obwalden, Schaffhausen, Schwyz and Thurgau.

[6]Cantons Aargau, Geneva, Jura, Neuchâtel and Uri.

[7]Cantons Appenzell I.Rh., Basel-Stadt, St. Gallen, Solothurn (since 2005), Ticino, Zürich and Zug (since 2008).

In addition to the cantonal criminal prosecution systems, there were *three systems of criminal prosecution by federal authorities*: a system of prosecution by federal prosecutors, in cases involving offences directed against the Swiss Confederation or that affected its interests, e.g. organised crime, white collar crime, money laundering and corruption (Gilliéron 2014, p. 171),[8] a system of prosecution by military prosecutors[9] and another system for the prosecution of contraventions of federal administrative law.[10]

4.1.3 The Unification of the Swiss Criminal Justice System

4.1.3.1 The New Swiss Criminal Procedure Code

As already mentioned, since 1 January 2011, the Criminal Procedure Code has unified the various systems of criminal procedure and the organisation of prosecutions as well as the criminal justice chain for the whole of Switzerland. The CrimPC regulates the prosecution and adjudication by federal and cantonal criminal justice authorities of offences under federal law. For criminal proceedings involving juveniles there is a special Juvenile Criminal Procedure Code[11] that is closely based on the CrimPC. At federal level, the work of the Office of the Attorney General of Switzerland is governed by the CrimPC. The military prosecution system and the prosecution of contraventions of federal administrative law are still governed by the same special rules that applied before 2011.

4.1.3.2 The New Criminal Justice Chain in Switzerland

The Criminal Procedure Code follows the PPS Model II and therefore leads, in line with current trends in Europe (Gilliéron 2014, p. 59), to the abolition of the system of examining magistrates, which was previously found in the cantons with an examining magistrate model or the PPS-Model I (see above Sect. 4.1.2). Therefore in the new Swiss criminal justice chain there are only two principal prosecution authorities (see Fig. 4.1).

The police investigate offences on their own initiative, in response to reports from members of the public and from authorities, and on the instructions of the public prosecution service. In doing so, they are subject to the supervision and the directives of the PPS (Art. 15 para. 2 CrimPC). The police, which include the

[8]Federal Act of 15 June 1934 on the Administration of Federal Criminal Justice (in force until 31 December 2010).

[9]According to the Military Criminal Procedure Code, SR 322.1.

[10]Federal Act on Administrative Criminal Law, SR 313.0.

[11]Swiss Juvenile Criminal Procedure Code of 20 March 2009, SR 312.1.

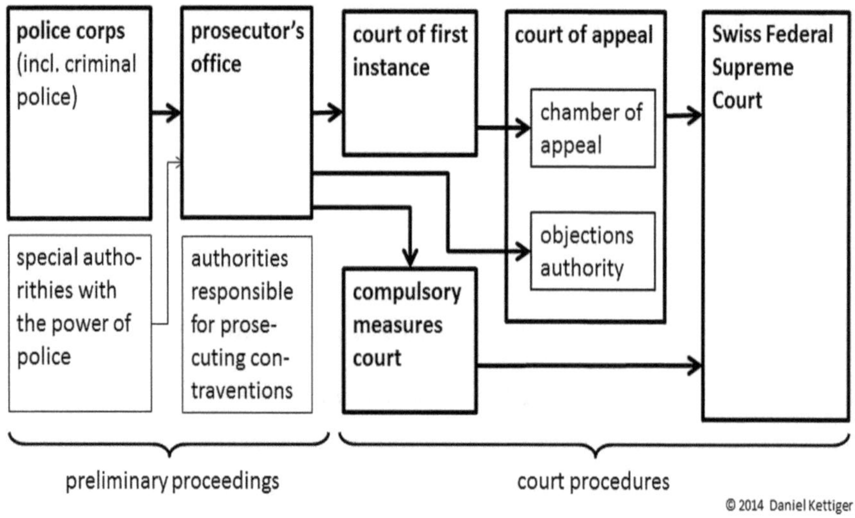

Fig. 4.1 Swiss criminal justice chain

criminal investigation and forensic specialists, are normally part of the cantonal police force, or in some cantons a city police force.

The public prosecution service is responsible for the uniform exercise of the state's right to punish criminal conduct (Art 16 CrimPC). It conducts preliminary proceedings, pursues offences within the scope of investigations, and where applicable brings charges and acts as prosecutor. So the public prosecutor in Switzerland assumes both the role of an examining magistrate and the role of the prosecutor as it is commonly understood.

For the prosecution of what are known in Switzerland as "contraventions",[12] cantonal law may delegate the preliminary proceedings to administrative authorities (Art. 17 para 1 CrimPC).

To counterbalance the enormous power that the PPS has throughout the preliminary proceedings, it was necessary to establish an impartial and independent judicial authority that checks the legitimacy and proportionality of compulsory measures (e.g. preventive detention, monitoring of telecommunications). Therefore every canton must have its *compulsory measures court*(*s*) (Art. 18 CrimPC). But a great number of compulsory measures still are within the competence of the prosecutor (e.g. searches of premises) or the police (e.g. observation of persons during less than one month).

The *canton of Basel-Stadt* has its own special system which does not follow the general Swiss model. The criminal investigation police are not part of the normal police force, but are a fully integrated division within the PPS.

[12]Minor criminal acts that are punishable only by a fine (Art. 103 of Swiss Criminal Code [SCC] of 21 December 1937, SR 311.0).

4.2 The Formal Position of the Public Prosecution Service

4.2.1 Status of an Authority Under the Swiss System of Separation of Powers

4.2.1.1 The Theoretical Background: Swiss Constitutional Law

The Federal Constitution (FC)[13] makes no mention of the constitutional status of the cantonal public prosecution services or other prosecution authorities; rather their organisation is basically an aspect of cantonal organisational autonomy (Art. 47 para. 2, Art. 123 para. 2 FC). This means that there are no specific constitutional requirements for the organisation of the PPS in Switzerland. Such requirements, however, are unnecessary, because international treaty law (in particular Art. 3, 5, 6 and 13 ECHR[14]) and the Federal Constitution (in particular Art. 29, 29a, 30 and 32 FC) lay down clear rules on the minimum standards that must be complied with in criminal proceedings and what decisions are reserved to judicial authorities, in particular in the form of procedural guarantees (Kettiger 2007 , p. 265ff). In addition, the guarantee of recourse to the courts (Art. 29a FC) applies to the orders issued by the prosecution authorities and to their investigative activities in individual cases; these orders and investigative activities are therefore subject to review by a judicial authority. Legal experts generally assume that the PPS is a constitutional "compositum mixtum", i.e. that the function it serves in the state places it somewhere between a judicial and an executive authority (Mettler 2000, p. 73f; Lienhard and Kettiger 2008, p. 6).

The PPS thus fulfils both prosecution and judicial functions in a broad sense but not a judicial function in the narrower sense of being able to set legal precedent (Kiener 2001, p. 319), despite having what are superficially quasi-judicial powers (Lienhard and Kettiger 2008, p. 21). Although its decision-making process is very similar to that of court judges, according to the prevailing expert opinion and legal precedent, the issuing of a *summary penalty order*[15] is not a judicial activity, as the decision has no legal authority and its binding effect as judgment depends

[13]Constitution of the Swiss Confederation of 18 April 1999; SR 101.

[14]Convention for the Protection of Human Rights and Fundamental Freedoms of 4 November 1950; SR 0.101.

[15]Art. 352 para 1 CrimPC: "If the accused has accepted responsibility for the offence in the preliminary proceedings or if his or her responsibility has otherwise been satisfactorily established, the public prosecutor shall issue a summary penalty order if, having taken account of any suspended sentence or parole order that must be revoked, it regards any of the following sentences as appropriate: (a) a fine; (b) a monetary penalty of no more than 180 daily penalty units; (c) community service of no more than 720 h; (d) a custodial sentence of no more than 6 months." The summary penalty order is a proposed and provisional judgment (Gilliéron 2014, p. 226). A written objection to the summary penalty order may be filed with the public prosecutor within 10 days. If the public prosecutor decides to stand by the summary penalty order, it sends the files immediately to the court of first instance for the conduct of a trial. If no valid objection is filed, the summary penalty order becomes a final judgment.

exclusively on the tacit or express consent of the defendant (Mettler 2000, p. 218ff; Kiener and Cupa 2012, p. 398ff). A similar situation arises with regard to the procedural arrangements in summary criminal procedure (plea bargaining); here again there is no judicial function in the narrower sense, as the arrangement is worked out in cooperation with the parties to the proceedings and only has the character of a request to the court (Brown 2003: 172ff). As a result, the PPS *is not in principle subject to judicial independence*, neither in the sense of a fundamental procedural right (Art. 30 para. 1 FC) nor in the sense of an institutional guarantee (Art. 191c FC) (Lienhard and Kettiger 2008, p. 21). It only acquires court status in exceptional cases and, even then only if it exercises the function of setting legal precedent in the narrower sense (e.g. when the Office of the Chief Public Prosecutor acts as first appellate authority); in this situation it must be institutionally independent, in particular from the executive (Kiener 2001, p. 319; Kiener and Cupa 2012, p. 401). Generally speaking, the issue of the independence of the cantonal public prosecution service *is not a question related to the functional or organisational separation of powers in the conventional sense* (Lienhard and Kettiger 2008, p. 21).

4.2.1.2 The Variations in Implementation

As discussed above, no constitutional restrictions have been placed on the organisational positioning of the cantonal prosecution services, and federal legislation imposes only one limitation, that the superior political authority or the supervisory authority must not be able to issue directives in individual cases (see Sect. 4.2.2). To this extent, the cantons are almost entirely free to decide how they wish to position their PPS in their structure and how the service is organised. Subject to these limited restrictions, the PPS may *be made subordinate to the executive or may be made part of the judiciary*. Making it part of the executive brings additional options when defining policy on law enforcement, while integration into the judiciary strengthens the position of the criminal justice system and thus the prosecution process as a whole. If an administrative committee of the court of appeal manages the judiciary in administrative terms and thus the public prosecution service as well, this has no adverse effect on judicial independence in subsequent appeal proceedings (Kettiger 2010). What must be considered when deciding on organisational positioning, and in particular in the case of the details of the organisational structure, is primarily the possibilities for working closely with the police (Blättler 2007).

In implementing the new criminal prosecution system, the cantons have made the most of their organisational freedom. In eight cantons, the PPS is fully integrated into the independent judiciary,[16] while in 16 cantons it is part of the cantonal administration and under the supervision of the executive.[17] Two cantons

[16]Cantons of Bern, Freiburg, Geneva, Jura, Neuchâtel, Nidwalden, Uri and Zug.

[17]Cantons of Aargau, Appenzell I.Rh., Appenzell A.Rh, Basel-Landschaft, Basel-Stadt, Glarus, Graubünden, Lucerne, St. Gallen, Schaffhausen, Solothurn, Schwyz, Ticino, Vaud, Wallis and Zurich.

have chosen a system in which the PPS, although part of the cantonal administration in administrative terms, is still subject to the supervision of the judiciary.[18]

4.2.2 The Personal Independence of the Prosecutor

Legal experts generally assume that the cantonal prosecution service—even if not subject to the guarantees of judicial independence—must have a special institutional and personal independence in view of its role in the prosecution process (Kiener 2001, p. 319; Kiener and Cupa 2012, p. 401; Lienhard and Kettiger 2007, p. 22). Nonetheless, it is occasionally argued that a PPS should be fully integrated into the executive and subject to its directives (Mettler 2000, p. 237ff; Trechsel 2005).

The new, uniform criminal procedure law now brings some clarity: Art. 4 CrimPC states that the prosecution authorities—including the cantonal prosecution service (cf. Art. 12 ff. CrimPC)—are independent in applying the law and bound solely by the law; this is however subject to the reservation of the statutory powers to issue directives. "As long as such powers to issue directives are not expressly stipulated in a formal federal or cantonal act, the cantonal prosecution service is independent in applying the law following the entry into force of the Criminal Procedure Code, without the need for any further legal provisions" (Lienhard and Kettiger 2007, p. 23). The dispatch[19] on the CrimPC also clearly states that in the future no supervisory authority of any nature or any other superior authority is permitted to exert any influence over an individual case that the PPS is dealing with: "The provision is clear that it relates to independence in the application of the law. As a result, interference by political authorities in the specific prosecution activities of the prosecution service are unreservedly excluded" (Bundesrat 2006, p. 1129).

On the other hand, it must be assumed that, *leaving aside individual cases*, a superior authority or supervisory authority may issue directives to the cantonal prosecution service, i.e. in a general, abstract or in a general, specific form that goes beyond administrative directives and also includes *legal directives*. However, a formal statutory basis is required (Art. 4 para. 2 CrimPC). In addition, the power to issue directives must be exercised with caution. In particular, where the cantonal prosecution service is part of the executive, it is the government's responsibility to set the prosecution authorities *criminal policy goals* and related priorities.[20] In this connection, it will also be permitted to issue *general directives on cooperation between the prosecution service and the police* (Lienhard and Kettiger 2007, p. 24).

[18]Cantons of Obwalden and Thurgau.

[19]A report by the Swiss government (Federal Council) on draft legislation.

[20]The Swiss Federal Supreme Court declared such general instructions and orders to be constitutional (see leading case/precedent of 21 October 1981, BGE 107 Ia 253, E. 3a).

4.3 The Internal Organisation of the Cantonal Prosecution Services

The federal law allows the cantons a very large degree of freedom in relation to the internal organisation of their prosecution services. The fact that this freedom has actually been used in implementing the new criminal prosecution system is shown by the following results of a study that the authors have carried out.[21]

Of the 26 cantons, 14 chose to organise their prosecution service *centrally* in one place, and 12 chose to organise it *decentrally* in two or more locations, the main reason being the size and the geography of the canton concerned.

The prosecution services in 18 cantons have a special *section for economic offences*, while only seven cantons—above all small cantons—have no special section for economic offences.[22] The three small cantons of Nidwalden, Obwalden and Uri have a joint section for economic offences, which is an organisational unit of the prosecution service in the canton of Nidwalden (Wolf 2011, p. 391).

Around 90 % of criminal proceedings are dealt with by means of a *summary penalty order*[23] (Gilliéron 2014, p. 226). The offences involved are primarily contraventions, in particular road traffic offences. In nine cantons, the prosecution service has a special section that is responsible for processing all or most of the summary penalty orders.[24]

The cantons may establish *a chief public prosecutor's or attorney general's office* (Art. 14 para 3 CrimPC). Five cantons have established an independent attorney general's office, controlling and supervising their generally decentralised prosecution services and representing the prosecution service before other cantonal authorities and in the Federal Supreme Court.[25] In the other cantons, the chief public prosecutor or attorney general is also the head of the prosecution service.

Most of the cantons provide in their legislation that a no-proceedings order, the complete or partial abandonment of proceedings, the suspension of an investigation or summary penalty orders *must be approved by a senior prosecutor* or an attorney general. Five cantons do not have any such rules, delegating all decisions in the preliminary proceedings entirely to the prosecutor in charge of the case.[26]

---

[21]Different descriptions of the status by Gilliéron (2014) or Arn et al. (2011) are due to definitions and actuality.

[22]Cantons Appenzell I.Rh., Appenzell A.Rh., Freiburg, Glarus, Graubünden, Jura, Neuchâtel and Schaffhausen.

[23]See footnote 15.

[24]Cantons Basel-Landschaft, Basel-Stadt, Jura, Lucerne, Neuchâtel, St. Gallen, Solothurn, Wallis and Zug.

[25]Cantons Aargau, Bern, Freiburg, Schwyz and Zurich.

[26]Cantons Geneva, Glarus, Neuchâtel, Schaffhausen and Ticino.

4.4 The Interface Between the Public Prosecution Service and the Police

4.4.1 The Position of the Police in the Cantonal Organisation

4.4.1.1 Basic Remarks

In Switzerland, policing tasks are assigned to the Federal Office of Police (fedpol), the military police forces, the transport police, the cantonal police forces and the numerous communal police forces—reflecting Switzerland's federal structures (Gilliéron 2014, p. 182f). Generally speaking, the cantons are responsible for the police (Haller 2009, p. 67). Each canton is in charge of its own police forces and has its own police code that regulates the cantonal police force and the communal police forces. However, cooperation is also established between the cantonal police forces through intercantonal agreements. In addition, the Conference of the Cantonal Justice and Police Directors and the Conference of Cantonal Police Commanders guarantee the coordination required by the Federal Constitution (Art. 57 para 2 FC).

The police forces belong to the executive branch. The cantonal police forces are fully integrated into their respective cantonal administrations and are subordinate to a cantonal department and to the government. In some cantons, the police force and the prosecution service are subordinate to the same minister but fully independent of each other.

4.4.1.2 The Multiple Roles of the Police

When it comes to the activities of the police in Switzerland, a general distinction is made between *criminal investigation* duties, and *public order and security* duties (Kettiger 2012, p. 4; Uster 2011, p. 204). In some cases, a further distinction is made in the field not involving criminal investigations between public order and security duties on one hand and *traffic policing* duties on the other hand. Criminal investigation activities in terms of the CrimPC is understood as any state activity involving investigation in the first phases of criminal proceedings and reporting to the investigating authority (normally the cantonal prosecution service) for the continuation for the prosecution process. The transport and public order and security police can also be responsible for criminal investigation activities, as they may also become involved in the investigation of offences (Gilliéron 2014, p. 183; Kettiger 2012, p. 5). Criminal investigation activities are exhaustively regulated by the CrimPC. The common element in all public order and security policing activities is that they primarily serve to avert specific dangers to public security, safety and order and risks to the environment (Uster 2011, p. 204). Public order and security policing activities are regulated by the cantonal police acts.

The police—in practical terms most police officers are members of the cantonal and communal police forces—have duties that involve both investigating crimes and averting dangers; the two areas of activity cannot be clearly separated in organisational terms—other than in the case of special services (Uster 2011, p. 204). This means that the majority of officers in any police force carry out criminal investigation activities for at least part of their duties, also the basic training given to the police primarily relates to security and traffic police duties.

4.4.2 A Principal and Agent Relationship

According to the law, the PPS has the lead over the whole of the preliminary proceedings (Art. 16 para 1 CrimPC). It may issue instructions and assignments to the police at any time or take over the conduct of the proceedings (Art. 15 para. 2, Art. 307 para. 2 CrimPC). The public prosecutor may also instruct the police to carry out additional enquiries after the investigation has been formally opened (Art. 312 para. 1 CrimPC). There are many investigative activities (e.g. a great number of compulsory measures) that the police may only carry out with the prosecutor's consent. Finally the prosecutor supervises the criminal investigation police (Art. 15 para. 2 CrimPC). The relationship between the prosecutor and police—to speak in terms of political or administrative science (Lane 2005)—is that of principal and agent. So the principal-agent theory may be used to explain problems in the relationship between the prosecutor services and the police.[27]

4.4.3 The Difference in Culture Between the Police and the Public Prosecution Service

The *criminal investigation police* in Switzerland are—with the exception of the police in Basel-Stadt—part of the cantonal police force or a city police force. Swiss police forces mostly have long traditions as (paramilitary) hierarchical organisations. Among their main values are law, order and discipline. One of the tasks of the police is enforcing the law—it is the police that exercise the state monopoly on the use of force. Most police officers (also police detectives) do not have an academic education. After completing secondary school and an apprenticeship unconnected with the police, they attend police school and start work as uniformed police officers in the police force.

The *public prosecution service* is either an independent agency of the public administration or is part of the judiciary (see Sect. 4.2.1.2). Commonly the current

[27]Such as the motivation (Behn and Robet 1995, p. 3018ff) of the police in criminal investigation.

cantonal PPS were founded in 2011 by merging the existing public prosecution service with the examining magistrates' authorities (the examining magistrates until the merger having the status of judges). So the culture in Swiss PPS is similar to the culture of a court. The expectations and values of judges focus on independence, on justice as a public service for the benefit of the parties to the court proceedings, and also very strongly on the human side of justice (humane, personalised, receptive) (Emery and De Santis 2014). Most assistant prosecutors and prosecutors are university graduates.

Given these circumstances, a "clash of cultures" may be expected when the police and prosecutors interact in the criminal justice process. From a theoretical point of view, this difference in organisational culture is likely to lead to basic distrust, which will affect cooperation. But according to results of new research, the reality seems to be rather different: prosecutors have high level of confidence in the police without regard of their own rating of work of the criminal police.[28]

4.4.4 The Prosecutors' Attitude to the Work of the Police

According to a current study,[29] the public prosecution services rate the work of the police in law enforcement with a grade of 5.0.[30] The work of police detectives and investigators was rated at 5.0, the work the forensic services being rated at 5.5. In contrast, the law enforcement work of uniformed police officers (i.e. police on patrol or riot police) was only given a grade of 4.5. Chief prosecutors gave the reason for this rather low rating for the riot police as primarily *inadequate training* with regard to law enforcement matters (in particular the procedural regulations) and a *lack of manpower* in the police.

15 of 26 PPS are of the opinion that the introduction of the new prosecution system and the new procedural law (CrimPC) has led to *changes in levels of cooperation with the police*. The main change is seen as the loss of the police's responsibility for conducting investigations independently or in giving the cantonal public prosecution service responsibility for conducting the entire preliminary proceedings. The possibility of issuing more precise instructions on investigation tasks is regarded as a positive development.

---

[28]In 2014 a survey by the authors in a cantonal prosecutor's office 21 prosecutors without leading function indicated the trust into police with an average index of 8.0 (out of 10) and thus higher than the average of Swiss population in a national survey with an index of 7.5 (Tresch and Wenger 2014, p. 102f).

[29]Survey by the authors (January 2015) asking the attorney general of the cantons.

[30]Swiss school mark system (grade system; Schulnoten): 6 = very good (A grade; sehr gut), 5 = good (B grade; gut), 4 = sufficient (D grade; genügend), 3 = insufficient (F grade; ungenügend), 2 = fail (schwach), 1 = total fail (sehr schwach).

Potential for *improving cooperation* in the law enforcement system is in particular seen in closer local cooperation or even in the organisational integration of the criminal investigation police into the cantonal public prosecution service (the Basel model), in a better legal training for police officers, in educating police officers to understand their specific role, and in increased communication.

4.5 First Experiences with the New Prosecution Model

Since its introduction on 1 January 2011, the Criminal Procedure Code has been widely criticised by experts, *primarily with regard to the law of criminal procedure*, which does not always seem to prove its value in practice (Donatsch 2012; Egli 2012; Jeanneret 2012; Kettiger 2012; Landshut and Schöning 2012; Schubarth 2012). In particular, the rules on participation in procedural hearings (Art. 147 CrimPC) where there is more than one accused person has been a matter of controversy (Schäfer 2012; Sprenger 2012) and there have even been calls for the rules to be repealed (SSK 2014). In addition, there are concerns as a matter of criminal policy (Riklin 2012, 2013; Schmid 2014) about the fact that around 90 % of convictions are secured by means of summary penalty order (see above Sect. 4.3). In another current study of the prosecution model,[31] criticism was often not directed towards the organisational model or the criminal justice process but towards the procedural law. The following remarks are limited to experiences of an operational or organisational nature.

So far, no systematic initial evaluation of the new prosecution system has been carried out and only a small number of papers have been published that consider the role of the public prosecutor (Summers 2012). Now, however, the first study on the assessment of the new prosecution system by the PPS is available. In the view of the chief cantonal prosecutors, the *main advantage of the new prosecution system* is that it avoids responsibility changing hands during the preliminary proceedings and thus leads to a gain in efficiency. Accordingly, it seems that the main objective of the new Criminal Procedure Code (Bundesrat 2006, p. 1107) has been achieved. Further advantages are seen in giving overall responsibility for the preliminary proceedings to one person, the public prosecutor, and in introducing a standardised system for the whole of Switzerland. The main disadvantages are regarded as the end to what was known as the "four-eyes" principle (i.e. that the examining magistrate/prosecutor could check each other's work) and system of quality control that it provided, as well as the increased level of bureaucracy.

[31] Survey by the authors (January 2015) asking the attorney general of the cantons.

4.6 Concluding Remarks

The new Criminal Procedure Code and the new, standardised prosecution model are applied in Switzerland since January 2011. The study conducted by the authors around four years after introduction reveal in general a positive picture. The main deficiencies in the Code appear to lie in the field of criminal procedure law, but not in the model introduced for PPS. However, only the opinions of the PPS are available. In order to obtain a more complete picture, the experiences of the police and the criminal courts within the criminal justice process must also be canvassed. In addition, the experiences of lawyers should also be evaluated. Whether the new prosecution model and the new Criminal Procedure Code are actually proving their value can probably only be comprehensively assessed in several years' time, based on a full evaluation of the Code. Whether a study of this type will be carried out is still uncertain at present, in autumn 2015. A comprehensive assessment would however be essential in order to avoid a situation in which Parliament, in a sense of unthinking activism, starts making changes as part of its day-to-day political business that harm the overall concept implemented in the Criminal Procedure Code.

References

Arn, Raphaël, Nicole Saurer and André Kuhn, ed. 2011. *Organisation der kantonalen und eidgenössischen Strafbehörden*. Helbing und Lichtenhahn: Basel.

Behn, Robet D. 1995. The Big Questions of Public Management. *Public Administration Review*, Vol. 55, No. 4 (Jul.–Aug., 1995), 313-324.

Blättler, Stefan. 2007. Die Stellung der Polizei im neuen schweizerischen Strafverfahren. *Zeitschrift für Strafrech*t (ZStrR), 243ff.

Braun, Robert. 2003. *Strafprozessuale Absprachen im abgekürzten Verfahren*. „Plea bargaining" im Kanton Basel-Landschaft? Verlag des Kantons Basel-Landschaft: Liestal.

Bundesrat. 2006. *Botschaft zur Vereinheitlichung des Strafprozessrechts vom 21. Dezember 2005*. BBl 2006 1085. Bern: Bundeskanzlei.

Donatsch, Andreas. 2012. Erste Erfahrungen mit dem Beweisrecht. *forumpoenale* 4, 235-246.

Egli, Isabelle. 2012. Protokollierungsvorschriften der schweizerischen Strafprozessordnung – ein Plädoyer für die Revision. *Aktuelle juristische Praxis* 5, 627-638.

Emery, Yves and Lorenzo De Santis. 2014. What Kind of Justice Today? Expectations Of 'Good Justice', Convergences And Divergences Between Managerial And Judicial Actors And How They Fit Within Management-Oriented Values. *International Journal for Court Administration* 6/1:63-75.

Gilliéron, Gwladys and Martin Killias. 2008. The Prosecution Service Function within the Swiss Criminal Justice System. *Eur J Crim Policy Res* (2008) 14:333–352.

Gilliéron, Gwladys. 2014. *Public Prosecutors in the United States and Europe*. A Comparative Analysis with Special Focus on Switzerland, France and Germany. Cham: Springer.

Haller, Walter. 2009. *The Swiss Constitution in a Comparative Context*.

Landshut, Nathan und Rolf Schöning. 2012. Die StPO in der praktischen Anwendung. In *Liber amicorum für Andreas Donatsch*, ed. Angelo Cavallo et al., 417-436. Schulthess: Zürich.

Lane, Jan-Erik. 2005. Public Administration and Public *Management. The Principal-Agent Perspective*. Routledge: Oxon

Lienhard, Andreas and Daniel Kettiger. 2007. Wege zur Aufsicht über den Bundesanwalt. *Justice-Justiz-Giustizia* 4.

Lienhard, Andreas and Daniel Kettiger. 2008. Die organisatorische Einordnung der Staatsanwaltschaft in die kantonale Behördenstruktur. *Justice-Justiz-Giustizia* 2.

Jeanneret, Yvan. 2012. Ordonnance pénale et procédure simplifiée: une autoroute semée d'embûches? *Jusletter* 13 February 2012

Kettiger, Daniel. 2007. Parteien—Rechtsunterworfene oder Kundinnen und Kunden? In *Akteure der Gerichtsbarkeit*, ed. Benjamin Schindler and Patrick Sutter, 245-282. St. Gallen: Dike.

Kettiger, Daniel. 2010. Zur Unabhängigkeit der Staatsanwaltschaft in der Justizorganisation. *Justice-Justiz-Giustizia* 4.

Kettiger, Daniel. 2012. Schnittstellenfragen der Schweizerischen Strafprozssordnung. *Jusletter* 13 February 2012.

Kiener, Regina. 2001. *Richterliche Unabhängigkeit.* Stämpfli: Bern.

Kiener, Regina and Basil Cupa. 2012. Hybrider Status – relative Unabhängigkeit. Zur institutionellen Stellung der Statsanwaltschaft. In *Liber amicorum für Andreas Donatsch*, ed. Angelo Cavallo et al., 395-416. Schulthess: Zürich.

Mettler, Christoph. 2000. *Staatsanwaltschaft*. Position innerhalb der Gewaltentrias, Funktion im Strafprozess und aufsichtsrechtliche Situation sowie ein Vorschlag zur Neuordnung. Helbing Lichtenhahn: Basel.

Riklin, Franz. 2012. Prozesserledigungsstrategien im Strafprozess und ihre Tücken. In *Liber amicorum für Andreas Donatsch*, ed. Angelo Cavallo et al., 499-516. Schulthess: Zürich.

Riklin, Franz. 2013. Rechtsstaatlichkeit von Strafbefehlen. *Neue Zürcher Zeitung*, May 6.

Schäfer, Michael. 2012. Die Teilnahme an Einvernahmen von Mittätern – Theorie und Praxis. *forumpoenale* 1, 39-44.

Schmid, Gian Andrea. 2014. Ohne rechtliches Gehör ins Gefängnis. *plädoyer* 2, 11-13.

Sprenger, Thomas. 2012. Teilnahmerechte der Parteien im Strafverfahren – wird die Ausnahme zum Grundsatz? *forumpoenale* 3, 167-172.

Schubarth, Martin. 2012. Chatroomproblematik und Versagen des Gesetzgebers. *Jusletter* 13 February 2012

Schweizerische Staatsanwälte-Konferenz SSK. 2014. Medienmitteilung, November 21.

Summers, Sarah. 2012. Presence, Absence, Dominance. Reflections on the Role of the Prosecutor in Switzerland. In *Liber amicorum für Andreas Donatsch*, ed. Angelo Cavallo et al., 517-529. Schulthess: Zürich.

Trechsel, Stefan. 2005. Wohin gehört der Bundesanwalt? *Neue Zürcher Zeitung* 2 October, 17.

Tresch, Tibor Szvircsev and Andreas Wenger. 2014. *Sicherheit 2014.* Aussen-, Sicherheits- und Verteidigungspolitische Meinungsbildung im Trend. ETH Zürich: Zürich.

Uster, Hanspeter. 2011. Art. 15. In Niggli, Marcel Alexander, Marianne Heer and Hans Wiprächtiger, 203-206. *Kommentar Schweizerische Strafprozessordnung*. Helbing und Lichtenhahn: Basel.

Wolf, André. 2011. Kanton Niedwalden. In *Organisation der kantonalen und eidgenössischen Strafbehörden*, ed. Arn, Raphaël, Nicole Saurer and André Kuhn, 387-402. Helbing und Lichtenhahn: Basel.

Chapter 5 Do Statistics Reinforce Administrative Centralisation? The Contradictory Influence of Quantified Indicators on French National Police

Anne-Cécile Douillet, Jacques de Maillard and Mathieu Zagrodzki

5.1 Introduction

Over the last few decades, the importance of quantitative indicators in policing has grown dramatically. These statistics are used for measuring both the current state and use of available resources, as well as the activities and results of the teams. Increased reliance on such tools derives mainly from an explicit will to improve the effectiveness of the force by assigning goals and monitoring results. The use of quantified performance indicators to measure and steer policing activities is a direct consequence of the rise of new public management, a trend that has recently taken over the policing world in France and elsewhere (Jones and Newburn 2009; de Maillard 2009), and is characterised by the implementation of "results-oriented management methods, based on goal-setting, performance measurement and appraisal, and new forms of control" (Bezes 2012, p. 17, our translation).

This chapter is an abridged and revised version of a paper published in *Politiques et Management Public* ("Une centralisation renforcée par le chiffre? Les effets contradictoires des indicateurs chiffrés dans la police nationale", 21 (4), 2014). The authors wish to thank the journal for authorising the present version.

A.-C. Douillet (✉)
Ceraps, University of Lille 2, Lille, France
e-mail: anne-cecile.douillet@univ-lille2.fr

J. de Maillard
Institut Universitaire de France, University of Versailles CESDIP, Versailles, France
e-mail: demaillard@cesdip.fr

M. Zagrodzki
UVSQ-CESDIP, Versailles, France
e-mail: mathieu.zagrodzki@gmail.com

A. Hondeghem et al. (eds.), *Modernisation of the Criminal Justice Chain and the Judicial System*, Ius Gentium: Comparative Perspectives on Law and Justice 50, DOI 10.1007/978-3-319-25802-7_5

Quantitative indicators appear particularly adequate for results-oriented management and "performance" comparison. "Numbers" (in French, "*le chiffre*") constitute an exchange, appraisal, and benchmarking tool for the actors involved.

This is a hugely debated and controversial trend, especially given the political use and low credibility of these statistics.[1] Some research seems to show that pressure to deliver has brought about policing practices focused on short-term results, easy cases, and rigged statistics in France (Mucchielli 2008; Matelly and Mouhanna 2007). Whatever the case may be, despite ongoing criticism, these metrics remain popular with media and political figures, because of a "shared political sense in matters of security" (Cos 2012, our translation).

Another question, beyond the political/politician use of "policing stats", is how they are being used by both the organisation itself and policing actors, and whether policing activities may not ultimately end up being governed by numbers. How are performance indicators used by the various components of policing? How significant are they considered to be? What is their influence on working practices and relationships? These questions can only be answered by exploring how policing is perceived on a statistical basis, how these data are read, and how policing is affected.

In the context of this chapter, the influence of quantified indicators on policing is to be analysed through how they affect the organisation. We intend to question their effects on hierarchical relationships: are performance indicators rather linked to central control and steering, or do they foster autonomy among agencies at various hierarchical levels? The organisational aspects of this questioning are obvious, and whether or not quantitative goal-setting fosters (de)centralisation matters all the more that policing has long been highly centralised in France. These questions, however, also raise highly political issues. Two aspects of policing that need to be better understood are goal-setting (where are planning and prioritising actually done?) and reporting (how much of police action actually transpires from indicators?).

In management literature, "results-oriented management" is associated with empowerment at every echelon (Biondi et al. 2008), which implicitly suggests a "participative", or at least devolved, process of goal-setting. Most studies on management reforms in police forces, however, conclude at an increase of centralisation, precisely because shared goals and priorities are attributed to rather disparate units, and also due to increased monitoring and reporting demands from top management (Collier 2006; Hough 2007). These studies also emphasise the fact that the logic of accountability has somewhat shifted in nature, from "community-oriented" (answering the needs of the population) to "management-oriented" (delivering to the upper echelons) (Loveday 2006). The use of performance indicators thus seems to follow a vertical pattern, from top to bottom, in which goals are set and resources allocated at the national level, which implies that controls become

[1]See for instance: Laurent Mucchielli, "Délinquance: la com' rituelle du ministère de l'Intérieur", 21 January 2011, *Médiapart*.

pervasive, feeding a vicious circle of increasingly direct interventions from the upper echelons. Hibou (2012, p. 113), analysing the expansion of "results-oriented management" in a broader sense, concluded quite bluntly that this logic requires "the centralisation of decision-making and an authoritarian brand of power".

In the case of the French police, the first conclusion that can be drawn from the research materials collected so far is that reporting activities have become a significant part of the overall work: more and more *Police Nationale* (national police) officers are busy churning numbers each day, as key performance indicators (KPI) reporting fundamentally seems to be about fuelling a self-feeding frenzy whereby more quantitative data have to be generated each day (1). Another finding is that increased reliance on performance indicators seems to bolster the centralisation tendencies of French police forces even further, every echelon being expected to report to some upper level of management (2). This way of reporting information upward, however, triggers all sorts of reactions and behaviours from the lower echelons, who tend to implement various adjustment strategies to cope with increasingly urgent demands from their hierarchy (3). Moreover, and however pressing the controls induced by the very use of performance indicators and objectives are perceived to be, they can only partially be achieved, given the many adjustments, arrangements, and downright cheating procedures that enable the rank-and-file to bypass the demands of management and generate a fragmentation process which contradicts the centralisation logic described previously (4).

This chapter is based on comparative research about policing management in France and Britain.[2] Data from four French police stations are examined—two of them from the Paris *Préfecture de Police*[3] (PP—Police Prefecture), and the other two from the Pas de Calais *Direction Départementale de la Sécurité Publique* (DDSP).[4] Police stations were chosen for accessibility reasons but also in order to have contrasted situations, in terms of population density, delinquency rates and police "performance". Interviews have also been carried out at the ministerial level, both at the *Direction Centrale de la Sécurité Publique* (DCSP—Central Directorate of Public Security) and at the headquarters of the *Direction de la Sécurité de Proximité de l'Agglomération Parisienne* (DSPAP—Directorate for Public Safety of the Paris area). The French part of the research, which is the focus of this chapter, involved 41 exploratory interviews (mostly at the central level, almost exclusively with superintendents) and 85 local field interviews (46 for the PP, 39 in Pas de Calais). The survey took place in 2012–2013.

---

[2]This research, called Refmanpol (*Réformes managériales des polices*), is funded by the ANR (Agence nationale de la Recherche).

[3]The *Préfet de Police* (police prefect) is in charge of policing in Paris. The job-holder is a senior civil servant, appointed by the President of the Republic and reporting directly to the minister of Interior.

[4]Pas de Calais is a department in northern France. DDSP: Departmental Directorate of Public Security.

5.2 Data Collection and Management: A Fast-Developing Activity Within the *Police Nationale*

As of 2013, the French national police was keeping track of 73 indicators, organised into 6 sections, one for each mission of the police: crimes and offenses registered by both police and gendarmerie forces[5]; solved cases; persons held in police custody; impleaded third-parties; use of resources; time spent on activities… These data are used to compile monitoring scoreboards at both the district ("*arrondissement*", one of the 20 subdivisions of Paris) and department levels (in this chapter, "department" and "departmental" refer to the "*département*", a French administrative division), making it possible to compare the results from each district. One of the reasons for the spectacular development of such indicators is of course technology, which fosters a logic of quantitative data digitisation, automatic recording, and immediate transmission. At a more fundamental level, the development of scoreboards and quantified indicators has to do with the managerial transformations taking place in public organisations, which tend to import standards and methods from the private sector, thus popularising tools and discourses on performance, with an emphasis on "getting results" (Roché 2008; Maillard and Savage 2012).

In this respect, a recent and symptomatic example is the use of the word "performance" in police-related pieces of legislation such as LOPPSI (*Loi d'orientation et de programmation pour la performance de la sécurité intérieure*—Framework and planning Act for Homeland security performance) in 2009, or the 28 July 2006 directive from the ministry of Interior to prefects as well as police and gendarmerie directors, with its emphasis on the "culture of performance". The production of indicators meeting planned quantitative goals is clearly encouraged by such a logic. Since quantified indicators are supposed to help improve team management and performance, further indicators are needed to either justify potentially disappointing results, show why the previous indicators did not perform as expected, or prove that no effort has been spared to get the best possible results. Thus it is that statistics generate more statistics, as the two logics—reporting and performance-driven management—seem to feed one another in practice.

While quantified indicators were rising to prominence, the police were assigned new responsibilities and tasks, and major changes occurred in their training, compensation, and appraisal processes as well. Today, establishing explicit goals and building performance indicators to evaluate the efficiency and effectiveness of the various units are defining elements of the work of managing officers. Ever since the 2001 piece of legislation that first introduced the logic of performance in public management (*Loi organique relative aux lois de finances*—constitutional bylaw on budget acts), the general director of the national police has been tasked with

[5]In France, public safety is entrusted to two distinct forces: the *Police Nationale* in urban areas, and the *Gendarmerie Nationale* in rural areas.

designing a yearly performance plan that includes specific goals and quantified indicators. In addition, the appraisal process of police superintendents (*commissaires*) was modified in 2004 to evaluate whether "results pertaining to objectives previously established in line with available resources" have been obtained. By the same logic, starting in 2010, managers heading central police stations are expected to elaborate "individual performance plans" that may result in bonuses, provided the goal(s) that have been jointly set with their superiors are reached. The whole policing organisation has seen the advent of performance-based compensation in 2004. The initial €5 m budget funding individual and group bonuses was gradually raised to reach €10 m in 2005 and €25 m from 2008 (Cour des Comptes 2013).

One proof of the growing importance of performance indicators is the massive creation of new specialised jobs within the police force, some of which are specifically devoted to data collection and processing. In Paris, each district has its own central police station, headed by a superintendent who, ever since the early 2000s, has been able to rely on an Operational coordination office (*Bureau de Coordination Opérationnelle*—BCO) that reports directly to him/her. One of the BCO's tasks is to collect and record statistical data, as well as answering requests for information from upper echelons. At DSPAP headquarters, a 15-strong team has been put together to monitor quantified indicators. In the Pas de Calais department, a dozen officers collect and process statistical data at DDSP, in addition to individual statistics managers in each police station.

5.3 Quantified Indicators and Increased Centralisation

Even though the aforementioned 2006 directive stressed the participative nature of the goal-setting process, KPI proliferation only reinforces the hierarchical structure of the *Police Nationale*. The French national police is structured around three nodes of hierarchical relationships: central/departmental, departmental/local, and within police stations. At each of these three levels, new management techniques tend to further promote the centralising tendencies of the French system.

5.3.1 From the Ministry to the Police Station: Reinforced Centralisation

Priorities are defined at the ministry of Interior, first and foremost. Once objectives have been set by DCSP in agreement with both the ministry and the general police directorate, they are passed down to the departmental level, which is supposed to make adjustments for local conditions. Itemising such national objectives is a complex process. Departmental directors have to take into account local conditions and national priorities without any opportunity for "local negotiation". In fact, their goal is to meet their own management's expectations, because their own appraisal process is at stake. Another element that tends to shore up centralisation is the fact that information has to be passed on to the central level at regular intervals—which used to be monthly, then weekly—not to mention weekly meetings with the *prefect* and thematic requests.

Statistical reporting is partly hierarchic by nature, since those reporting are held accountable and may be queried about their action. This puts generalised pressure on local actors, especially when black sheep may be identified. In this case, requesting statistics may be construed as a governance tool: the demand for numbers demonstrates control, while the reward system instils the idea that reaching one's goals is a good thing. One Chief of staff, when asked what happens when departmental objectives are not reached, initially answered "nothing!" before elaborating:

> If departmental objectives are not reached, there is a penalty, if I may say so, i.e. some collective bonuses awarded by the government may not be paid. Some departments are selected for bonuses when they have good results; for instance we did receive the bonus this year. So, that's another criterion to judge results (…) When a departmental director gets the bonus on a given year, he wants good results after that, not so much to get the bonus as to avoid not getting it. (December 2012).

Relationships between departmental directors and police stations are similarly impacted. The proliferation of digital monitoring systems creates an afflux of information at the departmental level. This allows departmental chiefs of staff to monitor police station activity on a daily basis and potentially call superintendents whenever they notice "abnormal" numbers or negative developments.

This situation is even more acute in Paris, especially ever since the *Préfecture de Police* (PP) got responsibility for Paris' three neighbouring departments. The PP's management and the *police prefect*'s cabinet are statistics-hungry organisational units. Hence, all police stations under PP's jurisdiction have stringent goals and priorities, even if it sometimes means involving suburban precincts in what are essentially Parisian issues. Statistics must be reported so that the implementation of these objectives may be monitored: the point of asking districts to specify the number of peddlers or prostitutes that have been arrested is to control that actions prioritised by the prefect are indeed being carried out (Maillard and Mouhanna 2015).

As a consequence, police superintendents—who used to enjoy a degree of real autonomy—now seem to be twice accountable, having to report to their management internally while being expected by their political and social environment to deliver on crime statistics and be able to communicate with local actors.

> I basically have three or four directors: the prefect, the public prosecutor, my administrative director, and the mayor. Those are my four bosses. That's where I take orders… well, directions at least, and then it's up to me to come up with the right mix. Note that the incentive system encourages us to favour ministerial instructions over local priorities. (superintendent, Préfecture de police, February 2012)

French centralisation gets all the more bolstered that there are no participatory dynamics to speak of. Only the superintendents' individual performance plans are defined by the concerned parties. The same logic—reporting to superiors, monitoring subordinates—is at work within police stations.

5.3.2 The Reinforcement of Internal Accountability Within Police Stations

Within police stations, quantified indicators can be used as a tool for measuring, monitoring, and controlling activities. Managing officers often have an in-house data management team. In any case, scoreboards and other aforementioned computer tools are updated on a daily basis by field officers, who thus pass on information to their management.

This reporting mania seems relatively new to sergeants,[6] who now have to account for their activities by delivering scoreboards at regular intervals—this is especially true for beat patrols. Sometimes, this can be supplemented by quantitative goals:

> We were expected to pass on information from the management and set goals for the commanding officers and ourselves. We had objectives for everything: fines, accidents, arrests; and at the end of each month, we had to hand in a report listing the recorded cases, the atmosphere at the brigade, sick leaves, arrests, roadside checks per officer... everything was minutely detailed on paper. We handed the report to the commander and went through it with him. He then wrote his own report, merging data from all brigades, and sent that to central management. (Junior officer, beat patrol, Préfecture de police, October 2012).

This logic of reporting is expected to reinforce dedication among middle managers monitoring operational teams. Information must circulate from the bottom of the pyramid to the top and support decision-making, from which scoreboard-based systematic reporting seems ideally suited. The ambition is to rationalise the police as an organisation, making it more transparent and accountable to itself, and making sure that management is able to monitor activities. However, such a project meets with critics and adjustment strategies within the police organisation, which reinforce its fragmentation rather than its centralisation.

5.4 Criticising the Logic of Bureaucracy

As we can see, the centralised system creates information-hungry central authorities that are constantly requesting data to support their planning and decision-making activities, and to monitor the subsequent implementation of their measures. The frequency of such requests, especially in Paris, often tends to irritate the rank-and-file, who perceive reporting as a time-consuming, routine, and useless activity (3.1). Uncooperative behaviours have even been observed, in particular when a given request cannot possibly be answered adequately (3.2). Quantitative data management (colloquially known as "*le chiffre*", i.e. "numbers", as in "meeting one's numbers") is perceived as a form of bureaucratic hassle, an unwieldy additional activity.

[6]Brigadiers or brigadiers-majors in the National police.

5.4.1 Urgent, Nagging Requests: The Ordeals of Centralisation

While information does get passed on, those who collect it may have some reservations, emphasising the ever-urgent, repetitive, sometimes groundless character of the requests. In terms of urgency, requests emanating from the central level may put staff under considerable pressure:

> The main constraint for us is deadlines. We are talking very tight deadlines. (…) I mean, typically, sometimes the deadline is a couple of hours or even less… sometimes 24 hours. (Chief of staff, territorial directorate, Préfecture de police, July 2012).

Besides, the same information will often be transmitted to various recipients, in a similar format but with a slightly different time-frame. Some staff are getting tired of producing the same information for different management units:

> We do a lot of one-off reporting on specific topics… The problem, however, is that the same stuff might be requested 4 to 5 times, from 5 distinct requesters. (Chief of staff, territorial directorate, Préfecture de police, April 2012).

Finally, the frequency and variety of inquiries originating from the central level tend to generate a fair share of weariness among staff. Requests keep pouring in, often perceived as "political" in nature and far removed from ground reality, triggering negative reactions:

> We realised that we were receiving quite a few requests the year before (elections)… We knew they were going to give us a hard time anyway. (…) We literally had to report about everything. (Officer, office of statistical analysis, departmental directorate, October 2012).

Centrally-designed requests do not necessarily make sense at the local level:

> And then there is this tendency to take a one-sided view of every problem. Prostitution is not confined to Paris; I'm not saying it doesn't happen in X, but it's confined to three Romanian hustlers operating on Y Square, period… certainly not a [major] trend, yet we are now conducting a study! (…) The whole team is going to have to churn out some kind of report. (Superintendent, Préfecture de police, July 2012).

The reporting process is made all the more complex by the hierarchical nature of the institution. It is a defining characteristic of the French police force that it has a great many layers of hierarchy, each of which is expected to report to the echelon above. Such a proliferation tends to stretch the temporality of the process and fuel tensions between the various levels.

5.4.2 Maintaining a Form of Organisational Opacity

One-off requests cannot be anticipated by the requestee, which can result in erroneous output. Under time pressure, lacking adequate data-collection resources, not even convinced of the legitimacy of the request, subordinate levels may be led to supply faulty information. Some do indeed question the quality and reliability of the information thus produced:

> For clever requests, we're going to look up the proper figures; but for stupid questions such as 'Boss, headquarters want to know the number of... pffff', I simply call my secretary: - 'Give me a figure between 0 and 100' (I swear!) - '37'. And let me tell you: 9 times out of 10, it's fine, we never hear about it again. (Superintendent, Préfecture de police, July 2012).

This is clearly not an entirely rational system with perfectly fluid information flows. At each and every level, requests get retranslated, reappropriated, even rejected sometimes. This mix of detachment from institutional tools and increasing reliance on quantified indicators actually fuels the proliferation thereof. Many actors have in fact informally developed their own makeshift quantitative tools, either for improved management effectiveness—when institutional tools (MCI, crime mapping...) are deemed unreliable—or in anticipation of potential criticism from above:

> I have designed my own tools, updated by the junior officer who is working with me. (...) I use that to justify myself. If I'm being blamed for a slump in activity, and for instance we had 16 staff guarding hospitals, or simply being present at some events, football games, whatever... this adds up, it's time you can't give for something else, so you can't do traffic checks, you can't arrest people, you can't secure places... because you're somewhere else. I need supporting evidence explaining why results are not that good (...). (Commanding officer, beat patrol, Préfecture de police, October 2012).

In other words, observing how information is produced yields insights on the centrifugal nature of policing, as well as (crucially) tensions between the top and the bottom, and on discrepancies between the synoptic ambition of central authorities and the actual ability of the system to produce relevant information, as evidenced by the use of quantified indicators in establishing objectives and monitoring teams.

5.5 Managing by Numbers: Quest of Conformity and Organisational Tensions

As we have seen, statistics put all levels of management under pressure by generating upward information flows. Rank-and-file officers feel pressured as well because quantified indicators mean that quantitative results are expected. Efforts to "meet numbers" ultimately generate arrangements to make sure management expectations are fulfilled (4.1). Those very numbers may also be a source of disagreement between the various hierarchical layers on the relevance of planned goals. The study does indeed reveal a number of organisational rifts hinging on the issue of performance indicators (4.2).

5.5.1 Tampering with Numbers: An Implicit Arrangement

It has been shown that crime statistics have become a key element in how the effectiveness of police forces is evaluated politically (Monjardet 2006; Mucchielli 2008). The more politicised police information is, the more likely it is to be tampered with. Both the police and political actors have an incentive to produce information displaying lower crime rates and higher clearance rates, and since this information is produced by the force itself, numbers may be "skewed" to suit the needs. As a consequence, tampering is known to be a rather common practice (Matelly and Mouhanna 2007).

Demands for "good numbers" from above may lead superintendents to fall back on compliance strategies that make full use of any leeway the system has to offer. Some managers did quote specific examples of pressure from their own management to produce better-looking results. Nothing is ever mentioned explicitly, of course, but they are expected to find "creative" ways of showing a decrease of criminal activities in their sector:

> When numbers look very, very, very bad, (your boss) won't get mad at you, he'll just ask for an explanation. 'How come…?'. You're supposed to realise that he is really admonishing you, but he's just calling you. That's what he did to me in the early days. (…) It would last three or four days maybe. Finally, you realise that he's piling up pressure on you and that you're expected to find a way to get those indicators to look greener. There are many different ways, each more or less tolerated and institutionalised. (…) So you display good results, and then you do your job as best you can. (Superintendent, 2012).

Frequent statistical reporting, then, tends to increase hierarchical influence and control: numbers travelling upwards may result in (not necessarily explicit) demands for better results. Still, ground officers do retain some leeway, which goes to show how paradoxical centralisation can be: while statistical tampering is a consequence of central orders that aim at reaching certain goals, tampering methods derive from myriad local practices developed by the police. From this perspective, policing is both undeniably centralised (centrally-defined goals must be reached) and deeply fragmented (each management level enjoys significant leeway in data recording and reporting). Moreover, this results-oriented logic tends to generate tensions in hierarchical relationships, the upper echelons being perceived as focused on quantitative goals only.

5.5.2 KPI Use as a Source of Institutional Divide

There is no doubt that statistical pressure increases distance between the various levels of management. In this respect, quantified indicators can be said to be contributing to organisational tensions within police forces. While junior and middle-ranking officers tend to be loyal to their superiors, they may occasionally keep their distances, or even strategically question their decisions. In police stations, for instance, some of them implicitly challenge the "productivity" goals set by superintendents, suggesting that teams had better "not overdo it" lest they should eventually be asked to do "even more", or telling their management that better results cannot be achieved:

> You might be forgiven to think that management always wants more. The problem is, you can do more and more for a while, but eventually... That's my position always. (...) We're not a private venture with numbers to make, however. That's not possible. (...) Sometimes we just have nothing to show. (Commanding officer, Préfecture de police, October 2012)

However, this rift does not appear to be quite as glaring as the one separating senior officers from junior officers (*officiers* vs. *gradés*). While superintendents and senior officers, especially those with a team management role, perform quite similar functions, there seems to be less continuity between senior officers and junior officers/rank-and-file. Junior officers with a direct management role will translate—i.e. transmit *and* transform—orders. These "men in the middle", as Monjardet (1996) put it, play a key role in the adjustment process that transfers management demands into field practices, sometimes increasing results-oriented pressure by setting even more ambitious goals in order to make sure management will be happy, sometimes negotiating the quantitative requests, emphasising the fact that staff safety might be put at risk. In one of the beat patrol units we met, everybody agreed on the precedence of safety rules over quantitative goals:

> I always tell colleagues–'I will never judge you on the number of arrests you'll bring back to me in a one-month period'. I do, however, focus on how many ID checks they perform. And I do have a zero tolerance policy on safety in ID check situations. (Junior officer, neighbourhood safety group leader, October 2012).

More often than not, junior officers consider instructions from above disguised encouragements to meet numbers, even though it may not be the case. One example occurred in a Paris district. As one captain was telling his staff to fine a group of youths who had gathered in the street—with a view to curb peace-disturbing behaviours—one of his junior officers, considering that this demand was essentially meant to improve statistics and that fining was not part of his team's missions, flatly did not even attempt to have his staff fulfil these instructions.

This goes to show that relationships within police stations remain quite distant, and communication rather uneasy. Orders from the top are often perceived exclusively through the cold prism of numbers. Hierarchy is discontinuous and laden with misunderstandings, and there is no real shared understanding of strategic orientations either. The issue of quantitative results is thus a debated one, prompting both negotiations and tensions between the various levels of management. More fundamentally, however, statistics is a professional identity defining issue. During our interviews, one consistent leitmotif from lower-ranking staff was the idea that management was focused on numbers first and foremost, whereas they were into real policing themselves, as a *junior officer* pointed out: "*Management work for their numbers, we work for victims.*"

5.6 Conclusion

Widespread reliance on quantified indicators has undeniably changed the way French national police operates. Our study shows that the proliferation of performance indicators acts as a booster for the organisational centralisation logic, both between the central and local levels and within police stations. Organisational integration within police forces has been reinforced by such methods as quantitative goal setting, systematic statistical reporting, and incentive and sanction systems. The centralised logic that was already prevalent within the institution has served as the backdrop for the development of KPI use, which was furthered by the deployment of more stringent mechanisms of accountability. All kinds of scoreboards and charts move their way up the hierarchical management ladder. Such centralised reporting generates frustration among staff, who complain about having to transmit data repeatedly without necessarily being given the means to produce relevant information or knowing what it will be used for.

Still, in each of these dimensions, the organisational thickness of the force leaves an imprint on how such tools are mobilised. Reappropriation, deflection, bypass, and avoidance strategies abound at each and every level of management. The present study shows the existence of a discrepancy between the will of the central echelons to steer and control the activities of the rank-and-file on the one hand, and the latter's ability to appear to meet the demands of management by patching together solutions that actually serve to conceal their real actions on the other. In this perspective, systematic use of quantified indicators essentially points at some form of organisational hypocrisy (Brunsson 2002): while indicators may be perceived as meeting a growing external demand for improved performance (the political organisation, in Brunsson's logic), actual KPI use is indicative of relatively stable institutional workings (organisational action), even though quantitative data management has prompted the creation of new tasks as well as new recording practices, and can be said to have induced extra tensions.

References

Bezes Philippe (2012), "Etat, experts et savoirs managériaux. Les producteurs et diffuseurs du *New Public Management en France* depuis les années 1970", *Actes de la recherche en sciences sociales,* n°193, p. 16-37.

Biondi, Y., Chatelain-Ponroy, S. et Sponem, S. (2008), "De la quantification comptable et financière dans le secteur public: promesses et usages de la gestion par les résultats», *Politiques et management public*, 26 (3), p. 113-125.

Brunsson, N. (2002), *The Organization of Hypocrisy,* Copenhagen, Copenhagen Business School Press (2nd Edition).

Collier, P. (2006), In Search of Purpose and Priorities: Police Performance Indicators in England and Wales.*Public Money and Management* 26 (3), 165-172.

Cos, R. (2012), "Les élus socialistes face aux chiffres de la délinquance. Dispositions, positions et prises de position partisanes sur les statistiques policières", *Mots. Les langages du politique*, n°100, p.107-122.

Cour des Comptes (2013), *Police et gendarmerie nationale: dépenses de rémunération et temps de travail*, Rapport public thématique.

Hibou, B. (2012), *La bureaucratisation du monde à l'ère néo-libérale*, Paris, La Découverte.

Hough, M. (2007), "Policing, New public management and legitimacy in Britain", in T. Tyler (ed.), *Legitimacy and criminal justice: an international perspective*, The Russell Sage Foundation.

Jones, T. & Newburn, T. (2009), "Le managérialisme et la nature des réformes policières en Angleterre et au Pays de Galles", *Revue française de science politique,* 49 (6), p. 1175-1196.

Loveday, B. (2006), "Policing performance: the impact of performance measures and targets on police forces in England and Wales", *International Journal of Police Science & Management*, 8 (4), p. 282-293.

Maillard, J. de (2009), "Réformes des polices dans les pays occidentaux. Une perspective comparée", *Revue française de science politique*, 59 (6), p. 1197-1230.

Maillard, J. de & Savage, S. (2012), "Comparing performance: the development of police performance management in France and Britain", *Policing & Society*, 22 (4), p. 363-383.

Maillard, J. de, Mouhanna, C., 2015, «Governing the police by numbers: the French experience», in J. Ross & T. Delpeuch (eds), *The Democratic Governance of Intelligence: New Models of Participation and Expertise in Policing*, Edward Elgar Publisher, 2015.

Matelly, J.-H. & Mouhanna, C. (2007), *Police. Des chiffres et des doutes*, Paris, Michalon.

Monjardet, D. (1996), *Ce que fait la police. Sociologie de la force publique*, Paris, La Découverte.

Monjardet D., 2006, "Comment apprécier une politique policière ? Le ministère Sarkozy (7 mai 2002-30 mars 2004)", *Sociologie du travail*, 48 (2), p. 188-208.

Mucchielli, L. (2008), "Le "nouveau management de la sécurité" à l'épreuve: délinquance et activité policière sous le ministère Sarkozy (2002-2007)", *Champ pénal/Penal Field* mis en ligne le 28 avril 2008. URL: http://champpenal.revues.org/document3663.html.

Roché, S. (2008), "Performance Management in France: A Police or an Electoral Issue?", *Policing*, 2 (3), p. 331-339.

Chapter 6
From Justice Archipelago to Security and Justice Chain: Strategy-Organisation Configurations in the Dutch Criminal Justice System

Stavros Zouridis

6.1 Introduction

From the end of the Second World War to the 1980s the organisations in the Dutch criminal justice chain led a relatively stable and quiet life (Brommet 2002; Bevers 2004). Triggered by the explosion of cases in the 1970s and 1980s many reforms have dramatically changed the structure, the performance, and even the very principles on which these organisations have been built. This contribution depicts some of the major reforms in the Dutch criminal justice chain. These reforms are analysed from the perspective of strategy-organisation configurations. The concept of strategy-organisation configuration refers to the more or less coherent mix of law enforcement strategy on the one hand and organisation principles, structures, and routines on the other hand. The strategy-organisation configuration perspective assumes that organisational reforms are never strategically neutral and that changes in law enforcement strategies affect the organisations involved.

Section 6.2 introduces the criminal justice system in the Netherlands and Sect. 6.3 sketches some major reforms in the Dutch criminal justice system since the 1980s. In Sect. 6.4 these reforms are analysed from the perspective of strategy-organisation configurations. Systemic legal reforms such as a renewal of the appeal system, the gradual development of a system of administrative legal protection and its insertion in the regular court system, and the integration of cantonal courts in the district courts are not included in this contribution (see for example Bovend'Eert 2008). The concluding section speculates on the next generation of reforms and the next strategy-organisation configuration.

S. Zouridis (✉)
Tilburg University, Tilburg, The Netherlands
e-mail: S.Zouridis@uvt.nl

A. Hondeghem et al. (eds.), *Modernisation of the Criminal Justice Chain and the Judicial System*, Ius Gentium: Comparative Perspectives on Law and Justice 50, DOI 10.1007/978-3-319-25802-7_6

6.2 The Dutch Criminal Justice Chain

This section briefly summarizes some key features of the Dutch criminal justice chain. It first outlines the criminal justice organisations in the Netherlands and the way these are connected. In order to illustrate the size and the case load of the organisations in the Dutch criminal justice chain this section also includes some recent facts and figures.

6.2.1 The Main Actors of the Dutch Criminal Justice Chain

Because of its broad range of tasks the police is a key actor in the Dutch criminal justice chain. Apart from specific tasks such as supervising non-Dutch citizens and deciding on licenses to owe a gun, the police is primarily responsible for crime control, public order, traffic, securing persons, and the general task of providing assistance to those who appeal on the police (article 3 of the Police Act 2012). Compared with other police forces the Dutch model of policing has been described as a predominantly civil model of policing (e.g. Pakes 2004). The Dutch police operates under the authority of the mayors and the public prosecutors (the articles 11 and 12 of the Police Act 2012). The authority of the mayor extends to maintaining public order in his municipality whereas the public prosecutor leads criminal investigations. The coordination between the authorities and police management takes place in regular meetings on the local, the regional, and the national level. The public prosecutor decides on the investigative actions to be carried out (article 148 of the Code of Criminal Procedure). Some actions require the authorisation of a pre-trial judge such as the decision to keep a suspect in custody for more than three days.

The public prosecutor has the exclusive authority to prosecute suspects. In this respect the Dutch legal system can to a large extent be characterised as an inquisitorial system (see Damaška 1986). The Dutch system is based on the principle of opportunity instead of the legality principle (e.g. Pakes 2004). The opportunity principle implies that the public prosecutor has the exclusive authority to prosecute or dismiss suspects. Recently victims and any other persons with an interest in the case may submit their case to the appeal court. The appeal court then decides whether the public prosecutor should prosecute a suspect (article 12 of the Code of Criminal Procedure). Criminal cases are only a relatively small part of the case load of the district courts and the appeal courts (only 25–35 % in 2013). In the Netherlands there are no special criminal courts or criminal appeal courts. The pre-trial judges that decide on investigative actions are members of the same courts as the judges who decide on the cases and the lawfulness of the investigative actions. After the court has ruled the public prosecutor is primarily responsible for the execution of court convictions (article 553 of the Code of Criminal Procedure). Prison sentences are carried out by the prison organisation, fines are collected by a central collection agency, and community services are implemented by the child protection agency and resettlement organisations.

6.2.2 Case Loads and Size of the Organisations in the Dutch Criminal Justice Chain

The police is the biggest organisation in the criminal justice chain.[1] In 2013 some 63,000 employees worked for the police organisation, whereas the public prosecutor's office employed almost 4,700 prosecutors and support staff. The number of police officers per 100,000 citizens is almost 300. Contrasted with other European countries the number of police officers per 100,000 citizens in the Netherlands is relatively low.[2] The total number of staff employed by the court organisation (including judges) was approximately 8,500 in 2013. Only 25–33 % of these employees deal with criminal cases. The organisations that carry out court decisions vary substantially in numbers of staff. The central collection agency has less than 1.000 employees but the prison organisation employs approximately 15.000 people.

In 2013 the police registered 1.09 million criminal offences. The overall clearance rate is 22.4 % which means that 244,000 criminal offences are cleared by the police. The public prosecutor registered 209,000 criminal cases in 2013 and it brought 114,000 cases to court. The public prosecutor also has two other options. It can either dismiss a case or impose an administrative penalty. In 2013 the public prosecutor imposed 42,000 administrative penalties and it dismissed 39,000 cases. The courts dealt with 93,000 cases in 2013. The conviction rate was 90 %. In 34,000 cases the courts decided that the suspect should go to prison, in 31,000 cases the suspect was convicted to community service, and in 25,000 cases the courts ruled that the suspect should pay a fine. The prison organisation dealt with an influx of 39,700 prisoners. Adults carried out 32,700 community services and juvenile delinquents carried out 11,100 community services. The central collection agency collected the administrative penalties imposed by the police and the 52,000 administrative penalties that were imposed by the public prosecutor. Finally, the central collection agency implemented almost 28,000 court decisions in which the courts ruled that a fine should be paid. These figures only include criminal offences. For example, the central collection agency also collected more than 10 million administrative traffic penalties. The numbers show some discrepancies due to different registration methods and time lags between the different steps (see also Algemene Rekenkamer 2013).

---

[1]These numbers were copied from the annual reports of the organisations involved and the overall picture sketched in a publication of the Ministry of Justice (Criminaliteit en rechtshandhaving 2013).

[2]http://ec.europa.eu/eurostat/statistics-explained/index.php/File:Police_officers,_average_per_year,_2007–09_and_2010–12_(per_100_000_inhabitants)_YB14.png.

6.3 Reforms in the Dutch Criminal Justice Chain

The first wave of reforms in the Dutch criminal justice system were initiated in the 1980s. These reforms were primarily triggered by a sudden explosion of the numbers of criminal cases. In 1975 the police registered approximately 453,000 criminal offences (Sociaal en Cultureel Planbureau 1998). Only five years later the number of criminal offences registered by the police had risen to 706,000 and this number rose to 1,094,000 in 1985. In ten years' time the number of criminal offences doubled and the growing case load blocked the criminal justice chain. The heterogeneity of the cases also increased. Organised crime, fraud, environmental crimes, and so on required a different approach compared to the traditional crimes. Several explanations for the rising numbers of criminal cases have been put forward. Economic trends such as growing unemployment went along with macro trends such as individualisation (Sociaal en Cultureel Planbureau 1998). The rising numbers are also endogenously explained. For example, several criminologists have argued that the registration behaviour of the police is the main cause of the rising numbers. It also appears that citizens' reporting behaviour has changed (Wittebrood and Nieuwbeerta 2006; Wittebrood and Junger 1999; Kester and Junger-Tas 1994; Van Tulder 1985). The rising numbers and the inability to effectively deal with case load caused political attention and political incidents. It gradually became clear that both citizens and political leaders expected a more effective criminal justice chain. Moreover, the position of magistrates in the Dutch society seemed to change because of a gradual process of democratisation. In a number of decades Dutch society transformed from the vertical and hierarchic pillar structure into a horizontal structure of individualisation (e.g. Van Gunsteren and Andeweg 1994). In order to regain its legitimacy it was considered that both the effectiveness and the responsiveness of the criminal justice chain should be substantially improved (e.g. Steenhuis 1984).

In this section some major reforms that occurred in the Dutch criminal justice chain since the 1980s are briefly sketched. A first type of reforms (Sect. 6.3.1) focuses on the overall structure of the links in the criminal justice chain (public prosecutor, courts, police). These reforms aimed at transforming loosely coupled criminal justice systems into coherent national organisations. A second type of reforms has been driven by ICTs (Sect. 6.3.2). These reforms have changed the everyday working processes in criminal justice organisations. The most recent type of reforms builds on the interdependencies within the criminal justice chain and beyond (Sect. 6.3.3).

6.3.1 The Overall Structure: From Archipelago to Coherent Organisations

The explosion of the case load, the political incidents, and the challenged legitimacy of the criminal justice system inspired many of the reforms from the 1980s to 2013. With regard to the overall structure of the criminal justice chain three reforms should be mentioned. First, almost all links in the criminal justice chain such as the public prosecutor, the courts, and the police have been scaled-up from the local and regional level to the national level. Second, the process of scaling-up has gone along with deliberate attempts to strengthen the autonomy of these links. Third, the establishment of more or less autonomous national organisations and systems accommodated reforms that promoted the coherence of management and policies within these organisations and systems (e.g. Brommet 2002). This triple reform process successively took place in the office of the public prosecutor, the court system, and the police.

Until the 1990s legal work in both the public prosecutor's office and the courts was very decentralised. For example, within the public prosecutor's office decisions on cases and priorities were made by the prosecutors themselves, the chief of the district office of the public prosecutor in the 19 districts and the five procurators general who were responsible for prosecuting cases in appeal. Tight managerial control by the Ministry of Justice on finance, housing, staff, and procurement sharply contrasted the decentralised professional structure (e.g. Brommet 2002; van der Bunt et al. 1985). The rising number of cases challenged both professional decentralisation and managerial centralisation. A committee was installed and this committee concluded that the lack of unity on the policy level, the attribution of authority to individual prosecutors and districts, and the lack of hierarchy were dysfunctional from a managerial perspective. The Committee observed a culture of individualism and particularism with regard to prosecution policy (Commissie Openbaar Ministerie 1994: VI). It concluded that the public prosecutor's office should be transformed into a coherent organisation led by a board of Prosecutors-general. The board should be responsible for the unity of prosecution policy and the implementation of these policies. It should also become responsible for the managerial control of the resources. The Minister of Justice and Parliament adopted this approach and on 1 January 1998 the new structure had been legally institutionalised.

The simultaneous reinforcement of the organisation character and its managerial autonomy also took place in the judiciary (e.g. Cleiren and Brommet 2000; Bovendt'Eert 2008; Mak 2008). These reforms were triggered by at least two perceived problems. First, the dual management structure was experienced as a barrier to effectively deal with the case load. The dual management structure refers to the judges who were managed by their court presidents and the support staff who were managed by a local manager who in turn accounted to the Ministry of Justice. The project 'ZM 2000' was initiated in 1994 to improve the management and control structure within the judiciary. Within the realm of this project a number of pilots and initiatives has been set up to connect the management of the judges with the management of the support staff and its resources. It appeared that these informal changes did not suffice. In 1996 Dutch parliament forced the state secretary of justice to form a committee on the future organisation and resources of the judiciary (Adviescommissie toerusting en organisatie zittende magistratuur 1998). This committee recommended to simultaneously improve the judiciary as an organisation and to strengthen its institutional independence from the Ministry of Justice. A council should be formed that managed the judiciary and guaranteed its institutional independence. Within each court a model of integral management should be developed as a replacement of the dual management system. On January 1, 2002 these legal changes were enacted. The principle of integral management was laid down in law (article 23 of the Judiciary Organisation Act). This principle implies that judges are also made responsible for the management of resources and the support staff. Nowadays courts are managed by governing boards. The members of this board are the president of the court, the chairs of each sector (private sector, criminal sector, administrative sector, cantonal sector) and a representative of the support staff. This board is expected to enhance the legal quality and a uniform application of law. It also manages the court's resources. The overall management of the judiciary is a responsibility of the Council for the Judiciary. This Council allocates and controls the financial resources and it supervises operational management. The council also draws up and implements policies with regard to ICTs, housing, staff/human resources, and other material resources. Finally, in case of appointments the council recommends both judges and members of the governing board to the Minister of Security and Justice. Because of judicial independence the responsibilities with regard to legal quality and uniform application of law are created as soft powers. The governing board is legally authorised to improve legal quality and a uniform application of law and the Council for the Judiciary supports these responsibilities of the local boards. In the end the court decisions should be made independently from the court management and the Council of the Judiciary.

The threefold reform process of scaling up, strengthening the organisation and the autonomy of the sector also took place in the police organisation (e.g. Fijnaut 2012). Until 1993 the police force was both functionally and geographically fragmented. Next to a national police force that operated both on a national level and in small communities each municipality above 25,000 inhabitants maintained its own police force. In 1993 the national and local police forces were integrated into regional police forces. The mayor of the biggest city in the police region became responsible for overall management of the police force. Overall management had to take place within the policy framework decided upon by a regional council. All mayors of the municipalities in the region as well as the chief public prosecutor were members of the regional council. Next to the regional forces a national police force was created for national tasks such as large-scale criminal investigations and terrorism. The allocation of resources took place on different levels. On the national level a model was developed to allocate the resources over the regional forces and the national department. Within the regions the regional council allocated the resources over local districts. Within municipalities the local meetings of the mayor, public prosecutor, and local police chief decided on the allocation of resources. Soon after the new structure had come into force the disadvantages of the regional police organisation became clear (e.g. Fijnaut 2012). The differences with regard to the policies on procurement, ICTs, staff, and so on hindered the efficiency of the police organisation and they also put up barriers for cooperation between the regional forces. The creation of regional councils was meant to strengthen the influence of all mayors in the region but in fact the mayors of small communities seemed to have lost power. After previous attempts to create a national police force failed a national force was created in 2013 (e.g. Fijnaut 2012). The management of the police force became a primary responsibility of the Minister of Security and Justice and the national head of police. Despite the establishment of a national police force the authority of both the mayor and the public prosecutor remained untouched.

With regard to the overall structure another reform should be mentioned. At the end of the 1980s an agency was established for the collection of fines. Until the 1980s the public prosecutor did not seem to bother whether court decisions were actually implemented or whether fines were actually collected. The growing numbers of cases that either never made it to court or never made it to actual implementation of the court decision increasingly threatened the legitimacy of the criminal justice chain in the 1980s (e.g. Steenhuis 1984). With the transfer of most of the traffic violations to the realm of administrative law and the simultaneous creation of a central collection agency this situation dramatically changed. Within a couple of years the percentage of fines actually collected was raised from 45 % to more than 95 % (see Zouridis 2000). Because of this success the central collection agency was also made responsible for the implementation of court decisions.

6.3.2 Working Processes Within Organisations: ICTs, Structural Differentiation, and Managerialism

Strengthening the coherence of the quasi-anarchistic links such as the public prosecutor and the courts while simultaneously scaling-up these organisations and providing them with autonomy enabled structural differentiation within the newly established organisations. After the centralisation of the public prosecutor's office the new council of procurators general started to further structurally differentiate the organisation. Gradually the smooth and easy cases were tapped off in an early stage by specific departments that specialised in large numbers of easy cases. The most severe cases of organised crime were also separated and went to a national department. The complex cases of fraud and environmental crimes were also tapped off and sent to a specific department (e.g. De Jonge and Van Nederpelt 2011). This process of case sorting and structural differentiation was first initiated in the office of the public prosecutor but gradually diffused in the whole criminal justice chain.

Taken together these structural reforms provoked a managerial orientation in an overwhelmingly legal environment. The discovery of management tools represents a cultural shift from a predominantly legal orientation on individual cases to a managerial orientation on working processes, quality and citizen satisfaction, and planning and control (e.g. Zouridis 2000; Mak 2008). The lawyers with management responsibility gradually familiarised themselves with management instruments such as output based allocation systems (e.g. Boone and Langbroek 2007).

In 2002, a planning and control cycle was introduced in the newly established organisation of the judiciary (Mak 2008). The use of management instruments has not been limited to finance but it also includes human resources management and operational management with regard to other support functions such as ICTs and housing.

All reforms mentioned above have been either supported by ICTs or provoked by new technologies (e.g. Zouridis 2000; Langbroek and Tjaden 2008). During the 1970s and 1980s several small-scale experiments with the use of ICTs have been carried out within the organisations of the police and the public prosecutor. From the start of the 1980s the first large scale systems were introduced in the criminal justice chain. These systems were used for the implementation of court sentences (e.g. Langbroek and Tjaden 2008). Primitive case management systems were also introduced in the 1980s and these systems were explicitly designed to connect the links in the criminal justice chain. For example, the BAS and COMPAS systems were case management systems that enabled the transfer of cases from the police to the office of the public prosecutor and from the public prosecutor to the courts. Apart from these systems ICTs played a major role in the implementation of fines and financial penalties (e.g. Zouridis 2000).

6.3.3 Interdependencies Between Organisations: Joining-up the Criminal Justice Chain and Beyond

The reforms on the level of the overall structure created more or less coherent national organisations such as the public prosecutor office, the national court organisation, and a national police force. The reforms also strengthened their autonomy and enabled structural differentiation on a national level. Driven by large scale ICTs and planning and control systems the working processes have been redesigned and, if possible, automated. A major shift in the emphasis of criminal justice reforms took place at the start of the new millennium. The managerial and reform emphasis gradually moved from the separate organisations and links in the criminal justice chain to the coordination of the criminal justice chain as a whole. The concepts of chain management and chain informatisation symbolised the shift of emphasis. The concept of chain management encompasses three simultaneous processes (Van der Doelen en Klink 2000). First, chain management refers to horizontal coordination on the national level. Ever since the organisations in the criminal justice chain have been organised on a national scale, their view also includes national ministries with which they have to deal. For example, national drug policy very much affects the criminal justice chain so the newly established national organisation for the public prosecutor's office also wants to connect with the health ministry in order to coordinate drug policy and its effects on law enforcement. Second, the newly established national organisations should be more or less coordinated with regard to their working processes and the mutual interdependencies. For example, if the public prosecutor decides to focus on specific priorities such as fraud or white collar crime these decisions affect the police but also the judiciary and the organisations that implement court decisions. Third, because of the legal authority of the mayor there is a need to coordinate the criminal justice chain on the local and regional level.

The concept of chain management encountered a serious difficulty in the criminal justice chain. Since the judiciary is legally and institutionally independent it cannot be made part of the criminal justice chain. For example, from a perspective of chain management it could make sense to achieve agreement between the judiciary and the prison organisation (or the public prosecutor) on the number of suspects that are sent to prison. From the perspective of judicial independence such an agreement is impossible. The judiciary can therefore only to a certain degree be included in a chain management perspective. Ever since the introduction of the principles of chain management the Ministry of Justice (now Ministry of Security and Justice) has struggled with the difficulty of including the judiciary.

As argued the reform emphasis shifted to interdependencies and chain management. Recently, the reforms that build on interdependencies also include adjacent organisations and sectors such as the tax authorities and local government. Two examples of these latest reforms can be mentioned. First, the concept of the security house has been developed to deal with both juvenile and adult recidivists (Peeters 2013). For example, in the Tilburg security house the public prosecutor's office cooperates with the police, the municipality, welfare and youth organisations. Collaboratively these organisations decide on the most appropriate way to react on the offences of recidivists. Second, the concept of the Regional Information and Expertise Centres (RIEC) has been developed to organise collaborative law enforcement with regard to organised crime. In these centres the police, the public prosecutor, the local authorities and the tax authorities develop a common understanding of the organised crime problem in their region. The threats commonly identified are then used as a basis for a collaborative approach using criminal law, administrative law, and tax law. Next to the RIEC the region of Noord-Brabant has further intensified a collaborative approach. Five major cities (Tilburg, Eindhoven, 's-Hertogenbosch, Breda, and Helmon), the provincial government, the police, the public prosecutor, the tax authorities (including the special criminal investigation department of the tax agency) and the military police have set up a task force to develop a concerted program to tackle organised crime in this region (Zouridis et al. 2013).

6.4 From Reforms to Strategy-Organisation Configurations

6.4.1 Strategy-Organisation Configurations

Policy strategies on the one hand and the structures and routines of public organisations are strongly connected with each other (e.g. Mintzberg et al. 1998). Public organisations and the principles on which these organisations are built can be regarded as expressions of specific strategies. For example, if policies aim at tailor made provision of public services a decentralised and professional organisation design seems better suited than a mass bureaucracy. If on the other hand policies are geared towards uniform implementation highly centralised organisations with automated decision making are more likely (e.g. Bovens and Zouridis 2002). Public organisations do not only express specific strategies. Organisations also shape strategies (e.g. March and Simon 1993). Strategies therefore also display specific organisation characteristics. It seems unlikely to expect a fixed and unambiguous strategy in a highly decentralised professional organisation. Taken together the policy strategies of public organisations and their organisational characteristics can thus be analysed as a configuration. The concept of configuration refers to a more or less coherent set of organisation principles and policy strategies. The configuration perspective does not necessarily assume an institutional equilibrium between strategy and organisation but it does predict a tendency towards alignment or equilibrium. Even though an institutional equilibrium is not likely to occur the use of ideal typical strategy-organisation configurations contributes to a better understanding of reform attempts and the underlying tensions that drive reforms. The reforms described above thus indicate changing law enforcement strategies. In order to make sense of these reforms and the strategic choices expressed by them the organisational change within the criminal justice chain can be understood as a succession of four different organisation-strategy configurations.

6.4.2 Incident Driven Legalism in a Criminal Justice Archipelago

Until the 1980s the predominant strategy-organisation configuration can be labelled as incident driven legalism in a criminal justice archipelago. The organisations in the criminal justice chain primarily reacted on the cases that were brought to their attention. The organisations were not driven by explicit law enforcement strategies. The number of crimes reported to the police was relatively small and the limited resources of the police also restricted its possibilities to detect and investigate crimes. Usually the police reacted on the cases that had been reported by victims or cases that they more or less coincidently discovered. In turn the public prosecutor reacted on the cases or incidents brought in by the police. The courts more or less uncoordinatedly responded on the case load caused by the public prosecutor. The organisations in the criminal justice chain were loosely connected on both the operational and systemic level. As a whole the criminal justice chain was driven by incidents. Because of the predominance of lawyers, an explicit law enforcement strategy that also included the use of organisation resources was outside the focus of these organisations. The police heavily relied on the public prosecutor with regard to criminal investigations because of the lack of legal knowledge within the police organisation. Resources were controlled on a national level without any connection with local law enforcement strategies. The criminal justice chain primarily focused on meticulous legal assessment of the cases that were brought to their attention and the organisations were more or less negligent to what happened outside their scope. The organisations in the criminal justice chain were also preoccupied with checks and balances within the chain. This preoccupation reinforced the archipelago structure within and between the organisations.

6.4.3 Policy Driven Managerialism in a Pillarised Criminal Justice Chain

The first wave of reforms led to a new strategy organisation configuration. The new strategy organisation configuration may be referred to as policy driven managerialism in a pillarised criminal justice chain. The reforms that focused on the overall structure have been led by the desire to control the processes and resources in the separate links of the criminal justice chain. The introduction of managerial tools such as planning and control, integral management, and performance based budgeting were all meant to achieve managerial control. The power of managers in the organisations increased at the expense of the power of the professional lawyers. Within the organisations the traditional layers between legal professionals and administrative support staff blurred because of the managerial focus. Coordination was also reinforced between the public prosecutor and the local mayor responsible for maintaining public order. Together with the local police chief these authorities set up a triangle meeting that facilitated a more targeted approach. Gradually the incident driven law enforcement strategy was replaced by a targeted law enforcement strategy. The police and the public prosecutor defined different types of crimes that required different approaches (e.g. the everyday crimes versus organised crime). The targeted nature of the law enforcement strategy also led to the discovery of target groups (e.g. recidivists) or target areas (the hot spots approach). The explicit law enforcement strategy also allowed for a strong connection with policy goals and political goals. Managerialism, increased control, and a purposive use of the criminal justice chain led to a new strategy-organisation configuration. In this configuration the criminal justice chain is to a large extent pillarised because of the emphasis on control on the level of separate links.

6.4.4 Information Driven Risk Management in a System-Level Bureaucracy

The next generation of reforms driven by ICTs again led to a new strategy-organisation configuration. ICTs were introduced to support the working processes and the work flows within the criminal justice chain. Gradually the organisations were built around the ICTs (e.g. Zouridis 2000). The judiciary lagged behind but the work flows of the police, the public prosecutor, and the agencies responsible for the implementation of court decisions were increasingly automated by the introduction of large scale information systems. Traffic violations were transferred from criminal law to administrative law in order to facilitate automated decision making and everyday cases were increasingly dealt with by automated systems. The management focus shifted from meticulous legal assessment of individual cases to the management of work flows. Applying the framework developed by Joan Woodward this transformation has been referred to as a transformation from unit batch processing to mass production to process production (Zouridis 2000). Legal assessment and legal knowledge gradually became less important because of the emphasis on managerial knowledge on work flows and production statistics. The new managerial focus on work flows and ICTs started within the separate links of the criminal justice chain but from the start of the new millennium onwards the focus shifted to chain management. The use of ICTs enabled the production of detailed statistics that gradually also transformed the law enforcement strategy underlying the criminal justice chain. New risk management techniques could be based on the large scale analysis of the production. The strategies and organisations had previously been infected with crime control goals but the use of ICTs enabled a much more efficient and targeted allocation of resources. The use of risk management techniques, prevention, and problem solving law enforcement has been extensively described by Sparrow (2000). The criminal justice chain increasingly became an instrument of criminal policies. The new strategy organisation configuration may thus very well be characterised as information driven risk management in a system-level bureacracy (see Bovens and Zouridis 2002).

6.4.5 A Coherent Criminal Justice Chain for Collaborative Law Enforcement

The final wave of reforms has only just started. Apart from the creation of a national police force that replaced the regional organisations these reforms widen the view of individual criminal justice organisations. The reform attention now shifts to the interdependencies both within the criminal justice chain and beyond. For example, chain management tools include joint information strategies and new coordination structures on work flows, types of cases, and the quality of the output. Collaborative law enforcement transcends the criminal justice chain. The differentiation of cases has reinforced the focus on problem solving and prevention both within the police organisation and the public prosecutor office. With the security houses, RIECs, and other cooperative bodies a new law enforcement strategy seems to evolve. The public prosecutor's office nowadays argues that its work is about meaningful interventions aimed at solving problems instead of prosecuting suspects (Openbaar Ministerie 2011). Each type of work load and each type of problem requires a different collaborative approach with a selected group of partner organisations and targeted intervention strategies. Repeated offenders are dealt with by security houses that carry out joint interventions to prevent recidivism. Combatting the increasingly undermining organised crime has become the focus of joint teams of the police, the public prosecutor, tax authorities, and local governments. Even though it is still too early to speak of a new strategy organisation configuration it seems that a coherent criminal justice chain increasingly focuses on a collaborative law enforcement strategy.

The collaborative turn seriously affects the position of the courts. Because the focus of the criminal justice chain has somewhat shifted away from criminal law and criminal procedure the courts have increasingly been pushed into the background of the law enforcement strategy. Traffic violations have been transferred to administrative law, the public prosecutor has acquired the power to impose administrative penalties for everyday cases, administrative penalties have been introduced in many other realms, and many public organisations have aligned their strategies with the criminal justice chain. The redirection of large numbers of cases away from the courts and the criminal justice procedure is still going on. Whether that development should be welcomed or lamented remains to be seen. There are signs that the redirection of cases comes at the cost of legal protection. For example, recent research of the procurator-general at the supreme court demonstrates that not all administrative penalties imposed by the public prosecutor would have led to convictions if these cases were submitted to courts (Procureur-Generaal bij de Hoge Raad der Nederlanden 2014).

6.5 Conclusions

The criminal justice domain in the Netherlands has been continuously reformed ever since the 1980s. More than three decades of reform have dramatically changed the face of the criminal justice chain. The archipelago of criminal justice organisations dominated by lawyers who primarily focused on legal scrupulousness of a more or less random sample of crimes has transformed fundamentally. It has become a policy driven and tightly controlled criminal justice chain that proactively involves other public organisations to combat crimes. It took more than two decades to achieve some managerial control on the criminal justice chain. As soon as the organisation structures allowed managerial control the criminal justice chain became interwoven with policy and political goals. Instead of passively dealing with incidents the criminal justice chain increasingly focused on problem solving. The emerging contours of a problem solving criminal justice chain and law enforcement strategy are still vague (e.g. Verberk 2011) but that should not withhold us to ask ourselves what will be the next strategy organisation configuration. Since legal protection and careful legal assessment seem to be the victims of the latest generations of strategy organisation configurations it is not improbable that collaborative chain management will trigger a renewed quest for checks and balances, legal protection, and rule of law standards.

References

Adviescommissie toerusting en organisatie zittende magistratuur, Rechtspraak bij de tijd, The Hague, 1998

Algemene Rekenkamer (General Accounting Office), Prestaties in de strafketen, The Hague, 2013

Begeleidingsgroep unitvorming bij gerechten en parketten, Unitvorming in de praktijk, The Hague, 1989

Bevers, P.J.J.M., Samenwerken binnen de rechterlijke organisatie, The Hague: Boom, 2004

M. Boone, Ph.M. Langbroek, Van Dieteren naar Delden, in: NJB 2007, 530-538

M. Bovens, S. Zouridis, From Street-Level to System-Level Bureaucracies, in: Public Administration Review, March/April 2002, vol. 62, number 2, pp. 174-184

P.P.T. Bovend'Eert, Rechterlijke organisatie, rechters en rechtspraak, Alphen aan den Rijn: Kluwer, 2008

E. Brommet, Van rechterlijke macht naar rechtelijke organisatie. Kroniek van achttien jaar verandering, The Hague: Ministry of Justice, 2002

H. van der Bunt, Officieren van Justitie. Verslag van een participerend onderzoek, Zwolle: H.D. Tjeenk Willink, 1985

C.P.M. Cleiren, E.C. Brommet, Managing and Delivering Justice in the Netherlands in the 21st Century, in: M. Fabri, Ph.M. Langbroek, The Challenge of Change for Judicial Systems, Amsterdam: IOS Press, 2000

Commissie Openbaar Ministerie, Het functioneren van het openbaar ministerie binnen de rechtshandhaving, The Hague, 1994

M.R. Damaška, The Faces of Justice and State Authority. A Comparative Approach to the Legal Process, New Haven and London: Yale University Press, 1986

Doelen, F. Van der, A. Klink, Strategie en verantwoording in een duale strafrechtketen, in: H.P.M. van Duivenboden, M. Van Twist, M. Veldhuizen, R.J. in't Veld, Ketenmanagement in de publieke sector, Utrecht: Lemma, 2000, pp. 115-130

H. van Gunsteren, R. Andeweg, Het grote ongenoegen. Over de kloof tussen burgers en politiek, Haarlem: Aramith, 1994

C. Fijnaut, Het nationale politiekorps. Achtergronden, controverses en toekomstplannen, Amsterdam: Bert Bakker, 2012

Kester, J.G.C., J. Junger-Tas, Criminaliteit en strafrechtelijke reactie: ontwikkelingen en samenhangen, Arnhem: Gouda Quint, 1994

Ph.M. Langbroek, M. Tjaden, ICT in de strafketen. De ontwikkeling en implementatie van nieuwe systemen bij het Openbaar Ministerie, in: PROCES 1008, 1, pp. 2-8

E. Mak, De rechtspraak in balans, een onderzoek naar de rol van klassiek-rechtsstatelijke beginselen en 'new public management'-beginselen in het kader van de rechterlijke organisatie in Nederland, Frankrijk en Duitsland, Nijmegen: Wolf Legal Publishers, 2008

L. de Jonge, A.T. van Nederpelt, Het Openbaar Ministerie werkt, leert en ontwikkelt, in: Strafblad, 2011, po. 41-47

J.G. March, H. Simon, Organisations (second edition), Cambridge (Mass.): Blackwell Publishers, 1993

H. Mintzberg, B. Ahlstrand, J. Lampel, Strategy Safari – Your Complete Guide Through the Wilds of Strategic Management, London: Pearson Education, 1998

Openbaar Ministerie, Perspectief op 2015, The Hague, 2011

F. Pakes, Comparative Criminal Justice, Portland (Or.), 2004

R. Peeters, The Preventive Gaze. How Prevention Transforms our Understanding of the State, The Hage: Boom, 2013

Procureur-Generaal bij de Hoge Raad der Nederlanden, Beschikt en gewogen. Over de naleving van de wet door het openbaar ministerie bij het uitvaardigen van strafbeschikkingen, The Hague, 2014

Sociaal en Cultureel Planbureau, Sociaal en Cultureel Rapport 1998, The Hague: 1998.

M. Sparrow, The Regulatory Craft. Controlling Risks, Solving Problems, and Managing Compliance, Washinton D.C.: Brookings Institution Press, 2000
D. Steenhuis, Strafrechtelijk optreden: stapje terug en een sprong voorwaarts (I), in: Delikt en Delinkwent, 14, 1984, pp. 395-414
Tulder, F. Van, Criminaliteit, pakkans en politie: schattingen met een macromodel, Den Haag: Sociaal en Cultureel Planbureau, 1985
Van Traa Committee, Inzake Opsporing, 1996
S. Verberk, Probleemoplossend strafrecht en het ideaal van responsieve rechtspraak, The Hague: SDU Uitgevers, 2011
Wittebrood, K., M. Junger, Trends in geweldscriminaliteit: een vergelijking tussen politiestatistieken en slachtofferenquêtes, Tijdscrift voor Criminologie, 1999, no. 3, pp. 250-267
Wittebrood, K., P. Nieuwbeerta, Een kwart eeuw stijging in geregistreerde criminaliteit. Vooral meer registratie, nauwelijks meer criminaliteit, Tijdschrift voor Criminologie, 2006, no 3, pp. 227-242
S. Zouridis, Digitale disciplinering. Over ICT, organisatie, wetgeving en het automatiseren van beschikkingen, Delft: Eburon, 2000
S. Zouridis, P.W. Tops, R. Peeters, Bestrijding van criminele ondermijning in Noord-Brabant. De taskforce-B5 als katalysator voor samenwerking, Tilburg, 2013

Part II
Trust and Cooperation in the Criminal Justice Chain

Chapter 7
The Concepts of Trust and Distrust in the Belgian Criminal Justice Chain

Jolien Vanschoenwinkel and Annie Hondeghem

7.1 Introduction

Different disciplines have attempted to study the two concepts of trust and distrust in different contexts, leading up to a so called 'conceptual confusion'. The great deal of approaches and perspectives have led to a lack of consensus concerning the meaning and operationalisation of trust and distrust (Misztal 2013). McKnight and Chervany (2000) explain this confusion as follows:

> One reason is that each discipline views trust from its own unique perspective [...]a disciplinary lens causes psychologists to see trust as a personal trait, sociologists to see trust as a social structure, and economists to see trust as an economic choice mechanism. However, the other reason is that trust is itself a vague term...depending on the context, we may think of many different things when someone uses the word 'trust' (p. 827).

Few of these trust studies, however, have focused on the collaboration among criminal justice agencies during the process of investigation, and therefore the definition and importance of (dis)trust within this specific context remains unclear. The question thus remains to what extent the concepts of trust and distrust and their effects can be applied to the criminal justice system as an interorganisational network.

Some studies predict the possible significance of trust in the process of investigation and prosecution, rendering further research into this topic interesting.

J. Vanschoenwinkel (✉) · A. Hondeghem
Public Governance Institute, KU Leuven, Leuven, Belgium
e-mail: Jolien.vanschoenwinkel@soc.kuleuven.be

A. Hondeghem
e-mail: Annie.hondeghem@soc.kuleuven.be

A. Hondeghem et al. (eds.), *Modernisation of the Criminal Justice Chain and the Judicial System*, Ius Gentium: Comparative Perspectives on Law and Justice 50, DOI 10.1007/978-3-319-25802-7_7

Cole (1985) studied the decision to prosecute and concluded that public prosecutors know which police officers to trust. Police officers, in turn, have a preference to work with a prosecutor who shares their vision, and the police officers might therefore even postpone the submission of a case. In addition, the study of Tasdöven and Kapucu (2011) on criminal justice agencies brought to light the possible significance of trust, since they argue it is "the most influential factor in the formation of informal relations" (p. 92). Benson and Cullen (1998) also point out that cooperation between criminal justice agencies finds its origin in personal relationships.

This chapter focuses on the Belgian criminal justice chain as an interorganisational network in order to study the topic of trust and distrust. More specifically, it looks into the relationship between the local criminal investigation department (local CID), the federal criminal investigation department (federal CID), the public prosecutor's office (PPO) and the examining magistrates (EM). This chapter focuses on the following research question as a starting point: what do trust and distrust mean for the police, the PPO and the EM? The following subquestions have been formulated:

- How do the police, the PPO and the EM reflect on our definition of trust?
- How do the police, the PPO and the EM reflect on our definition of distrust?

This chapter is therefore unique in terms of shedding new light on the concepts of trust and distrust within the Belgian criminal justice chain.

7.2 Definitions of Trust and Distrust. A Conceptual Confusion

Although trust has received a lot of attention in multidisciplinary organisational research (Oomsels and Bouckaert 2012), a concise and universally accepted definition remains absent, thus leading to 'conceptual confusion' (Kramer 1999; McKnight and Chervany 2006). In Table 7.1, we present several definitions, which illustrate the fact that different author's focus on different elements.

In order to construct a definition, the most common elements of the definitions presented below, are used. As a result we propose the following definition of trust:

> The willingness to be *vulnerable* based upon *positive expectations* of the *intentions or behaviour* of other actors in the context of an *institutional system*, which will lead to concrete *actions*.

Table 7.1 Definitions of trust

Source	Definition
Lewicki et al. (1998, p. 439)	"Confident **positive expectations** regarding another's **conduct**, and distrust in terms of confident negative expectations regarding another's conduct"
Edelenbos and Klijn (2007, p. 29)	"The concept of trust presumes a stable **positive expectation** (or prediction) of the intentions and motives of other actors"
Mayer et al. (1995, p. 712)	"The willingness of a party to be **vulnerable** to the **actions** of another party based on the expectation that the other will perform a particular action important to the trustor, irrespective of the ability to monitor or control that other party"
Deakin and Michie (1997)	"Trusting another actor means that one is willing to assume an open and **vulnerable position**. One expects the other actor to refrain from opportunistic behavior even if the opportunity for it arises without having any guarantee that the other party will indeed act as expected"
Ellis and Shockley-Zalabak (2001, p. 383)	"Positive expectations about the behavior of others based on **roles, relationships, experiences, and interdependencies**"
Rousseau et al. (1998, p. 395)	"A **psychological state** comprising the intention to accept **vulnerability** based upon **positive expectations** of the intentions or behaviors of another"

This definition contains five defining elements:

1. Willingness to be vulnerable
2. Positive expectations
3. Intentions or behaviour of another actor
4. Institutional system
5. Concrete actions

In the following each constitutive element of the definition of trust will be explained.

The first element concerns the **willingness to be vulnerable** and assumes an open position. Since the trustor depends on the trustee in a trust relationship, there can be a risk[1] that the trustee does not act in a way that is advantageous for the trustor. In this respect the trustor is vulnerable towards the trustee. The second element of the definition refers to **positive expectations**. These are based on the perceptions that people have of the other's intentions, behaviour and motives. The trustor hopes that the trustee will behave in his best interest (Bak 2005). The third element, **intentions or behaviour of another actor**, addresses the objects of trust.

[1]"Risk can be seen as the perceived probability of loss as interpreted by a decision maker. Uncertainty regarding whether the other intends to and will act appropriately is the source of risk" (Rousseau et al. 1998, p. 395).

In this research, the objects of trust are situated both at the macro level (trust in the criminal justice chain), the meso level (trust between criminal justice agencies) and micro level (trust between police officer/chief of police/PPs/EM) (Grimmelikhuijsen 2012). Trust does not only refer to what the trustor says or does, but also to the decisions that have been made (Lewicki et al. 1998). The fourth element is the **institutional system**. This element was added to the definition because of the judicial context. This is defined as "the aggregate of bodies, institutions and subsystems, as well as the principles, rules, norms, policies and values relating to the judicial sector" (IICA 1973, p. 14). The fifth and final element, **concrete actions**, refers to the behaviours that the trustor will eventually execute or avoid, based on positive expectations. Regarding a trust relationship, this can refer to actions such as organising regular meetings or sharing information, ideas, knowledge and best practices.

7.2.1 Definition of Distrust

Most studies see trust and distrust as opposing concepts on a continuum. However, recent trust studies, such as Van de Walle and Six (2013), tend to turn away from this trend as they consider trust and distrust to be two different constructs (Van de Walle and Six 2013).

We formulated the following definition of distrust: the unwillingness to be vulnerable based upon negative expectations of the intentions or behaviour of other actors in the context of an institutional system, which will lead to the avoidance of concrete actions.

Although the definitions of trust and distrust seem to be the opposite of each other, they can relate to different aspects in a relationship, making them two different concepts. Actors in complex interactions can relate to each other in different ways. This in turn implies that one actor can trust another regarding some aspects of the relation, but equally distrust that very same actor regarding other aspects. This depends on the context, role, experiences and tasks (Lewicki et al. 1998). Furthermore, Hill and O'Hara (2005a, b) argue that "low trust is not equivalent to high distrust and low distrust is not the equivalent of high trust" (p. 11). Additionally, trust and distrust have different characteristics and can have to some extent different antecedents.

Lewicki et al. (1998) try to clarify this aspect by combining trust and distrust, leading to four trust-distrust states as shown in Fig. 7.1. They indicate that "condition 4 is the most prevalent for multiplex working relationships in modern organisations" (Lewicki et al. 1998, p. 447).

Lewicki et al. clarify the four different quadrants as follows:

(1) **Low Trust/Low Distrust**: Relationships tend to start in cell 1 (Hill and O'Hara 2005a, b). Under these conditions an individual has no reason to be confident nor suspicious and watchful (Lewicki et al. 1998). Actors have little information about each other and have little interactions in this phase (Hill and O'Hara 2005a, b).

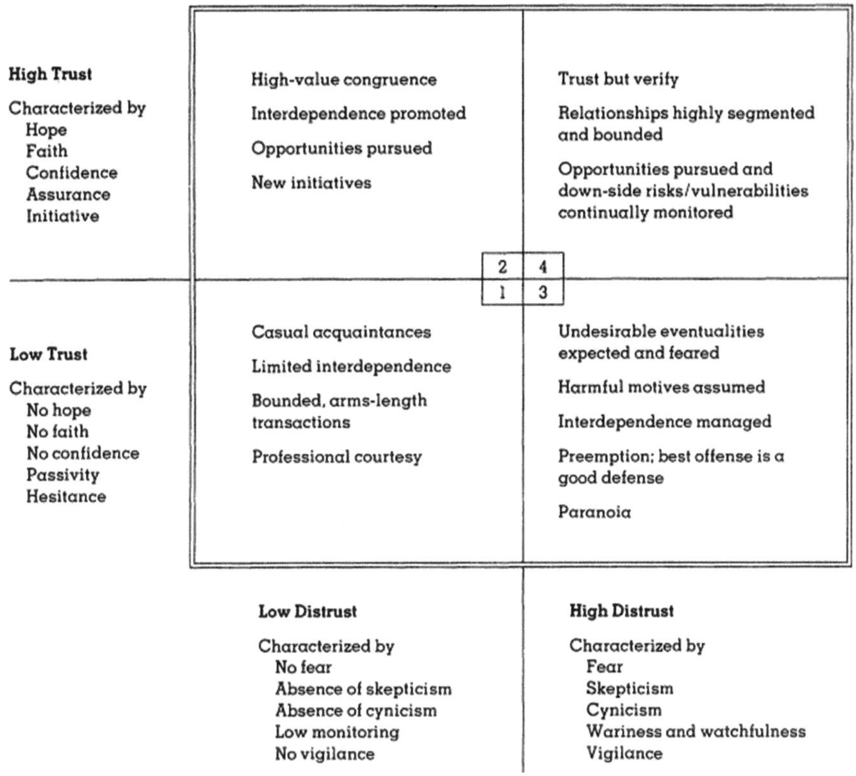

Fig. 7.1 Integrating trust and distrust: four social realities [*source* Lewicki et al. (1998)]

(2) **High Trust/Low Distrust**: Over time, the relationship can evolve into cell 2. This is usually the case after repeated positive interactions (Hill and O'Hara 2005a, b). An individual has reason to be confident in the other person and no reason to suspect him or her. Communication is complex and rich, reflecting awareness of each other.

(3) **Low Trust/High Distrust**: If the interactions are generally negative over time, the relationship can be situated in cell 3 (Hill and O'Hara 2005a, b). Under these conditions the actor has no reason for confidence in the other person and a good reason for suspicion and vigilance. These conditions make it very difficult to maintain effective interdependent relations.

(4) **High Trust/High Distrust**: Under these conditions actors have a good reason to be highly confident in another person regarding certain aspects of their relationship, but also have equally good reasons to be strongly wary and suspicious regarding other aspects (Lewicki et al. 1998). Parties have separate, as well as shared objectives (Hill and O'Hara 2005a, b). The relationship generates positive experiences, reinforcing trust, but also negative experiences, reinforcing distrust (Lewicki et al. 1998).

7.3 Methodology

Given the sensitivity of the trust topic we have chosen a qualitative approach. Qualitative research is best suited to respond to situations in which little information and knowledge is available (Maso and Smaling 1998). Furthermore, due to its explorative nature, the research does not seek generalisability, but strives for theoretical variation. For this reason, the typical as well as the atypical experiences and perspectives on trust and distrust will be described, so that the analysis is not distorted towards one perspective (Morce 1990, p. 139). Therefore, we have included even single opinions in the results.

The topics of trust and distrust were studied within the criminal justice context, as an interorganisational network. A strong and effective relationship among the criminal justice organisations is an essential component of investigation and prosecution. In order to deepen our understanding about trust and distrust, a closer look was taken at the Belgian criminal justice chain. The Belgian criminal justice chain has been subjected to fierce criticism, in turn leading to several reforms. A decade of public opinion research in Belgium revealed that, according to the public, the judicial system is beset by problems such as ineffectiveness, delays, injustice, non-prosecution, non-execution and lack of information sharing (Parmentier and Vervaeke 2011; Freyne 2009). These observations make the criminal justice chain in Belgium an interesting research field, in order to see which role trust/distrust can play.

In view of the stated aims of the research, a case study design has been chosen as our main research strategy. According to Yin (2009), "a case study is an empirical inquiry that investigates a contemporary phenomenon in depth and within its real-life context" (p. 14). A case study design has been applied to understand the real life phenomenon 'trust' and 'distrust' within the criminal justice context.

7.3.1 Sampling

Since the 1 April 2014, the judicial landscape in Belgium[2] has been drastically reformed. The three cornerstones of the reform were upscaling (from 27 to 12 judicial districts), mobility and management.

The case that we have used for this research is one specific judicial district.[3] This judicial district was a merger of several former judicial districts which have now the status of a "division". This district was chosen for two reasons. First, the influence of the reform on the organisation of the judicial district had to be limited.

---

[2]Law of 1 december 2013 *tot* hervorming van de gerechtelijke arrondissementen en tot wijziging van het Gerechtelijk wetboek met het oog op een grotere mobiliteit van de leden van de rechterlijke orde, *BS* 10 december 2013.

[3]The name of the judicial district is not mentioned due to reasons of confidentiality.

Second, the judicial district had to have an average score on all of the following criteria: caseload of the PPO, caseload of the local and federal CID, size of the local CID, size of the federal CID, and police capacity. Within this case the police, the PPO and the EM were selected as embedded cases (Carson et al. 2001, p. 96).

In Belgium there is an integrated police, consisting of a local and federal level. The local police carries out seven basic policing tasks: community policing, assistance, intervention, victim support, local investigations (focus of research), maintenance of law and order, and road traffic, under hierarchical supervision of the chief of police. The federal police is responsible for specialised judicial and administrative missions that reach beyond the local level. The federal level also provides support to the local police (Van den Wyngaert 2006). The federal police is headed by the judicial director (Dirjud). The PPO leads the preliminary investigation and is responsible for the prosecution. If a judicial investigation is required, the EM comes into play. The EM exercises judicial control over the course of events, such as the legitimate use of investigative powers, the use of intrusive investigative methods (interception of telecommunication, search of homes, etc.) and the progress of the investigation (Ballin 2012).

In total 8 different ***zones of local police*** were selected, striving for maximum variation on the following criteria: the size of the local police force, size of the CID, police capacity and years of service of the chief of police. First, the chiefs of police were contacted. Then through the snowball sampling method (Babbie 2010, p. 208), these interviewees were asked to refer to staff members who were willing to cooperate in the research. In some cases, however, the chief of police gave us certain names, making the cooperation no longer voluntarily.

For the ***federal police***, first the judicial directors (Dirjud) were interviewed. Next, again through the method of snowball sampling, the Dirjud were asked to contact the heads of the different divisions within the federal police. Within the divisions a sample was drawn from their members.

Because the amount of ***examining magistrates and public prosecutors*** for each division of the judicial district is limited, all of them were contacted.

In total 32 interviews were conducted as shown in Table 7.2.

Table 7.2 Number of interviews

Function of respondent	Number of interviews
Chief of police	8
Member of the local CID	13
Dirjud	2
Member of the federal CID	3
Public prosecutor	2
Examining magistrate	4
Total	32

7.3.2 Data Collection

Semi-structured interviews were conducted during a period of nine months, from march 2014 until November 2014. Although some of the interviews took place after the reform of April 1 2014, all the interviews relate to the period before the reform and therefore to the old structure.

Semi-structured interviews allowed for deviations from the interview guide (topic list) and enabled us to ask additional questions, as well as adapt the questions depending on the situation, the respondent and his/her answer (Hesse-Biber and Leavy 2010; Bryman 2008). Furthermore, semi-structured interviews pay great interest to the respondent's point of view. The interviews used for this chapter were part of a broader research[4] and therefore queried more topics than will be discussed in the following section.

In order to answer the research question the interviews will probe for the meaning of the dependent variables trust and distrust, as defined in the conceptual framework. In the interviews, the respondents were shown the definition of (dis) trust which was formulated by the conceptual framework.

Due to the sensitivity of the topic of trust in the judicial context, we must take into account the possibility of socially desirable answers, leading to a positive bias in the results, which could indicate that there is more trust between the Belgian criminal justice agencies than in reality, leading to a distorted view. We tried to avoid this by guaranteeing the anonymity of the research, but this does not mean the bias can be fully excluded.

7.3.3 Data Analysis

In total 32 interviews were analysed. The duration of the interviews lies between one and two hours. The recordings were all transcribed and analysed using NVIVO, a computer assisted qualitative data-analysis tool. First a basic set of codes was created based on the theoretical framework concerning the definitions of trust and distrust. However, during the coding process additional codes emerged.

7.4 Results

7.4.1 View of Respondents on the Definition of Trust

This section gives an answer to the first subquestion: how do the police, the PPO and the EM reflect on our definition of trust? In the interviews, the respondents

---

[4]Ph.D. research investigating trust between the police, public prosecutor's office and the examining magistrates in one judicial district.

were shown the definition of trust which was formulated in the conceptual framework. The respondents were able to reflect about the definition, which led to a variety of opinions. These ranged from completely agree to completely disagree or (dis)agree with certain aspects of the definition: vulnerable, positive expectations and perform concrete actions. In the following the different views will be discussed, elaborating on these different aspects.

22 out of 32 respondents agreed with the definition of trust as formulated in this research. These respondents had no negative comments on the various aspects highlighted in bold in the definition. Of these 22 respondents, 7 were rather compliant as they did not elaborate on their opinion and readily agreed with the definition. On the other hand, 14 other respondents did explain their view on the different aspects of the definition. 1 of the 22 respondents was rather negative at first, due to some misunderstanding of the definition. After further explanation, he formulated a more positive opinion. 1 out of 32 respondents questioned whether this was the right definition of trust, he therefore remained rather neutral and could not form a concrete opinion.

In addition, no respondent fully disagreed with the definition of trust, but 9 respondents disagreed with one or more aspects of the definition, namely vulnerability, positive expectations and concrete actions. All of these respondents were therefore rather sceptical towards our definition and elaborated on their opinion. The fact that respondents raised doubts about the applicability of the definition and the fact that their scepticism is directed to certain elements of the definition, can explain or even justify—to a certain degree—, the 'conceptual confusion' Kramer (1999) refers to. Because trust is such a complex, vague and personal concept, which can refer to so many different aspects in a relationship, the question can be asked if it is possible to formulate a universal definition that applies to everyone and in every context.

In what follows the aspects vulnerability, positive expectations and concrete actions will be discussed in more detail.

7.4.1.1 Vulnerability

26 of the 31[5] respondents agreed with the fact that they were 'vulnerable' towards their partner in the criminal investigation process. Initially it was rather difficult for the respondents to formulate an opinion on the concept 'vulnerability', which often led to additional explanations. This, however, resulted in more reflection on the concept and ultimately to different interpretations of the concept 'vulnerability':

- Not being able to execute certain investigation actions
- Dealing with someone else's flaws
- A decision that is not in line with your own expectations

[5]Because one respondent didn't have an opinion about the trust definition, the total of respondents for the results about trust will be 31.

- Vulnerability of the system
- Accepting criticism
- The possibility of being shot in the back
- Make concessions
- The vulnerability of a case when the responsibility is out of your own hands
- The uncertainty of what will happen with shared information
- Bear the ultimate responsibility of a file
- Making mistakes
- Vulnerability in the beginning of a relationship, not knowing what to expect
- Oral agreements
- Not knowing if agreements will be kept or executed correctly.

This list shows that 'vulnerability' is not only linked to the intentions and behaviour of the trustee as it usually occurs in the literature (Edelenbos and Klijn 2007), but also that in a judicial context trust can be related to the case, the system, and the uncertainty. Interdependency can play an important role in this matter. The criminal justice chain is characterised by a reciprocal dependency,[6] meaning that each actor (organisation) is situated in a vulnerable position in relation to the previous actor. The responsibility for the case shifts from one actor to another, placing the case in a vulnerable position. Furthermore there can be a lot of uncertainty concerning the information that is shared, agreements that are made and expectations, creating a lot of room for vulnerability.

5 of the 31 respondents did not agree with the meaning or the term 'vulnerability'. One chief of police did not think of vulnerability as a part of trust. Vulnerable meant for him to be putting oneself in a weak position. Even if this chief of police has positive expectations, he will never put himself in an inferior position in relation to the other, but instead will shield himself from harm by the other. He stated that "trust is good, but control is better" (Interviewee, 21 February 2014), emphasising the fact that he rarely trusts people. Two other respondents (one chief of police and one member of the local CID) did not agree with the term 'vulnerability', but they would be more open as a result of these positive expectations. This could indicate an aversion towards this laden term. Additionally it is imaginable that people, based on their function and the culture, struggle in admitting that they are putting themselves in a vulnerable position. This does not come as a surprise, knowing that only 1/3 (29, 73 %) of the integrated police in Belgium are women, it's predominantly a man's world (De Standaard 2013) and that men usually do not like to admit their vulnerability (Lippens 2009).

Furthermore, a member of the local CID indicated that after a certain time the feeling of vulnerability disappears, because one knows what to expect (Interviewee, 22 October 2014). This can be related to the opinion of another member, who stated that he has toughened over the years (Interviewee, 22 October 2014).

---

[6]A nuance has to be made, since it is possible to return to a previous actor in the chain, for example when additional investigative actions are necessary.

This tougher attitude can be explained by the factor 'intensity of the relationship', meaning the longer people know each other, the more they 'get' to know each other on certain levels. As stated by Adober (2003), frequent interaction can lead to the possible prediction of someone's behaviour and decisions, which in certain degree could eliminate some of this personal vulnerability. However, as stated before vulnerability is much more than not knowing what to expect and can also be linked to the case or the judicial system.

7.4.1.2 Positive Expectations

The second aspect highlighted in the definition was the 'positive expectations' towards the intentions or behaviour of another actor. 26 of the 31 respondents agreed with this element. Positive expectations are also linked to different aspects such as the behaviour of someone and the agreements that are made. For example, one member of the federal CID states that he is open and honest and that he expects no less from the other partners in the relationship (Interviewee, 20 October, 2014). Another member of the federal CID states that he expects that everyone in the relationship does everything in their power to successfully close the case (Interviewee, 20 October 2014). In line with this finding, an EM hopes that all agreements are respected (Interviewee, 11 July 2014).

Five respondents did not agree with the 'positive expectations'. Four out of five respondents stated that their expectations do not necessarily need to be positive. Even when they have negative expectations they still trust the other actor. A member of the local CID and a chief of police state the following:

> Sometimes I have negative expectations because I do not always agree with a decision the Public Prosecutor's Office made or with their view, but that doesn't mean that my trust in them will decrease….If you have positive or negative expectations towards the end result, the important thing is to know you can count on each other (Interviewee, 14 November 2014).

> If I place my trust in someone, it is also possible that a negative outcome results from the negotiation or conversation. But if you know the other is being honest and acts in the best possible way, even if you know the expected result can be negative,… (Interviewee, 28 October 2014).

These results correspond to the literature claiming that the object of trust does not only refer to what is been said or done, but also to the decisions that are made (Lewicki et al. 1998). This result shows that, especially in a judicial context, the object of trust often refers to the decision making process. This, however, is not surprising since the criminal justice chain is characterised by a series of decisions and actions (Bednarova 2011).

Finally, one EM indicates that the element of 'expectations' applies to his relationship with the police, but does not apply to the relationship with the PPO. He indicates that he does not have any expectations towards the PPO, but the PPO does have expectations towards the EM. This implies that he does not rely on the PPO during the judicial investigation. But in this case the expectations are solely linked to the ordering of certain investigative actions and the way they are executed. In our opinion this is a rather restricted view, since according to the literature expectations can also be linked to intentions, motives and behaviour of the other actor. For example, the EM can have expectations towards the prosecution by the PPO.

7.4.1.3 Concrete Actions

The third and final element of the trust definition is that, based on positive expectations, concrete action will be taken, such as sharing information, ideas, and organising meetings. These results can be discussed rather briefly. 30 of the 31 respondents agreed with or did not have any negative remarks about the aspect 'concrete actions' in the definition. One member of the local CID indicates that when there are positive expectations he will speed up while working on a file (Interviewee, 14 November 2014). One chief of police linked the concrete actions to acting correctly or honestly.

Given the previous results, it can be said that most sections of the definition were recognised. Based on the research results our definition of trust could be reformulated into the following definition:

> The willingness to *assume an open position* based upon *positive or negative expectations* towards the *intentions, behavior and decisions* of other actors in the context of an *institutional system*, which can lead to concrete *actions*.

7.4.2 View of Respondents on the Definition of Distrust

This part gives an answer to the second subquestion: how do the police, the PPO and the EM reflect on our definition of distrust. 20 of the 32 respondents agree with the definition of distrust. As was the case with the trust definition, they had no negative remarks about any of the components of the definition. 8 of these 20 respondents simply agreed with the definition without any further thoughts. The 12 other respondents elaborated their view.

Despite this general agreement the term distrust itself was considered to be formulated too harsh. Six of these 20 respondents wouldn't call it distrust, but defined it as wariness or cautiousness, being more distant, being less open and double checking everything. Seven respondents gave another interpretation such as a healthy cooperation, a strict professional cooperation, a negative image, lack of trust, institutional distrust, opportunism or frustration. The following quotes refer to the variety of meanings.

> On the basis of previous experiences trust will build, but it can also quickly disappear. If I find myself in similar situations I will think twice before trusting him again, but I wouldn't call it distrust, but a healthy way of cooperation. A fox is not caught twice in the same snare (Interviewee, 21 February 2014).

> A lack of trust is not necessarily distrust (Interviewee, 30 April 2014).

> Do you distrust someone if you are not happy with his way of working? If you don't agree with his way of thinking? That is not always distrust (Interviewee, 21 February 2014).

These results show that an aversion is expressed regarding the word 'distrust', because of its heavily-laden character. Therefore the question can be asked if it is justifiable to use the term 'distrust'. However, based on the previous results no conclusions can be drawn for the questions whether they experience distrust or not (degree of trust). It simply implies that they (do not) agree with our definition.

As was the case with the definition of trust, no respondent fully disagreed with the definition of distrust. The scepticism of 12 respondents was directed towards the different components: not being vulnerable, negative expectations and avoiding concrete actions. In what follows these aspects will be discussed in more detail.

7.4.2.1 Not Being Vulnerable

30 of the 32 respondents agreed with the fact that people would not place themselves in a vulnerable position if they have negative expectations. Due to these negative expectations, people will be more careful in the future, when deciding to take a risk by working together with the person that they have had negative expectations for. They develop a kind of fear and will be less open in the cooperation. As will be discussed later, this refers to an adjustment of their behaviour.

Only two respondents did not agree with the term 'vulnerable'. A chief of police referred to it as 'being less open' (Interviewee, 14 November 2014). Again, in the light of our definition, not being vulnerable means assuming a more closed attitude towards the trustee.

A member of the local CID stated the following: "being vulnerable counts for trust as well as for distrust. When you do something, you always put yourself in a vulnerable position" (Interviewee, 14 November 2014). Stating that even when she is distrustful towards someone, she still finds herself in a vulnerable position. This may refer to the fact that even if they distrust someone, in the light of their work, they cannot choose not to work together. Therefore some degree of vulnerability is always present. This will be further elaborated in this chapter.

7.4.2.2 Negative Expectations

31 of the 32 respondents agreed with the fact that distrust is related to negative expectations. The expectations are mostly linked to the results people would like to achieve or decisions that are made that are not always in line with peoples' wishes. Only one respondent did not agree with the negative aspect of the 'expectations', as shown in the following quote: "I would leave the negative out. It is based on the fact that you do not know what to expect. I cannot assess the situation" (Interviewee, 30 April 2014).

7.4.2.3 Avoid Actions

Concerning the last part of the definition, 21 of the 32 respondents agreed with the fact that certain actions would be avoided on the basis of previous negative expectations. People will avoid certain actions out of fear or because it will not lead to the desired result.

11 of the 32 did not agree. They all stated that in their line of work it is not viable to avoid certain actions or to avoid working together. In the worst case it can result in certain frustrations, but it is "part of the job" and "tomorrow is another day with new expectations". Again an explanation can be found in the uniqueness of the criminal justice chain which is characterised by a series of decisions and actions, making discussions and disagreement inevitable in this line of work.

> We cannot avoid certain actions, because it is not possible from our position. We cannot choose. If a crime occurs, you have to work with the magistrate that is of service. That's a choice we cannot make (Interviewee, 20 October 2014).

> Even though you had some negative experiences in the past, you cannot say "I will not execute this investigative action. If a EM says to interrogate all the people that occur in the file, you just do it" (Interviewee, 28 October 2014).

On the other hand the respondents do indicate that their behaviour can be altered due to the negative expectations, such as information that has been shared too late. In such a situation, people will be less open, more careful and only the desired magistrate will be contacted.[7]

So, despite the fact that there was some aversion towards the term 'distrust', there was a lot of agreement with the different aspects of the definition. However, based on some negative critique the definition of distrust can be reformulated as followed:

> The unwillingness to assume an open position based upon *negative or unknown expectations* of the *intentions, behavior, results and decisions* of other actors in the context of an *institutional system*, which will lead to the alteration of behaviour or avoidance of certain *actions*.

7.5 Conclusion

This chapter attempted to shed some light on the 'conceptual confusion' concerning the definitions of trust and distrust as used by Kramer (1999) and McKnight and Chervany (2006), within a specific, judicial context. A definition of trust and distrust was formulated using different components, based on several authors. The research conducted in one judicial district indicates that most respondents agree with the formulated definitions, and that the criticism was aimed at one or more components of the definitions. This indicates that (dis)trust is a concept which is

[7]This phenomenon is also called 'judge shopping' (Garner 2001, p. 481).

given a personal meaning. Therefore, formulating a universal definition of trust and distrust across disciplines could be a difficult, if not impossible challenge. In this respect the 'conceptual confusion' can be said to be to a certain degree justifiable, as in the judicial context as well other elements came to light, in comparison to other contexts. Therefore, not only the context needs to be taken into account, but also someone's personal attitude, agreeing with the statement of McKnight and Chervany (2000) of conceptual confusion. In the light of these research findings, we have adapted our initial definitions of (dis)trust

> Trust is the willingness to *assume an open position* based upon *positive or negative expectations* towards the *intentions, behavior and decisions* of other actors in the context of an *institutional system*, which can lead to concrete *actions*.

> Distrust is the unwillingness to assume an open position based upon *negative or unknown expectations* of the *intentions, behavior, results and decisions* of other actors in the context of an *institutional system*, which will lead to the alteration of behaviour or avoidance of certain *actions*.

This study has a number of limitations. First of all, only one judicial district was part of the research making it impossible to generalise these findings to other judicial districts. Thus other judicial districts should be included in the research. Hereby can be focused on the size of the judicial district, size of the local criminal investigation department, years of employment and the impact of the judicial reform. Secondly, only semi-structured interviews were conducted, which are sensitive to social desirable answers, creating a risk for a positive bias. Results should therefore be read with caution and complementary methods should be used to conduct further research into the topic.

Acknowledgment The authors want to thank Prof. Dr. Jeroen Maesschalck (KU Leuven, Leuven Institute of criminology) for his input to this chapter.

References

Adober, H. (2003). A decision-based explanation of trust in interfirm alliances. In R. Golembiewski, K. Mackenzie, & M. Afzalur Rahim, *Current Topics in Management* (pp. 143-162). New Jersey: Transaction Publishers.

Babbie, E. (2010). *The Basics of Social Research.* USA: Cengage Learning.

Bak, N. (2005). Would you buy an education from this teacher? Notions of trust and distrust in education. In S. Askvik, & N. Bak, *Trust In Public Institutions In South Africa* (pp. 183-196). England: Ashgate Publishing.

Ballin, M. (2012). *Anticipative Criminal Investigation: Theory and Counterterrorism Practice in the Netherlands and the United States* . The Netherlands: Springer.

Bednarova, J. (2011). The heart of the criminal justice system: a critical analysis of the position of the victim. *Internet Jourlan of Criminology*, pp. 1-46.

Benson, M., & Cullen, F. (1998). *Combating Corporate Crime: Locale Prosecutors at Work.* Boston: Northeastern University.

Bryman, A. (2008). *Social Research Methods.* Oxford: Oxford University Press.

Carson, D., Gilmore, A., Perry, C., & Gronhaug, K. (2001). *Qualitative Marketing Research.* London: Sage.

Cole, G. (1985). The Decision to Prosecute. *Law and society review*, 331-344.

De Standaard. (2013, november 08). Slechts 30 procent vrouwen bij politie. *http://www.standaard.be/cnt/dmf20131108_00829750.*

Deakin, S., & Michie, J. (1997). *Contracts, Co-Operation, and Competition: Studies in Economics, Management, and Law.* Oxford University Press.

Edelenbos, J., & Klijn, E. (2007). Trust in Complex Decision-Making Networks : A Theoretical and Empirical Exploration. *Administration & Society*, 25-50.

Ellis, K., & Shockley-Zalabak, P. (2001). Trust in top management and immediate supervisor: The relationship to satisfaction, perceived organizational effectiveness, and information receiving. *Communication Quarterly*, 382-398.

Freyne, T. (2009). De positie van de onderzoeksrechter op de helling: nood aan vernieuwde werkprocessen in het strafrechtelijk vooronderzoek. In M. Vanderhallen, E. Jaspaert, & G. Vervaeke, *De relatie in de strafrechtsketen tussen politie, parket, onderzoeksrechter en rechtbank* (pp. 177-197). Gent: Maklu.

Garner, B. (2001). *A Dictionary of Modern Legal Usage.* New York: Oxford University Press.

Grimmelikhuijsen, S. (2012). *Transparency and trust: an experimental study of online disclosure and trust in government.* Utrecht: Wöhrmann Print Service.

Hesse-Biber, S., & Leavy, P. (2010). *The Practice of Qualitative Research.* London: Sage.

Hill, C., & O'Hara, E. (2005). *A Cognitive theory of trust.* Washington: University Law Review.

Hill, C., & O'Hara, E. (2005). A Cognitive theory of trust. 1717-1796. Minnesota Legal Studies Research Paper No. 05-51 .

IICA. (1973). *A Hemispheric and Humanistic Projection in the 70's.* IICA.

Kramer, R. (1999). Trust and distrust in organizations: emerging perspectives, enduring questions. *Annual Reviews of Psychology*, 569-598.

Kroeger, F. (2012). Trusting organizations: the institutionalization of trust in interorganizational relationships. *Organization*, 743-763.

Lewicki, R., McAllister, D., & Bies, R. (1998). Trust and Distrust: New relationships and realities. *Academy of Management Review*, 438-458.

Lippens, V. (2009). Over mannelijke daders en slachtoffers: een gendergevoelige benadering van criminaliteit. In M. De Metsenaere, *In haar recht. Vrouwe Justitia feministisch bekeken* (pp. 107-122). Brussel: Vubpress.

Maso, I., & Smaling, A. (1998). *Kwalitatief onderzoek: praktijk en theorie.* Boom.

Mayer, R., Davis, J., & Schoorman, D. (1995). An Integrative Model of Organizational Trust. *The Academy of Management Review*, 709-734.

McKnight, H., & Chervany, N. (2000). What is Trust? A Conceptual Analysis and an Interdisciplinary Model. *AMCIS 2000 Proceedings*, (pp. 826-833).

McKnight, H., & Chervany, N. (2006). Reflections on an initial trust-building model. In R. Bachmann, & A. Zaheer, *Handbook of Trust Research* (pp. 29-52). UK: Edward Elgar Publishing.

Misztal, B. (2013). *Trust in Modern Societies: The Search for the Bases of Social Order.* UK: Blackwell Publishers.

Morce, J. (1990). Strategies for sampling. In J. Morce, *Qualitative Nursing Research: A Contemporary Dialogue* (pp. 126-145). London: Sage Publications.

Oomsels, P., & Bouckaert, G. (2012). Managing trust in public organisations: A consolidated approach and its contradictions. *Paper for the XVI IRSPM conference: Contradictions in Public Management: Managing in Volatile Times*, (p. 25).

Parmentier, S., & Vervaeke, G. (2011). In Criminal Justice We Trust? A decade of public opinion research in Belgium. *European Journal of Criminology*, 286-302.

Rousseau, M., Sitkin, S., Burt, R., & Camerer, C. (1998). Introduction to special topic forum: Not so different after all: A cross-discipline view of trust. *Academy of Management Review*, 393–404.

Tasdöven, H., & Kapucu, N. (2011). Network analysis tools and methods in analyzing coordinated response against organized crime. *Turkisch Journal of Police Studies*, 75-99.

Van de Walle, S., & Six, F. (2013). Trust and Distrust as Distinct Concepts: Why Studying Distrust in Institutions is Important. *Journal of Comparative Policy Analysis: Research and Practice*, 1-17.

Van den Wyngaert, C. (2006). *Strafrecht, strafprocesrecht en internationaal strafrecht in hoofdlijnen. 6de herziene uitgave.* Apeldoorn: Maklu.

Wehmeyer, K., Riemer, K., & Schneider, B. (2001). Roles and Trust in Interorganizational Systems. 14. Maastricht, bijdrage aan Eighth Research Symposium on Emerging Electronic Markets .

Yin, R. (2009). *Case study research: design and methods.* Thousand Oaks: Sage.

Chapter 8
Intra- and Interorganisational Trust in a Judicial Context: An Exploratory Case Study

Marloes Callens, Geert Bouckaert and Stephan Parmentier

8.1 Introduction

Delivering justice is a process in which various public and private actors need to cooperate, especially for juvenile proceedings. After an incident with a minor, a sequence of interactions will take place. First, a report will be filed to the police, based on which a police investigation will start. The public prosecutor gets involved by notification by the police, and will take the lead of the police investigation. Once the investigation is completed, the prosecutor can decide to refer the case to court. At the trial the judge will assess the evidence gathered by the police in the investigation stage, listen to the requisition of the public prosecutor and to the statements of the other parties involved, such as the counsellor representing the defendant. When the trial is concluded, a decision will follow and a sanction might be imposed.

The effectiveness and efficiency of the proceedings will depend on the way in which these interactions take place. Efficient information sharing between police, the judiciary and the social services, for example, is a crucial factor in solving complex criminal cases, or in finding the best measure to individual cases with complex psycho-social background problems accompanying for example drug

M. Callens (✉) · G. Bouckaert
Public Governance Institute, KU Leuven, Leuven, Belgium
e-mail: Marloes.Callens@soc.kuleuven.be

G. Bouckaert
e-mail: Geert.Bouckaert@soc.kuleuven.be

S. Parmentier
Leuven Institute of Criminology, KU Leuven, Leuven, Belgium
e-mail: Stephan.Parmentier@law.kuleuven.be

A. Hondeghem et al. (eds.), *Modernisation of the Criminal Justice Chain and the Judicial System*, Ius Gentium: Comparative Perspectives on Law and Justice 50, DOI 10.1007/978-3-319-25802-7_8

addictions (Vandam et al. 2010). Moreover, present society posing more complex legal matters increases the demand for effective management of the interactions between the judicial organisations (Koppenjan and Klijn 2004). Management of these relations is, however, not a straightforward matter, because of the multifaceted relations within such judicial network. This results in many current tensions in the relationships: faulty communication and inefficient cooperation between different members of a judicial system are often heard concerns (De Bruyn 2006; Depré and Hondeghem 2000).

To improve the quality, efficiency, and effectiveness of the judiciary and the other institutions related to the administration of justice there is a pressing need for improved justice chain management, i.e. "a quantitative and qualitative alignment of the efforts of all actors present in each layer of the criminal justice system" (Reynders et al. 2005, p. 158). There is a need for more communication between the different actors, for faster procedures, efficient information sharing, and a more cost-effective organisation (De Bruyn 2006; Depré and Hondeghem 2000).

8.2 Trust as an Organising Principle

One organising principle important to the alignment of the different connections in a judicial network is the presence of trust between the actors within the network (Bouckaert 2012; Edelenbos and Klijn 2007). Especially under conditions of complexity, trust is found to be important to allow sustained effective coordinated action (McAllister 1995). Trust, for example, should allow for organisational effectiveness, internal communication, and information and knowledge transfer (Seppänen et al. 2007).

On the other hand, inter-organisational trust isn't only ascribed positive features (Skinner et al. 2014). Also in a judicial context trust could have a double role, since other professional values inherent to the judicial system such as confidentiality of social services and lawyers, judicial autonomy, and hierarchical structures could be conflicting with the managerial value of trust. Arguably, close and blindly trusting relationships between the organisations making legally binding decisions about citizens could be problematic. Maintaining checks and balances between the different authorities serves the purpose of providing extra protection against careless work or abuse of power by others within the judicial chain: when internal trust increases, the amount of control between the actors can decrease (Castelfranchi and Falcone 2000).

Taking a closer look at the trust literature, and as highlighted in the previous chapter, there is a lot of conceptual confusion and little agreement on what trust means, and how it can be measured (McEvily and Tortoriello 2011). Trust appears to be an omnipresent influence in social life (Luhmann 1979), but at the same time, it remains fuzzy and elusive. A wide range of shared experiences between people are labelled as trust in daily life discourse, to grasp an otherwise difficult to describe aspect of human interaction. The same has taken place in academic work

(Blois 1999). The danger of these fuzzy concepts in academic discourse is that researchers may believe they are addressing the same phenomenon but are actually targeting quite different ones (Markusen 1999).

Numerous definitions of trust have been proposed, where reports are made of over 70 different existing definitions (Lyon et al. 2012) and the use of 38 different dimensions and 129 different measures of trust spread within the organisational literature alone (McEvily and Tortoriello 2011). Costa (2003) suggests that trust has a specific nature in every other context. To join all the different views, Dietz (2011) proposed a universal trust model (cf. Fig. 8.1), where "the sequence and dynamic is universal, but people's idiosyncratic preferences and influences and localised external conditions shape the content and process at each stage" (Dietz 2011, p. 219).

This trust process starts with the inputs available to the trustor (the person who needs to decide whether or not to trust) to base the following judgements on. These inputs come from various sources, and here the process will differ depending on the context. When no information on the person of the trustee (the target to be trusted) is available the trustor is convicted to use other arguments like common conventions or structural factors that determine the trustee's intentions and behaviours.

Based on the inputs the trustor then continues to make a judgement of the perceived trustworthiness of the trustee. This is a compilation of three factors: ability, benevolence and integrity, after Mayer et al. (1995), often abbreviated as ABI (cf. Fig. 8.1).

Based on the perceived trustworthiness the trustor will develop an attitude towards the trustee, which entails whether the trustor is willing to be vulnerable towards the trustee. This is the actual trust part, and has been defined as "a psychological state comprising the intention to accept vulnerability based upon positive expectations of the intentions or behaviors of another" (Rousseau et al. 1998, p. 395). Fulmer and Gelfand (2012) note the usefulness to distinguish between different types of targeted trustees: interpersonal, team, and organisation. Interpersonal refers to trust in a specific other such as a co-worker or co-workers.

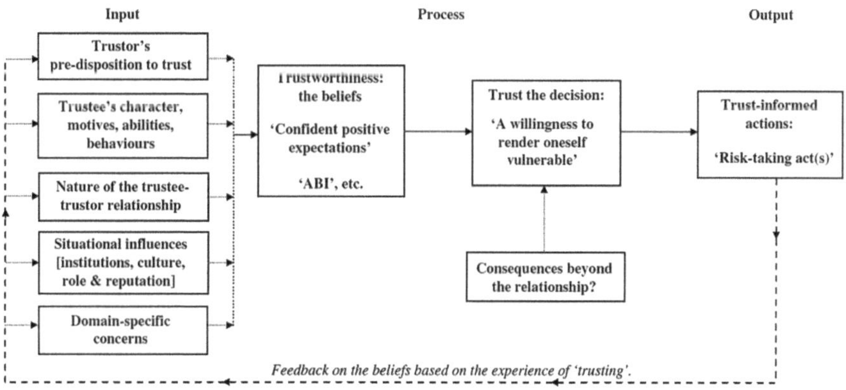

Fig. 8.1 A depiction of the trust process (*source* Dietz 2011, p. 219)

The team referent refers to trust in a collective of interdependent people pursuing a shared goal. The organisation referent refers to trust in the entity of an organisation.

Next in the trust process, the trust attitude should translate to actual risk taking behaviour (or the lack thereof). The consequences of this action will then be taken into account as an input of the next trustworthiness assessment. This way trust's cyclical dynamic continues through a feedback mechanism.

This process provides a good lens for investigating inter-professional relationships among the judicial services. Therefore, this chapter aims to apply this universal yet variform model to the juvenile justice context and has as its aim:

> To explore the manifestations of this trust process throughout daily interactions between the actors in the juvenile public prosecutor's office and the juvenile courts.

8.3 Setting and Context

In Belgium, different judicial chains deal with a specific branch of law and are organised accordingly. One segment of the judicial system where cooperation is of special importance is the juvenile justice system (De Bruyn 2006), dealing with cases in which minors are involved.[1] This case will therefore provide rich information on the trust phenomenon, since it is one of the judicial branches whose efficiency and effectiveness are expected to depend greatly on the cooperation among the organisations involved (De Bruyn 2006). Indeed, cooperation between the various actors is required to find a measure appropriate to the minor's personal situation rather than strictly apply legal rules, as it is in the adult criminal justice chain.

From the juvenile justice chain focus went to two judicial authorities: the juvenile public prosecutor's office and the juvenile court for a particular geographical area. Within these (sub)organisations of the judicial system, several professionals work together on the case files in which minors are involved, and they also need to interact for practical tasks such as organising hearings, holding meetings, etc. This cooperation takes place both within and across the entities. The different occupations are: juvenile public prosecutors, criminologist, secretaries from the secretary of the public prosecutor's office, juvenile judges, and registrars from the registry of the juvenile court.

[1]Under Belgian law, a minor is a person who has not yet reached the age of 18. Cases within the juvenile justice system are called 'protectional' cases because it involves on the one hand cases where the minor finds himself in an unstable home environment and needs to be protected by judicial action, and on the other hand the criminal cases, where the minor who committed the crime is presumed not to have reached a sufficient level of maturity to be held responsible. Juvenile courts may only impose protective and educational measures that are not penal in character (Youth Protection Act, April 8, 1965).

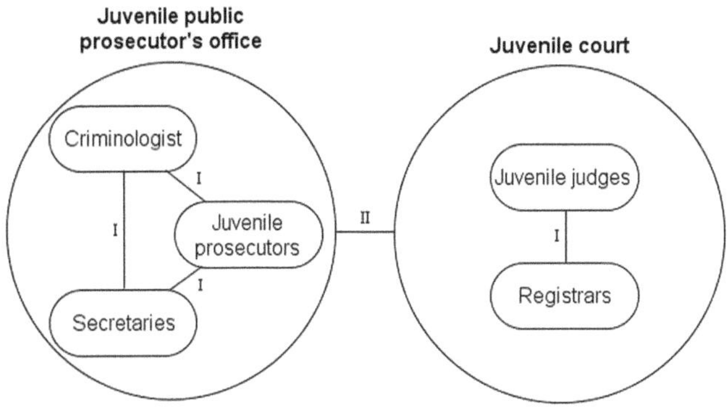

Fig. 8.2 The different positions held within the case organisations

8.4 Methodology

To allow for rich data collection a qualitative single-case study was performed to explore the trust process in the relationships between the juvenile prosecutor's office and the juvenile court. Case studies are widely used in organisational studies across the social sciences (Hartley 2004), and can be defined as "an empirical enquiry that investigates a contemporary phenomenon in depth and within its real-life context" (Yin 2009, p. 18).

8.4.1 Selection and Recruitment

Belgium has 12 judicial districts, each containing one or more judicial divisions, the level on which the juvenile justice chain is organised. The case at hand is part of the juvenile justice chain within one of these judicial divisions.[2] The units of analysis are the professional relationships within (edges I in Fig. 8.2) and between (edge II in Fig. 8.2) the juvenile public prosecutor's office and the juvenile court. Focusing on a particular segment was useful to reduce the heterogeneity of the case, which allowed the discovery of congruent patterns, and increases the internal validity of the study.

Due to the closed nature of the judicial system obtaining access for research can be hard. The advantage of selecting respondents from one single judicial district was that access to the case only needed to be given once. An additional advantage of contacting respondents within the same organisation is that it provides a deeper and more holistic understanding of the case, improving the internal validity of the study. External validity of the findings cannot be guaranteed by this methodology, this is, however, not the goal of a first exploration.

[2]The name of the district is withheld due to reasons of confidentiality.

The different positions held within the organisations are depicted in Fig. 8.2. In total, 9 individuals are employed within the organisations of the selected judicial division. As such there are 36 interpersonal connections within this network (16 intra-organisational (I) and 20 interorganisational ties (II)). Since trust is a directed sentiment towards another person, there are two directed trust assessments in one interpersonal connection. Two connected persons act simultaneously as a trustor and as a trustee, and the trust of person A in person B does not necessarily equal trust of B in A (see e.g. Golbeck and Hendler 2006). As such there are in this inter-organisational network a maximum of 72 trust valuations in place.

First, contact was sought with the president of the Court of First Instance, within which the juvenile court resides. A letter was sent containing the research plan and an indication of the selected members of the court. The same was done for the Crown Public Prosecutor, who is the head of the Public Prosecutor's office within which the juvenile public prosecutor's office is located. After permission for the study was granted by both, appointments were made with the available respondents. This resulted in meetings with six respondents directly from within the case. One registrar was unable to participate due to a temporary allocation to another department with a pressing shortage of personnel, the head of the secretariat of the public prosecutor's office was interviewed instead of the two youth secretaries due to practical availability, and one additional interview was obtained with the Crown Prosecutor of this district who had a more global perspective of the case. By comparing different respondents' perspectives on the same relationships we were able to triangulate the different data sources. All nine respondents gave full and informed consent for the cooperation to the study.

8.4.2 Data Collection

In-depth semi-structured interviews were administered, for which a general structure was set up about the main questions to be asked on each of the topics. The detailed structure was established during the interview, depending on the input of the interviewee (Drever 1995). The interview sections relevant to our aim probed the main dependency experienced in the cooperation within their organisation and in interaction with the partner organisation. Based on these received interactions, questions on the perceived trustworthiness within this interaction followed, as well as on the trust levels within these interactions. Then the respondents were asked if they could identify the factors they believed influenced the trust relations within their professional context. The respondents were queried about their experiences as a trustor, not as trustee.

8.4.3 Analysis

In total there were 9 h and 33 min of voice recordings to analyse, with an average duration of an interview of 1 h and 11 min. The recordings were transcribed and analysed with the computer assisted qualitative data analysis tool NVivo, version 10. A two-stage coding scheme was used, starting with a provisional list of codes based on the framework developed by Dietz (2011). This was the deductive stage. After this an inductive stage was included, where coding of the remaining relevant segments was done based on the data (Hennink et al. 2010). Through the iterative process of the two stages of coding, recurring themes emerged.

8.5 Findings

The findings are structured around the concepts of the theoretical framework: (a) the inputs, (b) the trustworthiness, and (c) the willingness to be vulnerable and the risk taking acts. The latter are treated together since during the analysis it appeared difficult to distinguish between a person's attitudes and behaviours, even though in the model they are separated. Other techniques seem more relevant to really distinguish between trusting intentions and behaviours of the trustee, such as experimental studies, instead of retrospective interviewing.

Quotes, translated from Dutch, are provided to demonstrate the discourse of the respondents concerning their personal experiences. We focus on the elements of the concepts recurring throughout the interviews. Consequently the trustor's predisposition to trust is not further discussed as well as the domain specific concerns, however, all discussed inputs have a domain specific interpretation as well.

8.5.1 Inputs

8.5.1.1 Trustee's Character, Motives, Abilities, and Behaviours

As predicted by the theoretical model, various attributes of the trustee were brought forward as inputs for the trust process in the juvenile justice setting. The most valued characteristics were flexibility, loyalty, and a willingness to help, to communicate and to listen. Some respondents argued these attributes are found in younger more than in elder colleagues, and that an ongoing rejuvenation of the judicial system eases cooperation. Hierarchical and distant individuals—a common style within the magistracy—are hence perceived harder to trust, for example, in open dialogue.

> Now, with the rejuvenation of justice, they are all young magistrates who look differently at their job and who want to cooperate. They don't want to take the decisions on

> their own, they want to deliberate. They enter the job very open-minded and not blinkered thinking 'I've done it like that for years and it will stay that way or I'll get tired.'. (Criminologist)

Only when the right personalities are in place, they feel able to depend on each other in the difficult daily context of their work. For example, flexibility is specifically necessary because of the unpredictable nature of their work, and mutual support because of the emotional strain within the job. This seems to confirm that in different contexts different characteristics can serve as a basis for trust. The following quotes illustrate the importance of flexibility and willingness to listen:

> I believe, definitely here at the registry, it is very important who is working here. It can't be just anyone sitting here. It's not like you give the people just something to process and that's it, it doesn't work that way. They need to have certain flexibility and that is very important because we are not dealing with just average issues here. And definitely here at the registry you have to receive people who are often angry, so you do need a certain personality to deal with that. (Registrar)

> Also the willingness, so the fact that every now and then, we need to vent, because of everything we deal with. And then we can talk to each other. So the willingness to listen from their side. (Juvenile Judge)

For all interactions taking place within their work environment, however, the respondents were generally very positive about the personality traits. We could therefore expect this factor to have a positive influence on the next step of the trust process, the assessment of the trustworthiness.

8.5.1.2 The Nature of the Trustor-Trustee Relationship: "We" Versus "They" Culture

A trust-inhibiting factor mentioned by six respondents is the effect of an ingroup-outgroup dynamic in their professional context. The separation between the public prosecutor's office and the court is prominent because of task divergence, physical distance of offices, unequal working conditions (e.g. stricter work hours for one than for the other), ivory tower attitudes, different views, and not having a clear picture on what the other's tasks are. This can create prejudices and conflicts between the entities. This did result in a higher assessment of intra-organisational trust (I) than inter-organisational trust (II).

> They have their arrangement just like us, with employees and registrars. We call and pass by there every day. This contact is good but you do feel it's another terrain, prosecutor's office and registry. [...] It's another system, with different hours, different operationalisation, different agreements, and you can feel that and always have. So concerning trust and distrust, what you are talking about, you do feel 'this person is from the prosecutor's office' or 'this person is from the registry' where you feel a certain distance. We call everyone but it's never a feeling like we are one. (Head of the secretariat)

However, this was not felt as problematic and the respondents even saw some benefits of this, since it keeps up the spirits and since it creates more cohesion within the own organisation.

> People are like that, you have your team, your own group where you feel safe and everything that is outside this is a bit different, and then they are a bit sceptic towards that. And that can cause a slight form of distrust. […] I think that is a healthy form, a little is ok. You can feel a bit the competition, the challenge and sometimes feel better than them. People gossip and that happens inevitably, as said, that's particular to human beings. (Head of the secretariat)

> Because there [in court] there is sometimes a different opinion, a different view. Sometimes cases are closed or decisions are made of which I think 'That's impossible, that's not logical, did you even read the file?'. That does not happen often, but sometimes it does. In general that is also a positive thing, because of this I have more trust in us than in them, that's what I believe. (Criminologist)

This culture might have some influence on the rest of the trust process, however, it is unlikely that it will have a decisive effect because it was not seen as a problematic effect of the environment by our respondents.

8.5.1.3 Situational Influences: Perceived Workload of the Trustee

A long-standing issue in the Belgian judicial system is that the workload for staff members is experienced as being too high. Also for the selected case this held true and it was seen as an important factor affecting trust. Each respondent was aware that the amount of information and files entering the organisation, the complexity of the tasks, and the lack of means, of good standard procedures and of digitalisation were putting an enormous strain on the people involved. Being concious about the difficult working conditions of their colleagues made them aware that mistakes are likely to happen, and that no one's work could therefore be fully trusted.

> Yes, the workload has an influence on the way tasks are being executed, that will definitely have an influence. I believe if more people and means would be available, and everyone could work more comfortably, then this should have a positive influence. It might also be that some people will say: 'ok, now we can relax' and then not necessarily will work better. But normally you could expect that if your work pressure decreases, one can work more concentrated, more focussed, and more precise, and that this will consequently have an influence on trust. (Public prosecutor)

The issue of the high workload and high work pressure was deemed vastly important and potentially has a quite large negative effect on the next step of the trust process. The inputs thus are mixed, with a positive effect of the personality traits, a negative effect of the workload and an ambiguous effect of the ingroup-outgroup culture. This will inevitably make the next step less straightforward.

8.5.2 *Perceived Trustworthiness*

8.5.2.1 Perceived Ability

Ability refers to "that group of skills, competencies, and characteristics that enable a party to have influence within some specific domain." (Mayer et al. 1995, p. 717). The statements on the ability of the trustees are, as expected by the concurrent positive and negative inputs, somewhat ambiguous. On the one hand the respondents feel the magistrates and the administration are highly competent and working to the best of their abilities. On the other hand they feel the pressure of the work at times drives them to the limits of their abilities, resulting in mistakes. As such the competence is estimated high, but the respondents realise the structural environment hinders the abilities, which leads to a negative assessment of the abilities.

> The only thing I can think of – but that is not really distrust, it's just because of the lack of capacity – is that files are not dealt with in time. It gets postponed because an inquiry has to happen, the cabinets are too full, then the case doesn't progress, and if the case doesn't progress we can't help the child forward. For example, but that's not distrust towards that person, that the person doesn't do their job, but just that you know there is no time to meticulously follow up on everything. (Juvenile Judge)

> Trust is there, yes, but you have to manage too. If there is something, like today we only have X (registrar) who came to have a look if I was here. If that person simultaneously has to handle the incoming phones calls, present the files, process the decisions, and all urgent faxes, well… Then you know it will become quite difficult. But it's not the person's fault, that's the influence of the amount of work, you see. (Juvenile Judge)

This, however, does not apply to all tasks which need to be relied on. For example, the criminologist expects the prosecuting magistrates to immediately take the correct action in urgent cases, when a notification of a child in need is received: "*They will ask the necessary investigations, will correctly bring the case to the judges, and if urgent action is needed they will again do the necessary.*" This suggests that perceived trustworthiness is indeed task specific.

8.5.2.2 Perceived Benevolence

Benevolence is "the extent to which a trustee is believed to want to do good to the trustor, aside from an egocentric profit motive." (Mayer et al. 1995, p. 718). We see a similar discourse arising for benevolence as for ability. The respondents are positive about the benevolent intentions of those working in both entities. For example, the schedules of all parties are taken into account before a person is summoned for a hearing, or they can count on it that documents arriving at the fax machine will reach their desk within the first 10 min after arrival. However, it is recognized that also these intentions cannot always be translated into benevolent actions, again as a consequence of handling too many things at once due to the understaffing of the organisations.

> Yes, well, they do take our concerns and needs into account, but I must say, sometimes there is so much to process that it's not always easy to do this. From my side as well as from their side. Actually, to be honest, we should have more personnel, both administrative and judges. Because I believe we do have a huge responsibility, but with too many files... (Juvenile Judge)

> We have to find a balance there; it's about what I would want to have in my files, and what is possible for them. We work with a limited amount of people in the administration and I would always like to receive perfect files with everything on order and as many copies as we need. But we always need to find a balance between what I absolutely need and what is reasonable for them, to get their work done. (Public prosecutor)

There was also a slight contrast between the perceived benevolence within the own organisation, and that within the other organisation, with a more negative appraisal of the benevolence of the outer entity.

> It happens that you call [the registry] and that they give you very little information. We have a common system with the registry, and we can look into that but we can't change anything in there. And then you expect something to be available in there but sometimes we need more clarification, and then I feel that people won't call them because you already know you will get a comment like 'You already know that don't you, you can access that too can't you?'. That they are reluctant to give information to us in the public prosecutor's office. (Head of the secretariat)

8.5.2.3 Perceived Integrity

Integrity involves "the trustor's perception that the trustee adheres to a set of principles that the trustor finds acceptable." (Mayer et al. 1995, p. 719). Integrity in this context was linked by the respondents to discretion, work ethics, conscientious decision making, honesty, responsibility, work motivation, and having the interest of the child as absolute priority.

> I believe the expectation is that we are all involved in the same philosophy and that for everyone the interest of the child is priority. And this should be the underlying principle for all decisions, in files as well as in the cooperation; this has to be the critical factor. (Public prosecutor)

> They are definitely aware that they are dealing with children and not with objects. So you don't just decide something about the life of a child. You have to take everything into account and often there is not a good solution for the child available. You have to choose the least bad option. Those are very tough decisions to make, also for them [the prosecutors]. And they deal with this upright and serene. (Criminologist)

The unanimous response was that they believed in the integrity of the others. No reports were made about a possible influence of the working conditions on the integrity, as was the case for ability and benevolence. We can conclude for perceived trustworthiness that the ambiguous trend continues throughout this step. Overall the respondents are positive about the ability, benevolence and integrity of their fellow staff members. However, they do admit that for some tasks the ability and/or benevolence are expected to be lowered by circumstances typical to their work environment, especially the high workload. These positive and negative expectations of the trustworthiness now form a basis on which to decide on the willingness to be vulnerable.

8.5.3 Trust as Attitude (and Behaviour)

A trusting attitude refers to the willingness to be vulnerable based on positive expectations of the trustee. Trusting behaviour refers to the risk taking acts that result from the willingness to be vulnerable. Since the research conducted made use of interviewing in which respondents rely on previous experiences to formulate their answer it becomes difficult to distinguish how the last part of the trust processes were experienced, and whether their attitudes had differed from eventual behaviour. Therefore, these two steps are considered together in this paragraph.

Two main vulnerabilities were eminent in the discourse of the interviews. First, there was the vulnerability in the communication with others. Asking or sharing information is risky since it can never be fully estimated what the outcome will be. The counterpart can decide not to give the information or can abuse the information they receive. Second, task delegation is a form of accepting vulnerability and risk taking. This can mean trusting others with a task you can hand over, or trusting their task performance without constantly checking up on them, which could otherwise be time-consuming.

The willingness to exchange information seemed diminished by a sometimes low estimation of the perceived benevolence.

> Therefore I think the intention to ask information; this will disappear because you already have a kind of distrust towards their reaction, a negative expectation. They say we can consult the system ourselves and this should be enough. (Head of the secretariat)

> When I have the file of a child and I need to know where we stand in the investigations, because not all items are in the file, then I need to see which magistrate is on the case, and each magistrate has their own administrative clerk, and then I need to go to them. You think ahead, oh no, I hope this person is not there and the other is, so I can ask them instead. That's typical; some people you rather avoid because you know they will grunt and sigh, they see you coming and already look like 'What do you want now…'. (Criminologist)

The willingness to take the risk of task delegation on the other hand seemed diminished by the lack of positive expectations about the abilities. The respondents felt double-checking remained necessary given the problematic working conditions of the one performing the task. Especially since a small mistake in address or name can have long lasting effects on the whole process.

> An advantage of distrust is that everything is double-checked. Because we are dealing with such sensitive issues, and we're only humans and humans make mistakes. And everyone makes mistakes, me too, the magistrates, the administration, everybody here makes mistakes. And you need to double-check because you know your colleague has prepared something in a hurry, it's probably going to be a job half done, I'm going to double-check it. And it's not a critique towards that person; it's just that you know the reality. And that's why you need a healthy portion of distrust to keep checking if everything is done correctly. (Criminologist)

Others however did not feel the need of checking everything, although they realised mistakes were going to occur. The reason for this was that they too, as a trustor, have a high workload and no time to double-check the work of their colleagues on top of that. This way, even though they have negative expectations of the perceived ability, they do pose risk taking behaviour due to their own limitations.

> When a file enters here with a requisition of the prosecutor, then we read that and see whether it is urgent, whether an immediate measure has to be taken. Here I have a file which needs such immediate measure. Then people need to get summoned. I just write on a piece of paper: invite parents, minor, lawyer. The registry will execute this. I receive the letters from them and I sign this off. And I haven't checked whether the address was correct, I can't do that, we can't deal with all everyday mail. I assume this is correct. And like that sometimes something can go wrong. (Juvenile Judge)

In general the respondents did not have many issues with a lack of trust, but the above examples do illustrate how especially the working conditions can influence both the expectations one has of the trustee and limit the freedom to behave appropriately to these expectations by the trustor.

8.6 Discussion and Conclusion

We have used the framework developed by Dietz (2011), which is a composition based on several seminal literature works, as a lens to explore the trust phenomenon within and between the Flemish juvenile prosecutor's office and juvenile court. This first exploration of organisational trust by a case study within the judicial sector yields several insights on the manifestation of the trust process in this context.

The first step in the process contains the different inputs that serve as information for the trustor to make judgements about trustee's trustworthiness. It was found that for the input referring to the trustee's character, motives, abilities and behaviours, the most valued personal characteristics were flexibility, loyalty, and willingness to help, to communicate and to listen. These traits were especially deemed important because of the irregular and emotional nature of the work. This finding supports the argument of Dietz that "influences and localised external conditions shape the content and process at each stage" (Dietz 2011, p. 219). It was also stated that such characteristics are easier found in the younger generations of staff. All respondents stated that personalities of the current team members were adequate for trust to emerge. A second input, but on the level of the organisation, was the separation between the two entities. Knowing the counterpart is from the same organisation has a positive influence on the trust process. This "we" versus "them" culture is a well-known phenomenon in the literature (Brewer 1999). The influence however is deemed small by the respondents. A last important input is the workload of trustees. In this setting the workload was generally estimated as considerable, and this was said to have a negative influence on the rest of the trust process.

Concerning the trustworthiness, parted into perceived ability, benevolence and integrity (ABI), the link with the inputs is made. Ability and benevolence are estimated high when it comes to the individuals' intentions or competencies, but due to the situational factor of the high caseload this is estimated low for certain tasks. The integrity of all counterparts is however estimated high irrespective of the high workload.

When we look at the last stages of the process, namely the trusting attitudes and behaviours of the trustor, the process does follow the logic of the perceived trustworthiness. For example, the fact that the benevolence was estimated to be lower at times, had an influence especially on the willingness to be vulnerable in the communication with others. Expecting the trustee to be less benevolent can make the trustor decide not to go into dialogue with this person. This can be problematic since the work of the judiciary depends greatly on the sharing of information. Expecting the trustee to be less able in his work prevents the trustor from delegating tasks to the others and from not doing constant double-checking of the other's work. This can again be problematic since this prevents them from working more time-efficient, which will again increase the workload and in turn can diminish trust even more. Interestingly, the respondents report to sometimes taking risks such as not double-checking the other's work, even though they don't have full positive expectations of the trustee. This is due to the equally high workload of the trustor. Such forced trust might be typical for the (Flemish) judicial context where behaviour is constrained by the task division and the high workload. This creates a dangerous situation, where no double-checks are performed although this would be desirable to avoid procedural errors from slipping into the process. These findings can contribute to the discussion on the complexity of the trust process, as well as to the discussion on the management of a judicial system.

The reader should keep in mind the following limitations of this study. The separate steps in trust process could not all be studied separately. It proved difficult to distinguish between ones trusting attitude and ones trusting behaviour when interviewing people on their general experiences. The last stage of the process of feedback of the output to the input was also not studied in detail. Past experiences were only mentioned sporadically as input for the trust process. Furthermore, the results were based on interviews in one judicial division. Although there are no indications this case differs from the average judicial division, the trust process could play out in a different way in other divisions depending on the specific context. The transferability of these findings to other contexts should be regarded with caution.

Acknowledgements The authors would like to thank The Belgian Science Policy (Belspo) for organising and funding the interorganisational attraction pole programme 'Justice & Populations' within which this project has taken place. The authors also thank Peter Oomsels, Graham Dietz and Barbara Lawrence for their important inputs on earlier versions of the manuscript.

References

Blois, K. J. (1999). Trust in business to business relationships: An evaluation of its status. *Journal of Management Studies*, *36*, 197–215. http://doi.org/10.1111/1467-6486.00133

Bouckaert, G. (2012). Trust and public administration. *Administration*, *60*(1), 91–115.

Brewer, M. B. (1999). The psychology of prejudice: Ingroup love and outgroup hate? *Journal of Social Issues*, *55*(3), 429–444.

Castelfranchi, C., & Falcone, R. (2000). Trust and control: A dialectic link. *Applied Artificial Intelligence*, *14*(8), 799–823. http://doi.org/10.1080/08839510050127560

Costa, A. C. (2003). Understanding the nature and the antecedents of trust within work teams. In B. Nooteboom & F. Six (Eds.), *The trust process in organizations Empirical studies of the determinants and the process of trust development* (pp. 105–124). Cheltenham: Edward Elgar.

De Bruyn, D. (2006). *De magistraat aan het woord. Een verkennend onderzoek naar de opvattingen van magistraten over hun functioneren in justitie en samenleving*. Antwerp, Apeldoorn: Maklu.

Depré, R., & Hondeghem, A. (Eds.). (2000). *Management, bestuur & beleid in de rechterlijke organisatie*. Brugge: die Keure.

Dietz, G. (2011). Going back to the source: Why do people trust each other? *Journal of Trust Research*, *1*(2), 215–222. http://doi.org/10.1080/21515581.2011.603514

Drever, E. (1995). *Using Semi-Structured Interviews in Small-Scale Research. A Teacher's Guide*. Edinburgh: SCRE.

Edelenbos, J., & Klijn, E.-H. (2007). Trust in Complex Decision-Making Networks: A Theoretical and Empirical Exploration. *Administration & Society*, *39*, 25–50. http://doi.org/10.1177/0095399706294460

Fulmer, C. A., & Gelfand, M. J. (2012). At what level (and in whom) we trust: Trust across multiple organizational levels. *Journal of Management*, *38*(4), 1167–1230. http://doi.org/10.1177/0149206312439327

Golbeck, J., & Hendler, J. (2006). Inferring binary trust relationships in Web-based social networks. *ACM Transactions on Internet Technology*, *6*(4), 497–529. http://doi.org/10.1145/1183463.1183470

Hartley, J. (2004). Case study research. In C. Cassell & G. Symon (Eds.), *Essential guide to qualitative methods in organizational research* (pp. 323–333). London: SAGE Publications.

Hennink, M., Hutter, I., & Bailey, A. (2010). *Qualitative Research Methods*. London: SAGE Publications Ltd.

Koppenjan, J., & Klijn, E.-H. (2004). *Managing uncertainties in networks: a network approach to problem solving and decision making*. London: Routledge.

Luhmann, N. (1979). *Trust and power*. Chichester: Wiley.

Lyon, F., Mollering, G., & Saunders, M. N. K. (2012). *Handbook of research methods on trust*. Cheltenham: Edward Elgar.

Markusen, A. (1999). Fuzzy concepts, scanty evidence, policy distance: The case for rigour and policy relevance in critical regional studies. *Regional Studies*, *33*(9), 869–884. http://doi.org/10.1080/00343409950075506

Mayer, R. C., Davis, J. H., & Schoorman, F. D. (1995). An integrative model of organizational trust. *The Academy of Management Review*, *20*(3), 709–734. http://doi.org/10.2307/258792

McAllister, D. J. (1995). Affect- and cognition based trust as foundations for interpersonal cooperation in organisations. *Academy of Management Journal*, *38*(1), 24–59. http://doi.org/10.2307/256727

McEvily, B., & Tortoriello, M. (2011). Measuring trust in organizational research: Review and recommendations. *Journal of Trust Research, 1*(1), 23–63. http://doi.org/10.1080/21515581.2011.552424

Reynders, D., Thomaes, S., & Devroe, E. (2005). Het openbaar ministerie in de beleidscyclus: naar een samenwerkingsdynamiek met de dienst voor het Strafrechtelijk beleid. In R. Depré, J. Plessers, & A. Hondeghem (Eds.), *Managementhervormingen in Justitie, van internationale ontwikkelingen tot dagelijkse praktijk* (pp. 153–183). Brugge: die Keure.

Rousseau, D. M., Sitkin, S. B., Burt, R. S., & Camerer, C. (1998). Introduction to special topic forum: Not so different after all: A cross-discipline view of trust. *Academy of Management Review, 23*(3), 393–404. http://doi.org/10.2307/259285

Seppänen, R., Blomqvist, K., & Sundqvist, S. (2007). Measuring inter-organizational trust—a critical review of the empirical research in 1990–2003. *Industrial Marketing Management, 36*(2), 249–265. http://doi.org/10.1016/j.indmarman.2005.09.003

Skinner, D., Dietz, G., & Weibel, A. (2014). The dark side of trust: When trust becomes a "poisoned chalice." *Organization, 21*, 206–224. http://doi.org/10.1177/1350508412473866

Vandam, L., Colman, C., Vander Laenen, F., & De Ruyver, B. (2010). Towards an integral and integrated drug policy: Pearls and pitfalls. In M. Cools, B. De Ruyver, M. Easton, L. Pauwels, P. Ponsaers, G. Vande Walle, … G. Vynckier (Eds.), *Safety, societal problems and citizens "perceptions": new empirical data, theories and analyses* (Vol. 3, pp. 239–262). Antwerpen: Maklu.

Yin, R. K. (2009). *Case study research: Design and methods* (4th ed.). Thousand Oaks, CA: SAGE.

Chapter 9
Managing the 'Overall Integrated Security Policy' at the Local Level: An Analysis of Inter-institutional Dialogue

Alice Croquet and Frédéric Schoenaers

9.1 Introduction

The traditional elements of public action are currently being challenged and revised (Hassenteufel 2008) with coproduction becoming an increasingly dominant theme (Gautron 2013). The new trend is towards a new government model developed at the local level, forged by different actors who manage public issues within a relatively wide remit for action granted by the State. In particular, the security sector illustrates this common tendency towards more partnerships and dialogue between various institutional sectors (Crawford 2001; Roché 2004).

Belgium has observed this "institutionalisation of collective action"[1] (Duran and Thoenig 1996, p. 582) in the security sector since the early 1990s (Cartuyvels and Hebberecht 2001). Within this movement the police reform of 1998 was an important turning point.[2] If this was focused foremost on the structural aspects of the police system (see Box 1), it was also an opportunity to revise police culture and institutional security policy. By implementing an 'overall integrated security policy' (see Box 2), the reform urged the police force to conceive public security

[1]Extracts from documents, policy statements and interviews quoted in this chapter have been translated by the authors for this purpose.

[2]Law of 7 December 1998 organising an integrated police service structured on two levels, *M.B., 5th January 1999*, p. 132.

A. Croquet (✉) · F. Schoenaers
Centre de Recherche et d'Interventions Sociologiques (CRIS),
University of Liège, Liège, Belgium
e-mail: acroquet@ulg.ac.be

A. Hondeghem et al. (eds.), *Modernisation of the Criminal Justice Chain and the Judicial System*, Ius Gentium: Comparative Perspectives on Law and Justice 50, DOI 10.1007/978-3-319-25802-7_9

management through the 'integral security' model, presented in 2000 by the Minister of Justice.[3] This concept is defined as a "global approach that takes into account all causes liable to threaten or promote security."[4] Based on a close relationship between the main actors of the 'security chain' (prevention, repression and follow-up), this model questions the hegemony of the police institution in security matters by including other actors who traditionally worked separately (Loubet Del Bayle 2006). At the local level, the overall integrated security policy organises a systematic dialogue between the local chief of police, the mayor(s) and the public prosecutor. Concretely, these actors are required to meet in an official body especially created for this purpose, in order to collectively and consensually determine an Area Security Plan (ASP).

Referring to the heuristic framework known as Sociology of Organised Action (Crozier and Friedberg 1977; Friedberg 1997), this chapter will investigate the dialogue process that governs the ASPs. It will question and challenge the 'collective' nature of this 'collective decision,' defined as a "process through which a group decides together an intent to act for itself or for an entity of which it is a part" (Urfalino 2005, p. 107). The decision-making process during the official body of dialogue will be analysed, using Urfalino's model of 'apparent consensus' (Urfalino 2007). Focusing on how is the legal requirement for inter-institutional dialogue implemented in practice, the research question of this chapter is thus the following: can we speak of 'apparent consensus' in the decision-making process regarding the Area Security Plans? To answer this question, it is necessary to pay particular attention to the preparatory steps of the dialogue council.

This chapter will first focus on the methodological and theoretical framework guiding the research. It will then analyse the decision-making process firstly by investigating each step individually and, secondly, by discussing the concept of 'apparent consensus'.

Box 1: The New Belgian Police Pattern

Before 1998, the Belgian police system was comprised of three main autonomous forces with distinct authorities, legislations and organisational principles: the municipal police, the gendarmerie and the judicial police. The police system was extremely decentralised and had multiple command centres (Bayley 1985), which induced the overlapping of skills and territories and therefore created structural dysfunctions between the different police forces.

The police reform[5] created an integrated police force that joined together the three old forces under the same legislation and the same police status.

---

[3]"Federal Plan of Security and of Penitentiary Policy" (*Doc. Parl.*, Sénat, 1999–2000, n°2-461/1).

[4]*Idem*, p. 13.

[5]Law of 7 December 1998, *op. cit.*

The new structure is split into two levels, the local and federal, which are functionally linked through various integration mechanisms. Currently, the federal police are responsible for the whole Belgian territory under the authority of the Ministers of the Interior and Justice. It is responsible for specialised and supra-local missions (e.g. organised crime and terrorism) and for giving support to the local police. The local police are divided into 195 areas in the Belgian territory. Each local police force is under the direction of the police chief. Among these 195 local police areas, some are constituted by only one city ('single city areas') and are under the sole authority of the local administration authority—the mayor—whereas others are constituted by several cities ('multi-city areas') and are under the authority of several local administration authorities. Each local police force is in charge of basic police missions (proximity, intervention, road safety, and so on) as well as some federal missions. For the accomplishment of its tasks, the local police force reports to both the administrative authority (for administrative police tasks such as public order) and the judicial authority, that is to say the public prosecutor (for the judicial police tasks such as crime and penal infractions).

Box 2: The Overall Integrated Security Policy

The 'overall integrated security policy' is structured around various plans which play intermediary roles between actors of different levels (local and federal police forces) and sectors (police, politics, and justice) of public action. The system relies on a political framework determining security priorities (the 'Note-cadre de sécurité intégrale'), defined every four years by the Ministers of the Interior and Justice. From this framework, the federal and local police forces elaborate a National Security Plan and various Area Security Plans (ASPs) respectively. At the local level, the ASP must integrate the crime policy of the public prosecutor as well as the concerns of the mayor(s). To this end, all these actors—the representative of the federal police force (the 'administrative director-coordinator'), public prosecutor, mayor(s) and local police chief—must meet in a dialogue council (the Area Security Council) in order to determine the ASP collectively.

The ASP therefore constitutes a local implementation of a nationwide policy. Concretely, its main function is to manage police activity and capacity in a strategic way for the next four years via the definition of internal priorities (organisational development such as communications and training) and external priorities (security matters such as theft, illegal drugs and so on).

9.2 Methodological and Theoretical Framework

On the methodological level, the analysis relies on an empirical study conducted from January 2013 to June 2014 in the whole Belgian territory (Flemish, Brussels and Walloon Regions). This chapter takes an inductive, bottom-up and qualitative approach at the micro-sociological level, anchored in the Grounded Theory Methodology (Strauss and Corbin 2004). It is based on three means of data collection consisting of in-depth semi-structured interviews (using a general interview guide), direct observation and document analysis. The text draws on meetings with 21 police representatives (1 administrative director-coordinator, 15 local police chiefs, 1 officer and 4 strategic analysts); 11 administrative authorities representatives (9 mayors and 2 mayor's chiefs of staff); and 6 judicial authority representatives (4 public prosecutors, 1 general prosecutor and 1 substitute). It also draws on observations of 9 Area Security Councils, 1 Police College of Mayors and 2 Police Councils. Finally, the analysis of administrative, legislative and police documents completes these data.

Assuming that actors show 'bounded rationality' (Simon 1955) and using a 'constructivist' or 'processual' conception of organisations, Sociology of Organised Action has contributed greatly to the theories of decision-making. It considers that "a decision is always the product of a concrete action system" which founds its rationality in the system of actors which produces it (Crozier and Friedberg 1977, p. 303). By focusing on the logics of action developed by actors during the negotiation of the ASP, a meta-model of this concrete system of relationships will be introduced. This chapter will attempt to describe the general 'rules of engagement' that occur in ASP management, while noting variations that occur in particular instances.

In order to elucidate the exact moment when the decision is made, the text draws from the concept of 'apparent consensus' defined by Urfalino (2007). The author describes the model of 'apparent consensus' in opposition to other decision-making systems such as the vote model by majority or unanimity, which suppose the counting of voices, even if only in an informal way (through a wave of the hand, nod of the head, etc.). In defining 'apparent consensus,' Urfalino determines six main constitutive characteristics. Firstly, the 'apparent consensus' is a method of collective decision-making relate to the exact moment of the 'adoption' of the decision or the exact moment when the decision is made (excluding both the process leading to the decision and the result of the decision). Directly linked with this, Urfalino specifies the impression of 'continuity' between the process and the adoption of the decision, in such a way that the decision is viewed as directly emerging from the discussion. The third characteristic of the apparent consensus method is the 'collective' nature of the observation of the consensus, that is to say that the decision is taken when the assembly collectively notes that there is consensus. To help explain his theory, Urfalino clarifies two concomitant meanings of the adjective 'apparent'. Firstly, 'apparent' is opposed to the real, implying that the consensus might be wrong or misleading. Secondly, 'apparent' also means 'perceptible' or 'evident' in such a way that the consensus appears to the participants like a 'phenomenon'. In this way, Urfalino fourthly stipulates that the apparent consensus does not require unanimity, but that some stakeholders "consent to not protesting against the consensus proposal" (p. 64). The fifth condition of the apparent consensus is the "importance of the quality of the decision" prevailing over the "sum of individual opinions" (p. 62). Finally, the sixth condition is "the contrast between the equal right to participate [in the decision] and the inequality of legitimacy of the influences" (p. 57). By considering each one of these conditions and their relevance in the practices of decision-making around the ASP, we will suggest to discuss the concept developed by Urfalino.

9.3 The Decision-Making Process

The structural framework of the ASP formation is explicitly formalised (Friedberg 1992) concerning its essential points: the institutional scene of exchange, the minimal required actors and the global expected results are all defined by legal texts. However, the modalities concerning the collective decision process itself (in terms of frequency of meetings, agreement degree and precise role of each actor) are reduced to a general requirement for 'systematic dialogue'[6] and 'consensus method'.[7] Given the minimal information found in the 1998 law, two facts can first be established about the stabilisation of the practices observed around ASP.

Firstly, the ASP development process is clearly under the sole leadership and initiative of the local police, which is the true driving force of the ASP. Consequently, it is not the Area Security Council (ASC) which prepares the ASP, as required by the 1998 Law. However, the degree of elaboration of the ASP varies according to the police areas: the smallest ones tend to face many problems related to daily and reactive police work and do not necessarily possess the capacity to form a strategic security plan really detailed. Even so, local police forces do not act with total autonomy because the Ministry of the Interior also plays a regulatory function in the ASP process, notably by promulgating new directives. The regulation of the action system (Friedberg 1992) is thus both 'internal' and 'external'.

Secondly, the ASC is not solely responsible for the entire decision-making process. The development of the ASP also takes place elsewhere. This is not an allusion to the two other official steps provided for in the 1998 Law: the Police Council (or Municipal Council for the 'single city police areas') concerning the parts of the plan which may have any consequences on the competencies of the police force; and the Ministries of the Interior and Justice who have the power to validate the ASP. Beyond these official ratifications, two other main stages of dialogue have to be described, as these actually prepare the ASC itself.

[6] Law of 7 December 1998, *op. cit.*, art. 35.

[7] Nota ZPZ 20 of 1st Augustus 2001: transition from a pentagonal dialogue and from a security charter towards an area security council and an area security plan, *M.B. 7 September 2001.*

In practice, the decision process of the ASP starts with the consultation of police authorities concerning their requests related to the security issues.

9.3.1 Consulting the Authorities: Preparation of a Collective Decision

Seeing that the local police chief is under the authority of both the mayors and the public prosecutor, the latter have to determine the priority missions and objectives they want to see included in the ASP.[8] With regard to the 'integral security' concept, this political leadership has to be done within the perspective of an "integration of the administrative and judicial police functions" (Bourdoux and De Valkeneer 2001, p. 40).

9.3.1.1 Police and Mayors: An Inverted Expertise

In most police areas, the consultation of the administrative authorities is characterised by a common tendency from which the intervention of each mayor varies in some ways. Generally speaking, the path defined by the 1998 law is inverted: the police force proposes some priority issues to the mayors, who are invited to give their agreement. Starting with this proposal, some mayors do add their own preoccupations concerning a precise security issue (concerning a particular phenomenon or disadvantaged area in their municipality) and ask for it to be integrated into the priorities already suggested. Nonetheless, a certain number of mayors more or less validate the priorities proposed by the police force.

> Generally, we greatly follow what the police proposed. (Mayors' chief cabinet, Walloon Region).

It makes sense that the proposal of priorities originally comes from the police staff with regard to the logics of action developed by these actors according to their structural constraints, resources and interests. We would argue that the police force could be rightfully considered the more expert actor with regards to public security, which can be demonstrated as follows: drawing up a security analysis of a territory is a demanding exercise that police forces often delegate to strategic analysts completely dedicated to this task. While security is an important issue in the municipalities, the mayors often do not have such expertise. This 'expert power' (Crozier and Friedberg 1977, p. 84), symbolising the mastery of particular knowledge and know-how, partly explains why mayors trust in the counsel given by the police force. Directly linked with this, the gathering of specialised information must be taken into account. The police institution owns various data, in particular (but not limited to) statistics, on which it is possible to draw up a security diagnostic in order to determine the security policy. This legitimates and justifies

---

[8]Law of 7 December 1998, *op. cit.*, art. 36.

the strategic choices that the police suggest to the mayors, who indeed gain almost all their security knowledge from the information that the police forces regularly report to them. Undeniably, the mayors also acquire information through the very close relationships they have with the citizens they represent and this broadens their expertise beyond that provided by the local police. By conducting a specific study which gives mayors a precise vision of the security situation in their city, some municipal departments (such as the Prevention Department) can thereby constitute an important source of expertise for the mayor.

> Police collects the main part of data, and all the descriptions are made towards them, it is their job to record the descriptions, etc. So, police force produces statistics allowing putting in evidence the most frequent issues, etc. (Mayors' chief cabinet, Brussels Region)

Besides, some contextual elements may be proposed to explain how the mayors get involved in the process. Firstly, in larger cities, security matters are more important than in small and rural cities. Logically, the mayors therefore tend to be more concerned with security management and to take personally part in the decision-making. Secondly, the single-city police areas are more likely to develop dialogue because the mayor plays a central role of coordination, whereas in the multi-city police areas the scale of action does not correspond to the municipality and, so, to the territory of action of each mayor.

In practice, thus, mayors are often de facto dependent on information and expertise from the police force, which constitute two 'sources of uncertainty' produced by the decision-making system (Crozier and Friedberg 1977). They express quite unanimously their need of the local police and see the police expertise as an established fact they appreciate. This inversion of expertise in the relationship between these two institutions is described by Smeets and Tange (2008): the police institution owns the technical knowledge that is necessary for the exercise of authority, and that is why it is able and entitled to play the role of *conseiller du Prince* who enlightens the mayors about the security situation. A police chief very eloquently mentioned the 'political intelligence' they have to deploy in order to anticipate the mayors' preoccupations and to guide them in security management.

9.3.1.2 Police and Public Prosecutors: A Judicial Vision of Security

In a trend that has become more common in recent years, the public prosecutors decide some security issues that they consider priorities for the whole judicial district they manage. This judicial authorities' leadership conveys the hierarchical nature of the relationship between these two institutions and the way that public prosecutors employ it. According to them, the local police force has to adapt its work to the criminal policy of the public prosecutor's department. The ASP thus represents an opportunity for the prosecutor to guide police action towards their own priorities.

> So, I make my priorities know in terms of criminal policy and I hope of course that these will be taken into account. […] Because the sanctioning policy has to be adapted to the criminal policy. Otherwise, the chain runs idle. (Public prosecutor, Walloon Region)

Understandably, the public prosecutors are mainly interested in judicial matters. Their preoccupations thus focus on the 'investigation' aspects as well as policy concerned with sanctioning by the local police, both of which greatly influence court activity. In contrast with the mayors, they show little interest in the other dimensions of police work (intervention, proximity, etc.) or toward incivilities and public disruption. Indeed, public prosecutors show interest in only the most pressing criminal issues (in terms of both number and gravity) that need to be discussed judicially, delegating the 'little problems' towards other regulation mechanisms (the Prevention Departments or Municipal Administrative Sanctions, for example[9]). In this respect, mayors sometimes feel treated unfavourably in the discussions because of the prevailing influence of the public prosecutors upon the security chain: the final decision over whether or not to prosecute rests with the latter. Beyond their legitimate authority, the public prosecutors therefore own a strategic structural position in the penal chain that grants them significant power in their relationships with the other actors. The feeling of being side-lined sometimes expressed by mayors is moreover emphasised by the distrust that public prosecutors may express towards the mayors' communication culture, which stands in contrast with their own secrecy culture.

At this stage of the decision-making process, the determination of security priorities is thus realised in a bilateral way, under the lead of the police staff: on the one hand, the administrative authorities' priorities, which often overlap with the police priorities, and, on the other hand, the judicial authorities' priorities, which pay attention to the most important criminal issues. Clearly, these two sources of priorities are the most important ones for the local police force, as the mayor(s) and the public prosecutor are its two authorities and thereby have a decision-making power regarding the ASP. However, with increasing frequency some police areas have invited other partners to play advisory roles in security matters. This integration of other stakeholder's demands in the dialogue process is realised through a 'decisional matrix' proposed by the federal police force (CGL 2004, 2007).

9.3.2 The Decisional Matrix: Elaboration of a Police Proposal

The 'decisional matrix' is a double-entry table into which a set of security issues are inserted on one side, and the different sources of information as well as the different demands of the stakeholders on the other.

To recapitulate, according to the 'integral security' concept, the first and most important framework of the ASP is the 'Note-cadre de sécurité intégrale,' which is

[9]Municipalities may sanction the non-respect of some infractions provided for in the municipal regulations, in conformity with the Law of 24 June 2013 referring to the Municipal Administrative Sanctions, which amends the initial legislation on the Municipal Administrative Sanctions (article 119*bis* and 119*ter* of the New Municipal Law codified by the Royal Decree of 24 June 1988).

restated in the National Security Plan (NSP) of the federal police force. All the priorities included in the area plans have to correspond with this national framework; in the case of deviation, a justification is required. To ensure correlation between the two levels, the administrative director-coordinator of the federal police force is in attendance at the ASC. Nonetheless, these national priorities are often seen as broad enough that each police area can find some relevant phenomena for its territory.

The matrix usually includes at least the priorities of the local administrative and judicial authorities, the priorities of the federal authorities (included in the NSP) and those detected by the police force through its sources of information. Generally, the police force will add some other sources into the matrix, such as the priorities of the population (from a victimisation survey), the Governor of the Province, the administrative and judicial directors of the federal police force, the Prevention Departments of the municipalities, and so on. The crossing of the two entries in the table produces some factors of greater or lesser importance on which the choices regarding security policy will be made. The number of chosen priorities differs according to the police areas. Nevertheless, three or four priorities are usually drawn: burglaries, road safety, nuisance of any kind, and drugs; the presence of other priorities is dependent on the particularities of the police area in question.

By definition, the decisional matrix is built on the voting model: "a decision—secret or public—taken by counting the individual wills of a number of individuals considered to be equal" (Pasquino 2007, p. 35). Each voice is valued and counted,[10] but is not sure to be represented in the final decision. In this respect, the ASP results from the addition of the wills of the different partners involved in public security management.

Meanwhile, the work of writing the security project policy is realised by the police. In most cases, the plan is communicated in advance to the members of the ASC so that they can prepare their commentaries for the Council, during which, according to the 1998 law, the ASP has to be determined. Often, it is also the police chief who organises the official meeting, either hosting it in the police station or suggesting to the mayors that they hold it in their municipal offices.

9.3.3 The Area Security Council: Adoption of a Collective Decision

In all police areas studied, the ASC is inaugurated and led by the President-Mayor of the Police College. After the approval of the minutes of the previous meeting, the president lets the police staff present the ASP. In most cases, the police start their speech by giving some contextual or explicative comments concerning the plan and their police area. Then, they present the security phenomena, which they propose

[10] In this regard, some police staffs insert a coefficient into the sources included in the matrix in order to weight the influence of the different stakeholders according to their statute in the Area Security Council (members provided for in the Law, extra partners, etc.).

as priorities, on the basis of the decisional matrix. After this, the President-Mayor gives the members the floor to express their opinion about the police proposal.

According to the police area in question and to the characters of the individuals present around the table as well as to the relationships (formal and informal) they maintain with each other (Thoenig 1994), discussions then follow that challenge or applaud the police plan to various degrees.

> That takes around two or three hours of meeting, but we observe that there is absolutely never, never, a questioning of the ASP by the partners or the various authorities. Yes, some demands of explanations, of precisions… (Mayor, Brussels Region)

Sometimes, members propose modifications to a priority; other times, they ask to add a new priority to the ASP. What follows is the exchange of arguments for or against the modification proposal and these discussions often focus on the police capacity. In some cases, the police staff expresses some conditions related to the integration of a new priority: "it is okay if you pilot this priority yourself" or "it is okay, but with the status of 'point of attention' instead of 'priority'." A public prosecutor related that she had once disagreed with the police proposal and she had threatened not to sign the document unless the policy was modified. As we have seen, to reach an agreement the stakeholders sometimes have to have recourse to the compromise method in which the actors negotiate the agreement conditions of the collective decision through 'concession bargaining' (Elster 1994, p. 229). If the discussion appears to have reached a stalemate, the President-Mayor formulates a new proposal that (in their opinion) incorporates the wishes and the conditions expressed during the debate, which he or she then submits for general approval. When no objection is expressed, the President-Mayor declares the security policy accepted and officialises the collective decision by circulating a document for the council members to sign.

To conclude, whereas the ASC is not solely responsible for the entire collective decision-making process, it is precisely the moment of the 'adoption' of the decision (Urfalino 2007). This is precisely what we have described in the proceedings of the ASC, which actually fixes the agreement—the act of signing is a key indicator of this—, in contrast with the two preceding steps of dialogue which prepare this agreement. However, beyond this first characteristic of 'apparent consensus,' does the modality of decision-making applied in the ASC follow this logic as defined by Urfalino? By considering the six conditions described above and their relevance in the practices of decision-making around the ASP (with regards to the logics of action employed by the actors during the preparatory steps), we would question the nature of the process.

9.4 The Decision by 'Apparent Consensus'

In the ASCs, the decision is often made when the assembly collectively notes that there is consensus. Indeed, the chairperson does not gauge members' faces for agreement, nor do they proceed to a vote of any form. It is only after the establishment of the 'apparent consensus' that each member formalises his or her agreement with the project by signing the document. Thereby, the decision-making in the ASC responds to the 'collective' nature of the observation of the consensus specified by Urfalino.

The impression of 'continuity' between the process and the adoption of the decision can be also applied in the ASC situation. Indeed, the security policy project of the police force leads to many discussions, including compromise and negotiation. The partners discuss the results of the matrix by specifying the precise involvement of each institution in the priority concerned, in compliance with their prerogative. This argument is also related to the fact that "the decision in question is not reducible to a yes/no alternative" (Urfalino 2007, p. 54). In this way, we attend many discussions in the ASC before achieving a consensual decision. Therefore, because various proposals can be formulated before the final state of the agreement, the decision seems directly emerge from the discussion.

Then, as we can observe in the proceedings of the ASC, the decision by apparent consensus does not result from unanimity or majority agreement but from the absence of expressed disagreement or protest. In other words, "what appears is not direct consensus, but the absence of expressed dissensus" (Urfalino 2007, p. 60). In this regard, the absence of expressed disagreement does not mean that silent members approve the decision. This fourth condition of the apparent consensus is perceptible in some ASCs, especially concerning the 'withdrawal' (Crozier and Friedberg 1977, p. 76) of some mayors: tardiness, silence during meetings, and physical absence or distractedness (looking through the window, phoning, sleeping and so on). However, the motivations for this lack of involvement are many and can be linked to various explanations.

Firstly, in some cases, the ASC enacts the work prepared before, on the basis of the decisional matrix summarising all the stakeholders' requirements. If all the members are satisfied with the results of the matrix, there is no reason to contest the police proposal. Especially, as this decisional tool relies on the vote system widely considered to be the most democratic mode of decision-making, it benefits from significant legitimacy. Nonetheless, in this way, this achievement of consensus challenges the fifth condition of the apparent consensus method defined by Urfalino: the "importance of the quality of the decision" prevailing over the "sum of individual opinions" (Urfalino 2007, p. 62). Indeed, whereas the decision-making mode in the council excludes the principles of the vote, the preparatory steps of this decisional moment precisely follow this logic of aggregation of preferences. Can we still speak of a consensual decision in this case? In close relation with this criterion of 'the quality of the decision,' it is worth noting the highly predictable and broad nature of the priorities in some security plans. These vague objectives are described by some actors as 'truisms,' present in every plan and 'pushing at open doors.' This also makes consensus easier because everyone can find a security problem in the final selection that he or she would like to see treated. These descriptions challenge the boundaries of the concept of apparent consensus. The contrast is indeed quite important in some ASCs where the legitimacy of the decision results from the debates between the stakeholders and where "the arguments replace the aggregation of the preferences" (Urfalino 2007, p. 63).

A second explanation of the renunciation of contest from some authorities may be found in the sixth condition underlined by Urfalino: "the contrast between the equal right to participate [in the decision] and the inequality of legitimacy of the influences" (2007, p. 57). Between the authorities and the local police staff, an inequality of interests and resources exists leading to some voices being differently weighted during the decision-making. As the preparatory step of consultation has showed, the police institution is often considered to be the most able and experienced in security matters. In this regard, although the mayors are legally entitled to decide some security priorities for the ASP, some of them prefer to follow the choices proposed by the police staff because they consider the latter to be a legitimate expert in such matters. Thereby, beyond the hierarchical links *in law*, there is sometimes an asymmetry of power *in deed* between the police institution and the administrative authorities. By appreciating the inequality of the influences in the decisional process, the apparent consensus concept helps explain the weak participation of some members in the council.

Finally, the relative withdrawal of some authorities in the collective decision-making may be related to the purpose of the ASP. Formally, the ASP is a police plan[11] implying the responsibility of each stakeholder.[12] Consequently, because the security policy directly impacts its work, the police institution is logically the most concerned in the collective decision and positions itself at the heart of the collective action right away. In this regard, although most ASP members attach importance to this level of dialogue (because it organises a meeting between them and is useful in terms of monitoring), many of the judicial and administrative actors concede that they deal with very little of the implementation of the security policy once the document is validated, except at the moment of yearly evaluations. In doing so, the authorities do not always respect one of the *sine qua non* conditions of the apparent consensus, considering that the ASP has to "bind the stakeholders in favour of its implementation" (Urfalino 2007, p. 49).

Beyond observations relating to the apparent consensus method, it is above all the 'collective' nature of the decision that we question here. If the ASP only involves the local police force in its enactment (Freeman and Sturdy 2014), the decision-making is not a "process through which a group decides together an intent to act for itself or for an entity of which it is a part" (Urfalino 2005, p. 107). However, these considerations may also highlight some situations where the police chiefs themselves do not consider the ASP a motivation for action, as they believe that the plan can never be actually implemented (notably because of a lack of human and financial resources). Consequently, the nature of the decision-making process can point to a lack of 'enrolment' (Callon 1986) of the actors in the ASCs, which could further lead to a lack of 'enactment' by the signatories.

---

[11]"Seeing that this Area Security Plan concerns the contribution of the local police to the integral security, under the direction of the local police authorities, this can be considered to be a 'Security Police Plan'" (CGL 2007, p. 3).

[12]"That is the reason for which the role of each actor into the police policy cycle must clearly appear in the local policy. This role, related to the responsibilities of each one in the realisation of the determined objectives, must be put in evidence." (CGL 2004, p. 3).

9.5 Conclusion

Reconsidering the decision-making process by focusing on what happens in the dialogue council as well as during the preparatory steps has clarified the various forms of collective decision-making realised around the ASPs. Although the two first steps of the decision-making process (bilateral consultation and decisional matrix) are entirely based on the vote system, the council can represent a space of negotiation and discussion over the results of the decisional matrix. In this instance, the concept of 'apparent consensus' sheds light on the various forms of dialogue practices. Its six realisation conditions are especially useful for testing the boundaries of this specific collective decision-making method, as well as for understanding the motivations leading the stakeholders.

Indeed, according to the participation of each actor in terms of communication of priorities and discussion inside the council, the legal requirement for inter-institutional dialogue is achieved differently. The differences among situations are quite significant: in some cases, the consensus is attributed to the broad nature of the priorities determined by the ASP while in others, the legitimacy of the decision results from the debates occurring in the ASC. These different configurations of dialogue should be understood with regard to the logics of action developed by the actors involved, notably in terms of unequal interests and resources in security matters. Notably, the lack of concrete implementation of the ASP can be a source of disinterest in the process.

The crucial element in this collective decision-making appears to be the role each actor has in this structure and so the impact this decision has on each partner's work. Therefore, what often determines the collective decision of the ASP is the "finalisation of the regulation," that is to say the "degree with which the participants integrate the results of their cooperation into their interactions and transform them into issues, on the one hand, and integrate them as goals of their action, on the other hand" (Friedberg 1992, p. 541). The Area Security Plan is obviously a police plan, but it is also a contribution from the local police force to the integrated security policy of the region; this is in the heart of the 'integral security' concept proposed by legal and official texts originating from the 1998 reform. In this way, this plan has to find connection in similar plans from the public prosecutor's departments and from the mayors' administrations.

References

Bayley, D. H. (1985). *Patterns of Policing. A Comparative International Analysis*. New Brunswick: N.J., Rutgers U.P.

Bourdoux, G. L., & De Valkeneer, C. (2001). *La réforme des services de police. Commentaire de la loi du 7 décembre 1998*. Bruxelles: Editions Larcier.

Callon, M. (1986). Eléments pour une sociologie de la traduction. La domestication des coquilles Saint-Jacques et des marins-pêcheurs dans la baie de Saint-Brieuc. *L'Année Sociologique*, *36*, 169–208.

Cartuyvels, Y., & Hebberecht, P. (2001). La politique fédérale belge de sécurité et de prévention de la criminalité (1990-1999). *Déviance et Société*, *25*, 403–426.
CGL. (2004). *Manuel du cycle de politique policière au niveau local*. Bruxelles.
CGL. (2007). *Manuel de rédaction du plan zonal de sécurité 2009–2012*. Bruxelles.
Crawford, A. (2001). Vers une reconfiguration des pouvoirs? Le niveau local et les perspectives de la gouvernance. *Déviance et Société*, *25*, 3–32.
Crozier, M., & Friedberg, E. (1977). *L'acteur et le système*. Paris: Le Seuil.
Duran, P., & Thoenig, J.-C. (1996). L'État et la gestion publique territoriale. *Revue Française de Science Politique*, *4*, 580–623.
Elster, J. (1994). Argumenter et négocier dans deux Assemblées constituantes. *Revue Française de Science Politique*, *44*, 187–256.
Freeman, R., & Sturdy, S. (2014). Introduction: knowledge in policy - embodied, inscribed, enacted. In R. Freeman & S. Sturdy, *Knowledge in policy. Embodied, inscribed, enacted* (pp. 1–17). Bristol: Policy Press.
Friedberg, E. (1992). Les quatre dimensions de l'action organisée. *Revue Française de Sociologie*, 531–557.
Friedberg, E. (1997). *Le Pouvoir et la Règle. Dynamiques de l'action organisée*. Paris: Seuil.
Gautron, V. (2013). La coproduction locale de la sécurité en France : un partenariat interinstitutionnel déficient. *Champ pénal/Penal Field, VII*.
Hassenteufel, P. (2008). *Sociologie politique : l'action publique*. Paris: Armand Colin.
Loubet Del Bayle, J.-L. (2006). *Police et politique. Une approche sociologique*. Paris: L'Harmattan.
Pasquino, P. (2007). Voter et délibérer. *Revue Européenne Des Sciences Sociales*, *45*, 35–45.
Roché, S. (2004). Vers la démonopolisation des fonctions régaliennes : contractualisation, territorialisation et européanisation de la sécurité intérieure. *Revue Française de Science Politique*, *54*, 43–70.
Simon, H. A. (1955). A Behavorial Model of Rational Choice. *Quarterly Journal of Economics*, *LXIX*, 99–118.
Smeets, S., & Tange, C. (2008). Conclusions. Polices locales et autorités administratives : je t'aime, mais… In J.-P. Henin & S. Smeets (Eds.), *Polices locales et autorités administratives. Je t'aime… moi non plus ?* (pp. 155–162). Bruxelles: Politeia.
Strauss, A., & Corbin, J. (2004). *Les fondements de la recherche qualitative. Techniques et procédures de développement de la théorie enracinée*. Fribourg: Academic Press Fribourg.
Thoenig, J.-C. (1994). La gestion systémique de la sécurité publique. *Revue Française de Sociologie*, *35*, 357–392.
Urfalino, P. (2005). La délibération n'est pas une conversation. Délibération, décision collective et négociation. *Négociations*, 99–114.
Urfalino, P. (2007). La décision collective par consensus apparent. Nature et propriétés. *Revue Européenne Des Sciences Sociales*, *45*, 47–70.

Chapter 10
Visible and Invisible Sentencing

Neil Hutton

10.1 Introduction

This chapter develops a conceptual approach which understands sentencing as a collective practice which is generated by a number of actors, not only judges. Sentencing is seen as a series of decision making practices which are made visible in publicly available accounts. This way of seeing sentencing has significant implications for understanding conventional accounts of discretion. This chapter argues that discretion is best understood as a mode of justification based on trust in the invisible work of actors. Sentencing guidelines add a more visible, rule-based form of accountability which does not replace discretion but works alongside it as a complementary mode of justification.

10.2 The Discourse of Individualised Sentencing

Most of the literature on sentencing is written by scholars working within a legal paradigm concerned to elucidate the formal legal status of sentencing and with formulating proposals to make judicial sentencing more "law-like" (Ashworth 1983; Roberts 2011; Frase 2013). The focus is understandably on the authoritative

N. Hutton (✉)
Law School, University of Strathclyde, Glasgow, UK
e-mail: n.hutton@strath.ac.uk

A. Hondeghem et al. (eds.), *Modernisation of the Criminal Justice Chain and the Judicial System*, Ius Gentium: Comparative Perspectives on Law and Justice 50, DOI 10.1007/978-3-319-25802-7_10

legal decision maker, the judge. Judges operate as independent individuals.[1] They are not bureaucrats whose task it is to implement government policy. They have no corporate voice nor corporate identity. It is not surprising, therefore, that sentencing is usually represented as a decision making process carried out by an individual actor, a judge. Judges are the authoritative performers of sentencing. They are legally responsible for the allocation of sanctions. They are also acutely aware of the need to justify their decisions. Sentencing decisions need to be presented as just decisions.[2] In their judgements, they frequently allude to their perceptions of the complexities of sentencing decision making, their obligation to consider all of the facts and circumstances of each individual case, and the unique nature of each case.

The judge is often portrayed as having the lonely job of deciding what type and severity of sanction is appropriate for a case. The judge has to reach a judgement about the seriousness of an offence, the harm it has caused and the appropriate penalty to achieve a range of aims, many of which are contradictory. The discourse of "individualised sentencing" argues that each case is unique and that a just sentence can only be reached by the consideration of the detailed facts and circumstances of each individual case. Judges craft a bespoke sentence which fits the distinctive combination of facts and circumstances which make up the case and which generates a sanction which achieves a "just" sentence. This at least is the view of sentencing presented by judges in the discourse of individualised sentencing.[3] On this judicial account of sentencing, sentencers are held to exercise very wide discretion. Individualised sentencing in non-guideline jurisdictions and even in some jurisdictions with guidelines (Hutton 2013b; Frase 2013) is not governed by many rules.

This discourse of individualised sentencing provides both an empirical description of how judges perform their sentencing work, i.e. their decision making, and a normative account of what is to count as a "just" sentencing decision. The practical and normative work used to generate sentencing decisions is variously described as "intuitive synthesis" (R v Williscroft), holistic craft work (Tata 2007) or "subjective rationalities" (Aas 2005). The public are invited to place their trust

[1]In political theory, judicial independence means that the judicial branch of government is independent from the executive and legislative branches. However, many public law scholars (Ewing 2013) now accept that this theoretical separation of law and politics is not sustainable in practice. Further, the fact that the judicial branch is independent does not absolve individual judges of the responsibility for ensuring that appropriate attention is devoted to ensuring a measure of consistency in sentencing. Sentencing policy, in UK jurisdictions at least is made, de facto, by judicial sentencing practices.

[2]To say that sentencing decisions are justified by claiming that they are just is more than a little awkward. This begs the question of what criteria need to be satisfied to deliver "justice".

[3]See this recent judgement of the High Court of Australia for a classic judicial articulation of individualised sentencing, PASQUALE BARBARO v THE QUEEN SAVERIO ZIRILLI v THE QUEEN [2014] HCA 2.

in the office of the judge. Judges are uniquely qualified to deploy these mysterious cognitive processes and thereby to deliver just sentencing decisions. On this account there is no gap between the ideal of justice and the practice of justice.

10.3 Sentencing as Collective Action

This discourse of individualised sentencing struggles to explain the extent of pattern and consistency found in sentencing, where there are few rules. How can the exercise of discretion by individual judges produce broad patterns of consistency in sentencing? Does it make sense to understand sentencing decisions as being the product of the agency of individual judges? Or alternatively, are these decisions somehow generated by neo-liberal ideology (Wacquant 2001), or by a Culture of Control (Garland 2001) and if they are, how do these structural explanations take effect at the level of courtroom sentencing decisions?

Sociology has long grappled with the duality of agency and structure. To what extent are actions determined by social structures and to what extent are they the product of individual agency? Structuration theories (Giddens 1986; Archer 2003) are sophisticated attempts to understand the interplay between these two levels. For Giddens, actions both reproduce existing structures and at the same time produce new structures. The aim is to avoid the stasis of over-deterministic structural theories while at the same time avoiding the loss of the idea of collective action which can be the result of an exaggerated focus on individual agency. Bourdieu's concept of habitus (Hutton 2006) is also an attempt to deal with this conundrum by delineating a zone between agency and structure within which the two interact with each other, but how they do so is not clear.

In this chapter, following the work of Latour (2005) sentencing is understood as collective action, as the product of the actions of human and non-human actors (Hutton 2013a). Sentencing is not exclusively a judicial function. The sentencing process starts at earlier stages of the criminal process (McConville et al. 1991; Stenning 2008) and requires the work of other criminal justice practitioners and the work of laws, professional rules, guidelines or memoranda, professional standards, formal templates and other documents designed to shape the practices of criminal justice professionals (see Bastard and Dubois 2015 this volume). Conventionally, human actors would be conceived as using, referring to, implementing or applying these documents. However, these documents make a difference in the world independently of the actions of human agents. Often, in the language of structural sociology, these non-human agents are seen as either providing resources for human actors or as constraints to the freedom of actors to do otherwise. However this is to privilege human agency as being the originator of action. It pre-supposes that if the "constraints" were not there, human actors would act differently. It implies that without these "things", social life would be otherwise. This may be true, but what "otherwise" would it be? Not the random maverick preferences of individuals. Individual agency does not pre-exist the world in which individual agents operate. The social world is generated by the interactions of people and things, by what Pickering has called "the dance of agencies" (Pickering 1995 in Cooren et al. 2006). This is another metaphor for the relationship between structure and agency, but this time the duality is scrapped. The search for the source of agency is halted. Understanding the production of social life is achieved by the empirical study of the exercise of agency by both human and non-human actors.

The work of sentencing may be described as a process of "qualification", that is a process of deciding whether a report of an event-in-the-world belongs to a legitimate category: whether the reported "unique" event qualifies as an example of some general class. Qualification is a means of moving from the particular to the general and the criminal justice process is a means of moving from a unique-event-in-the-world to a case which can proceed in court and from there to a sentence to be administered.

"Operations of qualification also constitute the basic cognitive operations of social interaction, social coordination requires a continuous effort of comparison, agreement on common terms and identification." (Boltanski and Thevenot 2006, p. 1)

What does sentencing look like from this vantage point? What can we see of the dance of agencies? The answer is that we can see the documents which are generated in the process of constructing a case. This begins with police officers and criminal law and ends with the release of the offender from obligations imposed by penal sanctions. Sentencing is thus continuous with the criminal justice process itself. The sentencing judge is presented with a case file containing specific pieces of information, prepared by other criminal justice actors to fulfil their professional and legal obligations (Hawkins 2003). So although a sanction is allocated to a unique individual citizen, sentencing is based on the information contained in the case file. Police officers generate a file containing information about the alleged offence, offender, witnesses and other evidence. This file is sent to the prosecutor's office where a decision is made about prosecution and further material added to the file. By the time it reaches the court, the case is a file of documents[4] which presents discrete pieces of information about the offence and the offender. In order for the case to proceed through the criminal justice process, certain legal requirements have to be met. A criminal offence has to be identified, evidence that the offence has occurred and that the offender committed the act has to be assembled etc. The compilation of a "case" can be seen as the production of a series of documents. Each document enables movement to the next stage of the process. Criminal justice professionals process information into existing classifications which provide them with an account which serves their professional purposes, for example, to demonstrate that the criteria for establishing a criminal offence have been satisfied, to ensure that the rules of evidence and procedure have been correctly complied with, to demonstrate that social work practice

[4]Latour notes the importance of documents or forms for the production of social life, "a form is simply something which allows something else to be transported from one site to another. Form then becomes one of the most important types of translations." Latour (2005) 223.

guidelines have been followed. These are all forms of public justification for their decision making. The unique event in the world becomes a series of defensible accounts which form a more or less familiar criminal case. The work of professionals can be seen as a series of visible translations from the particular unique event-in-the-world to a criminal case, which shares much in common with other cases. So the case documentation can be seen as a series of accounts which provide a public justification for decisions taken which can be checked and verified. The case is the outcome of a series of decisions and it is the only visible account we have of the decision making processes. As Hawkins notes, "past decisions are used as raw material for present decisions" (Hawkins 2003, p. 198).

The construction of the case carries with it an unavoidable sentencing function. By the time the case reaches court, the sentencing options are significantly narrowed because the unique event-in-the-world has now been translated through a series of decision making processes into a more or less typical sort of case. The research reported in McNeill et al. (2009) shows how social enquiry reports are written for the courts by social workers.[5] The report writers are required to comply with national standards for the production of reports which prescribe a format and style. Within these strictures there is scope for social workers to both second guess judicial decision makers and try to influence the judicial decision by their use of language. However, there was evidence that social workers developed a sense of the appropriate sentence for the case, a decision usually made on the basis of a routine assessment of the seriousness of the case and the record of the offender. There was scope in some cases to seek to nudge the court towards what might seem like an unlikely non-custodial sentence where the social workers felt there was scope to work with an offender with a long criminal record but also occasions where the social worker felt that there was simply no scope to work with an offender who was almost certain to receive a custodial sentence. The account provided in the SER performs a significant part of the work of sentencing. It is a further translation of the prosecution case into an account which is clearly focussed on a relatively narrow range of potential sentencing outcomes.

What the discourse of individualised sentencing describes as "unique" events in the world comprised of a singular set of facts and circumstances are translated into more or less routine criminal offences defined by particular pieces of evidence. Judges have no unmediated access to "what really happened". All they have is the information which has been presented to them in the documentation (and to what

[5]Social Enquiry Reports are now known as Criminal Justice Social Work Reports following the Criminal Justice and Licensing (Scotland) Act 2010. There is a revised template for social workers to complete. These changes accompany the introduction of a single community sanction, the Community Payback Order, to replace the previous range of community options. The essential functions of the report, to provide information for the court and advice on the appropriate requirements of the order remain much the same. Evaluation of these reforms is currently in progress.

was said in court[6]). An offender will usually appear in court and may in some circumstances give evidence or make a personal statement but more commonly most of the information about the offender will come from reports contained in the case file (van Oorschot 2014). These professional practices generate an element of consistency in sentencing. Most regular court practitioners will have a sense of "the going rate" for typical offences although this is always tacit and impossible to measure (as in non-guideline jurisdictions at least, there is no benchmark against which to distinguish warranted from unwarranted disparity).

If this sociological account of sentencing decision making is correct, it presents a challenge to the discourse of individualised sentencing and to conventional understandings of judicial discretion.

10.4 Discretion and Practice

Individualised sentencing is held to involve the exercise of wide discretion by judges. But what does discretion mean? It is often taken to refer to the practice of sentencing decision making, that is, to the cognitive processes exercised by judges. However, if sentencing decision making is not solely performed by judicial actors, but is more accurately conceived as a form of collective action described above, then discretion is not only exercised by judges but by all of the other actors involved in the decision making processes. In practice, the extent of discretion available to judges is much more constrained than the discourse of individualised sentencing would suggest. This chapter argues that discretion should be understood as a mode of accountability, that is, as a way of justifying sentencing decisions, rather than a way of describing the practice of decision making (Lipsky 1980).

Gelsthrope and Padfield quote the definition of discretion from the Oxford English Dictionary: "the liberty or power of deciding according to one's own judgement or discernment" (Gelsthorpe and Padfield 2003, p. 3).

This definition refers to the "liberty or power" available to a decision maker. In other words, this is a political and legal capacity: the capacity and/or authority to make a decision without providing an account based on demonstrating adherence to rules. Discretion then might be thought of as the absence of a requirement to refer to rules in the provision of an account of a decision making process. In other words, discretion is not the exercise of judgment itself, but the capacity or power to do so. Discretion operates in the space famously described as the "hole in the doughnut" by Ronald Dworkin. Decisions made within the doughy substance of the doughnut need to be justified by reference to rules. Decisions made in the space in the middle which is not governed by rules, are justified by reference to

[6]Where a trial has taken place, there will be much more oral communication available to the judge which will provide a richer narrative about the offence and the offender. However, this case file will continue to structure the event and the offender into a more or less typical example of a criminal case.

the exercise of professional discretion. In this space, accountability for the exercise of judgment rests on trust in the office of the decision maker, which in sentencing is the judge.

However, Gelsthorpe and Padfield identify another way of conceptualising discretion. They argue that the implementation of rules necessarily involves the interpretation of both facts and rules. This process of interpretation involves the exercise of discretion. So discretion and rules are not distinctive modes of accountability as Dworkin argued, but rather seen by Gelsthorpe and Padfield as decision making practices which are much harder to distinguish one from the other.

Hawkins also uses the term discretion to describe the practices performed by legal actors to "translate" words into actions. "To understand better how law works, how the words of law are *translated* into action, it is essential to know how legal discretion is exercised." (Hawkins 1992, p. 44 my emphasis).

There is a difference between conceiving of discretion as a legal capacity and discretion as an interpretive practice. These are not the same things. When describing discretion as an interpretive practice, Gelsthorpe and Padfield refer to discretion as the difference between "the formal position and the actual practice". In other words, discretion helps to understand the way in which law "in the books" is translated into actions in the world, to use Hawkins' terminology.

How can we research these practices? How can we find out how laws are implemented or how rules are put into practice? We can look at the outcomes of practices: the cases which have been compiled, the decisions which have been made, the reports which have been written, the judgements which have been delivered, etc. We can also interrogate the decision makers, report writers and case compilers and ask them about their perceptions of their actions. The interrogations focus on the meanings expressed by the actors. We try to see the social world which they are creating through their eyes. We are interested in how the actors make sense of both the rules and the facts and how they perceive themselves applying rules to facts to reach decisions.

"…where lawyers think in terms of the role of legal rules in achieving outcomes, social scientists tend to think rather in terms of decision goals or decision processes." (Hawkins 1992, p. 14.)

From a social science perspective, rules do not by themselves generate particular practices. Hawkins quotes Lempert, "rules are not inexorably influential" (Hawkins 1992, p. 18). That is, actors are not always oriented to rules when they act. For example, police officers may perceive a need to resolve a problem of disorder. They do not see themselves as implementing the law so much as solving a problem in a legitimate fashion. They need to be able to provide an account of their actions that is lawful. Rules are a means of generating an account which justifies the choice of a decision maker.

To return to the idea of sentencing as collective action, the documents produced by actors at each stage of the process can be seen as accounts which justify their decisions by reference to the relevant rules/templates/memoranda/codes of practice etc. by which their decisions are held accountable. All of these actors exercise discretion in both of the senses identified by Gelsthorpe and Padfield. They interpret rules and fact situations and make judgements about whether or not rules apply to the facts and if so how they should be applied. They also generate documents which provide legitimate justifications for their decisions. These are different but neither are accurate accounts of their decision making practices. They are different forms of justificatory accounts.

10.5 Visible and Invisible Work: The Generation of Accounts

"It is important to recognise the existence of interaction between the different parts of the system, that the 'output' of one stage provides the 'input' for another……" (Bottomley 1973 in Gelsthorpe and Padfield 2003, p. 11)

"No work is inherently visible or invisible. We always "see" work through a selection of indicators…" (Starr and Strauss 1999, p. 9)

Starr and Strauss make the apparently obvious observation that social scientists have no un-mediated access to the cognitive processes of actors. The work performed by actors is only visible through the traces that they leave behind. So the decisions made by police officers about arrest and charge are visible in the reports which they file, the decisions of prosecutors are made visible in the case files they prepare for court, the decisions of judges are made visible in the sentences which they pass (see also Tata 2007).

This is true of all social action. Action is not immediately visible, it is only made visible through its products. We see decisions, but not decision making. We see reports, but not the processes which were used to produce these reports. Our access to these invisible processes is only gained through the accounts provided either by observers or by the actors themselves. Observers' accounts are external perceptions, actors' accounts are post hoc narratives which may be their best good faith efforts in explaining their actions or may be justifications/idealisations/rationalisations. However, they should not be taken as objectively accurate descriptions of cognitive processes because actors do not have access to the methods by which their decisions are reached, only to stories of these processes. This does not mean that the accounts are not useful, just that they are not necessarily accurate. So invisible work is necessarily invisible. There are good reasons for its continued invisibility. There are limits to our capacity for knowledge of the world. Requiring the production of accounts cannot make all invisible work visible. It makes new public accounts visible, but leaves invisible work un-accounted for.

We cannot "know" how actors make decisions because we do not have direct access to their cognitive processes only to their accounts of their actions. As described above, sentencing decisions are generated by a chain of what Latour (2005) calls translations. Accounts are generated to move from one stage in the chain to another. These accounts are produced to satisfy a range of demands on professional decision makers. Legality is one of these demands but it is not so much the demand to produce any particular legal outcome as the need to ensure that an account is lawful. If work is invisible, then all we can do is trust the professional competence of the worker. If, however, it becomes visible, these visible traces are available as an account of the work and our trust can be founded on this account.

In the production of a "case" for the court, some elements of the work of criminal justice practitioners have been made visible, other elements remain invisible. Some information has been included and some excluded. The judge has no access to the invisible work of practitioners nor to information that has been excluded. The judge makes a decision on the basis of the material presented to the court. So criminal justice practitioners participate in sentencing through their work in constructing a criminal case file. Routine cases will frequently generate a routine decision, more or less predictable to regular court actors. While there is always, in formal legal terms, scope for the judicial decision maker to diverge from the going rate, this is likely to happen relatively infrequently. Where a report has been prepared for the court recommending a community sanction, much of the sentencing work has already been performed by the report writer. Although the court is of course not legally obliged to follow the recommendation of the report, recommendations will be followed in a substantial majority of cases.[7] In other words, sentencing decisions are the product of the work of a number of criminal justice actors performing their routine bureaucratic tasks within the cultural frame of the local courtroom.

10.6 Invisible Work and Accountability

Much of the work which goes into sentencing is invisible. For example, in Scotland, a Criminal Justice Social Work Report (CJSWR) is prepared through the completion of a standardised template and must contain prescribed items of information. However it also conceals invisible professional judgements made by the report writer, for example, about the "suitability" of the offender for a particular community sanction (McNeill et al. 2009). The sentencing decision of the judge is invisible in the sense that the propriety or justice of the sentence is asserted on the basis of a narration of relevant facts and circumstances. None of the "workings out", so to speak, are made visible.

[7]Hawkins (2003) gives an interesting example from the work of Padfield et al. (2003) of how routine bureaucratic decisions of one agency (the Prison Service) have an impact on the future decisions of another agency (the Parole Board). Decisions made by the Prison Service which allocated prisoners to open conditions appeared to have an influence on Parole Board decisions. The Parole Board released no prisoner who was not in open conditions, and only one prisoner who was in open conditions was not released by the Parole Board.

It is tempting to call this invisible work, holistic or craftwork (Tata 2007). The difficulty with this is that it tends to exaggerate the influence of individual cognitive work on sentencing outcomes. It is as if the individual judge somehow exists outside of the social context of sentencing. That the judge, as it were, begins the sentencing decision making process afresh, assessing information as if this information has not already been processed by other actors. Sentencing is seen as purely a matter of individual cognitive work.

Another form of explanation attributes routine sentencing practices to the judicial habitus (Hutton 2006). Habitus is a metaphor which allows the analyst to avoid awarding causal priority to either structure or action and thereby avoids the stasis of either structural or individual determination. However, a more fundamental problem with the metaphor is that it retains the split between structure and agency. The approach proposed here develops a sociological analysis of sentencing. That is not to say that sentencing decision making does not involve cognitive processes, nor to deny that individual judicial characteristics or values may have an impact on judicial sentencing practices. A sociological approach argues that sentencing is not reducible to matters of personality or cognition. It argues that sentencing is collective action, that is, the shared work of actors, human and non-human, engaged in criminal justice processes. The visible evidence of this work are the files produced by criminal justice practitioners which provide public justifications for their decision making. Most of the time, these processes generate routine decisions and there is modest scope in practice for judges to stray from the going rate. Of course, the "going rate" is neither fixed nor objective and in any given court culture it will accommodate a range or possible variations. There will also be cases which do not fit comfortably into routine categories. However, these are questions for empirical investigation and in the absence of agreed sentencing guidelines, it is very difficult to establish a benchmark against which variation in sentencing can be measured.

Phenomenological or interpretive accounts of discretion are important (Tombs and Jagger 2006; Jamieson 2013). They provide us with accounts of how judicial actors understand and explain their sentencing practice. These accounts are generated to justify particular decision choices. Hawkins calls these naturalistic accounts. They challenge the goal-directed rational choice approach to understanding decision making. A naturalistic approach focuses on the moral or symbolic meanings held by actors, and on how information is framed and interpreted. However these accounts are not necessarily accurate accounts of the cognitive processes through which sentencing outcomes are generated. They tend to exaggerate the role of the individual judge and conceal the collective practices of sentencing.

Sentences may describe their individual cognitive processes as "holistic", but this should be understood as their account of their thinking and not as an objectively accurate description of cognitive processes. Judges interpret more or less familiar accounts presented in court papers and translate these into the next stage of the criminal process which is a sentencing decision. Hawkins' naturalistic approach de-centres the individual from an understanding of decision making but there remains a focus on trying to describe the production of actions rather than the production of accounts.

10.7 Individual Differences in Judicial Sentencing

This does not mean that there is no scope for individual differences between judges (tough or lenient, retributive or rehabilitative etc.), that sometimes similar cases are treated differently and different cases treated similarly, that for certain classes of case, for example those around the custody threshold, there is more scope for variation and unpredictability, but it means that there is considerably less scope than the conventional discourse of individualised sentencing would suggest.

Attempts to generate more predictable sentencing decisions by the proliferation and narrower specification of rules will produce more elaborate justificatory accounts which demonstrate that the processes defined by the rules have been observed and performed. The rules may or may not be successful in generating particular actions by decision makers, but all we will know is that legitimate accounts have been produced to justify the outcomes. The outcomes may or may not be closer to those desired by the rule makers (if it is possible to determine their desired goals). This, however, is an empirical question.

The argument here is that rules produce not actions but justificatory accounts for actions. So rules produce a process or formal version of justice rather than a substantive account. Decisions in the criminal justice system proceed through the construction of accounts. These accounts are performed by actors. These actors need to ensure that their accounts can be defended against potential criticism by some supervising agency whether this be their line manager, their colleagues, or other agents in the system with whom they have to work, i.e. those who use their accounts to perform their own work in the criminal process. They will be aware to at least some extent that they need to be able to demonstrate that their decisions are compliant with the guidance which regulates their work and ultimately with law. They may or may not see themselves as implementing law, more likely they see themselves as generating accounts which are not unlawful. The extent to which their decision making is oriented towards implementing a legal rule is an empirical question but we should not assume that actors working in a legal context necessarily orient their actions towards implementing the letter of the law, even where from an external perspective it seems to observers that implementing law is the essence of their job. So police officers engage with an event which may require their intervention to restore or maintain public order/perceptions of safety. Their focus is on solving a problem and generating an account of their conduct which provides a legitimate justification for their actions.

In a non-guideline regime, using the method of individualised sentencing, the judicial decision simply expresses the propriety of the sentence for the case at hand and makes no reference as to how the case may be similar or indeed different from other cases. As with sentencing under a guidelines approach, cognitive actions and normative judgements are not made visible. Much of the impetus behind the sentencing reform movement which began in the United States in the 1970s (Frankel 1972) was a desire to make sentencing decisions more visible and therefore more accountable. Sentencing guidelines are a means of injecting accountability by establishing a relatively simple form of calculability which enables an account of consistency to be articulated. Visibility of sentencing work can only be generated through the production of these sorts of accounts. Criminal justice actors engaged in the process of generating a case could be required to produce different accounts of their decision making. These accounts will produce a different type of visibility, but still leave invisible that work for which no methods have been designed to generate visibility. In other words some sentencing work will always be invisible because it can only be made visible through the generation of accounts and accounts are always partial. This partiality is a problem for law which desires certainty. Individualised sentencing is one way of delivering certainty, but it is certainty based on a claim for authority in the office of judge who asserts the propriety of the sentence. Guidelines shift some of this authority to the abstract system of guidelines, so certainty comes from visible work which allocates a case to a classification or not and invisible work which places the case at a particular position on the range within the guideline (or departs from the guideline with reasons). Individualised sentencing and Sentencing Guidelines produce two different sorts of justificatory accounts for sentencing. Individualised sentencing claims justification based on trust in the invisible work performed by the office of judge. Sentencing Guidelines share this element of trust, but add to it, a claim for justification based on a public account of an acceptable range of variation within which judges are entrusted to exercise judgement.

10.8 Conclusion: Rules, Discretion and the Regulation of Sentencing Practice

Martha Feldman asks, "How can decisions be responsive to the relevant features of a context without being ad hoc, unsystematic or incomprehensible?" (in Hawkins 1992, p. 163)

Sentencing is a process which is constructed out of a series of accounts of decision making by criminal justice practitioners. Each of these accounts is a justification for the presentation of a particular framing of an event in the world to meet professional and legal requirements of the construction of a criminal case. Each account addresses the problem posed by Feldman. Each account produces a visible record of work that was used to generate the account. Much invisible work is involved in the decision making processes of criminal justice actors. This is the exercise of discretion. Formal accounts make work visible, the work of discretion is invisible. Law does not regulate practice it regulates accounts of practice. We can only have access to accounts of practice and to the outcomes of practice, we cannot have access to the internal cognitive processes of individual decision makers.

Regimes of calculation cannot make everything visible. Beyond visibility lies the invisible. In sentencing, the decision is where accountability ends and trust begins. How much of an account of sentencing choice is it appropriate to make visible and how much should remain a matter of invisible judgement? The degree of desired visibility is a matter of political choice and contest.

References

Aas, K. F. (2005) Sentencing in the Age of Information. London. Glasshouse Press.

Archer, M. (2003) Structure, Agency and the Internal Conversation, Cambridge University Press, Cambridge.

Ashworth, A, (1983) Sentencing and Penal Policy (George Weidenfeld & Nicolson Ltd).

Bastard, J. and Dubois, C. (2015) Making sense of decisions? Collective action in the early release process in Hondeghem, A., Rousseaux, X. and Schoenaers F. (eds) Modernisation of the criminal justice chain and the judicial system: New insights on trust, cooperation and human capital. Springer.

Boltanski, L and Thevenot, L., (2006) On Justification: Economies of Worth. Princeton University Press Princeton and Oxford.

Bottomley, K. (1973) Decisions in the Penal Process, Robertson.

Cooren, F., Thompson, F., Canestraro, D. and Bodor, T. (2006) "From agency to structure: Analysis of an episode in a facilitation process." *Human Relations* 59(4) : 533–565.

Ewing, K.D. The Resilience of the Political Constitution, 14 German Law Journal (2013), available at https://www.germanlawjournal.com/index.php?pageID=11&artID=1596 accessed 15.05.15.

Feldman, M. (1992) Social Limits to Discretion: An Organisational Perspective. in Hawkins, K. (ed) The Uses of Discretion, Oxford, Clarendon Press.

Frankel, M. (1972) Criminal Sentences: Law without Order. New York. Hill and Wang.

Frase, R., (2013) Just Sentencing. Oxford. Oxford University Pres.

Garland, D. (2001) The Culture of Control. Oxford. Oxford University Press.

Gelsthorpe, L. and Padfield, N. (eds) (2003), Exercising Discretion: decision-making in the criminal justice system and beyond, Willan Publishing, pp.186–219.

Giddens, A. (1986) The Constitution of Society. University of California Press.

Hawkins, K. (1992) The Uses of Discretion. Oxford. Clarendon Press.

Hawkins, K. (2003) 'Order, rationality and silence: some reflections on criminal justice decision-making' in Gelsthorpe, L. and Padfield, N. (eds) (2003), Exercising Discretion: decision-making in the criminal justice system and beyond, Willan Publishing, pp.186–219.

Hutton, N (2006), Sentencing as a Social Practice in Armstrong, S. and McAra,L. eds. "Perspectives on Punishment: The Contours of Control". Oxford: Oxford University Press.

Hutton, N. (2013a) From Intuition to Database: Translating Justice .*Theoretical Criminology* 17:3. pp109–128, doi:10.1177/1362480612465767.

Hutton, N. (2013b) The Definitive Guideline on Assault Offences issued by the Sentencing Council for England and Wales: The Performance of Justice" in Ashworth, A and Roberts J.V. Sentencing Guidelines, Oxford University Press Oxford.

Jamieson, F. (2013) Narratives of Crime and Punishment. A study of Scottish Judicial Culture. Unpublished PhD thesis University of Edinburgh.

Latour, B (2005) Reassembling the Social, Oxford, Oxford University Press.

Lipsky, M. (1980) Street-level Bureaucracy: Dilemmas of the Individual in Public Services. New York, NY: Russell Sage Foundation.

McConville, M., Sanders, A. and Leng, R. (1991) The Case for the Prosecution: Police Suspects and the Construction of Criminality. London. Routledge.

McNeill, F, Burns, N, Halliday, S, Hutton, N, and Tata, C. (2009) Risk, Responsibility and Reconfiguration: Penal Adaptation and Mis-adaptation. *Punishment and Society* 11(4) pp419–442. Sage, London.

Padfield, N., Leibling, A., and Arnold, H. (2003) "Discretion and the release of life sentence prisoners." in Gelsthorpe, L. and Padfield, N. (eds) (2003), Exercising Discretion: decision-making in the criminal justice system and beyond, Willan Publishing, pp.186–219.

Pickering, A. (1995) The Mangle of Practice" University of Chicago Press, Chicago.

Roberts, J.V. (2011) (ed), Mitigation and Aggravation at Sentencing . Cambridge. Cambridge University Press.

Star, S.L. and Strauss, A. (1999) Layers of Silence, Arenas of Voice: The Ecology of Visible and Invisible Work, Computer Supported Cooperative Work **8** 9–30.

Stenning, P. (2008) The Modern Prosecution Process in New Zealand. Wellington. Victoria University Press.

Tata (2007) Sentencing as Craftwork and the Binary Epistemologies of the Discretionary Decision Process, *Social Legal Studies* vol. 16 no. 3 425-447

Tombs, J. and Jagger, E. (2006) "Denying Responsibility: Sentencers' Accounts of their Decisions to Imprison", *British Journal of Criminology* 46 (5): 803–821.

van Oorschot, I (2014) Seeing the Case Clearly: File-Work, Material Mediation, and Visualizing Practices in a Dutch Criminal Court, Symbolic Interaction Volume 37, Issue 4, Pages 439–623.

Wacquant, L. (2001) 'Deadly Symbiosis: When Ghetto and Prison Meet and Mesh', in *Punishment and Society*, 3: 95–133

Cases

PASQUALE BARBARO v THE QUEEN SAVERIO ZIRILLI v THE QUEEN [2014] HCA 2

R v Williscroft **[1975] VR 292**

Chapter 11
Making Sense or/of Decisions? Collective Action in Early Release Process

Joséphine Bastard and Christophe Dubois

11.1 Introduction

In Belgium, since the 1st of February 2007, Sentence Implementation Courts (SIC) have been responsible for granting early release to prisoners serving a sentence of more than three years. Far from the traditional idea of a ritualised justice (Garapon 2001), this court "does not judge" but makes decisions. These decisions are not produced through the syllogistic reasoning of some judges mechanically applying general rules to specific cases (Beccaria 2006). They rather depend on complex organising processes, enacted by various professional groups: SIC magistrates, prison governors, prison clerks, Prison Psychosocial Team (PST), and Prison Central Administration (Halliday et al. 2009). Those professionals are producing and making sense of diverse documents (Freeman 2006).

This chapter looks at the process through which judicial decisions are made by the SIC. It aims at accounting for the cooperation between the stakeholders. The formal coordination between the professional groups will be depicted, as well as their concrete practices and interactions. In doing so, we will emphasise the importance of documents as "boundary objects" (Star and Griesemer 1989) supporting professionals' cooperation. We will also analyse how "sensemaking" (Weick et al. 2005) underlies collective action across time and space along the sentence enforcement process.

J. Bastard (✉) · C. Dubois
Centre de Recherche et d'Interventions Sociologiques (CRIS),
University of Liège, Liège, Belgium
e-mail: josephine.bastard@ulg.ac.be

C. Dubois
e-mail: c.dubois@ulg.ac.be

A. Hondeghem et al. (eds.), *Modernisation of the Criminal Justice Chain and the Judicial System*, Ius Gentium: Comparative Perspectives on Law and Justice 50, DOI 10.1007/978-3-319-25802-7_11

11.1.1 Theoretical Framework

Our main assumption is that the court's decisions are coproduced by professional groups involved in the early release process, rather than automatically produced by the mechanical application of the 2006 Act.[1] Cooperation and "sensemaking" will be our main analytical concepts. Sociological definitions of cooperation usually highlight the ideas of collective action, interdependent relationships, and reciprocal adjustments. Following Friedberg (1997, p. 3), we will study the "processes of organisation that shape, stabilise, and coordinate the behaviour and strategic interactions of a certain number of actors whose interdependence makes cooperation indispensable, but who all preserve some degree of autonomy and continue, for many reasons, to pursue divergent interests".

Cooperation along the sentence execution chain is made necessary by the rules and the procedure, requiring interdependent relationships between various groups of actors. In order to account for the process through which these rules are concretely enacted, we will firstly focus on the documents that are produced, processed, (re)interpreted, and then transmitted. Whatever their nature (evidence, written recommendation, or record), these documents are useful tools for describing collective action processes. Secondly, the concept of "sensemaking" will help us in analysing the incremental decision-making process underpinning the court's work. This concept reveals how (groups of) actors construct reality through communication processes and out of ambiguity, "when a flow of organisational circumstances is turned into words and salient categories" (Weick et al. 2005, p. 409).

11.1.2 Methodology

The aim of the present study is to account for formal and substantial cooperation between groups of professionals involved in the decision-making of the SIC, focussing on prisons and courts. The in-depth field study took place in two French-speaking SIC and in two prisons. In total, 64 semi-structured interviews were conducted, in the courts (n = 23), at the central administration (n = 20), and in prison (n = 21). Extensive notes were taken while observing judges, prison governors and clerks at work (n = 6), and during hearings (n = 8). Finally, we also analysed case files before the hearing (n = 8). Based on an inductive approach, the qualitative data collected were progressively used to refine and update the assumptions and findings, allowing us to highlight the importance of cooperation in the decision-making process of the court.

[1]May 17 2006, "External legal position of persons convicted to deprivation of freedom and the rights accorded to the victim in the framework of the modalities of the execution of sentence", *Moniteur Belge* 15.06.2006, p. 30455.

11.2 The Legal Coordination by the 2006 Act

In Belgium, following the *Dutroux Affair* in 1996 (Walgrave and Varone 2008), the conditions of early release are enacted in the External Legal Position Act of 2006. As a consequence, SIC (Sentence Implementation Courts) have replaced the former "Parole Commissions"[2] and are responsible for granting conditional release (Bauwens et al. 2012), electronic monitoring (Beyens and Roosen 2013), semi-detention, and provisional release in view of expulsion or extradition (De Ridder et al. 2012) to prisoners serving a sentence of more than three years. However, since the implementation of the 2006 Act is not yet fully achieved the Minister of Justice, via the DMD (Detention Management Department at the Prison Central Administration, or "Direction Gestion de la Détention"—DGD), remains responsible for granting *provisional release* to prisoners serving a sentence of up to three years.

The judicialisation of early release is not complete. It is still a hybrid system where judicial and administrative decisions coexist. Indeed, the 2006 Act states that the Minister of Justice, via the DMD, is responsible for granting short prison leave (such as "*permission de sortie*", of up to sixteen hours maximum, and "*congé pénitentiaire*", up to 36 h maximum) (articles 4–9[3]). Short prison leave is a turning point for the prisoner: it is an opportunity to reconnect with society and his/her family, but also to look for a job, a flat, some professional training and employment that can be part of his/her "reintegration plan". In this paper, we will see that DMD and SIC decisions are interdependent, with short prison leaves providing a gradual transition to early release.

Each chamber of the SIC is composed of a professional judge (the President) and two non-professional assessors, one specialised in prison matters, and the other in social reintegration. Belgian prisoners become eligible for early release between one and two thirds (for legal recidivists) of their sentence (articles 21–26). When eligible, the prisoner submits an application form to the prison clerk's office. The prison governor must provide a (positive or negative) written recommendation within the next two months. Before writing his/her recommendation, he meets with the prisoner during a conference.[4] He can also mandate the PST[5] to write a psychosocial report (Snacken 2007, p. 199), and a justice assistant[6] for

[2]The laws of 5th and 18th March 1998 established these commissions.

[3]The article of the law in this section refers to the Law of May 17 2006, "External legal position of persons convicted to deprivation of freedom and the rights accorded to the victim in the framework of the modalities of the execution of sentence", *Moniteur Belge* 15.06.2006, p. 30455.

[4]The conference consists of the legally required meeting between the prisoner applying for early release and the prison governor.

[5]The Psychosocial Teams are part of the Prison Service. They are responsible for diagnosis and "pretherapeutic actions, including motivating prisoners to accept treatment upon early release" (Snacken 2007, p. 170).

[6]The Houses of Justice were introduced in 1998 in every Belgian judicial district, essentially to coordinate probation, early and conditional release supervision, victim support, and mediation. The justice assistants fulfil these tasks.

social enquiries (Beyens and Scheirs 2010). The prison governor gathers these documents and sends them to the public prosecutor of the SIC, who also writes a recommendation (articles 49–51).

The three magistrates of the SIC examine the case file before the hearing. Finally, the hearing brings together the court, the prisoner and his/her lawyer, the prison governor, the public prosecutor, and, ultimately, the victim and the justice assistant (articles 52–53). According to the law, the court can grant an early release insofar as the following counter-indications are not present in the case (article 47): (1) the lack of the prisoner's reintegration plan; (2) the risk of committing new serious offences; (3) the risk of causing further distress or offence to his/her victim(s); and (4) his/her efforts to pay debts to the civil parties. One more counter-indication was added in 2013[7]: the effort of the prisoner to compensate the civil parties, which is redundant when the fourth counter-indication is considered. Those counter-indications can nevertheless be balanced by the imposition of conditions, such as the obligation of having daily employment. No appeal may be issued on the substance of a judgement, but well on the legal aspects of the judgement. The Court of *Cassation* is then competent to decide (articles 96–97).

In their daily practice, the Presidents of the SIC organise their jurisdiction independently from each other (Anleu and Mack 2008). The division of labour between the president and the assessors is different from one chamber to another. The application of Article 59 of the 2006 Act illustrates how local variations (localisms) and autonomy prevail. This article indicates that in exceptional circumstances, the SIC may grant short prison leave within a two-month period of time, if and only if this leave constitutes a useful means to granting the early release requested. "Article 59" is a major resource for SIC, since periods of short prison leave are often blocked by the DMD.[8] However, every SIC chamber manages and interprets the many "Article 59" requests addressed to them in their own way.

Various bodies are involved in the early release process: SIC, prison clerks and governors, psychosocial teams (PST), DMD, prisoners, lawyers, and the Houses of Justice. If localism prevails at the SIC level, the same statement can be made at the prison level. An attempt at standardising some procedures has been set by the Central Administration. As an example, the Ministerial Circular n°1794 of 7 February 2007 provides some detail about the meaning of counter-indications, the staff conference composition, and it gives forms and a basis for the prison internal procedure. However, prison practices are locally adapted while still meeting the law's requirements. Prison governors can decide which staff will carry out some specific procedures, how information will be passed on to the prisoner, how a form is completed, etc. The way procedures are translated into concrete practice depends on local contingencies (Dubois and Vrancken 2014).

[7]Law December 15, 2013 "diverse disposition in order to improve the victim' status in the framework of implementation of sentences", *Moniteur Belge* 19.12.2013, p. 99993.

[8]Quantitative study of DMD decision-making showed that the decisions made were positive for 55.8 % of requests that had received a positive recommendation from the prison governor (Mine and Robert 2014, p. 285).

Beyond legal prescription, the law sets out the role of the stakeholders in the early release procedure, without specifying every role in detail. Nor does it define the absolute meaning of the counter-indications: what should be understood by "the risk of new serious offences"? What evidence can be provided for this? And how is the court's decision passed on to the prisoner and the various actors preparing his/her file? There lies the issue of cooperation within the sentence execution process.

11.3 Formal and Substantial Dimensions of a Collective Action Process

The case files examined by the SIC are prepared inside prison. Prison clerks, prison governors, and the PST receive, process and exchange information through meetings and documents. We will now look closer at these groups' interdependency and at their respective key resources and functions.

11.3.1 The Prison Clerks, Bandmasters of the Legal Procedure

The prison clerks' office, composed of one to four clerks in charge of the SIC matter, is responsible for managing the procedure. This consists primarily of calculating the prisoner's eligibility dates[9] and initiating the early release procedures, but also of assembling the case file. The case file is composed of legal documents (recommendation, requests, hearing convocations, etc.), and of judicial documents (the judgement and description of the offence by the public prosecutor; the record of short prison leaves previously granted by the DMD and the SIC). The clerks' office centralises and dispatches documents that are passed through the prisoner (his application file), the DMD (short prison leave approval or denial), the governors (written recommendation), the PST (PST file, victim record), the Houses of Justice (attestation of the conditions for an eventual reintegration), and the SIC (judgements). This is the first key facility handled by the clerks: monitoring the timescales, they centralise the communication and drive the coordination between the actors involved in the process.

In some prisons, clerks are personally informing the prisoners about the procedure, the timescale, and what they have to do. Where such information is directly communicated to the prisoner by a clerk rather than by a prison guard, the length of the procedure may be reduced, because a clerk can discern whether

[9]Calculating the dates of eligibility is a complex exercise (Beernaert and Vandermeersch 2008, p. 75).

an application will be viable or not. This expertise is a second key facility of the clerks: acting as gatekeepers, they can be the first filter in the early release process.

> It is easier to go and see the prisoner directly. (…) We can talk to them quickly, I tell them that they can apply if they are ready. Since I give the information personally, half of them are filling the application form. (A prison clerk)

They also ensure the prisoner's rights are respected as the prisoner depends on them to move his/her application file forward and update it frequently, recording the various administrative and judicial decisions concerning him. In doing so, they "establish the prison as a legal entity" (Salle and Moreau de Bellaing 2010, p. 164).

> We have to respect many deadlines, regardless of our opinion. (…) We have to execute the legal procedure and the decisions. Our role is to make it work. (A prison clerk)

Keeping in contact with groups both inside (prison governors, the PST, prisoners) and outside the prison (DMD, Houses of Justice, SIC) is the third key facility of the clerks. For example, they have regular contact with the court's clerks: they exchange files, hearing schedules and judgements. These three key facilities make clerks powerful: concretely enacting the procedure, the coordination between the various groups of actors depends on them, so that the files can be processed on time.

11.3.2 The Prison Governors, Strategic Brokers

A prison's management staff is usually composed of four to twelve governors, according to the size of the prison. The governor, who is responsible for the prisoner's detention, has to write a positive or negative recommendation for every request. To do so, they meet with the prisoner during the conference. They can also mandate the PST to provide a psychosocial report if necessary, and mandate the House of Justice to lead certain social investigations. They then base their written recommendation on the information inscribed in the documents and collected during the meeting(s) (with the prisoner, the PST, the clerk, the guards). Later in the process, during the hearing to decide whether leave or early release is granted, they orally update their recommendation, according to the evolution of the prisoner's situation.

The conference consists of a meeting between the governor and the prisoner. Usually, this is the place to discuss the prisoner's general situation, the state of the requests sent to the DMD, etc. Early release processes are not linear. The prison governor looks at the reintegration plan, he gives advice to increase the chances of success. Many governors conceive the conference as an opportunity to work on the requests and files, but also with and for the prisoner. In the following example, the governor advises a prisoner, as he knows that his case file fits with "Article 59", and that the court's magistrates could be sensitive to some arguments.

A conference: Alex (I)

Alex's request for electronic monitoring (EM) is being discussed during the conference. His lawyer is not present. The DMD had previously granted Alex a one-day prison leave that was successful. But the DMD is now refusing to grant Alex a weekend leave, blocking any conditional release application.

The prison governor explains to Alex that he has to apply again for a weekend leave: *"I will write a positive recommendation. But you should submit an "Article 59" [request] to the court. The main justification to be developed is that your reintegration plan is only missing a test of cohabitation at your mum's. And you have to insist on the fact that the DMD keeps refusing the weekend leave requests"*.

Along the preparation of the file, prison governors can give some information, explanation and advice to the prisoners about the procedure. Their knowledge of the case, inscribed in various documents, is a first key resource.

In meeting with the prisoner before and at the hearing; reading and interpreting judicial, administrative, social and psychosocial documents in order to write their recommendation; and transmitting this recommendation to the court: prison governors are experiencing interactions between various professional groups, both inside the prison and with the SIC. Their "boundary spanning" position is a second key resource, "possessed by an actor participating in several related systems of action. As a result, [they] can play the indispensable role of intermediary and interpreter between different and even contradictory logics of action" (Crozier and Friedberg 1980, p. 41).

Along their career, prison governors become familiar with judicial and administrative routines, categories, expectations, and reactions that comprise the courts' jurisprudence. Their experience is a third key resource as it enables the prison to react "to the data or problems that have been previously perceived, recognised and understood by its members, who must then integrate them into the causal maps that they construct from experience and that provide them with their representations and scenarios for interpreting the world" (Friedberg 1997, p. 58).

> Since we have no access to the Court, the governor is a relay person. After the hearing, he gives us a quick feedback of whatever has been said, so that we can have an insight on what happened. (Social worker PST)

While writing their written recommendation, prison governors have to collect and make sense of various documents produced by different professional groups (DMD, SIC, PST, Houses of Justice) using different languages, tools, and guided by different professional and institutional norms (Hutton 2006). Governors not only summarise and assemble the information out of these documents, but they also translate, compare, make sense of them, in the light of the information collected during the conference. Beyond the procedure, the governors are enacting the substantial dimension of the files, making sense of various documents, and feeding the justification of the SIC's decision downstream. In doing so, prison governors are brokering substantial knowledge on the prisoner's situation to the court and on the court's expectations to the prisoner.

11.3.3 The Psychosocial Report, a "Boundary Object"

The psychosocial teams are composed of 15–25 members, psychologists and social workers, who are responsible for evaluating the prisoner. They are subordinate to a double hierarchy: the local prison governor and the central psychosocial department. As previously mentioned, they are mandated by the governors to write a psychosocial report, whose content depends on what the governor has requested.[10] Having no direct contact with the court, the PST can influence and inform the final decision through his written report and via the governor who takes part in the hearing.

The PST takes part in the preparation of the prisoner's request for the DMD, and contributes to the elaboration of his/her reintegration plan. Above all, the key resource of the PST lies in the psychosocial report. It influences the governor's and the public prosecutor's recommendations and the court's decision by providing them with material (risk evaluation, criminogenesis, anamnesis, the prisoner's attitude towards the victim(s) and towards the facts, etc.). Making this material available, the psychosocial report plays a big role in the labelling process, framing the file. The document produced by the PST will be examined by the governors, the DMD, the public prosecutor and the court in order to produce their recommendation, inform their decision and justify it, although the influence of the psychosocial report can remain invisible in the SIC judgement.

> Everybody knows that the PST report plays a central part in the whole process. (Prison governor)

The psychosocial report illustrates the role of "boundary objects" (Star and Griesemer 1989) in a decision-making process. Boundary objects pass information from one group to another: "Both plastic enough to adapt to local needs and the constraints of the several parties employing them, yet robust enough to maintain a common identity across sites. [...] They have different meanings in different social worlds, but their structure is common enough to more than one world to make

[10]The request might concern the prisoner's familial and personal situation, a comparative description of the facts as viewed by the public prosecutor and by the prisoner, the prisoner's attitude towards the facts and the victims, his behaviour during his detention, some investigation about his personality, his reintegration plan, his social situation, and most of all, the risk of re-offending. The reports are very different (from 1–50 pages), depending on their author, the offence, the offender, the sentence, etc.

them recognisable, a means of translation" (Star and Griesemer 1989, p. 393). Because they do not require any consensus, the different groups of actors using boundary objects can make sense of them in and according to their local context of action. The substantial information the psychosocial report carries is neither received nor perceived in the same way by every stakeholder. Every professional uses, translates and makes sense of the report in his/her own way, according to his own professional practices, language, tools and constraints. In that respect, the psychosocial report is "plastic". But the report is also "robust", as it is part of a routinised process: if the 2006 Act barely mentions the PST, we can observe that both the DMD and the court request it in the files, and that SIC will be reluctant to make a decision if the report is not included. The psychosocial report is a boundary object, "revealing point of exchange between two professional groups working within the criminal justice system." (Halliday et al. 2009, p. 407).

This section depicted how the clerks, the prison governors and the PST took part in the incremental production of prisoners' case files. From a formal point of view, they are collecting information, inscribing it in documents, receiving these documents, making sense of them, and moving them forward. From a substantial point of view, these professionals are progressively labelling both the prisoner and his case file. In the following section, we will consider this substantial dimension as a collective process of "sensemaking".

11.4 A Collective Process of "Sensemaking"

Taking place at the end of the early release process, every hearing is partly determined by the coordination of the procedure by the clerks, the (sometimes strategic) mediations by the governors, the "boundary object" produced by the PST, and the reading of the file by the SIC members (public prosecutor and magistrates). Three judges are responsible for making the decision, in the light of the legal counter-indications already mentioned. Partly due to the nature of these counter-indications, their judgement is based on common sense (Thévenot 1992), discussion and deliberation (Elster 1998), rather than on general rules syllogistically applied to specific cases (Beccaria 2006). They then focus progressively on the elements to be worked on by the prisoner. The judgement is written after the hearing by one of these magistrates justifying their decision with, among other things, the material included in the psychosocial report and the governors' recommendation. When the decision is negative, the justification is addressed to every stakeholder, indicating how to improve the prisoner's file for a future request.

The hearing is the place for discussing and updating the reintegration plan and the recommendations that the public prosecutor and the governor may have been writing weeks or months earlier.

A hearing: Alex (II)

Only a few days after his conference by prison governor I, Alex's hearing takes place in the absence of both his lawyer and prison governor I, the latter being represented by one of his colleagues, prison governor II.

As advised by prison governor I, Alex asks the court to grant him a weekend leave under "Article 59", in order to try out the living arrangement with his mother. Alex relays the arguments that governor I has told him: the DMD keeps refusing the granting of the weekend leave, and his reintegration plan is ready but still misses the test of cohabitation. As an answer, the court president underlines that the prison governor's written recommendation on a weekend leave was negative. Alex explains that at the conference prison governor I had promised to write him a positive recommendation for his next request.

Prison governor II, who is attending the hearing, says that he is not aware of this. The magistrates have received the reintegration plan, the written recommendation, and the psychosocial report. But they are missing some crucial information to grant a weekend leave via Article 59: the positive recommendation. According to Alex, this positive recommendation has not yet been added to the file. After the hearing, the information is checked and the weekend leave can be granted via the use of Article 59.

The hearing reveals the importance of cooperation between stakeholders. Communication is a major element of cooperation within the prison and within the court as much as between both these entities. Because of their broker position, the communication process strongly depends on the prison governors, as illustrated by Alex's case. The sharing of information between colleagues (prison governors in this case) is another decisive aspect of the collective action process, which also relies on meetings and documents to make coherent sense.

Despite the fact that the SIC depends on all the other professional groups involved in the process, it has some autonomy to make decisions. A failure in the formal dimension of the collective action chain upstream does not automatically involve a negative decision downstream. Judges have been developing their own strategies to react quickly when a missing document prevents them from granting an early release (using the fax, going to the clerks' office). Sometimes, if the magistrates realise at the hearing that the prisoner is not eligible for a conditional release, or that the file does not meet the required criteria (the lack of a reintegration plan for example), they then indicate in their decision the required time needed before a new request can be made. The court also handles the substantial dimension of the process when contradictory information or miscommunication between the prison governors occurs, as in Alex's case. If their judgement partly relies on the "translation" of various documents by the PST and prison governors, they still can read the original documents composing the case file.

Moreover, the hearing reveals how the prisoner's file has been progressively framed and labelled.

From the case file to the hearing(s): labelling Charly

Charly has a heavy criminal and prison background. Having served many sentences, he was previously granted two conditional releases, which were later revoked. He has been imprisoned since 1995; his sentence (for murder, robbery and drugs offences) will expire in 2023. Since 2007, Charly has been heard ten times by the SIC. His case file mentions two PST reports, wherein five other reports are also mentioned. After a few rejections of his requests, the court asked for a psychiatric report in 2010. In 2011, the court granted Charly three one-day leaves, using Article 59. Although eligible for short leaves since 2002, none had been granted to Charly by the DMD. Thanks to the short leave granted by the court, Charly has been setting up a reintegration plan. The SIC granted him a semi-detention measure in September 2011, then electronic monitoring in March 2012. On two subsequent occasions, the court refused to grant him a conditional release, as he did not have a stable job.

By May 2014, and his 10th hearing, Charly has found a flat and professional training. The court granted him a conditional release, after he had been subject to electronic monitoring for more than two years.

Charly's case file provides traces from the multiple conferences, hearings, decisions, and from the work carried out by the PST. All these documents indicate that Charly's release consisted of a long process of requests, refusals and adjustments leading to new requests, refusals, etc. The psychosocial team first mentioned that more time was needed to make an evaluation; then they and the governor recommended that Charly should go through the early release options progressively; the DGD refused every leave request; the court required a psychiatric report, before using the "Article 59" strategy.

Charly's case shows how "sensemaking" is distributed through multiple actions along the processing of the file (Weick et al. 2005). The "labelling and categorising" operated by professionals is progressively inscribed in documents and marked by the work already done upstream. This work mainly consists of qualifications both about the prisoner (his/her psychological state, his/her behaviour in prison, his/her reintegration plan, etc.) and from the professionals (the difficulties encountered, their concerns, recommendations, advice, expertise, etc.). Documents are the recipients of a "labelling" process, where every written contribution must be understandable by every stakeholder. In such a long process, the file is *re*composed throughout the elaboration of the reintegration plan and the evolution of the prisoner: some steps in Charly's process are omitted when they are considered as meaningless regarding his actual situation. "These changes through time progressively reveal that a seemingly correct action 'back then' is becoming an incorrect action 'now'" (Weick et al. 2005, p. 413).

11.5 Conclusion

A legal decision needs some justification. If the final decision lies in the judgement of the SIC, this decision is emerging all along the construction of the file. Just like in a criminal court, it "depends on the ability of the criminal process to communicate expectations and cues which guide judges in answering the question 'what type of case is this?'" (Tata 1997, p. 413).

The hearing and the files reveal how "sensemaking" is a nonlinear and collective process: "In sensemaking, action and talk are treated as cycles rather than as a linear sequence. Talk occurs both early and late, as does action, and either one can be designated as the 'starting point to the destination'" (Weick et al. 2005, p. 412). The visible dimension of this process lies in various documents; its invisible dimension leads to the hearings, where decisions are to be taken. Such a collective decision-making process is both procedural (progressive trajectory of the prisoner's request and file, according the deadlines and requirements) and substantial (incremental translation of information into documents, such as the psychosocial report, the governor's and public prosecutor's recommendation, the social enquiry, the previous decisions of the DMD and SIC). Charly's case underlines the cyclical aspect of "sensemaking". Every stage, meeting and document, including the hearings, implies the framing of the case. The qualification follows and is adapted to the evolution of the prisoner, his mental state and his reinsertion plan.

Coordination as prescribed by the law, and documents as material, are necessary but not sufficient to concretely enact the early release process. The different groups of actors need to share some common understanding of the counter-indications. The meaning of "a lack of social reintegration", or of the "risk of committing new serious offences", will vary according to the case file they have to deal with, but also according to the request and to the prisoner. This means that the various stakeholders need some flexibility in their way of working. In Alex's case, the lack of communication between the prison governors did not constitute a definitive obstacle for the "Article 59" strategy conceived by the first governor to be performed by the SIC. Alex's file, the preparation of the reintegration plan, the rejection of a previous request by the DMD, and his cooperation with the PST; all these factors are contributing to the collective decision finally made by the court. These elements are brought together and given sense by the professionals involved in the process. It is through meetings and documents that these elements are elaborated and discussed with the prisoner, then communicated to the court, where they will be (partly) validated or not.

Meetings and documents compose the collective action process conceived as "organisational sensemaking". The decision of the SIC is the output of a retrospective process (Weick et al. 2005, p. 411) woven by actors who are memorising some effective solutions and adjusting their actions to the available clues. In Alex's case, the back and forth movement of the documents and of the oral communications incrementally allowed his case to be categorised according to previous experiences and recollections of other prisoners. But "sensemaking" is also retrospective because it always consists of interpreting, bracketing and labelling already existing facts, documents, information: "A mistake follows an act. It identifies the character of an act in its aftermath. It names it. An act, however, is not mistaken; it becomes mistaken" (Paget 1988: 56, quoted by Weick et al. 2005, p. 412).

References

Anleu, S. R., & Mack, K. (2008). The professionalization of Australian magistrates: Autonomy, credentials and prestige. *Journal of Sociology*, 44(2), 185–203.

Bauwens, A., Robert, L., & Snacken, S. (2012). Conditional release in Belgium: how reforms have impacted recall. *European journal of probation*, 4(1), 19–33.

Beccaria, C. (2006). *An Essay on Crimes and Punishments* (242 p.). The Lawbook Exchange Ltd.

Beernaert, M.-A., & Vandermeersch, D. (2008). *Le tribunal de l'application des peines et le statut externe des condamnés à des peines privatives de liberté de plus de trois ans* (162 p.). Kluwer.

Beyens, K., & Roosen, M. (2013). Electronic Monitoring in Belgium: A Penological Analysis of Current and Future Orientations. *European Journal of Probation*, 5(3), 56–70.

Beyens, K., & Scheirs, V. (2010). Encounters of a different kind Social enquiry and sentencing in Belgium. *Punishment & Society*, 12(3), 309–328.

Crozier, M., & Friedberg, E. (1980). *Actors and Systems: The Politics of Collective Action* (341 p.). The University of Chicago Press.

De Ridder, S. D., Beyens, K., & Snacken, S. (2012). Does Reintegration Need REHAB? Early Release Procedures for Prisoners without a Legal Permit of Residence in Belgium. *European Journal of Probation*, 4(3), 21–37.

Dubois, C., & Vrancken, D. (2014). Restorative detention or 'work on self'? Two accounts of a Belgian prison policy. *Ethnography.*

Elster, J. (ed). (1998). *Deliberative Democracy (Vol. 1)* (294 p.). Cambridge University Press.

Freeman, R. (2006). The Work the Document Does: Research, Policy, and Equity in Health. Journal of Health Politics. *Policy and Law*, 31(1), 51–70.

Friedberg, E. (1997). *Local Orders: Dynamics of Organized Action* (330 p.). Jai Press Inc.

Garapon, A. (2001). *Bien juger : Essai sur le rituel judiciaire* (352 p.). Odile Jacob.

Halliday, S., Burns, N., Hutton, N., Mcneill, F., & Tata, C. (2009). Street-Level Bureaucracy, Interprofessional Relations, and Coping Mechanisms: A Study of Criminal Justice Social Workers in the Sentencing Process. *Law & Policy*, 31(4), 405–428.

Hutton, N. (2006). Sentencing as a social practice. In S. Armstrong & L. McAra (Eds.), *Perspectives on Punishment* (pp. 155–174). Oxford University Press.

Mine, B., & Robert, L. (2014). Le processus décisionnel relatif aux permissions de sortie et aux congés pénitentiaires. *Revue de droit pénal et de criminologie*, 3, 267–287.

Salle, G., & Moreau de Bellaing, C. (2010). Les grincements d'un rouage de l'État. *Terrains & travaux*, n° 17(1), 163–180.

Snacken, S. (2007). Penal Policy and Practice in Belgium. *Crime and Justice*, 36(1), 127–215.

Star, S. L., & Griesemer, J. R. (1989). Institutional Ecology, `Translations' and Boundary Objects: Amateurs and Professionals in Berkeley's Museum of Vertebrate Zoology, 1907-39. *Social Studies of Science*, 19(3), 387–420.

Tata, C. (1997). Conceptions and Representations of the Sentencing Decision Process. *Journal of Law and Society*, 24(3), 395–420.
Thévenot, L. (1992). Jugements ordinaires et jugement de droit. *Annales. Économies, Sociétés, Civilisations*, 47(6), 1279–1299.
Walgrave, S., & Varone, F. (2008). Punctuated Equilibrium and Agenda-Setting: Bringing Parties Back in: Policy Change after the Dutroux Crisis in Belgium. *Governance*, 21(3), 365–395.
Weick, K. E., Sutcliffe, K. M., & Obstfeld, D. (2005). Organizing and the Process of Sensemaking. *Organization Science*, 16(4), 409–421.

Part III
Human Capital in Historical Perspective: Belgian Magistrates

Chapter 12
Prosopography, Crisis and Modernisation of Justice—"Belgian Magistrates": An Introduction

Xavier Rousseaux

The abstruse term of prosopography relates to an approach towards social reality through biographical research.[1] Yet, unlike biographies, as they are known to the general public, which usually focus on a renowned individual,[2] the prosopographical method articulates around a socio-professional group studied from the perspective of individuals' biographic paths and the multiple aspects of their integration within society (alliances, networks, recruitments, positions, honours, estates ...). This principle of collective biography is widely based on the analysis of interpersonal networks through the way they are built, structured and reproduced. This method also lies on the epistemological and technological developments that now enable large-scale automation of data crossing, which used to be performed manually in the past. For instance, the set or graph theories, the study of networks or the progress made in IT, both in hardware (computing power and storage capacity extensions) and software, especially the developments in the field of relational database management systems (RDBMS).

[1]L. Stone, 'Prosopography', *Daedalus* 100, 1971, pp. 46–79.

[2]However we must mention the original and controversial attempt of Alain Corbin to write the biography of an anonymous person (*Le Monde retrouvé de Louis-François Pinagot. Sur les traces d'un inconnu, 1798–1876*, Paris, 1998, Reprint Flammarion, coll. "Champs", 2002) and the methodological reflections of Jean-Luc Mayaud ("'Recherches pinagotiques'. À propos du Monde retrouvé de Louis-François Pinagot", *Ruralia* [En ligne] 03, 1 June 1998, consulted 22 August 2014. URL: http://ruralia.revues.org/60).

X. Rousseaux (✉)
Centre d'histoire du droit et de la justice, UCL, Louvain-la-Neuve, Belgium

A. Hondeghem et al. (eds.), *Modernisation of the Criminal Justice Chain and the Judicial System*, Ius Gentium: Comparative Perspectives on Law and Justice 50, DOI 10.1007/978-3-319-25802-7_12

These innovations open the way to a renewal of prosopographical work. Indeed, some disciplines, especially the history of older periods, for which documentation is scarce, scattered and fragile have long depended on the common thread of name lists, enriched with all sorts of possible sources. The specialists in ancient and medieval periods are familiar with them. However, nowadays, the method does not consist in producing paper files, enriched by their author throughout a life of hard work, neither in publishing bulky dictionaries, constantly annotated by anonymous researchers who add their personal findings. Research is based on creating a smooth data collection, organisation and enrichment tool. Available to the public thanks to a web-based access, such databases are likely to be further populated by thousands of connected researchers. Prosopography, which has become a full-fledged discipline, now has its own manuals,[3] specialised periodical[4] and websites.[5]

A quick analysis of definitions provided on websites and in specialised books highlights to what extent this method concerns contemporary social groups. Among these prosopographical initiatives, researchers have particularly focused on "judicial officials" or "legal professionals", as they provide a variety of information on the long process that gave birth to professions critical to the Modern State.[6] The world of legal professionals, in which are intertwined historical fields of research such as history of law, political history, and social history and social sciences such as demography, social anthropology and elite sociology, based on methodologies that have been previously mentioned, has many advantages. This is a population that has been closely linked with the use of writing since the Middle Ages and is therefore largely documented.

These professionals come from religious and lay elites, both in the old regime and in 19th–21st century middle class circles, and have proved to be surprisingly stable as socio-professional groups and as a political elite, at least until the middle of the 20th century. This group brings together—more or less—all those who are related to establishing standards, solving disputes and regulating conflicts, which are critical practices for ensuring society works properly. From a long-term perspective in the West, this sphere of law played a critical role yet again in the creation of the modern State. The legists of the prince and the parliamentarians in the Middle Ages (F. Autrand), high civil servants in Burgundian Low Countries,[7] Belgian magistrates

[3]K.S.B. Keats-Rohan (ed.), *Prosopography approaches and applications: a handbook*, Oxford, 2007 (Prosopographica and Genealogica 13).

[4]Prosopon.

[5]http://prosopography.modhist.ox.ac.uk/directory.htm.

[6]F. Autrand, *Prosopographie et genèse de l'État moderne, actes de la table-ronde CNRS et ENSJF, Paris, 22–23 octobre 1984*, Paris, ENSJF, 1986. V. Bernaudeau, *La justice en question. Histoire de la magistrature angevine au XIXe siècle*, Rennes, Presses Universitaires de Rennes, 2007.

[7]C. Thomas, *Le visage humain de l'administration. Les grands commis du gouvernement central des Pays-Bas espagnols (1598–1700)*, Brussels, Académie royale de Belgique, 2014; C. Bruneel, J.P. Hoyois, *Les grands commis du gouvernement des Pays-Bas autrichiens. Dictionnaire biographique du personnel des institutions centrales*, Brussels, Archives générales du Royaume, 2001.

from the French Revolution until the Empire (J. Logie), lawyers in the French Republic[8] or the magistracy at the time of the Liberation (A. Bancaud) were all judicial bodies that strongly contributed to the major changes in Western society.[9] From the 18th century onwards, a professionalisation movement of legal professions developed. This was highlighted by Hervé Leuwers for lawyers.[10] This movement resulted in closing off the circles of law, gradually restricting the practice of law to specific categories of individuals. These "legal professions": lawyers, notaries, magistrates or registrars, have essentially been defined by a common training: a law university diploma and shared professional practices.

The idea to study Belgian magistracy has been inspired by the progress made in research on law and by current debates. In the 1960s and 1970s, a multidisciplinary approach to law emerged, one of the contributions of which has been to draw the attention to the law in action within the law in book. Renewing the study of law by contextualising the way it was put into practice in a society resulted in shifting the focus of analysis from texts to the stakeholders, that is to say judges. Belgium has dealt with several scandals involving the judicial system since the 1980s, which have gradually led to an increasing atmosphere of distrust between the judicial sphere, the political world and "public opinion". The topic of defiance between the populations and judicial authorities has given rise to a debate. The corporatist character of the magistracy has been put forward within this debate to justify the body's alleged inability to follow the changes in society. Both approaches have drawn the interest of researchers in the fields of legal practice and sociology. Historians will soon follow in their steps. Indeed, they have set out to analyse the origins of Belgian magistracy's emergence and to find out whether this corporatist interpretation matched reality.

After preliminary studies, two individual research projects have established a first state of knowledge. As a history enthusiast, Jacques Logie, the vice-president of the Brussels Commercial Court (*tribunal de commerce*) had undertaken to write a thesis on the magistracy of "Belgian" departments when "Belgian" territories were attached to France, during the late 18th-century revolutions. He published a synthesis of his work in 1995. On the other hand, Jean-Pierre Nandrin, holder of a history degree and a bachelor in law, undertook an innovative study on the emergence of magistracy in the early days of Independent Belgium. He reconstructed the first appointments in the body (1832) and carried out a research on justices of

[8]G. Le Beguec, *La République des avocats*, Paris, Armand Colin, 2003.

[9]F. Autrand, *Naissance d'un grand corps de l'État: les gens du parlement de Paris (1345–1454)*, Paris, Publications de la Sorbonne, 1981; J. Logie, *Les magistrats des cours et tribunaux en Belgique, 1794–1814. Essai d'histoire politique et sociale*, Paris–Genève, Droz, 1998; A. Bancaud, *Une exception ordinaire. La magistrature en France, 1930–1950*, Paris, Gallimard, 2002.

[10]H. Leuwers (ed.), *Juges, avocats et notaires dans l'espace franco-belge. Expériences spécifiques ou partagées (XVIIIe-XIXe siècles)*, Brussels, Archives générales du royaume, coll. Justice & Société, 2, 2010.

the peace (*justices de paix*) until 1848.[11] Together with Xavier Rousseaux, he performed a first exploration within the framework of a research project on the "Belgian" sphere throughout the Revolutions (1780–1830).[12] The objective was to identify the role of judicial officials in the transformations of the elites between the late 18th-century revolutions and the Belgian revolution in 1830.

Later on, the idea of an ambitious project emerged when these two pioneers, who unfortunately passed away too soon, joined forces with young researchers from the Centre d'Histoire du Droit et de la Justice (UCL-CHDJ) in Louvain-la-Neuve and the University of Namur: build a relational database, entitled "Prosopography of the Belgian magistrates in the 19th century (1830–1914)". This project initiated by Jean-Pierre Nandrin (Saint-Louis University, Brussels, USL-B), Xavier Rousseaux (Catholic University of Louvain, UCL) and Axel Tixhon (University of Namur) within the framework of the development of an integrated history of justice has benefited from the support of the Fonds national belge de la recherche scientifique (Belgian Fund for Scientific Research, FRS-FNRS) since 2005. It provided the opportunity to recruit several researchers in 2005–2007—Françoise Muller (UCL), Anne Roekens and Bénédicte Rochet (University of Namur) and the IT engineer Xavier Cuvellier (USL-B)—in order to structure historical data and create the tool. The first step consisted in setting up the database architecture, which was carried out by Françoise Muller with the support of Aurore François and Frédéric Vesentini (UCL-CHDJ). Thanks to a FNRS post-doctoral mandate, Vincent Bernaudeau (University of Angers) joined the USL-B team and brought his prosopographical expertise. In particular, he handled the preparation, organisation and publication of proceedings for the conference that was hosted by the University of Namur on 14–16 December 2006.[13] The project's ambition was to create a specific tool that could be adapted to other prosopographical data and other national spheres. In this perspective, the conference aimed at gathering prosopographical experiences in different groups, reflecting on the issues and contributions of these research projects for understanding the emergence and structuring of socio-professional identities in the long-run and analysing the underlying methodologies for the development of such approaches. Therefore, the last day of the conference widened the scope of participants to the FNRS

[11]J.P. Nandrin, *La justice de paix à l'aube de l'indépendance de la Belgique (1832–1848). La professionnalisation d'une fonction judiciaire*, Brussels, Publications des Facultés universitaires Saint-Louis, 1998. Id., *Hommes et Normes. Le pouvoir judiciaire en Belgique aux premiers temps de l'indépendance (1832–1848)*, 4 vol., Louvain-la-Neuve, UCL, Ph.D. thesis in History, unpublished, 1995.

[12]X. Rousseaux, J.P. Nandrin, "Le personnel judiciaire en Belgique à travers les révolutions (1780–1832). Quelques hypothèses de recherches et premiers résultats", in P. Lenders (ed.), *Le personnel politique dans la transition de l'Ancien Régime au Nouveau Régime en Belgique (1780–1830)*, Kortrijk, Anciens Pays et Assemblées d'État, 1993, pp. 13–69.

[13]V. Bernaudeau, J.P. Nandrin, B. Rochet, X. Rousseaux and A. Tixhon (eds.), *Les Praticiens du droit du Moyen-Âge à l'époque contemporaine. Approches prosopographiques (Belgique, Canada, France, Italie, Prusse)*, Rennes, Presses Universitaires de Rennes, 2008.

Contact Group "Sources and methods for the history of social control from the Middle Ages to present day", in which archivists, legal professionals and historians participated. Under the guidance of the Director General of the Belgian State Archives, Karel Velle, a first version of the "Magistrates" database was presented at this occasion.

The prosopographical project's scope had gradually widened beyond the 19th century. For the late 18th century and the first half of the 19th century, this was made possible by integrating the data collected by our dearly departed Jacques Logie in the framework of his Ph.D. at Paris-IV University on Belgian magistracy under the Revolution and the Empire. Thanks to the research carried out by Catherine Goffin (University of Namur), the link between magistracy in the 1830 Belgian Revolution and its roots through the periods of the Directory, the Consulate and the Empire (1795–1814) has been re-established[14]. For the first half of the 20th century, the initial project was integrated in a research programme, financed by Belgian Scientific Policy, on the Sociopolitical History of Justice Administration in Belgium (1795–2005). It was part of the team managed by Pr. Jean-Pierre Nandrin at USL-B concerning the history of Belgian magistracy in the 19th century and during the Second World War.

Besides, a second FNRS post-doctoral research position enabled the UCL team to recruit David Niget (University of Angers, University of Quebec in Montreal) in order to develop an additional research axis on a specific type of magistracy, juvenile court judges (*juges des enfants*), a position created in the first half of the 20th century. With the development of similar projects, especially the French magistrates database created by Jean-Claude Farcy,[15] the project has been presented in specialised conferences on "digital humanities", an emerging discipline.[16]

New dimensions were still explored in the database through specific research. Additional research has also been carried out on Belgian military magistracy since 1830, thanks to the work carried out by Eric Bastin[17] and Laurence Montel. After an exploratory study carried out by Laurence Montel and Enika Ngongo,[18] a new project which started in July 2014 aims at integrating all colonial Africa's

[14]C. Goffin, "Les magistrats dans les départements réunis sous le Directoire (an IV-an VIII): corps social à part entière?", in E. Berger (ed.), *L'acculturation des modèles policiers et judiciaires français en Belgique et aux Pays-Bas (1795–1815)*, Brussels, Archives générales du Royaume, 2010, pp. 99–107.

[15]*Annuaire rétrospectif de la magistrature. XIXe-XXe siècles*, http://tristan.u-bourgogne.fr:8080/.

[16]Université de Dijon, Journée d'étude, "Base de données et histoire de la justice", 10 juin 2010, http://tristan.ubourgogne.fr/CGC/manifestations/09_10/10_06_10.html.

[17]E. Bastin, *La justice militaire en Belgique de 1830 à 1850. L'auditeur militaire, "valet" ou "cheville ouvrière" des conseils de guerre?*, Louvain-la-Neuve, Presses universitaires de Louvain, 2012.

[18]L. Montel, "Le contrôle des magistrats dans le Congo léopoldien, d'après les registres du Service du personnel d'Afrique (SPA) (1885–1908)", in B. Piret, C. Braillon, L. Montel, P.L. Plasman (dir.), *Droit et justice en Afrique coloniale. Traditions, productions et réformes*, Brussels, Publications de l'Université Saint-Louis-Bruxelles, 2013. pp. 51–78.

"magistrates" under "Belgian" mandate, from the Congo Free State until the end of the United Nations mandate on Ruanda-Urundi.

In August 2014, a biographical sketch was drawn up in the database for 6283 people, among whom about 4313 were Belgian magistrates who served in courts and tribunals in Belgium and Africa. Besides, several hundreds of jurisdictions have been listed and their staff have been located on a timeline.

The research work was mainly focused on collecting data through the various produced sources: official directories, specialised press or archive sources. After spending a great deal of energy in order to collect and verify data and solving time-consuming technical challenges, we are starting to exploit the collected material.

The interest of such a project is not only purely scientific in nature. Understanding the extent of collective mind-sets and individual competences or analysing an institution's way of working in its early days, in a period of crisis or once it is fully established also gives the opportunity to offer better guidance to individuals and the structures on which the State is founded. The contribution of a historical sociology of magistracy also emphasises how present day decision-making can be influenced by past methods (path dependence).

Chapter 13
Prosopography in the Digital Age: Current Situation, Prospects and Perspectives in the Light of the Forthcoming "Belgian Magistrates" Application

Aurore François and Françoise Muller

As Claire Lemercier and Emmanuelle Picard have pointed out, prosopography is experiencing a "second vogue",[1] accompanied by fertile reflection and discussion on its definition, methods and tools. An essential part of this revival is the use of computer tools, which expand the range of potential possibilities within any one project. Could it be possible to include the gathering of ID data sheets, the historical tracing of professional careers, the networking of players and the inclusion of these in an institutional context, all within the same tool? In any case, this is the challenge taken up by the database entitled "Prosopography and Directory of Belgian Magistrates", which we profile here.

At its name implies, this project has a resolutely generic perspective. It is a 'directory' in that it sets out to list as comprehensively as possible all the members of the judiciary who practised in the territory. It is 'prosopography' in that it aims to move beyond the function of biographical directory and to provide researchers with a tool that can support a prosopographical approach to bodies of information, the boundaries of which they are free to define themselves.[2]

[1]C. Lemercier and E. Picard, "Quelle approche prosopographique?" in L. Rollet and P. Nabonnaud (eds), *Les uns et les autres... Biographies et prosopographies en histoire des sciences*, Nancy, Presses universitaires de Nancy, pp. 605–630.

[2]The article by Claire Lemercier and Emmanuelle Picard cited above offers a quality discussion of the issues related to the definition of a prosopographical corpus.

A. François (✉)
Laboratoire de recherches historiques, UCL, Louvain-la-Neuve, Belgium
e-mail: aurore.francois@uclouvain.be

F. Muller
Centre d'histoire du droit et de la justice, UCL, Louvain-la-Neuve, Belgium
e-mail: francoise.muller@uclouvain.be

A. Hondeghem et al. (eds.), *Modernisation of the Criminal Justice Chain and the Judicial System*, Ius Gentium: Comparative Perspectives on Law and Justice 50, DOI 10.1007/978-3-319-25802-7_13

While the project was originally intended to cover the ordinary Belgian judiciary from 1830 (independence) to 1914, it rapidly extended beyond these boundaries to include other judiciaries (military tribunals, juvenile judges), territories (colonial judiciary) and time frames (from 1795 to the second half of the 20th century for certain institutions). The database is in fact fed by a number of projects that provide it with the human and technical resources necessary for its development.[3] The initial project and its successive enlargements have produced a number of methodological challenges: how to manage the evolving nature of the data, their at times uncertain nature, or the unstable nature of the institutions in which the players themselves evolved? The present contribution will focus on three points: after describing (I) some methodological questions that we faced and the solutions applied, we will provide (II) an overview of the application as it is today, and conclude (III) with a more proactive opening towards the future.

13.1 A Prosopographical Database: Methodological Issues, Technical Choices

13.1.1 Men, Institutions and Relationships…

Since the launch of the project, the research team has focused on the relational model in seeking to structure the data relating to the judiciary. Formalised by Codd in 1970, this data structuring model based on set theory has many qualities, one of the first of which is its accessibility for the non-expert public.[4] Not requiring prior training in its technical aspects, it permits easy dialogue between researchers.

By making it possible to represent multi-feature, inter-linked data, the relational model has been found to satisfactorily represent the multitude of realities which form the context in which members of the judiciary operated: their multiple

[3]The "Prosopography and Directory of Belgian Magistrates" database was created in 2005 as part of a project of the Fund for Collective Fundamental Research (FRFC) submitted by UCL, FUSL and FUNDP. The project was originally focused on the ordinary courts between 1830 and 1914. Since then, additional funding has made it possible to expand the time frame both downstream and upstream as well as to include the military judiciary and the juvenile judiciary. The application was first integrated into the Just-His portal of IAP P6/01 "Justice and Society: The Sociopolitical History of Justice Administration in Belgium (1795-2005)" http://www.digithemis.be/. The PAI funded the major recasting of the application in 2010. 2014 marks the beginning of a four-year project dedicated to the colonial judiciary (Congo and Ruanda-Urundi) from 1885 to 1962. This extension of the spacial-temporal framework will require an adaptation of the application to the specifics of colonial data. For documentation on the initial project, see A. François, "Capitaliser les ressources sur l'histoire socio-politique de la justice belge (1797–2005). Le portail just-his.be" in F. Clavert and S. Noiret (eds.), *L'histoire contemporaine à l'ère digitale*, PIE-Pieter-Lang: Brussels, 2013, pp. 95–106.

[4]The theoretical foundations of the relational model were stated by Codd: E.F. CODD, 'A Relational Model of Data for Large Shared Data Banks' in *Communications of the ACM*, vol. 13, No. 6, June 1970, pp. 377–387.

personal features and attributes of course, but also information relating to the institutions in which they functioned, and not forgetting the archival references from which the data are taken.

13.1.2 Time Management and the Evolving Nature of the Data

The modelling of time as proposed by so-called *temporal* databases provides an answer to this essential concern of historians to place objects within time markers. The literature distinguishes at least three temporal types: the *moment,* that is an "isolated point on the time axis"; the *interval,* a period of time between two points in time, the lower and upper bounds, included or not, which refer us to the concepts of *terminus post quem* and *ante quem* that historians are familiar with; and finally the *period or duration* or "amount of time that cannot be localised on the time axis".[5]

In any biographical or prosopographical work, researchers are faced with these types of data, sometimes in a hybrid manner: some events are associated with a moment described in more or less precise manner (a birth, graduation, the publication of a book, …), and some situations are deemed "valid" for a more or less specified interval of time (the exercise of a function, membership in an association, marital status or wealth, political or religious belief, and so on).

Situating data in time, in terms of moments, intervals or durations in a relational model makes it possible to associate objects with a multitude of events or situations involving other objects (e.g., a person associated with a number of functions performed and whose career can be reconstructed in this way), or combining two similar objects in different temporal contexts (e.g. a person performs the same function in the same institution, but during two different periods).

To account for this variable dimension (which is sometimes coupled with imprecise sources), a system that combines effective date, post quem date and ante quem date was devised.[6] Each data item liable to change is associated with a data interval. For each date, the encoder chooses "effective", "post quem" or "ante quem", according to whether the date is certain or not and depending on whether the date marks the beginning or end of the activity. This simple system makes it possible to cover all cases. The ante quem and post quem dates appear in italics and are accompanied by a tooltip explaining their principle to the user.

Additionally, the sources do not always give dates in the classic day/month/year format. It was therefore necessary to include the option of date formats "month/year", "year" and even "± years", a way of managing dates with which data scientists are not familiar.

---

[5]C. Souveyet and R. Deneckère, Conception de bases de données. Aspects temporels, On line: *Techniques de l'ingénieur*, 1998. http://www.techniques-ingenieur.fr/res/pdf/encyclopedia/42309210-h3268.pdf.

[6]The choice between the three types of dates also applies to single events.

13.1.3 *Uncertain, Inaccurate or Inconsistent Data*

The archival material is full of uncertain, inaccurate or contradictory data, including the dating of events or situations. It is not rare, or indeed very frequent, depending on the periods and the type of material, to be confronted for the same object with very imprecise data, including chronological data, or even conflicting data. Our preferred option in this situation is to:

- recover as much data as possible, even when very imprecise (for example by allowing incomplete data format);
- mention the uncertainty of some data, where applicable;
- record the multiple or competitive nature of versions for one and the same feature (e.g. attaching multiple locations or dates of birth to the same person);
- document each data item with the sources attesting to it[7];
- where possible, arbitrate between conflicting data by assigning certainty coefficients.

13.1.4 *The Succession of Regimes*

The extension of the database downstream—namely to the judiciary in place in "Belgian" territory during the French period (1795–1814) and the Dutch period (1814–1830)—also posed a methodological problem around the very definition of its component objects. Take for example the Brussels Court of First Instance (*tribunal de première instance*), a court that has retained this name without discontinuity from the French period to the present day. One option would have been to ignore the specifics of each system, and to create a single object passing through the different periods and a one single function for the member of the judiciary exercising one and the same function in this institution during several regimes.[8] Another option, however, has been preferred. This is based on the principle that an

[7]Managing conflicting data is a particularly delicate task. When faced with such data—whether the spelling of a name or date of birth which varies from one source to another—which one should we choose? Given that this choice is not that of the encoder, it was decided that several data can be introduced for one and the same field, even those, like date of birth, which a priori can contain only one value. Then we had to address the problem of displaying the results of a query including contradictory data. The issue was resolved by associating a confidence level to each data item. In addition, encoders are free to justify their choices in a "comments" box next to each field. Between two different degrees of confidence, the computer of course displays the data at the highest degree. In some cases, however, it is impossible to determine which data item presents the greatest level of reliability. This situation requires an arbitrary choice, placing one confidence level lower than the other, and indicating the choice made under "comments". In the detailed display of a particular person, the user can view the different data encoded for the same field.

[8]Following this philosophy, the function of judge exercised, for example, by a member of the judiciary from 1813 to 1833 would have constituted a single step in his career path.

institution, while keeping its name and its staff, but existing in different countries, each with its specific political organisation, its own way of recruiting members of the judiciary, and varying competences, should be dealt with as several distinct technical objects. We therefore opted for a dividing into individual regimes, and given the complexity of the French system, sub-dividing out the Directory, the Consulate and the Empire. This device has been complemented by the possibility to link two jurisdictions, in order to describe the replacement of one by the other. In this way any personnel remaining in place during a change of regime are attached to different functions, performed in institutions that are considered to be distinct.[9]

13.2 The Database: Current Structure and Functionalities

As we have explained, the database, but also the web application that makes its content available, needs to be able to allow for and give account of the dynamics of human relations, themselves embedded in a changing institutional context. In other words, the structure as defined must be able to recreate a both synchronic and diachronic picture of the career of a member of the judiciary, of a group of such members, or of a particular court. To this end, the database has been developed in a pattern of four main parts that will be examined in turn: the management of people, the management of courts, the management of appointments and the management of the references. In the web application, each component has one or more ad hoc search engines.[10]

13.2.1 Management of People

The study of people is constructed around five categories of data: personal, socio-professional, political, intellectual and relational. The personal data, essentially identity, provide an individual's family name, given name(s), places and dates of birth and death, nobility title, honorific title(s), address(es), state of wealth, language skills, religious and philosophical convictions and sentence(s). The socio-professional data consist of the university degree(s), the career path and the activities of the person, that is associations, committees or commissions to which he belonged. The political tendency and the mandates that a person held provide

[9]To continue the previous example, the career of a member of the judiciary exercising from 1813 to 1833 as a judge at the Brussels Court of First Instance would be structured in three stages (French, Dutch and Belgian regimes).

[10]More advanced users have the option of interrogating the database (implemented in PostgreSQL) directly in SQL.

Données intellectuelles

Publication(s) de la personne

Crahay Louis, *Traité des contraventions de police contenant l'exposé des principes généraux qui les régissent et le commentaire du titre X, livre II du Code pénal et de plusieurs lois spéciales*, Bruxelles, Bruylant
Crahay Louis, *Coutumes de la ville de Maestricht*, Bruxelles, Gobbaerts, 1876
Crahay Louis, "Mendicité, vagabondage et dépôts de mendicité. Commentaire législatif de la loi du 6 mars 1866", dans *La Belgique judiciaire*, n°33, 1866, La suite se trouve dans le n°34, p. 529-540
Crahay Louis, *Coutumes du comté de Looz, de la seigneurie de Saint-Trond et du comté impérial de Reckheim*, Bruxelles, Gobbaerts, 1871, En trois volumes, publiés entre 1871 et 1897
Crahay Louis, *Essai sur l'histoire du droit coutumier de l'ancienne ville de Maestricht*, Bruxelles, Gobbaerts, 1876, 95p.
Crahay Louis, *Principes généraux de la coutume liégeoise*, Bruxelles, Gobbaerts, 1884, 139p.
Crahay Louis, Descamps Louis, *Encyclopédie des juges de paix, des greffiers et des officiers du ministère public près les tribunaux de police*, s.l., 1901
Crahay Louis, *Coutumes du Duché de Limbourg et des autres pays d'Outre-Meuse*, Bruxelles, Gobbaerts, 1889, 72p.
Crahay Louis, *De la dévolution et de la mainplévie dans le droit coutumier liégeois*, s.l., s.d.

Autobiographie

Crahay Louis, *Histoire des Crahay par Louis Crahay*, 1891

Publication(s) sur la personne

Muller Françoise, Nandrin Jean-Pierre, *Regard sur la société élitaire belge du dix-neuvième siècle. L'autobiographie du conseiller de cassation Louis Crahay (1834-1904)*, Bruxelles, Commission royale d'histoire, 2014, Bulletin de la Commission 2013

Fig. 13.1 Intellectual data of Louis Crahay, counsellor at the Court of Cassation

the 'political' category. The intellectual data correspond to publications relating to a person, obviously both those written by the person[11] as well as those written about him, giving us in this way a list of the literature referring to the member of the judiciary in question (Fig. 13.1).

Finally, the relational data show links of kinship, marriage, friendship or enmity between people, enabling the data to be processed in a network approach.

This part has intentionally been entitled "management of people", not "management of members of the judiciary". This more general heading is explained by the fact that, via the relational database, the database includes people from outside the judiciary. These are mostly relatives of the members of the judiciary or politicians. These people have not been regarded as secondary inputs. They are encoded similarly to the members of the judiciary. The difference occurs when specifying the profession: depending on whether the person is or is not part of the judiciary, the program classifies the person in one or other of the categories. Right now, the database contains 6283 persons, namely: 4313 members of the judiciary and 1970 non-members.[12] Thus it would be easy to extend the content of the database to other professional categories such as lawyers or politicians.

There are currently three types of research possible on people: simple search, advanced search and search by keywords. The search engines concerned, which do not give complete satisfaction, are to be reviewed.

[11]The intellectual data distinguish autobiographies from the other publications concerning the person, telling us very quickly which members of the judiciary have left their memoires.

[12]In March 2015.

II. Place dans la hiérarchie des juridictions

A. Juridictions de rattachement

Il y a 2 scénarios possibles de rattachement pour cette juridiction :

Cour supérieure de justice Bruxelles > Tribunal de première instance Tournai

Juridiction	Juridiction de rattachement	Date de validité du rattachement
Tribunal de première instance Tournai	Cour supérieure de justice Bruxelles	14/10/1830 - 03/10/1832

Cour de cassation Belgique > Cour d'appel Bruxelles > Tribunal de première instance Tournai

Juridiction	Juridiction de rattachement	Date de validité du rattachement
Tribunal de première instance Tournai	Cour d'appel Bruxelles	04/10/1832 - 31/12/1974
Cour d'appel Bruxelles	Cour de cassation Belgique	04/10/1832 - aujourd'hui

Fig. 13.2 Management of courts (upper courts)

13.2.2 Management of Courts

Courts and men are intrinsically linked: the history of one cannot ignore the history of the other. This has proved the most complex part of the project to complete. The application needed to be able to provide three types of information, at a given date or over a given time interval: (1) locating the particular court within the pyramid of courts; (2) telling us precisely what functions existed at that time in the particular court; (3) providing a listing of people holding office in that court during the period or at the date desired.

An example: the user wants to know the situation of the Tournai Court of First Instance in Tournai between 1830 and 1850. Since he or she did not specify month or day, the application assumes that the request relates to the period "1/1/1830 to 31/12/1850". It will inform the user that there are two courts with that name, one under the Dutch regime, the other under the Belgian regime. The user selects the second and then obtains the data sheet concerning this court. After some general information on the court in question (creation date, deletion date, competences, etc.), the user is informed about the court's place in the hierarchy of courts (Fig. 13.2).

The application draws the user's attention to the fact that, during the requested period, there were two possible hierarchical scenarios. We see that, from 1830 to 1832, the Tournai Court of First Instance was attached to the Upper Court of Justice in Brussels and that this latter court was, at that time, the highest court in our judicial system. In 1832, we observe that the "Upper Court" (*cour supérieure*) becomes "Appeal Court" (*cour d'appel*) and that this Court is itself attached to the Court of Cassation, created in October 1832. It should be noted that the courts are mentioned with hyperlinks and users can navigate from one jurisdiction to another,

B. Juridictions rattachées

Juridiction de niveaux -1 :

Afficher 25 éléments Rechercher:

Juridiction	Juridictions rattachées	Date de validité du rattachement
Tribunal de première instance Tournai	Justice de paix Antoing	14/10/1830 - *31/12/1914*
Tribunal de première instance Tournai	Justice de paix Ath	14/10/1830 - *1967*
Tribunal de première instance Tournai	Justice de paix Celles	14/10/1830 - *31/12/1914*
Tribunal de première instance Tournai	Justice de paix Ellezelles	14/10/1830 - 10/03/1848
Tribunal de première instance Tournai	Justice de paix Flobecq	10/03/1848 - *1967*
Tribunal de première instance Tournai	Justice de paix Frasnes	14/10/1830 - *1967*
Tribunal de première instance Tournai	Justice de paix Lessines	14/10/1830 - *1967*
Tribunal de première instance Tournai	Justice de paix Leuze	14/10/1830 - *1967*
Tribunal de première instance Tournai	Justice de paix Péruwelz	14/10/1830 - *1967*
Tribunal de première instance Tournai	Justice de paix Quevaucamps	14/10/1830 - *1967*
Tribunal de première instance Tournai	Justice de paix Templeuve	14/10/1830 - *1967*
Tribunal de première instance Tournai	Justice de paix Tournai (1er canton)	14/10/1830 - 15/05/1847
Tribunal de première instance Tournai	Justice de paix Tournai (2e canton)	14/10/1830 - aujourd'hui

Affichage de l'élement 1 à 13 sur 13 éléments

Fig. 13.3 Management of courts (lower courts)

always between 1830 and 1850, as the date filter is kept.[13] One also observes that in 1832 the Upper Court of Brussels changes not only its name, but also its scope, losing the Flemish legal districts that come under the responsibility of the new Appeal Court in Ghent created in 1832.

After displaying the courts on which the Tournai Court of First Instance depends, the application indicates the courts for which the Court of Tournai acts as a higher court (Fig. 13.3). Again, the date filter is applied and, in our example, the user will see all the justices of the peace in the judicial district of Tournai between 1830 and 1850.

The application then provides information on the functions provided in the court during the requested period. These functions can change, either with the creation of new functions (e.g. that of juvenile court judge (*juge des enfants*) in 1912[14] or first substitutes to the public prosecutor (*premiers substituts du procureur du Roi*) in 1920[15]), the decrease or increase in personnel or the discontinuance of a function (e.g. that of the place of vice-president of courts of first instance in 1849[16]). In this way the application provides a list of existing functions. By clicking on a function (Fig. 13.4), one obtains details of it, namely the evolution of the number of seats (with the accompanying legislative references) and a list of people holding this position (with, next to them, their dates of office). This list can be sorted by name or date.

[13]When a filter "date" is activated in this way, the user always has the option to remove it with a single click and view the court over its entire period of existence.

[14]Act of 15 May 1912 on the protection of children, *Moniteur Belge*, 27 May 1912.

[15]Act of 31 July 1920 concerning salary increases for members of the judiciary, *Moniteur Belge*, 13 August 1920.

[16]Law of 15 June 1849 concerning the reduction of the personnel of courts and certain tribunals, *Moniteur Belge*, 21 June 1849.

Fig. 13.4 Evolution of a function (Chamber president at the Court of Cassation)

This part has required a census of all legislation establishing, modifying or discontinuing a function or a court. Particular attention needs to be paid, however, to the time gap between the enactment of an act and its application. For example, an act reducing irremovable judicial staff could be implemented only by not replacing a retiring judge. The effective discontinuation here could take place many years after the enactment of the act. Such was the case for one of the two positions of chamber president at the Court of Cassation, which was discontinued by an act of 1849 but with the holder remaining in office until his retirement in 1857. In this case, 1857 is considered the date of termination of the function, the source of this information being the 1849 Act (Fig. 13.4).

It must be noted that one must first encode the courts before one can attach people to them. To date, the database includes 680 courts.[17]

The extension of the database to the Congo confronts us with many inaccurate data, reflecting the process of construction of a judicial apparatus in a country with shifting borders. Far from 19th century Belgium with its stable judicial apparatus with well-established contours inherited from the Napoleonic period, the Congo—especially the Congo Free State—confronts us with at times temporary and/or peripatetic courts, which are also particularly complex. Let us illustrate our point with a few examples: an order of 20 November 1897 establishes a military tribunal (*conseil de guerre*) at Banzyville. Its jurisdiction is "determined to the north, east

[17]In March 2015.

and south by the Ubangi District, to the west and south-west by a line from the river immediately downstream of Mokwangai station and meeting longitude 20° east of Greenwich meridian at its intersection with 4° latitude north".[18] What we have therefore is a military tribunal established in a particular locality—Banzyville—but the jurisdictional boundaries of which are particularly unclear. Sometimes it is the place that cannot be precisely located, as illustrated by legislation couched in the following form: a military tribunal is established "in the capital of the northern zone of the Cataractes district". This capital, like others, cannot be identified for the simple reason that it was never fixed… It was not until the early 20th century that a real regional organisation was introduced in the colony. Before that, one is faced with temporary and theoretical boundaries that are particularly difficult to process. The final example of these colonial particularities: the jurisdictional area of a Congolese court may extend over a particular zone, but exclude a particular territory. These exclusions have also to be taken into account in one way or another in the database. In this way the extension of the database poses a new challenge requiring an adaptation of the application structure to these data.

13.2.3 Management of Appointments

If the study of a social group requires knowledge of its members and the legal rules governing its operation, it also requires us to take account of the practices found within it. The management of appointments focuses on practices observed in judicial appointments. Which minister appointed a particular member of the judiciary to a particular function? Who were the other candidates for the same function? What was their seniority on the bench at the time of the appointment? Their age? What opinion did the judicial and political powers-that-be hold about these candidates? And so on. All these questions are addressed in this part of the database that is adapted for the three types of appointment that existed in Belgium until recently: direct appointment by the King (for the lower judiciary and public prosecutors), appointment by King upon presentations made by a judicial body and a political body[19] (for vice-presidents and presidents in the courts of first instance and for counsellors), and election by the counsellors (for chamber presidents and the first presidents).

In the case of direct appointment, one has simply to select the names of all the candidates and that of the Minister of Justice, and the program automatically imports from the "management of people" part the political tendency of each protagonist, where known. It then goes on to establish whether or not there is a

[18]Official Bulletin, Congo Free State, 1898.

[19]The judicial body is always the Court where the place is vacant while the political body is the Senate for the Court of Cassation and one of the provincial councils of the jurisdiction concerned for the Appeal Courts (there is a complex system of alternating between the various provincial councils).

correspondence between the political tendency of the named candidate and that of the Minister, and the percentage of candidates of each tendency.[20] The same features are available for appointments made upon presentations. In addition, the lists of candidates submitted by the judicial and political bodies are studied down to the voting details. The study of elected offices focuses on the persons' seniority in the court. The database is programmed to calculate the age and length of service in the Court by each counsellor at his date of election. This because length of service appears more important here than age, at least, this is the assumption made.

While this offers a significant research potential—especially concerning the issue of "political appointments"[21]—this part entails, in return, heavy and tedious encoding work, which is why until now just 138 appointments have been encoded. Given the sensitive information it contains, this section also calls for particular vigilance with regard to the protection of privacy (see below).

13.2.4 Management of References

"References" should be understood here as synonymous with "sources." To enable users always to verify information themselves, the one, or several sources of information are routinely mentioned. This constraint, although demanding, is necessary for a critical use of the sources by the user. An encoding system adapted to the different sources has been implemented.

Moreover, it is possible to link every reference to one or more documents, in the form of a pdf file or digital photographs. These can be texts, like a royal appointment order or an Act modifying the jurisdiction of a court, but also a representation of a member of the judiciary (portraits, busts, photographs, etc.), or a document containing a person's family tree. It is conceivable—with due respect for legislation on intellectual property—to scan the archives, giving users direct contact with the document.[22]

---

[20]In fact, a double calculation is made. The first relates to all candidates, including those whose political views are unknown. The second calculation applies only to those whose political views are known, while indicating the percentage of unknown data. Besides political tendency, this part is used to encode the opinions given by the authorities consulted. The opinion is taken in its entirety, the encoder also mentions whether it is favourable or unfavourable, and ticks, from a predefined list, the criteria put forward.

[21]Regarding appointments to the Court of Cassation, see: F. Muller, *La Cour de Cassation à l'aune des rapports entre pouvoirs. De sa naissance dans le modèle classique de la séparation des pouvoirs à l'aube d'une extension de la fonction juridictionnelle 1832–1914/1936*, Bruges, La Charte, 2011 (Justice et Société).

[22]With the "comments" fields that can be filled for any field of the database, the encoder can add useful information. Take the example of the Act of 25 October 1919 amending temporarily the judicial organisation and proceedings before the courts'. This law establishes the single judge system in Belgium. This information does not transpire from its title. A user wanting to know when the single judge system was initiated in our country can find it by entering 'single judge' in a keyword search, the encoder having taken care to indicate this under 'comments'.

13.3 Some Challenges Posed by the Extension of the Space-Time Framework

The obtaining of the research project "Belgafrican Magistrates Social Networks (1885–1962)" marks the beginning of a new era for the database. While providing the wherewithal to make certain improvements to the application and thus to further increase its potential by making it increasingly generic, the complexity of the data to be incorporated represents a challenge.

The jurisdiction part lies at the heart of the application, as the criterion for being viewed as a 'member of the judiciary' is attachment to at least one jurisdiction. Unfortunately, this part in its current state does not support well the African data and, to a lesser extent, the more recently encoded data on the Belgian military tribunals.[23] We have mentioned earlier the complexity of the African data. It will now be possible to add certain characteristics of jurisdictions: peripatetic jurisdiction or not, temporary jurisdiction or not,[24] and so on. Right now the indication of the competences (civil, criminal, appeal, military, etc.) of a particular jurisdiction does not make allowance for changes over time. It will be necessary to make this data more dynamic by adding a date range to each competence. But the heart of the problem lies particularly in creating a module for managing jurisdictional areas. This will be useful both for the Congo and for military justice, but also if, one day, there is a wish to incorporate the 2014 revision of Belgian judicial districts.

One goal of the "Belgafrican Magistrates Social Networks" project is to shed light on the constitution of "colonial science" in Belgium and on the intellectual networks active in the legal journals. For this, the relational data will need to include a new type of relationship, namely the intellectual link between two people. Until then, relational data were envisaged in terms of "concrete" links, i.e. people related by kinship, marriage or friendship/enmity. From now on relational data will be able to connect two people who do not know each other (one of them might even be dead when the relationship is created) but who share and develop a common understanding of a given topic.

The constant expansion of the research object, which originally involved a "distant" period (1830–1914), raises questions concerning the protection of privacy. A system of protection for the most recent data will have be set up so that only researchers authorised to access such data will be able to consult it.

Such changes, in particular those concerning the jurisdictions, require significant re-engineering to transform the existing data structure into one able to meet

[23]An example: the military tribunal for the province of Antwerp, created in 1831, also includes from 1899 the province of Limburg. This change needs to be managed in such a way that this military tribunal represents just a single entry in the database.

[24]Military tribunals in time of war or assize courts are temporary jurisdictions. It is not possible to create a new jurisdiction in the database every time they meet. The indication "temporary" suffices, and the period during which the court meets will be deduced from the judges attached to it.

these new requirements. Such a project must be accompanied by the management of already encoded data and their migration, as well as adapting all encoding and consultation interfaces.[25] If the prosopography of the 21st century seeks to take into consideration ever more complex subjects, those working with it need to be particularly vigilant to the constant and rapid evolution of computer tools on which it is based. Well beyond the issue of dematerialisation of archives, the design of prosopographical databases confronts historians with multiple—and sometimes new—concerns, from the structuring of data from large and diversified corpuses to the maintenance and to the security of these new tools.

[25]This will have an organisational impact alongside the technical impact, because during this period of technical adaptation and data migration, researchers and encoders attached to the project will be unable to access this data.

Chapter 14
Conflicts, Tensions and Solidarity Within the Judicial District: A Socio-Professional Study of the Judiciary of the "Belgian" Departments Under the French Directory (1795–1799)

Emmanuel Berger

The turbulent history of Belgian justice during the French period (1795–1815) has been the subject of much debate and controversy, testifying to the magnitude of the breaks with the past that the Revolution brought with it. The questions raised focus, among others, on the export of the French judicial model, the practices of the new courts, the election of judges, and the establishment of the system of the people's jury. The overturning of the justice system of the *Ancient Regime* poses in particular the question of continuities and breaks with the former order, of resistance to and support of the Republic by existing judges.[1] Significant advances have been made in this area over the past 20 years thanks to the work of both general and legal historians like Xavier Rousseaux,[2] Marie-Sylvie Dupont-Bouchat, Fred Stevens,[3] Axel Tixhon,[4] Jacques Logie,[5] Jean-Pierre Nandrin[6] and

[1]E. Berger (dir.), *L'acculturation des modèles policiers et judiciaires français en Belgique et aux Pays-Bas (1795–1815)*, Brussels, Archives générales du Royaume, 2010.

[2]X. Rousseaux, M.-S. Dupont-Bouchat and C. Vael (dir.), *Révolutions et justice pénale en Europe. Modèles français et traditions nationales (1730–1830)*, Paris, L'Harmattan, 1999.

[3]F. Stevens, "Het tribunal criminel te Antwerpen (19 September 1794–19 februari 1795). Een nieuwe 'Bloed Raed' op het einde van de 18e eeuw?", in *Acta Falconis*, 1983, 83, pp. 176–221.

[4]A. Tixhon, "L'activité du tribunal correctionnel de Namur durant la période française (an IV—1814)", in *Annales de la société archéologique de Namur*, 1998, vol. 72, pp. 291–341.

[5]J. Logie, *Les magistrats des cours et des tribunaux en Belgique (1794–1914)*, Geneva, Librairie Droz S.A., 1998.

[6]X. Rousseaux and J.-P. Nandrin, "Le personnel judiciaire en Belgique à travers les révolutions (1780–1832). Quelques hypothèses de recherches et premiers résultats", in *Le personnel politique dans la transition de l'Ancien Régime au Nouveau Régime en Belgique (1780–1830)*, Kortrijk, Anciens Pays et Assemblées d'Etat, 1993, pp. 13–69.

E. Berger (✉)
University of Namur, Namur, Belgium
e-mail: emmanuelberger@hotmail.com

A. Hondeghem et al. (eds.), *Modernisation of the Criminal Justice Chain and the Judicial System*, Ius Gentium: Comparative Perspectives on Law and Justice 50, DOI 10.1007/978-3-319-25802-7_14

myself.[7] Thanks to this research, the area which is now Belgium is probably today one of the European territories whose legal history is best known for the revolutionary and Napoleonic period. Belgium stands out also for the development of a prosopographical database covering the entire French period, conceived as part of a larger project, "Prosopographie des magistrats belges 1795–1960" ("Prosopography of Belgian Magistrates").[8] This project set out to provide both synchronic and diachronic views of a particular court or judge and of relational networks. The data produced for the French period have been gathered mainly from the records produced by Jacques Logie.[9] Information technology has made it possible to rationalise the data collected by Logie and to interrogate the database on the social origins, professional careers, political opinions and financial resources of the members of the judiciary. Most importantly it opens the possibility of cross-comparing the activity of the courts with the profiles of the individual judges who composed them. In this article, I shall focus on the identity and penal practices of judges and prosecutors serving under the Directory (*Directoire*), in the key jurisdictional area created by the Revolution, that is, the legal district (*arrondissement judiciaire*).

According to the Constitution of Year III (1795), the judicial district was a place of both prosecution of offences and punishment of crimes. It was in the chief city of this district that the sessions of the grand jury (*jury d'accusation*) and the correctional (i.e. minor offences) court (*tribunal correctionnel*) took place. The grand jury was responsible for determining whether there was sufficient evidence of guilt to place the accused before the criminal court of the department. The task of the correctional court was to try minor offences, those for which the punishment did not extend to the loss of civil rights (*peine infamante*), the death sentence or penal servitude (*peine afflictive*) but exceeded the value of three working days or three days in jail. Prison sentences were not to exceed two years. As a pivot and relay in the judicial system, the judicial district represents one of the cornerstones of the criminal organisation of the Directory.[10]

The chief judge of the district was the director of the grand jury (*directeur du jury d'accusation*), appointed every six months from among the elected judges of the civil court of the department. As an officer of the judicial police, he directed the prosecution of all offences (*infractions*) together with the justices of the peace

[7]E. Berger, *La justice pénale sous la Révolution. Les enjeux d'un modèle judiciaire libéral*, Rennes, Presses universitaires de Rennes, 2008.

[8]See the contribution of Aurore François and Françoise Muller in this volume.

[9]J. Logie, *Les magistrats des cours et tribunaux en Belgique (1794–1814). Essai d'approche politique et sociologique*, PhD thesis for Université Paris IV, prosopographical index, 1995. The data were encoded under the direction of Catherine Goffin (C. Goffin, 'Les magistrats dans les départements réunis sous le Directoire (an IV-an VIII): Un corps social à part entière?' in E. Berger (dir.), *L'acculturation des modèles policiers et judiciaires français en Belgique et aux Pays-Bas (1795–1815)*, Brussels, Archives générales du Royaume, 2010, pp. 99–108).

[10]Berger, *La justice pénale…*, pp. 24–27.

(*justice de paix*), who fell under his supervision. He also chaired the meetings of the grand jury held every ten days and chaired the correctional court together with two justices of the peace. Following the liberal principles of the penal model of the Revolution, the powers of the public prosecutors were limited to requesting the application of the law and enforcing judgments. Unlike jury directors, prosecutors—known at the time as 'government commissioners'—were appointed and could be dismissed by the Directory. While the limitation of the powers of the commissioners was motivated by the desire to preserve the independence of the judiciary from the influence of government, it proved to be a great source of conflict and tension between independent judges aware of their popular legitimacy and commissioners required to apply the penal policies of the Directory.[11]

In the Belgian departments, tensions related to the prerogatives of judges and commissioners were increased by the recent annexation of these territories to the Republic. The territory that was to become Belgium was as a result administered by a number of so-called French "insiders" sent by Paris and therefore perceived as "foreigners" by the people. In his remarkable thesis, Jacques Logie traced the development of the new judicial organisation and the process of selecting judges. Shortly after the annexation of Belgium on 9 Vendémiaire Year IV (1 January 1795), people's representatives Pérès and Portiez, succeeded by Bouteville, proceeded to the first appointments starting on 7 Frimaire Year IV (28 November 1795). The appointment of judges was viewed as a transitional measure pending the elections of Germinal Year V (March–April 1797) (Table 14.1).

On the eve of the first judicial election, in Year V, the proportion of French judges was 24 %. This is explained both by the need to fill the positions vacated by the many refusals and resignations that followed the first appointments[12] and by the political desire to place Frenchmen from the interior in each jurisdiction. The authorities were suspicious of the conservatism of the Belgian judiciary and prompted their countrymen to accept judicial office in the Belgian departments. To promote their arrival, the Directory decided on 26 Frimaire Year IV (17 December 1795) to allocate an advance of 10,000 livres in assignats as travel expenses.[13] The need to have trusted men in key positions explains the high proportion of French judges (36 %) among chairmen and public prosecutors (*accusateurs publics*) in criminal courts as well as commissioners of the department level and their assistants (*substituts*). In the theoretically less sensitive jurisdictions such as district and civil courts, the French made up only 23 % of the judiciary. Here it should be said that this proportion met the earlier instructions of the Committee of Public Safety (*Comité de Salut Public*) that the people's representatives should not exceed a maximum of 25 % Frenchmen for government appointments.[14]

[11]Ibid.

[12]Just over half (58 %) of judges refused their appointments (Logie, *Les magistrats des cours* ..., p. 117).

[13]Ibid., p. 172.

[14]Ibid., p. 111.

Table 14.1 Proportion of French members of the judiciary in the nine Belgian departments

	Before the first judicial elections of Year V/1797		At the end of the directory (Year VIII/1799)	
	No. French	% French	No. French	% French
Civil court judges (dept.)	43/186	23	19/202	9
Criminal court chairmen (dept.)	5/9	56	3/9	33
Public prosecutors (dept.)	7/9	78	3/9	33
Commissioners (dept.)	6/9	67	8/9	89
Substitutes (dept.)	5/9	56	4/9	44
Commissioners (district)	8/35	23	12/35	34
Total	74/302	24	49/273	18

The differentiated presence of French judges according to the level and type of court would increase at the end of the Directory. At that time, in November 1799, just 11 % of electable functions (civil court judge, chairman of the criminal court and public prosecutor) were occupied by Frenchmen from France itself. Conversely, they had increased to 45 % in the positions appointed by the government (commissioners and assistants). This trend is visible at judicial district level where in Year VIII (1799) 34 % of commissioners were Frenchmen but just 9 % of the civil court judges, from whose ranks the jury directors came. The extent of this imbalance shows the limits of the various laws that authorised the Directory to bypass the election process and appoint judges directly. If, in the Belgian departments, the government used this prerogative to appoint nearly a quarter of the judges, these numbers are swollen by the particular circumstances of the department of Deux-Nèthes in which all the judges were appointed following the cancellation of the elections in Year V (1797).[15] The Belgian courts in fact present a varied landscape, populated mostly by 'local' judges deriving their legitimacy from their being elected, and by government commissioners, the instruments of the new regime, a significant portion of whom came from metropolitan France. It remains to determine what were the effects and consequences of this imbalance both in the organisation and in the practices of the penal jurisdictions of the legal district. For this, I will study a sample of eleven legal districts, the archives of which for the Directory period have been particularly well preserved (Table 14.2).

For all legal districts together, the proportion of Frenchmen from metropolitan France among the jury directors (17 %)[16] and the government commissioners (37 %)[17] corresponds to that recorded by Jacques Logie. The situation varies greatly, however, from one legal district to the next. Some (Waremme and Liège) had no French judge at all, while others (Nivelles and Turnhout) exhibit a greater

[15]Ibid., p. 219.

[16]I.e., 16 out of 94 jury directors.

[17]I.e., 10 out of 27 government commissioners.

Table 14.2 Presence of French members of the judiciary during the Directory

7 Frimaire Year IV/28 November 1795 to 18 Brumaire Year VIII/9 November 1799 (47 months)					
Departments	Legal districts	Jury directors		Government commissioners	
		No.	Duration (months)	No.	Duration (months)
Dyle	Brussels interior	1	2	0	0
	Nivelles	1	6	3	29
Jemappes	Mons	0	0	2	14
Deux-Nèthes	Mechelen	6	21	0	0
	Turnhout	3	11	2	21
	Antwerp	2	2	1	24
Scheldt	Ghent	0	0	2	17
Lys	Bruges	3	16	1	1
Ourthe	Waremme	0	0	0	0
	Liège	0	0	0	0
Total		16	58	11	106

metropolitan presence. This presence in fact varies greatly depending on judicial function. As in the previous results, the French are well represented among the government commissioners. In Nivelles, Turnhout and Antwerp they occupy their office for much of the Directory and in Ghent and Mons for a significant part of the regime. For jury directors, the situation is reversed. With the exception of Malines, Bruges and Turnhout, French judges of the departmental court never held the six-month position of jury director.

This finding can be explained by the extremely reduced number of judges from the "interior". On the eve of the Consulate, the latter represented a tangible presence only in the departments of Deux-Nèthes (5), Lys (4) and Forêts (4).[18] This relative weight could explain the higher proportion of French jury directors in Bruges (Lys), Mechelen (Deux-Nèthes) and Turnhout (Deux-Nèthes). The disaffection of the judges from metropolitan France is also explained by factors common to all Belgian members of the judiciary. In generally, the post of jury director aroused little enthusiasm. Besides the heavy workload (investigation of every offence committed in the legal district, the judgment of minor offences and meetings of the grand jury), judges appointed as jury directors were required to leave the capital city of the department to reside for six months in that of the legal district. The sometimes long travelling times involved had the effect of separating families. They also posed financial problems in that the judges concerned had to pay for their housing.[19] Finally, in the Flemish or German-speaking districts, it could be inappropriate to send French judges with insufficient knowledge of the local language.

[18]Ibid., p 236

[19]Ibid., pp. 143–144.

It is, however, interesting to note that such obstacles do not seem to have discouraged all judges "from the interior". One such case was Jean Tourn from Geneva who was employed in the Douai district during the Revolution. After serving as chief clerk (*chef de bureau*) in the central and upper administration of Belgium and then in the Governing Council, he was appointed judge in the Departmental Court of Deux-Nèthes on 7 Frimaire Year IV (28 November 1795).[20] Re-elected until the end of the Directory, he served twice as jury director of the legal district of Turnhout: from Prairial to Messidor Year V (2 months) then from Brumaire to Floréal Year VI (6 months). While Jean Tourn probably had some knowledge of Flemish before arriving in Belgium, the conditions for the exercise of his functions in the little city of Turnhout remain no less enigmatic. Tourn's case is not unique. Leaving aside François Louis Huttin, Desmyter[21] and Jean-Louis Carlier, all from Dunkirk, the six other French directors of the jury come from regions with no apparent relations with the Belgian legal districts: the Creole Guillaume Filleul, a native of Saint-Domingue, was director of the jury in Bruges between Floréal Year VII and Brumaire Year VIII (6 months), and Jacques Camus, a native of Metz, sat in Mechelen between Messidor Year IV and Floréal Year V (11 months).[22]

If we go on to analyse the geographical origin of the government commissioners from the "interior", the heterogeneity observed for judges disappears: eight of the eleven commissioners are natives of the Nord department.[23] This tells us that the Ministry of Justice deliberately favoured the appointment of individuals from the border areas. This is a consistent policy, with "northerners" appointed throughout the Directory. This choice is explained in part by greater ease in these territories of recruiting commissioners ready to travel to the Belgian departments. But the main reason was the requirement to have personnel sufficiently familiar with the areas in which they performed their duties. A minimal knowledge of local languages and customs was essential for controlling the penal activities of the courts. And while the government was in favour of integrating the commissioners within local populations, excessive proximity could prove compromising.[24] Jean-Antoine Chaix, a native of Geneva and commissioner to the district of Mons, learned this to his cost. Appointed in Brumaire Year VI (November 1797), he was dismissed on 29 Nivôse Year VII (18 January 1799) on suspicion of *protecting the caste of*

---

[20]Ibid., prosopographical index, pp. 339–340.

[21]Desmyter's first name is not known.

[22]The other judges are Edem Bourdault (dept. Haute-Marne) in the legal district of Antwerp, Jean-René Maloigne (dept. Seine) in the legal district of Nivelles, Pierre-Alexandre Lefèbvre (dept. Somme) in the legal district of Brussels-interior and Etienne Arbeltier (dept. Haute-Marne) in the legal district of Mechelen.

[23]The three correctional court commissioners from other departments are: Etienne Martin Chompré (born in Paris), commissioner in Mons and then Aalst; Jean Antoine Chaix (born in Geneva and then a lawyer in Paris), commissioner in Mons; and Antoine Jean Bazire Lacoudraye (dept. of Vienne), commissioner in Ghent.

[24]Ibid., propoposographical index, pp. 40–41

nobility, frequenting their homes, and visiting in their remand centres priests sentenced to transportation.

The issue of the integration of judges in their legal districts is fundamental to the study of the impact of the repressive policies adopted in Paris. At the end of the Directory, 86 %[25] of Belgian civil court judges had resided in the department before taking office, with 58 %[26] established in its chief city.[27] In the legal districts covered by my study, I arrive at similar results, with 83 %[28] of jury directors already resident in the department of the legal district in which they were appointed and 64 %[29] in the chief city of their jurisdiction. However, significant variations appear from one legal district to another. In Brussels, Nivelles, Mons, Ghent and Liège the majority of the directors of the jury (86 %) resided in the chief city.[30] In Mechelen and Antwerp only half of the judges lived there.[31] Finally, no judge came originally from Waremme or Turnhout.[32] These variations can be explained by several factors. First, most of the chief cities of the legal districts studied were also those of the departments. It follows that judges living there were more numerous than in the other legal districts. Conversely, it was more difficult to find men to serve as judges in less densely populated rural districts and those like Waremme with no strong legal tradition. The limited presence of jury directors from Antwerp and Mechelen is due to the cancellation of the elections of Germinal Year V and the subsequent difficulties faced by the Directory in constituting the departmental court.[33]

Despite the government's interference in judicial elections and the appointment of French judges, the majority of jury directors originated from the legal districts in which they performed their duties and were therefore relatively close to litigants. This strong trend is even more interesting given that Minister of Justice Genissieu had explicitly forbidden on 6 Ventôse Year IV (25 February 1796) that jury directors be overly integrated into local populations. When Charles Lambrechts was appointed Minister of Justice, the arrangements made with regard to the hierarchy (*ordre du tableau*) and the appointment of native jury directors had visibly not come to an end. On 3 Floréal Year VI (22 April 1798), the minister reminded those concerned, in a circular, of the absolute need to respect the *invariable order of the table*. This circular does not seem to have produced the desired effect, with Lambrechts again condemning on 16 Fructidor Year VI (2 September

[25] I.e., 175 out of 202 judges.

[26] I.e., 118 out of 202 judges.

[27] Ibid., p. 236.

[28] I.e., 58 of the 70 jury directors whose place of residence I have been able to determine.

[29] I.e., 45 of the 70 jury directors whose place of residence I have been able to determine.

[30] I.e., 36 of the 42 jury directors whose place of residence I have been able to determine.

[31] I.e., 8 of the 16 jury directors whose place of residence I have been able to determine.

[32] Not one of the 10 jury directors whose place of residence I have been able to determine.

[33] Ibid., p. 237.

1798) *the arbitrary arrangements of some courts* [produced by] *self-interest and unfortunately sometimes esprit de corps.*

If the government condemned the *esprit de corps* of civilian courts that enabled jury directors to serve in the legal districts of their place of residence, it did not hesitate to operate in the same way with its own representatives. At the end of the Directory, 83 %[34] of the Belgian commissioners to the correctional courts were appointed in their department of birth and 57 %[35] in the chief city of their legal district. These percentages, similar to those obtained for the jury directors, would likely be higher if data on place of residence were available. Moreover, contrary to legal district judges, appointed on a temporary basis, the government representatives are characterised by relative stability. In this way, 11 of the 35 correctional court commissioners remained in office throughout the Directory.[36] In the departments of Dyle and Ourthe, these personnel were particularly permanent, in four and three out of five legal districts respectively. If such stability can be explained both by reasons of political loyalty and legal competence, it also gave the Directory an effective tool for promoting its penal policies and maintaining public order within the district.

To understand the different dynamics surrounding the relationship between the jury directors and the government commissioners, I will go on to analyse the execution in the Belgian departments of the legislation on the religious police and specifically the issue of non-juror priests. The law of 7 Vendémiaire Year IV (29 September 1795) demanded that ministers of religion recognise that *sovereignty lies with the universality of French citizens* and that they promise *submission and obedience to the laws of the Republic.* Any individual not making this declaration was liable to a fine of 500 livres and from three months to one year imprisonment. The oath requirement made the law highly unpopular and aroused considerable resistance among both priests and ordinary citizens. The disobedience movement rapidly became a national matter, creating many tensions within the judiciary.

Given the low number of French jury directors (14 %), it is not easy to compare their repressive activity with that of their Belgian counterparts. Based on the selected legal districts, the French judges do not stand out from the others for excessive zeal. When the law of 7 Vendémiaire Year IV was published—on dates in the months of Floréal and Prairial Year V (April and May 1797) depending on the department—the first correctional courts to prosecute priests who refused to make the declaration of submission were those of Liège and Brussels, both chaired by Belgian judges. In Liège, Jean Lemoine handed down the first judgment on 25 Floréal Year V (14 May 1797). Paul Delchef, the parish priest of Saint-Nicolas-aux-Mouches was sentenced

[34]I.e., 19 of the 23 government commissioners to the correctional courts whose place of residence I have been able to determine.

[35]I.e., 13 of the 23 government commissioners to the correctional courts whose place of residence I have been able to determine.

[36]Note that two of the commissioners are French: Jean Jacques Bernard Laroche (leg. distr. Louvain, dept. Dyle) and Etienne Martin Chompré (leg. distr. Aalst, dept. Scheldt).

to three months imprisonment and a fine of 500 livres. In the following days and throughout the month of Prairial, the Liège Correctional Court pronounced another twelve convictions. In Brussels, Englebert Joseph Ippersiel pronounced the first sentence on 3 Prairial Year V (22 May 1797) against the priest of the Hôpital Saint-Jean, Joseph François De Hase. At the sessions of 6 and 7 Prairial, the court sentenced five other Brussels priests. Following his conviction, De Hase appealed to the criminal court of the Dyle. On 13 Prairial, the latter acquitted the priest on the grounds that the law on religious police was not constitutional and not enforceable in the Belgian departments. The sentence caused a political earthquake insofar as the judges were challenging the prerogatives of the Directory with respect to the publication of laws. They were also taking the liberty of suspending the execution of the laws—constituting a case of misconduct in public office (*forfaiture*)[37]—and challenging the legitimacy of the Directory's religious policy. At the judicial level, this judgment of the criminal court led to a general paralysis of prosecutions until the coup of 18 Fructidor Year V (4 September 1797).[38]

The controversy caused by the enforcement of the law of 7 Vendémiaire Year IV originated in the repressive activities of the chairmen of the correctional courts of Liège and Brussels, Lemoine and Ippersiel. These were not, however rabid Jacobins[39] and had many things in common: early collaboration with the French regime, electoral legitimacy in Year V and professional careers continuing until their death. They matched the general profile of judges during the Directory: 61 % of judges came from the elections in Year V and 80 % were law graduates. If Lemoine and Ippersiel exercised administrative functions at the time of the second

[37]Art. 644 of the Code of Offences and Penalties (*Code des délits et des peines*): "guilty of misconduct in public office (…): 4°. Any judge interfering with the exercise of legislative power, by making regulations, or stopping or suspending the execution of the law within his jurisdiction."

[38]On the De Hase case and the problem of non-juror priests, see: E. Berger, "La justice républicaine face aux prêtres insermentés sous le Directoire. Le cas des 9 départements belges", in E. Wenzel (dir.) *Justice et religion. Regards croisés: histoire et droit*, Editions universitaires d'Avignon, 2010, pp. 57–69; J.-L. Halpérin, "Cassation et dénonciation pour forfaiture dans les départements réunis sous le Directoire", in R. Martinage and J.-P. Royer (dir.), *Justice et institutions françaises en Belgique (1795/1815). Traditions et innovations autour de l'annexion. Actes du colloque tenu à l'université de Lille II les 1, 2 et 3 juin 1995*, Lille, L'Espace juridique, 1996, pp. 245–258.

[39]A law graduate, Lemoine was a member of the municipality of Herve in Year III. He was appointed deputy judge of the Civil Court of Ourthe on 27 Frimaire Year IV and served as effective judge until the elections of the year V. Re-elected in Germinal, Lemoine continued to hold office throughout the Directory. Appointed judge at Huy in Brumaire Year IX then at Liège in Nivôse, he died on 27 March 1807 (Logie, *Les magistrats des cours* … prosopographical index, p. 234). Ippersiel was a former lawyer at the Council of Brabant who was chief clerk at the Central and Higher Administration of Belgium. Appointed judge of the Court of Dyle on 28 Frimaire Year IV, he was re-elected in Year V and sat, like Lemoine, until the end of the Directory. He continued his career until his death in 1830, occupying successively the functions of president of the Court of Nivelles (Year VIII), of Brussels (Year VIII) and counsellor to the Imperial Court of Brussels (1813) (Logie, *Les magistrats des cours* … prosopographical index, p. 204).

occupation, their election in Year V and the continuation of their careers after the fall of the Directory reflect the moderation of their political views.[40]

The law enforcement initiative of the Liège and Brussels courts was in fact due less to the zeal of the judges than to the alacrity with which each departmental administration decided to publish the law of 7 Vendémiaire Year IV. The departments of Ourthe and Dyle were the first to publish the law, on 29 Germinal and 1 Floréal Year V respectively (18 and 20 April 1797). The controversy that arose shortly afterwards with the case of the priest De Hase led the other departmental administrations and the municipalities to suspend implementation of the law until the legislative body had ruled on the removal or retention of the oath. The virtual absence of correctional sentences after Prairial V (May 1797) does not signify that the jury directors gave up enforcing the law. In danger of being accused of misconduct in office, and subject to intense pressure from the Minister of Justice, government commissioners and the public prosecutor, several judges sought to cope with this totally new situation. In Mons, Judge Nicolas Marie Joseph Perlau had taken over as jury director in Floréal (early May 1797), that is, at the time of publication of the law of 7 Vendémiaire Year IV. A former lawyer at the Council of Hainaut, he had been appointed national commissioner to the district court of Ath in Year III and judge at the departmental court of Jemappes on 7 Frimaire Year IV (28 November 1795).[41] He had just been elected in Germinal Year V when the first accusations against non-juror priests reached the justices of the peace (*juge de paix*). Faced with the refusal of the latter to act *on the grounds of the possible suspension of this law by the legislature*, Perlau reminded them that one of the fundamental principles of the judicial organisation of the Revolution was that it was not for the judge to interpret the legitimacy of the law but that he had, like an automaton, to ensure its immediate implementation.[42] In line with his duty, Perlau tried the Capuchin Pierre-Joseph Rinchon on 9 Fructidor Year V (26 August 1797), sentencing him to three months in jail and a fine of 500 livres. This judgment remains exceptional, however, to the extent that among the legal districts studied this is the only sentence pronounced by a correctional court before the coup of 18 Fructidor.

The correspondence between the members of the judiciary shows Perlau's uncomfortable position. While urging the justices of the peace to activate prosecutions, his efforts seem not to have convinced the commissioner to the civil court of the department, Simon Nazaire Chenard. The latter considered, with regard to the Rinchon judgment, that *it is ridiculous that we have begun to take action against such an insignificant person when we are culpably inactive against abbots whose*

[40]With the exception of Deux-Nèthes, populated by Jacobin judges, the other Belgian departments consisted mostly of conservative and moderate Republicans (Logie, *Les magistrats des cours …*, p. 239).

[41]Ibid., proposographical index, pp. 284–285.

[42]Letter addressed to the justice of the peace of the legal canton of Ath on 25 Prairial Year V (AE Mons, fonds du tribunal correctionnel de Mons, registre de correspondances du directeur de jury de Mons no. 8, lettre no. A237).

offences are much older and for which society demands vengeance.[43] Summoned to explain the slow progress of the prosecutions, Perlau had already expressed his dismay to the public prosecutor, Joseph Giraud.[44] The jury director's discouragement reflects the need to find a compromise with the population of Mons, given the risk to public peace and order. He assures Giraud: *this becomes very serious, to the extent of undermining (…) security and public tranquillity and particularly that of government officials.*[45] Faced with pressure from his superiors and the unpopularity of the law, Perlau for a moment contemplated resignation. He would, however, remain in office until the end of his semester, in Brumaire Year VI (November 1797).[46] The discomfort and the impasse described by Perlau reveal the precarious position of the jury director, being required, as a government agent, to execute a law that was rejected by the majority of citizens who had elected him. Perlau's attitude is in fact characteristic of moderate Republicans, who had sided with the new regime but were attached to the interests of the local population. Like other moderates such as Lemoine and Ippersiel, he would remain in post throughout the Directory and serve in the court of Mons until his death in 1824.

The penal proceedings described in Brussels, Liège and Mons were, as I have said, exceptional. In the other legal districts, the courts, mostly chaired by Belgians, remained silent, waiting patiently for the outcome of discussions in the Legislature. The study of the legal district of Mechelen suggests that this strategy was also followed by the French judges. Martin Louis Joseph Lebrête from Douai held there the post of director of the jury from Prairial to Thermidor Year V (3 months). A lawyer of Jacobin opinions, he had been chief clerk to the Government Council during the second occupation. Appointed judge of the Court of Deux-Nèthes on 7 Frimaire Year IV, he was re-elected in Germinal Year V by the seceding assembly whose operations were ultimately not validated. Despite this, the Directory appointed him to the same office on 23 Fructidor. Lebrête's political convictions had little influence on penal activity at the Mechelen Correctional Court since no non-juror priest was judged during the months in question. The primary cause of this inertia was, as in Mons, to be found in the attitude of the justices of the peace.

Shortly after the publication of the law of 7 Vendémiaire by the municipality of Mechelen, Lebrête enjoined the justices of the peace of the legal district *to execute the above laws.* He finished his circular letter by seeking to convince himself that *your zeal for the public good, and the dedication to and execution of duty required of you by the law assure me that you will neglect nothing.* The doubts expressed regarding the enthusiasm of the justices of the peace to pursue such cases were

---

[43]Letter to Justice Minister Merlin dated 12 Fructidor Year V (AN BB18 400/DD4218).

[44]Letter to public prosecutor Joseph Giraud dated 27 Prairial Year V (AE Mons, fonds du tribunal correctionnel de Mons, registre de correspondances du directeur de jury de Mons n° 8, lettre n° A240).

[45]The insurrectionary atmosphere caused by the law of 7 Vendémiaire Year IV is clearly described by public prosecutor Giraud to Merlin in his letter of 28 Prairial Year V (AN BB18 400/DD4218).

[46]Letter written on 12 Fructidor Year V by the commissioner at the civil court of the department of Jemappes, Simon Nazaire Chenard, to Merlin (AN BB18 400/DD4218).

quickly confirmed. At the session of 14 Prairial Year V (2 June 1797), the Mechelen Correctional Court was due to judge Vanbenghem, secretary to the archbishop of Mechelen. However, that day Lebrête received a letter sent to him by one of the justices of the peace composing the court. The latter declared that he could not sit because he had undertaken the investigation of the Vanbenghem case and announced that his six associate justices (*assesseurs*) had refused to replace him. Three had tendered their resignations, two had reported sick and the sixth justified his absence by his summons as witness for the accusation. The various absences making it impossible to fill the place of the justice of the peace, the court judges found themselves insufficient in number and were forced to postpone the trial. Indeed, the trial session came at the worst possible time as, since that morning, news of De Hase's acquittal by the criminal court of the Dyle had spread throughout the city. The justice of the peace's assessors were not going to venture to try a priest with the legitimacy of the law of 7 Vendémiaire Year IV now in question. The paralysis of the correctional court provoked the resumption of religious services which had stopped since the arrest of Vanbenghem, and when Lebrête dared mention the resumption of proceedings, he was confronted with a chain reaction of resignations by police commissioners, justices of the peace and their associates, immediately affecting the proper functioning of all judicial activities, both civil and criminal.

In letters to the Minister of Justice, Lebrête denounces *the enforced stagnation* of the court caused by *resignations or the alleged apologies* (…) *tendered at the last moment.* Now, *the public service is made a laughing stock of by a certain class of fanatics which believes itself triumphant.* He relates in particular the recent events and rumours: the department of Sambre and Meuse had suspended the execution of the law, the criminal court of the Dyle had released De Hase, the city of Antwerp and several cantons of the legal district of Mechelen had refused to publish the law on religious police. Faced with these obstacles, Lebrête assured Merlin of his firmness.[47] Three weeks later, however, the assurance displayed by the jury director was unable to withstand the reality on the ground. Given the risk of paralysis of the entire judiciary, Lebrête decided, like other Belgian magistrates, temporarily to suspend the prosecution of non-juror priests.[48]

Faced with the failure of the courts to act, the government commissioners initially expressed their dismay, like Pierre-Joseph Vanderveken in Brussels, Pierre François Joseph Delneufcourt in Mons and François Joseph Auguste Sayavedra in Mechelen.[49] The reactions and statements by the three Belgian members of the judiciary may well be explained in part by their political beliefs. Vanderveken and

[47]Letter to the Minister of Justice dated 15 Prairial Year V (AN BB18 563/DD3929).

[48]Letter to government commissioner Sayavedra attached to the Mechelen correctionnal court, 7 Messidor Year V (AN BB18 563/DD3929).

[49]In Brussels, on hearing the judgment of the court of Dyle, Pierre-Joseph Vanderveken, from Louvain, was outraged (Letter to the Minister of Justice dated 14 Prairial Year V (AN BB18 284/DD 3877)). In Mechelen, the Brussels judge François Joseph Auguste Sayavedra addresses himself directly to the Directory (Letter to the Directory dated 15 Prairial Year V (AN BB18 563/DD 3929)).

Delneufcourt had been Vonckistes and were viewed under the Directory as Jacobins.[50] Sayavedra himself had belonged to the Brussels Surveillance Committee in Year II and was a member of the Antwerp criminal court in Year III.[51]

Despite their attachment to the Republic, the three judges could not ignore the local pressures and the legal uncertainty caused by both the judgment of the Dyle court and the legal challenges. Following the quashing of De Hase's sentence, Vanderveken seemed less eager to prosecute offenders and asked the Minister of Justice whether he should *continue to bring to court those priests who are in violation of the law* [7 Vendémiaire Year IV].[52] Sayavedra asked Merlin for instructions for replacing the assessors who have resigned. In Mons, Delneufcourt affirmed that ministerial directives are not required *to fire my zeal. Already the court where I serve has condemned Rinchon to 3 months imprisonment and a fine of 500 livres. It is pursuing the other priests targeted by the law. It is important that no law be violated in a Republic.*[53] However, his enthusiasm ignores the fact that the conviction and sentence of Pierre-Joseph Rinchon was the only one imposed by the Mons Correctional Court. Chenard, the commissioner at the departmental civil court, was little impressed by this sudden bout of repressive action, which he deemed *ridiculous.*[54]

It has to be said that the wait-and-see behaviour of the Belgian government commissioners differed little from that of their French counterparts. The commissioner to the Ghent Correctional Court, Antoine Jean Bazire Lacoudraye, filed on 23 Thermidor Year V (10 August 1797) a detailed and pessimistic report on the state of prosecutions against non-juror priests: *throughout my legal district, the law of 7 Vendémiaire is violated. In several cantons the government commissioners are complaining of this violation. In every one of them the justices of the peace authorise it by their failure to take action. Some of them, when priests are brought before them, give judgments which are highly injurious to the law and very likely to alienate the minds and the hearts of all. The same conduct is exhibited by the priests and justices of the peace of the neighbouring departments.*[55] If Lacoudraye denounces the apathy of the justices of the peace, he admits himself, in the same report, to having ordered the provisional release of the pastor of Our Lady of Ghent. The French magistrate in fact admits that he is resigned to staying the proceedings and explains: *I could have required an arrest warrant to be issued against each defendant. This would have been the best policy* (…) *but being*

[50]Logie, *Les magistrats des cours…*, prosopographical index, pp. 119–120 and 369–370.

[51]Ibid., p. 315.

[52]Letter to the Minister of Justice dated 14 Prairial Year V (AN BB18 284/DD 3877).

[53]Letter to his friend at the Tournai correctional court, dated 14 Fructidor Year V (AE Mons, fonds du tribunal correctionnel de Mons, registre de correspondances du commissaire du gouvernement, lettre no. A263).

[54]See footnote 42.

[55]Letter to the Minister of Justice dated 23 Thermidor Year V (AN BB18 400/DD 4375).

assured that the jury director [Charles Massez] *would not accept my request, I feared that, in forcing him to express his position publicly, I would procure further advantage to those who openly attack the law and encourage those who have not yet dared violate it.* Lacoudraye's statements fully reflect the constraints facing the commissioners, whether Belgian or French. Required to ensure the implementation of the law, they were powerless to influence the conduct of the jury directors towards the non-juror priests. Charles Massez could hardly be suspected of clericalism. A former temporary representative of Ghent in 1792 and an owner of national property, he was deemed to be of "democratic" opinions from the time of the Brabant Revolution.[56] The reserved attitude of the jury directors most loyal to the Republic was also pointed at by Delfneucourt: *there is disgust among the highly patriotic judges who are holding off until the Legislature has ruled in one direction or another.*[57]

With the Directory's religious policy never so unpopular as it was at that moment, the majority of government commissioners seem to have accommodated themselves to the inertia of the jury directors. Seeking solutions, the provisional release of non-juror priests represented, in their view, a compromise that made it possible to conciliate the public opinion of the legal district while assuring the government of their dedication.[58] This strategy was also followed in the legal districts of Brussels, Mons and Aalst.[59] With the coup of 18 Fructidor, the *entente* displayed by commissioners and jury directors throughout Year V continued but changed in nature. The coup allowed the government to take a tougher stance against its opponents. The Court of Cassation, purified of certain former members, quashed the judgment of the Dyle criminal court[60] and prosecuted three judges of the court for misconduct in public office. On the legislative front, the two assemblies, similarly purified, put an end to the debate on religious freedom. With regard to the policing of worship, Article 25 of the law of 19 Fructidor retained the declaration required by the law of 7 Vendémiaire Year IV but replaced the content with an *oath of hatred to royalty and anarchy, and attachment and loyalty to the Republic and the Constitution of Year Three.* From now on, the legitimacy of the oath could no longer be challenged and the directives from the Minister of Justice clearly indicated that any delay in the prosecution of offenders would not be tolerated. Increased government surveillance along with the end of the legal uncertainties surrounding the policing of religious practice encouraged jury directors and government commissioners to try non-juror priests. This awakening of repressive activity produced a rapid increase in the activity of the correctional courts starting

[56]Logie, *Les magistrats des cours...*, prosopographical index, p. 254.

[57]Letter to the Minister of Justice dated 14 Thermidor Year V (AN BB18 400/DD 5190).

[58]Lacoudraye's correspondence testifies repeatedly to his concern to win over public opinion (Letter to the Minister of Justice dated 23 Thermidor year V).

[59]Berger, *La justice pénale...*, p. 70.

[60]On 7 Pluviôse Year VI, the criminal court of the department of Scheldt sentenced De Hase to three months imprisonment and a fine of 500 livres (State Archives at Beveren, Assize Court of West Flanders, register of judgments No. 14).

in the early months of Year VI. 54 % of religious cases were handled by the correctionnal courts in Year VI,[61] against 21 %[62] in the previous year.

If the increase in lawsuits is due in part to the trying of the cases initiated in Year V and temporarily postponed, the main explanation is the sanctions applicable to judges and government commissioners who proved recalcitrant. In all their correspondence Ministers of Justice Merlin and Lambrechts reminded their counterparts of the application of Article 26 of the Law of 18 Fructidor Year V (4 September 1797) which provides for a sentence of two years in irons for members of the judiciary who refused to execute or hindered enforcement of the legislation on the policing of religion. The threat of punishment does not however appear to have undermined the relations of solidarity between the judicial officers of the district, as attested by the few cases of resistance to ministerial directives. In the legal district of Aalst, the correctional court courageously acquitted, on 3 Frimaire Year VI (23 November 1797), the parish priest of Resseghem, Vanransberghe, accused of celebrating mass on the first and second additional days of Year V (17 and 18 September 1797) without taking any oath. Jury director Jacques Lievin Joseph Vandeputte accepted the defence arguments based on the fact that, as the laws on the policing of religious practice had not been published in the municipality, they could not be applied.

In the eyes of the Minister of Justice, this was a *ridiculous pretext*,[63] whereupon Lambrechts asked the commissioner to the Aalst Correctional Court, Etienne Martin Chompré, to provide him with precise information *on* [the] *character and* [the] *political conduct* of the judges in his district in order to determine whether Article 26 of the law of 19 Fructidor was *likely to be executed*.[64] A former president of the Jacobin Club of Marseilles, Chompré had then been elected clerk of the revolutionary court and imprisoned after Thermidor as a terrorist. At the time of the crisis of non-juror priests, he was therefore one of the most fervent supporters of the Directory, expressing repeatedly his aversion towards the *fanaticism* of the Belgians.[65] At the same period, his opinion on judges was equally negative.[66]

Despite his many criticisms and a certain lyricism, Chompré was wisely circumspect about the man held directly liable for the acquittal of the priest Vanransberghe. In response to inquiries from Lambrechts, he downplayed Vandeputte's fault, describing him as *a man of gentle morals but weak character, with few resources, and holding office out of necessity*. Chompré's explanation sums up the dilemma of judges I have constantly encountered in my study: *he would like to please the government and not to displease his colleagues and the individual patriots of this town,*

[61] I.e., 42 cases out of 78.

[62] I.e., 16 cases out of 78.

[63] Letter to the commissioner of the criminal court of the department of the Scheldt, Lacoudraye dated 12 Frimaire Year VI (AN BB18 294/DD 2774).

[64] Letter to the commissioner of the criminal court of the legal district of Aalst, Chompré, dated 12 Frimaire Year VI (AN BB18 294/DD 2774).

[65] Letter to the Minister of Justice dated 4 Thermidor Year V (AN BB18 294/DD 2774).

[66] Letter to the Minister of Justice dated 28 Prairial Year V (AN BB18 294/DD 2774).

who want only those laws of the Republic that do not antagonise their opinions and their system of distancing themselves from our constitution.[67] The correspondence between Lambrechts and Chompré produced the desired effect. On 29 Frimaire (19 December 1797) and 11 Nivôse Year VI (31 December 1797), the Aalst Correctional Court pronounced the conviction of four priests. In the months that followed these verdicts, Vandeputte's equivocal attitude in the Vanransberghe case did not damage his career. A former lawyer at the Council of Flanders and appointed a judge on 20 Nivôse Year IV (10 January 1796), he remained in office until the end of the Directory, as did 61 % of the judges elected in Year V.[68] This permanence echoes the careers of other judges we have encountered earlier, such as Lemoine, Ippersiel and Perlau. The study of the judicial district enables us to understand the reasons for this stability. Its basis lies in the solidarity established within the jurisdiction among the judicial officers, whether Belgian or French, government commissioners or jury directors. The strength of the relationships and of the understanding between them was certainly variable, but it definitely allowed a number of the judiciary to ride out the storms of the Revolution.

[67]Letter to the Minister of Justice dated 21 Frimaire Year VI (AN BB18 476/DD 7419).

[68]Like Lemoine, Ippersiel and Perlau, Vandeputte's career lasted well beyond the fall of the Directory. After becoming a judge at the court in Ghent in Year VIII, he remained in office after the purification of 1811 and under Willem I. Vandeputte died in office in 1825 (Logie, *Les magistrats des cours*... prosopographical index, p. 365).

Chapter 15
Magistrates of Congo (1885–1960): Prosopography and Biography as Combined Tools for the Study of the Colonial Judicial Body

Laurence Montel, Enika Ngongo, Bérengère Piret and Pascaline le Polain de Waroux

15.1 Introduction

Since the start of the twenty-first century, the study of "colonialism" in Belgium has experienced new impulses.[1] A few major topics of the Leopoldian this colonial history (1885–1908) are thus well known today (the 1885 Berlin Conference, the "Scramble for Africa", "Red rubber" and the "Casement Report"). Other aspects of this this colonial history have also been widely studied, such as religious missions, teaching, the economy, social movements or military history. Nowadays, the

[1]X. Rousseaux, "Vers une histoire post-coloniale de la justice et du droit en situation coloniale?", in Ch. Braillon, L. Montel, B. Piret and P.-L. Plasman (ed.), *Droit et justice en Afrique coloniale: tradition, production et réformes,* Brussels, Université Saint-Louis, 2014, p. 11; P. Van Schuylenbergh, "Trop plein de mémoires, vide d'histoire? Historiographie et passé colonial belge en Afrique centrale", in P. Van Schuylenbergh, C. Lanneau and P.-L. Plasman (ed.), *L'Afrique belge aux XIXe et XXe siècles. Nouvelles recherches et perspectives en histoire coloniale*, Brussels, P.I.E. Lang, 2014, p. 44.

L. Montel (✉)
University of Caen, CRHQ—UMR 6583, Caen, France
e-mail: laurence.montel@unicaen.fr

E. Ngongo · B. Piret · P. le Polain de Waroux
Centre de Recherches en Histoire du Droit et des Institutions, Saint-Louis University, Brussels, Belgium
e-mail: enika.ngongo@usaintlouis.be

B. Piret
e-mail: berengere.piret@usaintlouis.be

P. le Polain de Waroux
e-mail: pascaline.lepolain@usaintlouis.be

A. Hondeghem et al. (eds.), *Modernisation of the Criminal Justice Chain and the Judicial System*, Ius Gentium: Comparative Perspectives on Law and Justice 50, DOI 10.1007/978-3-319-25802-7_15

judicial body and its staff is also one of the fields of study that is gaining importance.[2] However, this research is not as rich as that relating to the former British[3] and French empires.[4] This issue is central to the history of Belgian colonisation, which has too often been associated with—or even reduced to—the Leopoldian model, the stereotype of a far-away idea of justice.[5] Besides, it is known that, for the colonising state, the law and its application ensured the control of the conquered territories and their populations. To the colonial state, they were tools to maintain its position of domination, which explains their importance for the history of imperial societies.[6] This also justifies why it makes sense to study magistrates. Indeed, together with the police and the military, they were agents of this domination, yet with nuances that still need to be determined. Lastly, studying this exploring this field of study seems all the more critical today as it provides the opportunity to analyse the history of metropolitan states with new angles of approach, at a time when model transfers, techniques and practices between the homelands and the colonies are studied in both directions. Following this renewal in colonial legal studies and the positive results of the project entitled "Prosopographie des magistrats belges 1795–1960" (Prosopography of Belgian Magistrates), it was decided to widen the scope to overseas territories. This took place in the framework of the "Belgafrima: prosopographie des magistrats coloniaux belges" project, which has been followed by the "Belgafrican Magistrates Social Networks" project since July 2014. The objective of these projects is to study the collective profile of the judicial body and legal institutions in the Congo Free State (CFS, 1885–1908), in Belgian Congo (1908–1960), and in Ruanda-Urundi under Belgian administration (1924–1962), as well as to analyse it from the point of view of social networks.

[2]Rousseaux, "Vers une histoire post-coloniale de la justice et du droit en situation coloniale?", p. 15.

[3]M. Semakula Kiwanuka, "Colonial policies and administrations in Africa: the myths of the contrasts", in *African Historical Studies*, 3-2, 1970, pp. 295–315.

[4]M. Fabre, "Le magistrat Outre-mer, un élément capital de la stratégie coloniale", in *La Justice et le droit: instruments d'une stratégie coloniale, Rapport fait à la mission de Recherche Droit et Justice*, 2001; M. Fabre, "Les justices coloniales: clones imparfaits du système judiciaire métropolitain", in *Quaderni Fiorentini*, 2005, no. 33/34, t. II, Milan, 2005; B. Durand, "Le Parquet et la Brousse. Procureurs généraux et Ministère public dans les colonies françaises sous la Troisième République", in *Staatsanwaltschaft, Europaische und Amerikanische Geschichten*, Frankfurt am Main, Max-Planch-Institut, Klosterman, 2005, pp. 105–137; F. Renucci (ed.), *Dictionnaire des juristes ultramarins (16e-20e siècles)*, December 2012; J.-Cl. Farcy, "Quelques données statistiques sur la magistrature coloniale française (1837-1987)", in *Clio@Themis*, no. 4, March 2011.

[5]P.-L. Plasman, "Un État de non-droit? L'établissement du pouvoir judiciaire au Congo léopoldien 1885–1889", in Ch. Braillon, L. Montel, B. Piret and P.-L. Plasman (ed.), *Droit et justice en Afrique coloniale: tradition, production et réformes*, Brussels, Université Saint-Louis, 2014, pp. 27–28.

[6]Rousseaux, "Vers une histoire post-coloniale de la justice et du droit en situation coloniale?", p. 15.

Predictably, many questions have been formulated in the project's development phase, and they relate to the specificities of the colonial territory. For instance, from which intellectual and social circles did these magistrates come? Why did they decide to enter the colonial administration? What were the different steps in their careers? Do we observe the gradual emergence of a homogeneous socio-professional group sharing common training and experience? How did these magistrates, through their publications, contribute to the development of a "Congolese" law and judicial thought? Though the research project focuses on the people, it also aims at further developing knowledge of the overseas organisation and judicial map, which are still difficult to picture as a whole. Besides, the use of the database created by the "Prosopographie des magistrats belges 1795–1960" project (referred to here as the "Belgian Magistrates" database) will simplify the comparative and relational study of metropolitan and overseas justices regarding staff and organisation. To what extent were the bodies of metropolitan and colonial magistrates separate or in relation with each another? What, if any, were the mutual influences of both judicial systems? For instance, we know that the overseas colonial model was inspired throughout its existence by the metropolitan model (importance of the prosecution office, types of jurisdictions and functions)[7] and that conversely, some transformations of metropolitan justice were inspired by African innovations, especially during the disrupted periods of war and post-war, when techniques worked out in Africa were applied in the motherland.[8]

During the exploratory process, between 2011 and 2013, priority was given to studying how this judicial body and its first magistrates were established at the time of the Congo Free State.[9] All the official information concerning the jurisdictions and magistrates in office during this period was added to the "Belgian Magistrates" database, that is to say, for 112 jurisdictions and nearly 350 magistrates.

The progress made on the project entitled "Belgafrima: prosopographie des magistrats coloniaux" will be presented in two phases. We will first deal with the project's state of progress, with methodological and technical issues that are still to be solved and that determine the way the information is entered into the database. The second part will be devoted to presenting the first results and potential future developments.

[7]Plasman, "Un État de non-droit?" p. 37; B. Piret, "Les structures judiciaires 'européennes' du Congo belge. Essai de synthèse", in P. Van Schuylenbergh, C. Lanneau and P.-L. Plasman (ed.), *L'Afrique belge aux XIXe et XXe siècles. Nouvelles recherches et perspectives en histoire coloniale*, Brussels, P.I.E. Lang, 2014, pp. 163–178.

[8]The procedure involving a single judge after World War One, for example (Loi du 25 octobre 1919 modifiant temporairement l'organisation judiciaire et la procédure devant les cours et tribunaux, *Moniteur Belge*, 9 November 1919).

[9]L. Montel, "Le contrôle des magistrats dans le Congo léopoldien, d'après les registres du Service du personnel d'Afrique (SPA) (1885–1908)", in Ch. Braillon, L. Montel, B. Piret and P.-L. Plasman (ed.), *Droit et justice en Afrique coloniale: tradition, production et réformes*, Brussels, Université Saint-Louis, 2014, pp. 51–78.

15.2 From Project Design to Database Population

15.2.1 State of the Sources and Accessibility: Printed Sources

The most easily accessible sources are the printed sources: the *Bulletin officiel de l'État Indépendant du Congo* (*BO de l'EIC*), the *Bulletin officiel du Congo belge*, the *Bulletin officiel du Ruanda-Urundi*, the *Annuaire du Congo belge*, and the *Recueil mensuel de l'État Indépendant du Congo*,[10] published by the government, as well as the legislation, jurisprudence and doctrinal compilations which were generally written by the colonial magistrates themselves.[11] These documents contain many texts related to the organisation and judicial personnel: new jurisdiction or transferred jurisdictions, jurisdiction delimitation, appointments of agents, etc. Moreover, the practising magistrates in Congo during the 1920s could for instance be listed in the *Annuaire du Congo belge*, whereas the legal practitioners who left for Belgian Congo during the 1930–1960 period were mentioned in the *Bulletin officiel du Congo belge*. These sources enable us to identify the main reforms and regulatory texts that framed the judicial system. Nevertheless, the information they provide is limited in various ways. Periods of war and transitional periods are often not documented. For example, the *Bulletin officiel du Ruanda-Urundi* was only available between 1924 and 1962—although Belgium was administering the territories from 1919.[12] Besides, decrees and orders for judicial and other matters were not systematically registered in these publications. This is a certain fact for the Congo Free State and the Belgian Congo periods until 1914, which we will be taken as examples here. Indeed, the 1891 *BO de l'EIC* contains a long report to the king on the "Works carried out in Congo", praising the judicial administration which "had managed to replace anarchy with the rule of law".[13] This report indicates that ordinary justice was carried out in Lower Congo, "where the State authority is consolidated", whereas Upper Congo, beyond Stanley Pool, was subjected to military justice: "Military tribunals (*conseils de guerre*) were established in Équateur-Ville, Nouvelle-Anvers (Bangala), Basoko (Arouwimi), Stanley Falls,

[10] *Recueil mensuel des ordonnances, arrêtés, circulaires, instructions et ordres de service, État Indépendant du Congo*, Gouvernement local, Boma. Located at the library of the Belgian Federal Public Service Foreign Affairs (FPS FA) in Brussels.

[11] Such as: A. Lycops and G. Touchard, *État indépendant du Congo*; *recueil usuel de la législation des conventions internationales et des documents administratifs avec des notes de concordance*, 7 t. 1–7, Brussels, P. Weissenbruch, 1903–1913; O. Louwers, *Lois en vigueur dans l'État indépendant du Congo. Textes annotés d'après les instructions officielles et la jurisprudence des tribunaux*, Brussels, P. Weissenbruch, 1905. Rearranged and entitled *Codes et lois du Congo belge*, then later updated by Pierre Piron and Jacques Devos (1943–1960), these compilations remained reference works until Congolese Independence in 1960.

[12] W. R. Louis, *Ruanda-Urundi, 1884–1919*, Oxford, Clarendon Press, 1963.

[13] "Rapport au roi-souverain sur l'œuvre au Congo", in *BO de l'EIC*, 1891, p. 171.

Lomami, Lusambo, Luluabourg, Western Kuango, Ouellé and Katanga".[14] But the decisions to create these jurisdictions were not registered in previous *Bulletins*. Therefore, it is quite difficult to determine when some of the jurisdictions were actually in exercise.

Furthermore, the *Bulletins officiels* contain insufficient details to ensure a clear and complete understanding of the changes in judicial organisation. Indeed, the existence of some previous texts is revealed only by decrees based on or abolishing them.[15] Likewise, similar temporary jurisdictions may have existed without being mentioned in the printed sources. If they had already been suppressed by the time of the major judicial reform that took place in the mid 1890s, this fact is easy to explain. Another challenge is related to the changes in court names, the jurisdictions of which varied, notably in the first phase of the colonisation. The colony's judicial map was more flexible than that of the motherland: multiple factors led to a regular reworking of jurisdiction boundaries, mainly conditions related to the territory's occupation such as conquest, state of war or rebellions and progress towards territorial control.

Lastly, these sources provide insufficient details to determine the career paths of all the magistrates who held office in the African territories, at least for the Leopoldian period. Indeed, they only partly referred to appointments and transfers. The BO only scrupulously reported appointments to the *Conseil Supérieur du Congo* (High Council of Congo), which is probably partly due to their honorary character. They also report on a regular basis, yet imprecisely, the appointments to the courts of appeal (*cours d'appel*) and first instance (*tribunaux de première instance*) in Lower Congo. Lastly, it is pointless to try using these sources to reconstruct the whole careers of colonial magistrates, who were often transferred to other positions and combined several appointments. Whereas the monthly digests of the Boma government only partially complete those gaps from 1895 onwards, other written sources offer a wealth of information.

15.2.2 State of the Sources and Accessibility: Written Sources

It is particularly difficult to access primary sources, since the 600 personal files of magistrates in office in the Belgian overseas territories after 1908 cannot be accessed freely. Therefore, it is necessary to work with unrestricted sources, which

[14]Ibid., p. 172.

[15]For example: the Decree of 27 April 1889, on the reorganisation of the repressive justice begins with "reviewed the Decree of 8 April 1889" which is not recorded in the volume. Similarly, the *BO* of 1897, in its first article, refers to the revocation of the Decree of 5 August 1892, creating a territorial court at Matadi, and of the Decree of 14 April 1894, extending to the district of Cataracts the jurisdiction of the territorial court of Matadi: these two decrees do not appear in the *BO*.

were often incomplete. Indeed, some information is only available for certain periods. For example, a *registre du personnel judiciaire en congé* was preserved, but only covers the years 1947–1952. Royal decrees and ministerial orders related to staff appointment, as well as local government decrees, were not preserved as continuous series in the archives of the *Service du Personnel d'Afrique* (SPA).[16] By way of comparison, the records of the SPA which were kept over time by the Department of Foreign Affairs in Brussels, managing the judicial system at this time, are far more complete.[17] These have been preserved in full from 1885 to 1913 and provide a wide array of information on the Department of Foreign Affairs' agents, to which the judicial staff (e.g. the magistrates) pertained.[18] They make up for the absence of most of the personal files of the agents of the Congo Free State who stopped serving the CFS after power was handed over to Belgium. These files were probably destroyed by the colonial administration when the agent died or when the CFS disappeared.[19]

These SPA records are made up of two-page information sheets for each individual, covering the agent's *terme*, which referred to the period he served in Leopoldian Congo. Each time an agent was re-enlisted, a new sheet was drawn up in the current record. The number of sheets for a single agent, distributed over one or more records, reflected the length of his career. The notes added on the right edge of the sheet by the department's clerks make it easy to reconstruct the agents' careers: each sheet indicates the record and sheet numbers corresponding to other positions of the agent. The sheets are made up of a table with ten columns, topped by a header about the agent. They contain the following information which is critical to feeding the prosopographical database: surname, firstname, date of birth, marital status and parentage, start date of the *terme*, dates of appointment to main functions, transfer dates, dates of departure to the motherland for holiday periods, and even, as required, the cause and date of death (useful to calculate the death rate in office and to compare it with the metropolitan rate).[20] All these elements enable us to reconstruct the main structure of career paths, with the major changes and transfers as well as the types of positions held. In addition, they provide sociological data that sheds light on the profile of the hired magistrates: nationality,

[16]FPS FA, SPA, registers 195 to 232.

[17]"Décret du 30 octobre 1885", in *BO de l'ÉIC*, 1885, pp. 25–29.

[18]"The 'notes' were scrupulously recorded until 1912 then became more messy until their final abandonment in 1914". Montel, "Le contrôle des magistrats dans le Congo léopoldien", p. 52.

[19]We regret the absence of other personal files after we have seen the example offered by the file of Edgard Vanderschueren. However, it sheds essential light on SPA records, in particular because it captures even better how and why those records were produced and kept. Personal file 'Edgard Vanderschueren', FPS FA, SPA (162) 194, box n° 57 file n°35; Montel, "Le contrôle des magistrats dans le Congo léopoldien", p. 55.

[20]FPS FA, SPA, register 892; Montel, "Le contrôle des magistrats dans le Congo léopoldien", p. 55.

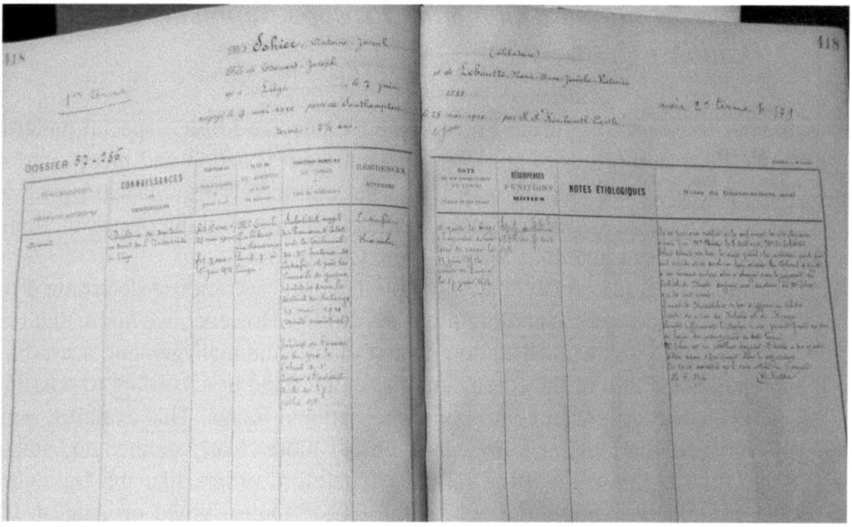

Fig. 15.1 SPA records—first *terme* of Antoine Sohier

university training, occupation before departure, address. These records also included decorations awarded to staff and any disciplinary sanctions, as well as short appraisals written by their superiors. This reveals the usefulness of in-the-field assessment in order to further optimise the use of human resources in the framework of a typical metropolitan recruitment process, which was still based on the agents' moral qualities, recommendations and a short interview (Fig. 15.1).

Towards the end of the period, and in the last volume in particular (SPA 96), the contents of the records gradually diminished. The *Notes* column was not systematically filled in any more, and quite often, the positions held in Congo by the agent were not mentioned. The information provided was often limited to the indication *agent de l'ordre judiciaire* (agent of the judiciary). Though more detailed information would be required in order to reconstruct the history of the judicial staff as a whole and the way they were assessed, these vague occupational indications are not detrimental to feeding the database.[21]

In spite of their usefulness for the magistrates' careers, the SPA records as a whole are not adapted to establishing the judicial map and the hierarchy of jurisdictions, since the information they contain are related to the staff, not the courts and the associated judicial functions. As explained below, this gives rise to some difficulties, as new data need to be entered into the "Belgian Magistrates" database.

[21]Indeed, in most cases, they are not related to magistrates, but to lower-ranking agents. The latter have not yet been taken into account for the current project work.

15.2.3 Adding Colonial Data to the Prosopographical Database

To complete the work of Aurore François and Françoise Muller, special patterns of colonial cases and issues of consecutive database translation and incorporation must be reasserted. The judicial map is not yet completely established owing to the state of the art in this research field and the constant reworking of jurisdictions' delimitations and headquarters, at least for the CFS period.

At the time, the judicial occupation of the territory was indeed determined by the background of conquest and dominion of territory. However, we know that territorial remodelling was a constant component of colonial management, according to the financial situation of the colony and the motherland or according to possible contradictory stakes of social control and international image. This explains, incidentally, why jurisdictions for Europeans were far more clearly defined and stable than those for the natives and the military. Therefore orders like the following could be formulated towards the end of the CFS: "Order issued on August 14, 1905, no. 35, suppressing the Albertville (Toa)'s military tribunal and attaching this jurisdiction's territory to the military tribunal established in the administrative centre of the Tanganika-Moero sector"—without mentioning any specific location.[22] This probably meant that the administrative centre, not definitively established, could be relocated. Such a formulation implied that judicial power would follow in the steps of administrative power, without requiring the issue of a new order. This administrative practice, which was frequent for military justice and of historic interest, makes the task of data entry more complex since all administrative variations have to be tracked, before the entry of personal data in the data base. In addition, some non-identical designations between BO and SPA records had made it difficult to link some of the personal data to the appropriate jurisdictions.

The process of data entry has also had to deal with the great flexibility of employment that Belgian colonial magistrates coped with, as did all European colonial officials. In most cases, agents accumulated numerous functions and had to replace colleagues on sick leave or on holiday. This issue of *ad interim* positions is crucial for imperial administration studies[23] but hard to incorporate into the database. On the one hand, it is often hard to identify the date of the beginning and end of those additional functions. On the other hand, as judicial positions must be pre-encoded in the database, all the *ad interim* positions have to be pre-encoded too.

---

[22] *Recueil mensuel des Arrêtés, Circulaires, Instructions et Ordres de service*, Boma, Imprimerie de l'État, August 1905, p. 142.

[23] On the interim, cf. for example, Farcy, "Quelques données statistiques sur la magistrature coloniale française", p. 2 and B. Durand, "Les magistrats coloniaux entre absence et errance", in B. Durand and M. Fabre (dir.), *Le juge et l'outre-mer. Les roches bleues de l'Empire colonial*, Lille, Centre d'histoire judiciaire, 2004, pp. 47–70.

Lastly, the SPA records as well as personal files contain some "sensitive" information about the agent such as assessments by his superiors, potential sanctions, relationships and political preferences.[24] Although information that is strictly identity-related can be encoded and partly disclosed, that is not the case for more personal data. Of course, these can be used in the context of scientific research if they are rendered anonymous. However, it seems questionable to make them accessible to any Internet user, without restriction of access, since this data could be used for purposes other than research which could even be polemic or malicious in nature. This issue is related to the right to oblivion. It is deeply rooted in Belgian colonial history, which is still subject to passionate debate nowadays. But the objective set by creating this database for the research community must preserve it from this kind of diverted use. This is why setting up a technical system and an adjustable control protocol for accessing data is necessary.

The way the data will be used is another issue. We can now report provisional results from the 112 created jurisdictions: the *Conseil supérieur de l'EIC* (CFS High Council), six courts of first instance, 35 regional courts and 70 military tribunals. These data cover the whole judicial system from 1885 to 1908, even though new records could still be provided in the field of military justice, using the *Recueils mensuels*. They have enabled us to enter the careers of all 350 magistrates listed in the SPA records. This data is of course incomplete for the moment. Therefore, we will explore possibilities rather than presenting conclusions.

15.3 Database Processing

The results from the first queries make it possible to outline trends in terms of the recruitment, training, career path and retirement of magistrates in Congo, all results likely to be compared with those carried out by Jean-Claude Farcy on French colonial magistracy.[25] This study will provide the opportunity to specify, confirm, qualify or even reject items that were hitherto only hypotheses, such as the nationalisation of the administrative framework that took place from Congo's handover of power to Belgium in 1908.[26] This aspect will be presented here. Next to this general overview, the purpose is also to unravel the internal dynamics of this judicial body and the networks that were built upon. In order to introduce this subject, we will deal with a few major individuals of the colonial world of the time, such as Antoine Sohier (1885–1963), an iconic figure of the Belgian colonial magistrates.

[24]Personal files can be accessed after authorisation.

[25]Farcy, "Quelques données statistiques sur la magistrature coloniale française".

[26]L. H. Gann and P. Duignan, *The rulers of Belgian Africa 1884–1914*, Princeton, Princeton University Press, pp. 164–181.

15.3.1 The Four Steps in the Career of Magistrates in Congo

15.3.1.1 Recruitment

The magistracy in the CFS widely differed from that of Belgium at the time due to the several nationalities of the people in its ranks. Unlike its metropolitan counterpart, the magistracy was not only made up of Belgian staff. Among the 350 magistrates currently listed in the database, twenty Norwegians, three Danes and more than fifteen Italians have been counted. Other nations were also represented in this body, though in less significant number: one Swede, one Frenchman, three Swiss, two Romanians and one American from Boston. The last had a degree in Law from the Christiana University (Oslo) and was a lawyer in the small city of Grimstad before he was enlisted to serve in the CFS. His recruitment could therefore be related to the Norwegian magistrates.[27] These foreign officials were not confined to low-ranking positions. On the contrary, several of them occupied the most important seats in the CFS such as the Italian Giacomo Nisco, who was appointed president of the Boma Court of Appeal before he became the general consul of the Leopoldian State in Italy. Further it seems that only the non-Belgian officials had previously held judicial positions. Therefore, many of them trained their young colleagues, especially the Belgians.

This multinational composition of the Congolese magistracy is related to the national political context. Leopold II, who did not manage to convince Belgians of the opportunity of his colonial project or to recruit staff for his African administration among his subjects, had no choice other than to hire foreigners. He opted for "small" countries with no on-going colonial project in Sub-Saharan Africa and mainly enlisted staff from Scandinavian countries and Italy. They filled magistrate positions, but also positions in the central administration in Banana at first, then in Boma (capital of the CFS from 1886), in local administration and in the *Force publique* (Congo's police force). The fact that foreigners held high-ranking positions was also a consequence of the complex diplomatic situation in Congo. The young state, which was created in the wake of the International Berlin Conference in 1885, was closely watched by the great colonial powers, such as Great Britain and France and was particularly subject to criticism. This occurred, for instance, during the Stokes-Lothaire case in 1895–1896, which had such an impact that it triggered the reform of the judicial institution. In this context, the Court of Appeal that took on the case was reinforced with two counsellors (*conseillers*, magistrates), an Italian and a Swede. The Secretary of State Van Eetvelde underlined this and said: "It seemed fitting that this Court of Appeal be made up of people from different nationalities".[28]

[27]About foreigners present in the CFS, see the works of Lilian Nielsen devoted to Danes and the book by R. Giordano, *Belges et Italiens du Congo-Kinshasa. Récits de vie avant et après l'indépendance*, Paris, Karthala, 2008.

[28]"Rapport du secrétaire d'État, E. Van Eetvelde, au Roi-Souverain, le 21 mai 1897", in *Bulletin Officiel*, 1897, pp. 192–193.

When Belgium took over power from the CFS in 1908, the colonial government engaged in replacing the administration's high-ranking foreign officials with Belgians. Even if no law required that new magistrates be Belgians, nearly all the new recruits came from the motherland. This development can be followed thanks to the *Rapports annuels sur l'administration du Congo belge*. About 58 % of the magistrates were Belgians in 1909 and they accounted for 82 % of the staff in 1911, then 89 % in 1913. By that time, only a few foreigners remained in office among colonial magistrates. They were generally migrants who had lived in Belgium or had been trained there: for instance, the Romanian Chirila Adreiu, who was a lawyer in Brussels and later became Matadi's deputy public prosecutor in 1905.[29]

The recruitment policy for 1908 and the following years showed a second trend. Candidates for Congo started to be recruited among civilians whereas Leopold II had given priority to the military. Indeed, at the time of the CFS and during the first years of the regime in particular, magistrates and civil servants mainly came from the Belgian army. Camille Coquilhat, for instance, had left his position as *adjoint d'État-major* (vice-chief of the Army staff) to carry out "pacification missions" on the Congolese territory before becoming vice-general governor of the CFS.

15.3.1.2 Training

On searching the database, it is striking to observe that most colonial magistrates were very young. They had barely graduated, had just obtained their law degree or had worked as lawyers for a few years in Brussels, Charleroi or Liège. The Liège bar, in particular, counted among its ranks distinguished colonial magistrates, one of whom was Antoine Sohier. Some worked for an administration, such as a municipality, a ministry or the prison service. Others served in the Congolese administration. Though they had followed training in Belgian law or that of another country, but only a few already had experience as magistrates. Jacques de Lichtervelde is an exception to the rule. He resigned from his position as a judge of the Brussels Court of First Instance to become a judge at the Stanleyville Regional Court in 1906. Since the Belgian and Congolese magistracies were autonomous entities, he had to give up his career in Brussels and his retirement pension.[30] This example highlights the lack of incentives offered to Belgian magistrates to leave their positions in Belgium.[31]

---

[29]Fonds SPA, register no. 94, sheets 243 and 355; register 95, sheet 504.

[30]A. Sohier, *Les rapports entre les magistratures coloniale et métropolitaine. Discours prononcé à la Conférence du Jeune Barreau de Bruxelles*, Brussels, 1926, p. 13.

[31]This situation came to an end with the promulgation of the Act of 10 August 1921 which allowed Belgian magistrates who left for Congo to preserve their years of service as well as their promotion opportunities. This stipulation facilitated the departure of experienced magistrates to Belgium such as Joseph Derriks who left the Huy Court of First Instance to preside over the Court of Appeal in Élisabethville in 1924.

Most of those who became colonial magistrates had no experience in the administration of justice of Congo. Before the *École coloniale* (Colonial School) and the *Université coloniale* (Colonial University) were created,[32] they trained themselves by reading the few books that existed about these subjects, for instance, *État indépendant du Congo. Historique, géographie, physique, ethnographie, situation économique, organisation politique* by Alphonse-Jules Wauters. As a result, they learned their functions on the job. The magistrates hired by the CFS had to carry out a traineeship that spanned over three years at most.[33] They were appointed on a temporary basis and carried out their mission while being supervised by an experienced official. However, due to the lack of staff, this training was often limited. In most cases, the young magistrates were quickly on their own at the head of a prosecution office or a jurisdiction.[34]

At the end of the traineeship in the field, the applicant took an examination, which included the presentation and defence of a dissertation on a subject related to law or legislation that was specific to Congo to be freely selected by the applicant.[35]

15.3.1.3 Career

Careers in Belgian Congo could in no way be compared to careers in the motherland. Whereas serving as a magistrate in Belgium implied engaging in a guaranteed and lifelong career, this was not the case for colonial magistrates. Indeed, their career in Congo did not last more than two or three *termes* (mandates), on average. Afterwards, they left Africa where the living conditions were harsh for both the body (disease, climate, etc.) and the mind (no contact with the relatives, absence of intellectual circles, etc.). This is why a colonial career was considered to be complete after having served for eighteen years.[36]

[32]The *École coloniale* (Colonial School) was founded in 1903 and the legal section welcomed its first students in 1911. The *Université coloniale* (Colonial University) was created in 1920. C. Van Leeuw, *L'administration territoriale au Congo belge et au Ruanda Urundi. Fondements institutionnels et expérience vécue 1912–1960*, Louvain-la-Neuve, Université catholique de Louvain, 1981, p. 143.

[33]"Décret du Roi Souverain du 21 avril 1886 concernant l'organisation judiciaire", in *Bulletin Officiel*, 1896, p. 104.

[34]In 1926, when Antoine Sohier saw that the magistrates in Congo were insufficiently trained, he proposed replacing the traineeship in Africa by a one-year training period in Belgium, during which the would-be magistrates would learn the various aspects of the job with the help of experienced magistrates. His proposal was turned down, however. Sohier, *Les rapports entre les magistratures coloniale et métropolitaine*, pp. 18–19.

[35]"Décret du Roi Souverain du 21 avril 1886 concernant l'organisation judiciaire", in *Bulletin Officiel*, 1896, p. 104 and the following one. Few theses have been preserved. Only around 50 of them, defended in the 1930 s, can be found in the fonds *Justice* (FPS FA library).

[36]A. Gohr, "Organisation judiciaire de Congo belge", in *Les Novelles. Corpus Juris Belgici. Droit colonial*, t. 1, Brussels, Picard, 1936, p. 107.

On top of these elements, which were common to many colonial careers, magistrates in Congo carried out their functions in trying conditions. In view of the constant lack of workforce, they had no choice but to cope with a workload that should have been distributed over several people. Above all, the legal provisions framing their occupation did not guarantee they would keep their position indefinitely once appointed, an advantage that magistrates in Belgium did have. Provisionally appointed magistrates could be transferred, without their agreement, to any district within the remit of the administrative centre they were attached to, or even to any location in Congo if required by an urgent situation. Even definitively appointed magistrates could be transferred. However, this decision had to be motivated by an urgent situation and could only be temporary.[37] Judicial staff in Congo thus had to be very flexible as to the location of their assignments.

According to the "Belgian Magistrates" database and the SPA records, during their first mandate, the magistrates would be assigned to courts in Boma or not far from the capital in order to be closely supervised by their superiors. For their subsequent mandates, they were sent to more remote locations and carried out various functions: investigating offences, making and applying rulings, administration of the public prosecution office.[38] Throughout their careers, Congo magistrates held various positions, serving as judges or prosecutors, from civil justice to military justice, or even both simultaneously.

15.3.1.4 Retirement

When they had completed their entire career in Congo, the colonial magistrates could retire when they were around 50 years old. However, in view of their age and the modest amount of the retirement pension they were entitled to,[39] most of them had to start a new career when they returned from Congo. Analysis of the data shows that this new career path would differ according to the period when the magistrate retired.

Among the magistrates who retired at the time of the Leopoldian regime, many were later appointed to positions in the central administration of Congo, which was based in Brussels. At the same time, many honorary (retired) magistrates were appointed to the boards of companies and organisations created by Leopold II or people close to him, for instance, the *Compagnie du Congo pour le Commerce et l'Industrie* and *Intertropical-Comfina*.

---

[37]This principle was established by the Decree of 21 April 1896 before being embodied in articles 18 and 18A of the Colonial Charter. In this regard, read especially: Gohr, "Organisation judiciaire du Congo belge", pp. 111–113. This situation is not unique to the Congo. French colonial magistrates are also removable, read: Farcy, "Quelques données statistiques sur la magistrature coloniale française", p. 22.

[38]Montel, "Le contrôle des magistrats dans le Congo léopoldien", p. 66.

[39]Although the amount of this retirement pension cannot be estimated, Antoine Sohier considered that it did not meet the needs of a magistrate and his family. A. Sohier, "L'organisation de la magistrature congolaise", in *Revue de Droit et de Jurisprudence du Katanga*, 2nd year, no. 2, p. 45.

In the wake of the handover of power to Belgium, the colonial authorities wished to put an end to the management methods used by the CFS and tried to establish a new administration in Congo. The old magistrates were not reintegrated into the central administration. Therefore, they chose to apply for magistrate positions within the Belgian judicial bodies. They managed to highlight their abilities and their previous experience and were appointed to important positions, like Fernand Waleffe, a former judge at Matadi's *Tribunal d'État* (State Court), who became counsellor and later *Président de chambre* of the Court of Cassation.

However, magistrates who returned to Belgium in the wake of the First World War experienced more difficulties embracing a career as magistrates in Belgium. Those who succeeded were assigned to lower-ranking positions. For instance, Iwan Grenade, who was a State prosecutor in Congo, became judge at Stavelot's *Tribunal de paix* (Justice of the Peace) in 1920, thus a lower status. According to Antoine Sohier, Grenade was not the only magistrate to experience such a situation.

> Some of them applied for positions, but their applications were turned down and their experience was not taken into account. Others managed to be appointed, but more often than not, their years of service were disregarded. They had to accept low-ranking posts.[40]

This explains why many magistrates who came back from Congo during the inter-war period took a new turn in their careers. Although it is particularly difficult to follow their change of occupation, it is to be noted that many of them, like Fernand Dellicour, a former general prosecutor, became university lecturers. They provided lessons on Congo's law and institutions to students of Belgian universities and the Colonial School. They thereby provided a full-fledged training to future Belgian Congo magistrates. Obviously, several retired magistrates from Congo took another path and did pursue successful careers as magistrates in Belgium. For example, Jean De Muylder became counsellor at the Brussels Court of Appeal and Antoine Sohier was appointed President of the Court of Cassation.

15.3.2 Antoine Sohier, from the Lukafu Court of First Instance to the Court of Cassation

Antoine Sohier (1885–1963), who led his life and career between two continents, offers an interesting case study. Analysing the professional career of this magistrate will enable us to highlight all the possibilities of studying the interconnections and perspectives the database will offer. Indeed, this individual's career reflects and suggests the presence of important networks of influence that only an in-depth study could confirm. Antoine Sohier did not serve under the CFS regime, but he arrived in Congo during the "in-between" period that started from 1908 and went on until the early 1920s, during which the structures and the officials established by Leopold II remained in place, in spite of the change of regime. Sohier's

[40]Sohier, *Les rapports entre les magistratures coloniale et métropolitaine*, pp. 17–18.

Fig. 15.2 Antoine Sohier

career fits in line with that of his predecessors, which makes it representative for the CFS magistrates' experience and paves the way towards the development of investigations of the database.

Born in Liège on 7 June 1885, Antoine Sohier was granted a law degree from his hometown's university in 1908. Following in the footsteps of his predecessors who graduated from the same university, such as Eugène Jungers, Octave Louwers or Fernand Dellicour, he soon engaged in a colonial career. Supported by his law professor Gérard Galopin, as were many former students,[41] Antoine Sohier decided to leave for the Belgian Congo to serve as a magistrate after completing an eighteen-month traineeship as a lawyer in Liège.[42] Appointed as *substitut suppléant* (substitute) for the state prosecutor on 10 May 1910 he boarded the *Kenilworth Castle* in Southampton en route to his new destination. Antoine Sohier was only twenty-two years old at the time. He was among the young Belgians who left for Congo to nationalise the colonial magistrates after Belgium took over power from the CFS (Fig. 15.2).[43]

15.3.2.1 Colonial Magistrate

When he arrived in Katanga on 8 July 1910 Sohier was welcomed by the public prosecutor Sigvald Meek,[44] a Norwegian magistrate with high standards of work ethics that inspired Antoine Sohier during his training.[45] The young magistrate

[41]F. Dellicour, "Gérard Galopin", in *Biographie coloniale belge,* t. IV, Brussels, Institut royal Colonial belge, 1955, col. 328–331.

[42]A. Sohier, "Un début de carrière judiciaire. Souvenirs et réflexions", in *Journal des Tribunaux d'Outre-Mer,* no. 100, 15 October 1958, p. 145.

[43]Fonds SPA, register no. 895.

[44]J. Sohier, "Sigvald Meek", in *Biographie coloniale belge,* t. VIII, Brussels, Royal Academy for Overseas Sciences, 1998, col. 283–288.

[45]"Chronique: dans le monde judiciaire", in *Revue de droit et de jurisprudence du Katanga*, no. 9, 15 July 1925, p. 254.

started his career with a traineeship at Lukafu's first instance prosecution office and the prosecution offices of the districts that were attached to the town. Less than a year later, in April 1911, he was appointed deputy judge at Étoile (which was later called Élisabethville) Court of First Instance and deputy judge at the Kiambi Court and the Tanganika-Moëro military tribunal. These first assignments enabled him to appreciate the versatility and the mobility that serving as a magistrate required. He ended his traineeship by being appointed definitively as deputy public prosecutor on 14 October 1912. After his first mandate, which would be followed by six others, Antoine Sohier realised how difficult it was for young magistrates to shoulder the heavy workload that was assigned to them without having received the adequate training to cope with it. On 14 December 1914, Antoine Sohier returned to Congo, accompanied by his wife Cécile Gulikers, with whom he had six children. During this second mandate, he was appointed public prosecutor at the Élisabethville Court of First Instance on 11 April 1915.

As shown in the database, throughout his career, Antoine Sohier climbed up the judicial system's ladder. On 5 December 1922 he was appointed deputy general prosecutor and later became general prosecutor on 15 May 1925, thereby following in the steps of his colleague and mentor from Liège, Fernand Dellicour, who started his career working for the Congo Free State in 1906 and retired early for personal reasons. According to the tradition, a ceremony was organised to celebrate the first assignment of the new general prosecutor on 27 June 1925. For Antoine Sohier, this marked the beginning of an assignment he kept until he left the colony in 1934.[46] In that, he stood apart from many of his colleagues who were very mobile throughout their careers.

Probably to make up for "the magistrates' lack of common spirit"[47] which he criticised many times,[48] Antoine Sohier in September 1924 created the *Société d'Études Juridiques du Katanga* (Katanga Legal Studies Society) and became its president. This association's purpose was to "study colonial law and to cooperate in its development, help maintain the traditions of the various judicial occupations and to strengthen the fraternal bonds between their members".[49] It was made up of several honorary members (whose title was granted by the Society), actual members (holders of a Ph.D. in law living in Katanga) and corresponding members (holders of a Ph.D. in law living in other provinces of the colony).[50] In view of its composition, we can assume that this Society had an influence on the colonial judicial world beyond the borders of the province. Antoine Sohier celebrated this success in the speech he gave for the Society's first anniversary. He was delighted

---

[46]Ibid., p. 255.

[47]Sohier, *Les rapports entre les magistratures coloniale et métropolitaine*, pp. 13–14.

[48]These criticisms are especially present in: Sohier, *Les rapports entre les magistratures coloniale et métropolitaine.*

[49]"Société d'études juridiques du Katanga—Statuts", in *Revue de droit et de jurisprudence du Katanga,* no. 4, 15 February 1925, p. 102.

[50]"Éditorial", in *Revue de droit et de jurisprudence du Katanga,* no. 1, 15 November 1924, p. 1.

to see that, "over the course of this first year, our weekly meetings have been increasingly followed, our relations with other colonial legal practitioners and foreign associations multiplied […]".[51] If we can assume that this newly created network forged closer ties between its members, it also raises many research questions for which answers can be found through the future use of the database. Indeed, it will enable us to measure the geographical and social reach of the network and the basis on which it is set up. For instance, it will highlight whether or not the different members have previous links and provide information about the strength of social cohesion.

The foundation of the Society coincided with that of the *Revue Juridique du Katanga*. This periodical, which resulted from the collaboration between Antoine Sohier and the president of the Court of Appeal Joseph Derriks, was the showcase of the Society, aimed at promoting "the management and development of legal publications".[52] This periodical, which was considered by the general governor as a "formidable judicial tool",[53] is a guide and a reference source to amend and supplement "the gaps of the science of law".[54] As from 1927, it became the *Revue Juridique du Congo belge,*[55] which shows how its scope widened. Even if this periodical's success suggests that certain trains of thought and, possibly, a Katanga legal current emerged, it was not only judicial circles that were interested in these publications. The very existence of this periodical had been made possible by the funding of industrial companies such as the *Union Minière* (Mining Union) or the *Compagnie foncière* (Property Company) and the *Comité Spécial du Katanga* (Katanga Special Committee). This enabled them to take part in the development of a colonial law that was critical to the colony's future.[56] Nevertheless, the existence of these bonds between private companies and the creation of juridical periodicals raise the question of the existence of broader networks. Indeed, beyond the judicial network, it questions the presence of a Katangese network and the place of the judicial network within it. Towards this issue, the database will lay the groundwork of an answer through the lens of the magistracy.

In 1933, a little before he left the colony, Antoine Sohier created the *Bulletin des Juridictions Indigènes et du Droit Coutumier Congolais*, the purpose of which is clearly stated in the title. Presented as a supplement to the *Revue Juridique du Congo belge*, this publication aims at providing a guide to the hundreds of jurisdictions created by the 26 April 1926 decree. In line with its founder's philosophy,

[51]"Société d'Etudes juridiques. Fête du premier anniversaire", in *Revue de droit et de jurisprudence du Katanga,* no. 1, 15 November 1925, no. 2, p. 51.

[52]E. Lamy, "Antoine Sohier", in *Biographie belge d'Outre-Mer,* t. VIII, Brussels, Royal Academy for Overseas Sciences, 1998, col. 392.

[53]"Société d'Etudes juridiques. Fête du premier anniversaire", p. 53.

[54]Ibid.

[55]After the Independence of Congo in 1960, it took the name *Revue juridique d'Afrique centrale*, then was renamed *Revue juridique du Congo* in 1964 and *Revue juridique du Zaïre* in 1967.

[56]"Société d'Etudes juridiques. Fête du premier anniversaire", p. 51.

this periodical defended the idea that a more in-depth knowledge of customs was necessary to supervise and guide customary law. By creating this *Bulletin*, Antoine Sohier showed the central role he considered native jurisdictions had to play in the colony's future.[57] In order to ensure this periodical's survival, the editing board had to rely on the collaboration of the colony's magistrates and missionaries, who could share their knowledge of customs and their experiences, as a source of content for the articles. The support this bulletin received testifies once again to the fact it met an actual need.[58] It was published until 1962, when it was merged with the *Revue Juridique*.

Besides creating, managing and maintaining these two periodicals, Antoine Sohier also collaborated with dozens of periodicals, among them *Congo* and *Zaïre*. These writings were characterised by a strong will to raise magistrates' awareness about customary law. This major field of interest took on its full meaning in the book *La pratique des juridictions indigènes*, "the first major essay on customary law",[59] which Sohier wrote in 1932. He thereby put his *leitmotiv* into practice: "study the native customs in order to learn their practices and teach them".[60] Through the interest he showed for this other branch of colonial law, Antoine Sohier shed light on a series of stakeholders, such as native judges, who often have remained hidden in the background. However, it is a pity that this aspect, which is a full-fledged part of the judicial history of Congo, cannot be taken into account in the database, which is currently focused on Belgian judges.

Like many colonial magistrates, Antoine Sohier ended his career after serving for eighteen years. In the farewell speech he gave upon leaving Africa, he expressed his sadness at leaving what he called "a great judicial family" and recollected how difficult it was to be so far away from Africa when he was on holiday: "the bonds of fraternity that connected the colonial agents could be strongly felt and the day of departure was no exception".[61] Even if these bonds were indeed built in the colonial judicial circles, their degree, nature and extent cannot be highlighted by a systematic study of the magistrates' profiles.

15.3.2.2 Metropolitan Magistrate

In spite of the fears he expressed concerning the possibilities of pursuing a career in the metropolitan judicial bodies after returning from Congo, Antoine Sohier returned to Belgium in order to take care of his children's education. Since there

---

[57]"Chronique: le départ de monsieur le procureur général Sohier", in *Revue de droit et de jurisprudence du Katanga*, no. 2, 15 February 1932, p. 67.

[58]"Éditorial", in *Bulletin des juridictions indigènes et du droit coutumier congolais*, no. 1, January 1933, p. 1.

[59]Lamy, "Antoine Sohier", col. 393.

[60]A. Sohier, "Fondons des cercles d'études juridiques", in *Journal des tribunaux d'Outre-Mer*, no. 37, 15 July 1953, p. 123.

[61]"Chronique: le départ de monsieur le procureur général Sohier", p. 68.

was no guarantee for him to enter the Belgian judicial system, Sohier was forced to accept a lower-ranking position than the one he had reached in Congo. Yet, unlike his colleague Ferdinand Dellicour, whose position he had taken over in Congo, he managed to be reintegrated into the judicial body. On 11 July 1934, he started a new career as a public prosecutor in Arlon. He kept that position until 1937, when he was appointed counsellor (magistrate) at Liège Court of Appeal.[62]

On 8 February 1946, Sohier became counsellor (magistrate) at the Court of Cassation. After serving for twelve years, he was appointed chamber president in 1958 following the unanimous vote of his colleagues. In March 1960, he became the president of this supreme jurisdiction.[63]

Throughout his career in Belgium, Sohier produced a large number of publications as well.[64] Following the success of the *Journal des tribunaux* for the metropolis. In 1950, following the success of the *Journal des Tribunaux*, he founded the *Journal des Tribunaux d'Outre-mer* for which he worked as an editor until 1961. This periodical gave him the opportunity to deal with all the legal and judicial issues in Belgian Congo. He regularly published articles on jurisprudence, civil and penal proceedings as well as native customs. Besides, he wrote many articles in other periodicals, such as the *Bulletin de l'Institut Royal Colonial belge* of which he had been a member since 1930. On top of the periodical articles, he also wrote textbooks that mainly consisted of a summary of his experiences and knowledge related to colonial realities. Among these publications, a few stand out, like the important chapter regarding obligations and contracts in colonial law in *Novelles* (1948), *Le traité élémentaire de droit coutumier du Congo belge* and the publication, with various collaborators, of *Droit civil du Congo belge* (1956).[65] At the end of his life, this magistrate left behind him an important bibliography which reflected the values and fields of interest he had focused on throughout his career[66] and the importance of the colonial magistracy in its own training.

15.3.2.3 Bridges Between Belgium and the Colony

The bonds that Antoine Sohier maintained with the Belgian colony were not restricted to this specialised literature. They remained central to his professional life. He was appointed a member of the *Conseil colonial* (Colonial Council) in 1951 and took part in the advisory commission set up by the 24 June 1955 decree to study the reforms in judicial law to be implemented in Belgian Congo. From

[62]Lamy, "Antoine Sohier", col. 394–395.

[63]Ibid., p. 392.

[64]Currently more than thirty articles by Antoine Sohier are listed in the EPrints database on http://www.just-his.be/eprints [consulted on 9 September 2014].

[65]Lamy, "Antoine Sohier", col. 393.

[66]The complete bibliography of Antoine Sohier can be found in *Bulletin des séances de l'ARSOM*, Brussels, 1965, fascicle no. 1, pp. 165–183.

1955 onwards, Antoine Sohier published many articles on colonial legislation, customary law and magistracy anonymously. We can assume that his new remits made him less prone to openly express his opinions. Besides, in the period that preceded the colony's independence, he was appointed to the *Conseil de législation* (Legislation Council), the mission of which spanned from 1959 to 1962. Lastly, three of his children engaged in careers in Congo.

Beside his purely legal and judicial activities, Antoine Sohier taught customary law at the *Institut universitaire des territoires d'Outre-Mer* (University Institute of Overseas Territories). Sohier, who was familiar with the lack of practical training available to future colonial magistrates, based his classes on examples out of his personal experience in order to prevent miscarriages of justice.[67] He also worked for the periodical sessions of the *Institut colonial international* (International Colonial Institute), the *Institut des civilisations différentes* (Institute for different civilisations) and accepted the position of vice-president of the *Association internationale de droit africain* (International African Law Association, IALA) founded and established in Paris in 1959.

Antoine Sohier died in Brussels on 22 November 1963. He summarised his long, mixed and eclectic career as follows:

> I was a magistrate in Africa and the motherland and worked as a judge and a prosecutor. [...] I would say that, in spite of its diversity, I feel like I have had only one single career.

15.3.3 Additional Information

Certainly, the first results of queries of the "Belgian Magistrates" database provide detailed information about the organisation of the magistracy in Congo during the Leopoldian period and the first years of the colony. They also highlight networks that require further analysis in order to measure their scope and implications. Among these, we can cite the Liège network, which counted in its ranks Fernand Dellicour, Eugène Jungers, Octave Louwers and Antoine Sohier. All these distinguished magistrates went to Congo after having been trained and encouraged to leave by Professor Gérard Galopin. A second network emerged around the Élisabethville Court in the 1910s. Mainly led by Antoine Sohier and Joseph Derriks, its views were reflected in the *Revue juridique du Katanga* and the *Revue des juridictions indigènes* as well as through the publication of doctrinal books (Fig. 15.3).

These are only the first results of an extremely promising tool. Further feeding the database will enable researchers to make the most of its potential and to investigate the questions raised in this chapter as well as new ones. We would like to underline two of them: the study of mobility of magistrates in the overseas Belgian territories and between the motherland and the overseas territories, as well

[67] These examples are particularly present in: Sohier, *Les rapports entre les magistratures coloniale et métropolitaine.*

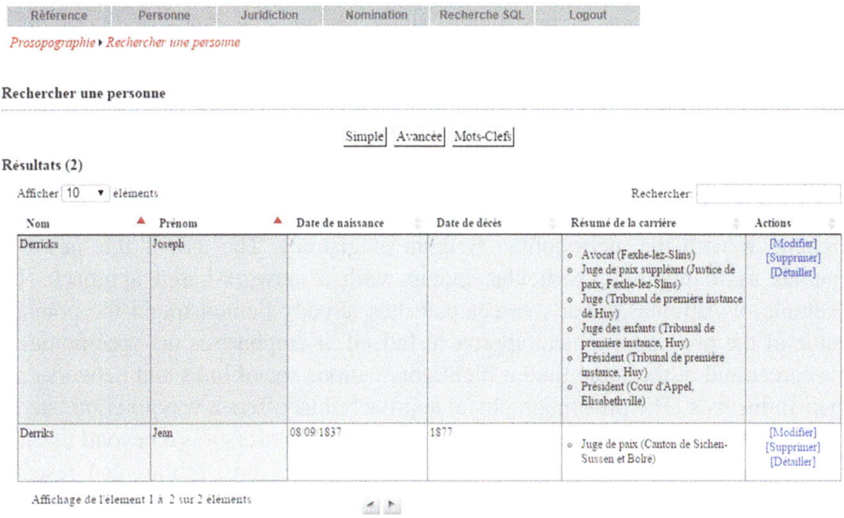

Fig. 15.3 Screenshot of the database "Prosopographie des magistrats belges" ("Belgian Magistrates") showing <Person search—Derriks>

as the recruitment of magistrates in Ruanda-Urundi. Were they appointed among the inexperienced applicants, as was the case for the CFS, among foreign magistrates in order to offer guarantees to the League of Nations, or among seasoned magistrates with experience in colonial jurisdictions? This thematic should make it possible to refine the analysis of the recruitment policy for magistrates in Belgian Africa.

15.4 Conclusion

This prosopographical project to the judicial organisation of the Belgian colonies focuses on the stakeholders of the legal system, who have long remained hidden in the background. Authorisation to study personal files that could not formerly be accessed has been granted, which will enable researchers to make the most of the project's potential. Two angles of approach will be used: group biography and network analysis. The knowledge gained regarding the CFS, based on the analysis of the *Bulletins Officiels*, the *Recueils mensuels* and the records of the *Service du Personnel d'Afrique*, will thereby be extended and seen from a wider perspective. The objective will now be to populate the "Belgian Magistrates" database further for both Belgian Congo and Ruanda-Urundi. The more systematic use of a database makes this colonial research project fit in the digital era and provides it with a better international visibility. In a discipline where English is the main language of communication, the next step towards this internationalisation will be the translation of the database fields into English.

The database makes it possible to study the judicial maps of States under Belgian control and the careers of Belgian magistrates who served overseas. The possibility to tap into new sources thanks to this tool unequalled in Belgium will provide major opportunities for a better understanding of this judicial body, the way it was built and the career paths it entailed. Comparative data is available for foreign magistracies, such as that of the British and French empires.[68] The prosopographical data will also make it possible to establish the similarities and discrepancies with the metropolitan Belgian magistracy. The use of this new tool enables us to highlight particular careers with a network-based approach. The example of Antoine Sohier's career path has already demonstrated the potential value of the prosopographical approach. Indeed, it emphasises the specificities of his career and at the same time it highlights various social links and networks and their influences. The prosopographical approach thus offers a way to eliminate the shortcomings of the biographical approach. It enables users to go beyond the simple individual experience and opens the way to new possibilities and research hypotheses.

The "Belgian Magistrates" database and the research methods it makes possible will lead to the emergence of a "connected" colonial history, filled with linked experiences and viewpoints. This wide-ranging research and documentation project will therefore contribute to knowledge in a vast emerging field of study.

[68] A. Allott, J.-P. Royer, E. Lamy et al., *Magistrats au temps des colonies*, Villeneuve-d'Ascq, L'espace juridique, 1988; Farcy, "Quelques données statistiques sur la magistrature coloniale française".

Chapter 16
Belgian Magistrates and German Occupiers: A Diachronic Comparison (1914–1918/1940–1944)

Mélanie Bost and Kirsten Peters

From the French period studied by Jacques Logie[1] to the post-1945 period analysed by Eva Schandevyl,[2] its sociological composition was one of the most stable characteristics of Belgian magistracy as a body.[3] The practices of social reproduction and endogamy, associated with closed recruitment methods, enabled the establishment of dynasties of magistrates. Even if the politicisation of appointments may have added some diversity—in certain periods—to the judicial body, its social homogeneity nonetheless remained strong. Most of the magistrates who attained high-ranking positions in the magistracy in the first half of the twentieth century came from the upper spheres of the French-speaking middle class or nobility. For *outsiders*, access to the highest positions was closed off.

[1] J. Logie, *Les magistrats des cours et des tribunaux en Belgique (1794–1814): essai d'approche politique et sociale*, Genève, Droz, 1998.

[2] E. Schandevyl, "Changements ou continuité? Rapports de force linguistique et (im)mobilité sociale dans la magistrature bruxelloise après la Deuxième Guerre mondiale", in V. Bernaudeau, J.-P. Nandrin, B. Rochet et al. *Les praticiens du droit du Moyen Age à l'époque contemporaine. Approches prosopographiques (Belgique, Canada, France, Italie, Prusse)*, Rennes, Presses universitaires de Rennes, 2008, pp. 255–270.

[3] In this text, we give the words 'magistrate' and 'magistracy' the meaning used in the civil law system, namely: all members of the judiciary: judges, prosecutors, investigating judges, juvenile court judges, justices of the peace....

M. Bost (✉)
Cegesoma and Royal Military Academy, Brussels, Belgium
e-mail: melanie.bost@cegesoma.be

K. Peters
Saint-Louis University, Brussels, Belgium
e-mail: kirstenmareke@yahoo.de

A. Hondeghem et al. (eds.), *Modernisation of the Criminal Justice Chain and the Judicial System*, Ius Gentium: Comparative Perspectives on Law and Justice 50, DOI 10.1007/978-3-319-25802-7_16

Unlike France, where sudden shifts in regime and consecutive purges led to a sociological renewal of the body, in Belgium the political stability of the country also contributed to strengthening that of the judicial body.[4] Yet, this stability was brutally threatened on two occasions. During both world wars, the establishment of a foreign power disrupted the balance of powers and jeopardised the independence of magistrates.

This chapter, based on Belgian and German sources,[5] combines for the first time the research results from two researchers active in the PAI research program "Justice and Society". These results will compare the impact of German occupations on the judicial body from two perspectives: the appointment policy in the judiciary and the measures of control taken against some of its members. The means used by magistrates in their own defence will also be examined. The comparison, which has never been made before for the judicial history of Belgium,[6] enables us to identify specificities and to outline a few invariants in the occupation policy and in the behaviour of magistrates. It also enables us to measure the influence of the first occupation experience on the second one.

Finally, this study offers another illustration of the interest of the "Belgian Magistrates" database created by the "Prosopographie des magistrats belges 1795–1960" project. Personal data (geographical origin, language, wealth etc.), socio-professional trajectories in peacetime, but also relational data that shed light on the networks of which individuals are part and political data have proved to be particularly valuable. They help to explain why some magistrates were discriminated by the German authorities, be it positively (they were promoted) or negatively (they were targeted by disciplinary or penal measures). On the other hand, individual employment histories during the two world wars may have had important consequences in terms of careers. If some are immediately visible—like premature

[4]Regarding the impact of the Third Republic on the social recruitment of magistrates, see C. Charle, "État et magistrats. Les origines d'une crise prolongée", in *Actes de la Recherche en Sciences sociales*, XCVI, 1993, no, 1, pp. 39–48.

[5]The Belgian sources used are mainly the appointment and disciplinary dossiers of the magistrates preserved in the Belgian national archives (AGR, *Ministère de la Justice. Secrétariat général. Dossiers de nomination des magistrats et greffiers de l'ordre judiciaire, et des officiers ministériels*, 1830–1953, and AGR, *Ministère de la Justice: Secrétariat général, 2e section* et *Ministère de la Justice, Secrétariat général, Service du personnel de la magistrature, Dossiers des magistrats*, 1953–1980). The main German sources used are the reports of the civil administration active in Belgium in 1914–1918 (*Verwaltungsberichte des Verwaltungschefs* kept in *Geheimes Staatsarchiv Preußischer Kulturbesitz*, Berlin) and those from the military administration active during the second occupation (Bundesarchiv-Militärarchiv, RW/36 in Freiburg).

[6]In general, the comparison between the two German occupations is still insufficiently developed. Some examples are: B. Majerus, *Occupations et logiques policières. La police bruxelloise en 1914–1918 et 1940–1945*, Brussels, Académie Royale de Belgique, 2008, and P. Nefors, "'*Quand les fils de novembre nous reviennent en mai* …'"14–18" als gedragsbepalende factor tijdens de tweede Duitse bezetting", in P.-A. Tallier and P. Nefors (eds), *Quand les canons se taisent: actes du colloque international organisé par les Archives de l'Etat et le Musée royal de l'Armée et d'Histoire militaire (Bruxelles, 3–6 novembre 2008)*, Brussels, Archives générales du Royaume, 2010, pp. 569–590.

ends of careers—more subtle impacts, like retirement without authorisation to bear the professional title and/or to wear a decoration, require understanding of the events and the specific dynamics of war.

16.1 The Two Occupations and the Judicial Landscape

During both occupations of the country, the Belgian magistracy kept on carrying out its work. Considered as the preeminent public service, judicial authorities needed to continue to dispense justice. The need to maintain judicial authorities was subject to a general consensus among the doctrinal authors specialising in international law (*occupatio bellica*). Before the country was invaded, the Belgian authorities wrote instructions in accordance with this consensus, recommending that the judicial system should be maintained, and planned legal provisions for the second occupation that punished dereliction of duty (the "Bovesse" Act of 5 March 1935).[7] All in all, the fact that national judicial authorities carried on their activities suited the occupying forces, who were anxious to maintain order in the occupied territory and to save their own resources at the same time.

As the main legal framework guiding the relations between the occupied and the occupiers, the 1907 Hague Convention entrusted the latter with responsibility to administer the occupied territory provisionally. Pursuant to the Convention, ratified by both countries, the occupying force was responsible for keeping public order and upholding public life. Within the framework of its mission, the occupying power had to respect local laws, unless that was absolutely impossible.

Any comparison between occupation under the totalitarian regime of the National Socialist Party and under the constitutional monarchy of Wilhelm II must obviously be made carefully. The totalitarian character of the regime in Nazi Germany led to the second occupation having a more strongly political nature.[8] The occupation regime was different in each of the wars as well. However, many similarities can be detected when we consider in isolation the attitudes of the institutions officially designed to supervise the Belgian judicial system.

[7]K. Peters, "Les abandons de poste dans la magistrature lors de la Seconde Guerre mondiale", in *Cahiers d'histoire du temps présent*, no. 24, 2011, pp. 163–186.

[8]Historian Herman Van Goethem underlines the fact that the broad interpretation of the Hague Convention of 1907, which was applied during both occupations, had much more problematic consequences under the second occupation with its far stronger political character than in 1914–1918. This broad interpretation (or *maximalistic interpretation* as Herman Van Goethem calls it) concedes the obligation for the local administration to execute German orders even contrary to Belgian law and the Constitution, if this legislation is "absolutely necessary" and promulgated in order to preserve "quiet and order". In far more cases than in 1914–1918, orders published to maintain or restore order suited the political and military aims of the Germans at the same time. (H. Van Goethem, "La Convention de La Haye, la collaboration administrative en Belgique et la persécution des Juifs à Anvers, 1940–1942", in *Cahiers d'histoire du temps présent/Bijdragen tot de Eigentijdse Geschiedenis*, no. 17, Brussels, 2006, p. 121f.).

In the 1914–1918 occupation, the German authorities opted to maintain Belgian administrative services and established a civil administration in charge of supervising them. Belgian public services continued to deal with current affairs under the direct supervision of the Germans. Within the civil administration, the *Justizabteilung* (Judicial Department), made up of a few legal practitioners, was in charge of supervising the Ministry of Justice and relations with the judiciary. Since the judiciary was an independent power, the relations with it were more complex. The German authorities intervened in judicial life in many ways. Acting as a substitute for the executive power, the civil administration occasionally sent circular letters to public prosecutors (*procureurs du Roi*), but these were rare and the Belgian prosecution offices were in fact fairly autonomous in their capacity to define their penal policy. The general governor, who took over royal prerogatives, exerted the power of pardon which allowed him to intervene in the carrying out of punishments. Furthermore, the German military often interacted with the Belgian judicial authorities through its own courts, which were in charge of enforcing martial law and applying occupation decrees. The scope of action of the German military justice constantly extended during the occupation, as thousands of decrees were issued to organise control over the population and the exploitation of the occupied territory's resources.

The magistrates, as a condition of keeping their salary and positions, were compelled to sign a statement of loyalty.[9] This statement established the basis for the compromise that enabled judicial cohabitation to work. Magistrates would keep their positions and be free to deliver rulings as they saw fit as long as they acknowledged German authority and its prerogatives according to international law and refrained from perpetrating any hostile action against the occupier. However, magistrates lost some of their authority to German military justice. They first lost their jurisdiction over all individuals, Germans or Belgians, who were related to the occupation authorities, and the subject-matter within their competence was gradually reduced.

During the second occupation of the country, the German authorities opted for a military administration.[10] This administration did not directly control Belgian ministries and could therefore operate with a reduced staff. As for judicial matters, the assignments and profiles of the people in charge of the *Gruppe Justiz* were nonetheless quite similar to their predecessors in the *Justizabteilung*. The heads of the staff, Wilhelm van Randenborgh and Walter Hartz, were reserve officers and professional magistrates in civil life. They carried out the surveillance of the Belgian magistrates.

On 10 May 1940, the German intentions to maintain the established Belgian institutions and to only act as a supervision government were announced in Belgium through a proclamation made by the German Army's Commander-in-Chief, von

[9]A. Meyers, "La Magistrature et l'Occupation. Discours prononcé à l'audience solennelle de rentrée du 1er octobre 1919 de la cour d'appel de Liège", in *Journal des Tribunaux*, 1919, col. 542.

[10]The introduction of a civil administration in July 1944 did not bring about radical changes, however, since it was short lived.

Brauchitsch, which specified that "local authorities will be allowed to carry on their activities on the condition that they behave loyally towards the German Army".[11] In his notice to the press in Western occupied territories, von Brauchitsch stated that orders from German heads of the military would have the force of law during the occupation and that they "took precedence over local laws".[12]

The main difference in comparison with the first German occupation lay in the organisation of the Belgian authorities. In 1914–1918, of the three branches of government, only the judiciary was allowed to carry on its activities in the occupied territory. The national legislative power was suspended. Only the occupying authority was allowed to enact new laws and it alone could judge what should be defined as an absolute impediment of enforcing Belgian laws in accordance with international law, as ruled by the Court of Cassation after turbulent legal debates.[13] The legislative situation was therefore relatively clear. On the one hand, national laws were applied as long as they were not amended or repealed by the occupying force and they were ratified by Belgian courts and, on the other hand, the occupation orders were ratified by the military courts of the Germans. The military administration sometimes tried to have its orders applied by Belgian courts, but these attempts failed in a great majority of cases, at least for penal courts. Magistrates proved very reluctant to accept a cooperation that would risk compromising them.

By contrast, from 1940 until 1944, the institutional landscape was somewhat more complex. The secretaries general of Belgian ministries, by way of a delegation system—the limits of which were subject to interpretation until the end of the war—carried out *ad interim* the executive and legislative powers. Yet, any order issued by these Belgian senior officials first had to be submitted to the occupying authority for approval. This system was very beneficial for the German power.[14] The *Militärbefehlshaber* resorted to his executive power as soon as he considered Belgian laws were insufficient and issued orders that had the force of law. These orders even took precedence over Belgian law. However, the occupiers preferred that unpopular German measures be taken by the secretaries general, hoping that local laws would be better accepted by the population.[15] Another essential conse-

[11]"Proclamation à la population de la Belgique", in *Heeresgruppen-Verordnungsblatt für die besetzten Gebiete*, no. 1, 10 May 1940, p. 2.

[12]"Notice destinée à toute la presse dans les territoires occupés de l'ouest", in *Heeresgruppen-Verordnungsblatt für die besetzten Gebiete*, no. 1, 10 May 1940, p. 16.

[13]On the positions of the Belgian Court of Cassation during the first German occupation, see: M. Bost, "Tour à tour malmenée, divisée, triomphante: parcours de la Cour de cassation de Belgique pendant la Première Guerre mondiale", in M. Houllemare and P. Nivet (eds), *Justice et guerre de l'Antiquité à la Première guerre mondiale. Actes du colloque (Amiens, 18-20 novembre 2009)*, Amiens, Encrage, 2011, pp. 183–194.

[14]M. Van Den Wijngaert, *Het beleid van het comité van de secretarissen-generaal in België tijdens de Duitse bezetting 1940–1944*, Brussels, Paleis der Academiën, 1975, p. 29.

[15]H. Umbreit, "Les pouvoirs allemands en France et en Belgique", in E. Dejonghe (ed.), *L'occupation en France et en Belgique 1940–1944, Actes du colloque de Lille, 26–28 avril 1985* [*Revue du Nord*, 1987–1988], vol. 1, Villeneuve d'Ascq: Revue du Nord, 1987/1988, p. 26.

quence of the secretary-general system was that it created an intermediary between the occupying force and the judicial power that did not exist in 1914–1918. At the time, the Chief Public Prosecutor of the Court of Cassation, Georges Terlinden, was the direct contact person for the head of civil administration, von Sandt, with whom he discussed the questions of principle. In the years 1940–1944, direct interactions between the two powers only took place on very rare occasions; they communicated through the secretary general of the Ministry of Justice.

One main difference of the second occupation was that institutions of the Third Reich other than the military were established in Belgium, which accentuated the confusion. The most important example of this is the German police forces. A part from the military police organs such as *Feldgendarmerie* and *Geheime Feldpolizei*, an additional threat for the magistrates consisted in the presence of the *Sicherheitspolizei-Sicherheitsdienst* (*Sipo-SD*), whose activities had the most intimidating impact. The *Gestapo*, as the *Sipo-SD* was also known in Belgium, was an institution that was intrinsically independent from the military administration. Evaluating the relation between the *Sipo-SD* and the military occupying power is complicated. On the one hand, sources clearly show that there was a high degree of collaboration. Concerning *Gruppe Justiz*, *Sipo-SD* regularly sent information collected from their informers about the (political) attitudes of magistrates. There is also evidence for the interference of the *Sipo-SD* in many affairs, such as the arbitrary incarceration of magistrates without previously taking advice from the military administration, which often ran contrary to the aims of the *Gruppe Justiz*. To put it simply, *Gruppe Justiz* was interested in the preservation of the Belgian justice administration, as long as it was aligned to the objectives of the military administration, whereas the mission of the *Sipo-SD* was intervention in cases concerning people or movements considered subversive. This meant that, besides tracing ordinary criminals, the *Sipo-SD* concentrated on pursuing Jews,[16]

[16]The Brussels judge, Henri Buch (1910–1972), was the only Jew active in the judiciary in 1940. There is evidence that Buch resigned from his office shortly before the German administration was established in Brussels. The exact circumstances of his departure are unknown at this stage, partly as Buch's personal file is unfortunately missing among the magistrates' dossiers. What we do know is that Buch participated in the Battle of Belgium in May 1940, went into hiding from 1941 onwards, was very active in the clandestine communist party and was one of the leaders of the *Partisans armés*, an armed resistance movement. What is interesting about Henri Buch's case is that the report made about him at the *Sipo-SD* apparently did not take into account that he was Jewish, but exclusively his political background as a communist. On 5 July 1944 he was arrested, incarcered and tortured in Breendonck and was later deported to the Dutch and German concentration camps of Vught, Sachsenhausen, Oranienburg and Schwerin. (J. Gotovitch, *Du rouge au tricolore, Les communistes belges de 1939 à 1944: un aspect de l'histoire de la Résistance en Belgique*, Brussels: Labor, 1992, p. 488; and, concerning Buch's appointment as a magistrate in 1936, L. Saerens, *Vreemdelingen in een wereldstad. Een geschiedenis van Antwerpen en zijn joodse bevolking*, Tielt: Lannoo, 2000, p. 335f).

Freemasons,[17] communists[18] and members of resistance movements. The first three of these persecuted groups were relatively underrepresented or even non-existent in the Belgian magistracy at that time. But there were more than 50 examples of magistrates who gave support to (or who were active members of) a resistance movement. For this reason, many of them were tracked by the *Sipo-SD*.

16.2 A First Type of Interference: Appointments in the Judiciary

16.2.1 1914–1918

"We are on 14 September 1917 and we are still the same age as we were on 14 August 1914."[19]

In the occupation of 1914–1918, the magistracy succeeded in avoiding German interference in appointments for a long time. Of course, the length of the occupation confronted the magistracy with the tricky issue of replacing staff who died or reached the age of retirement. In the absence of the Belgian legitimate authority, and to counter any attempt to interfere on the part of the occupying power, the magistracy discreetly elaborated a replacement strategy by using all the possibilities for substitution allowed by the 1869 Act on judicial organisation. Over the course of the occupation period, many magistrates reached the legal age of retirement, especially officials with leading positions.[20] The magistrates adopted a consistent attitude regarding this issue. They voluntarily postponed their resignations

[17]Almost nothing is known about Freemasons in the Belgian magistracy. It is extremely difficult to obtain any information about this subject, primarily because of the secret character of freemasonry and consequently the lack of publicly visible sources, but further because of the particular danger linked to divulgation as Freemasons in years 1940–1944. Among the thousands of magistrates' files we have examined, only one single file concerns a subject related to freemasonry: a magistrate from Namur was discharged in 1946 for having been a member of the anti-Masonic league *L'Épuration* during the German occupation. (cf. AGR, *Ministère de la Justice, Secrétariat général, Service du personnel de la magistrature, Dossiers des magistrats*, 1953–1980, no. 665.).

[18]There were very few substantially "left minded" magistrates. The best documented exception is Baron Adrien van den Branden de Reeth from the Brussels court, who openly sympathised with communism after having been a central character in the Resistance during the war. (Cf. AGR, *Ministère de la Justice, Secrétariat général, Service du personnel de la magistrature, Dossiers des magistrats*, 1953–1980, dossier no. 2461, and "Dossier concernant le baron Van den Branden de Reeth", in Archives de l'Etat à Anderlecht, Tribunal de première instance de Bruxelles, Dossiers politiques, no. 156).

[19]G. Terlinden, "Jubilé professionnel de Monsieur le Premier Président Du Pont, 14 septembre 1917", in *Bulletin de la Cour de cassation de Belgique*, 1917, p. 13.

[20]For instance, Eugène Dupont, first president of the Court of Cassation, was 78 years old when the Germans retreated in 1918. Armand Hénoul, Chief Public Prosecutor in Liège, was 76 years old at the time.

until the war came to an end, when the legitimate power would be able to approve their departure and to appoint new officials.[21] By continuing to serve beyond the legal term, these magistrates took part in the patriotic effort.

During the first years of the war, German authorities tolerated that option. They did not seem particularly interested in the appointments of magistrates. The stability of Belgian public services was rather beneficial for the Germans. Retirements and replacements were expensive and the occupying authorities would rather not bear such expenses since it was impossible to tell how long the occupation would last. The situation changed in the wake of the administrative separation of the country decreed in March 1917.[22] During the summer of 1917, the newly acquired power of the activists[23] in the Flemish Ministry of Justice encouraged some of their followers to propose their application for vacant positions. This was an opportunity for them, knowing they were hated by the judicial hierarchy, to create a more favourable environment by establishing magistrates who supported Flemish claims.[24] Therefore, as soon as he arrived at the Ministry in July 1917, the new secretary general, Flor Heuvelmans,[25] asked chief public prosecutors to provide him with a list of vacant positions and to summon the courts in order to review the applications, so as to provoke a domino effect that would free low-ranking positions.

From Le Havre, the Belgian government reacted by issuing a decree-law which laid down that the measures taken by the occupiers (including the appointments) would automatically become void as the country was gradually liberated.[26]

[21]There is a revealing exception to this trend, which highlights the power and sovereignty stakes related to the issue of appointments in the magistracy: the resignation request from the judge of the Court of Appeal of Brussels, Charles Diercxsens, who was 72 years old, submitted in September 1914, was accepted three months later by the Belgian Minister of Justice and by the German general governor in Belgium. However, he was only replaced in 1919.

[22]The decree that administratively split the country into two unilingual regions—Flanders governed from Brussels and Wallonia governed from Namur—was an important step in the *Flamenpolitik*, the German policy that favoured the Dutch-speaking community in Belgium. It led to the division of central ministries to Brussels and Namur. Most Belgian civil servants resigned and some of them were deported. The German civil administration was also split into two entities. (P. Delforge, *La Wallonie et la Première Guerre mondiale: pour une histoire de la séparation administrative*, Namur, Institut Destrée, 2008).

[23]This term referred to the minor fraction of the Flemish Movement who chose to collaborate with the occupying force in the First World War to achieve their linguistic claims.

[24]Verwaltungsbericht des Verwaltungschefs für Flandern für das Halbjahr August 1917 bis Januar 1918 (GSaPK, 32458, 474 vs-475 vs).

[25]Flor Heuvelmans, an important member of the Flemish Movement in Antwerp, was a police magistrate in that town when he agreed to become the secretary general of the Flemish Ministry of Justice. During the occupation period, he opted to collaborate with the occupiers when they organised the 'flamandisation' of the University of Ghent in October 1916. The transformation of the French-speaking university into a Dutch-speaking one was the most important goal of the Flemish Movement before the war.

[26]*Arrêté-loi du 8 avril 1917 déterminant l'effet des mesures prises par l'occupant et des dispositions prises par le gouvernement*, in *Moniteur belge*, 1917, pp. 338–340.

Everywhere in occupied Belgium, the heads of judicial bodies resisted. The judicial authorities, which felt threatened, let the German authorities know that they did not acknowledge the occupying force's power to appoint magistrates. In order to strengthen this position, Chief Public Prosecutor Terlinden wrote a list of arguments which he transmitted unofficially, during the summer of 1917, to von der Lancken, a German diplomat, the chief of the Political Section of the General Government, who was respected by the high magistracy for his intelligence and courtesy.[27] The main argument was drawn from international law: the occupiers, who only had a de facto power that was temporary in nature, were not allowed to appoint magistrates for life.[28]

The appointments issue, beyond the patriotic aspects it entails, also relates to the status of the magistracy. "…forcing magistrates who swore an oath to sit with individuals appointed by the Germans and who did not would be contrary to the fundamental rules of their institution. This would harm the status of Belgian magistracy and violate its independence.[29]"

For Belgian magistrates who lived in a closed occupational environment, this threat was as much professional as political in nature. The appointment of activist judges without respecting the rules in the matter was perceived as a real intrusion.

The Terlinden notice also warned the German authority. These appointments would have harmful consequences on the judicial authorities' ability to carry out their duties. Legally appointed magistrates would consider these appointments as non-existent and the decisions taken by the appointed individuals as lacking any authority and value.

According to the Chief Public Prosecutor, this opposition stopped appointments for a few months among magistrates and notaries.[30] But at the turn of 1918, soon after Flanders' autonomy was proclaimed, the resistance lost the battle. Several appointments of officials recruited among Flemish activists were promulgated. At the end of January 1918, the first three activist justices of the peace (*juge de paix*, "proximity magistrate") were appointed.

The Germans seemed to play a secondary role in this process and only helped the activists to satisfy their claims. The archives of the *Raad van Vlaanderen*[31] (the Council of Flanders) showed that some members suspected the occupying

---

[27]Palais de justice de Bruxelles, *Archives du parquet de la Cour de cassation*, boîte X, 2 (I). Terlinden was unofficially inspired by a study co-signed by the judge at the appeal court, Professor of International Law Ernest Nys, and by the judge at the Court of Cassation, Édouard Remy (E. Nys and E. Remy, "La nomination de magistrats et de notaires par l'occupant", in *Belgique judiciaire*, 1919, pp. 5–10.).

[28]The doctrine reinforces this theory. Terlinden quotes the German legal adviser Franz de Holtzendorff, who was against the appointment of judges by the occupier (*Éléments de droit international public*, Paris, Rousseau, 1891, p. 179).

[29]Palais de justice de Bruxelles, Archives du parquet de la Cour de cassation, box X, 2 (I).

[30]Ibid.

[31]The consultative body of Flemish activists to the occupying power.

authority to have intentionally delayed the appointments.[32] On his part, the head of Flanders administration, Alexander Schaible, criticised the limited number of valid applications. By the end of January 1918, the *Raad van Vlaanderen* was only able to propose four applicants to justice of the peace positions, among whom only three were appointed.[33] In Wallonia, the situation was totally different. Unlike Schaible, the head of the German administration Edgar Haniel, who did not have to deal with the activists' pressure, shared the reluctance of the magistrates. As was mentioned in his bi-annual report for June 1917–January 1918, "this is of no particular interest (…) as long as courts work normally", especially because such appointments could have very undesirable consequences, even if suitable applicants should be found.[34]

The appointments of activist magistrates were a first and prominent blow against the judicial organisation. The response of the judiciary was also radical. As Chief Public Prosecutor Terlinden had announced in his note to von der Lancken, the newly appointed magistrates were not warmly welcomed by their counterparts. When the new police magistrate of Antwerp, Henry Quakkelaer, came before the tribunal of Antwerp to take the oath, Prosecutor Augenot pretended to have no "réquisitoire" to do, whereas Vice-President Maquinay invited Quakkelaer to get out. A notary named Hallewyn, from Kontich (province of Antwerp), also freshly appointed by the German General Governor, was rejected in the same way. Once in place, the judicial work of the new Judge Quakkelaer was deliberately stymied. The judiciary counterattacked with its traditional weapon—legal process: the Chief Public Prosecutor of Brussels, Barthelemy Jottrand, ordered the Public Prosecutor of Antwerp to systematically appeal Quakkelaers' decisions.[35] In doing this, the judiciary exposed itself to sanctions. In France, the Chief Public Prosecutor of Douai, who appealed all the judgments of the Maubeuge Court set up by the occupier, was arrested and taken hostage in April 1915.[36]

Undoubtedly, this Belgian judicial offensive constituted an act of open resistance against the occupier's policies. The magistracy's tolerance threshold was reached. It was hostile to any intrusion by foreign elements on the judicial body.

We cannot fail to establish a link between the appointment issue and the judicial strike that began two weeks later. The *Flamenpolitik* was then, again, a cause of rupture between Belgian justice and occupiers. At the end of 1917, the Flemish

[32]Ligue nationale pour l'unité belge, *Les archives du Conseil de Flandre (Raad van Vlaanderen)*, Brussels, Dewarichet, 1928, p. 30.

[33]Verwaltungsbericht des Verwaltungschefs für Flandern für das Halbjahr August 1917 bis Januar 1918 (GSaPK, 32458, 474 vs-475 vs).

[34]The report highlights the menace announced by Terlinden with regard to the newly appointed judges (Verwaltungsbericht des Verwaltungschefs für Wallonien für das Halbjahr August 1917 bis Januar 1918. Haniel, 30. Januar 1918 (GSaPK, 32458, 30/391 verso).

[35]B. Jottrand, "Le pouvoir judiciaire et l'activisme séparatiste. Discours prononcé à l'audience solennelle [de la Cour d'appel de Bruxelles] du 4 décembre 1918", 15 December 1918, p. 9.

[36]A. Deperchin, *La famille judiciaire pendant la Première Guerre mondiale*, Université Lille 2, unpublished doctoral thesis in Law, 1998, p. 414.

activists declared Flanders politically autonomous. Sustained by a wave of popular indignation against this act of dismantling of the national political structures and under the influence of some politicians, the Brussels Court of Appeal, on 7 February 1918, urged the Chief Public Prosecutor to prosecute the main activist leaders, as initiators of an attack against the form of government.

One day later, following this demand, the Brussels prosecutor's office arrested two activist leaders, Auguste Borms and Pieter Tack. They were freed by the Germans a few hours later. On the orders of the latter, who were furious about this action against their politics, the Court of Appeal's first president and two presidents of the chambers were deported to Germany, while all the judges of the Court were suspended *sine die* for having participated in a political manifestation.

It did not take long before the Court of Cassation retorted with panache. On 11 February 1918, the Belgian supreme court, condemning this flagrant violation of the independence of justice, decided to suspend its functions. Following this example, all jurisdictions under the general government went gradually on strike, a protest movement which lasted until the armistice.[37] The Germans were forced to install their own judicial system to ensure the security of their armies in the occupied territory.

Most probably, the previous intervention in appointments to the magistracy played an important role in triggering the magistrates' strike. Why should magistrates do their duty if the body was diseased?[38] The hostile reaction against the newcomers indicates some radicalisation among magistrates. In the earlier years of the occupation, they had been more cautious and mostly favoured circumvention strategies and compromises with the occupiers.

During the 1930s, as the possibility of a second occupation of the country was seriously contemplated, the honorary Chief Public Prosecutor of Brussels, Jean Servais, suggested the delegation of competence in judicial appointments to chief public prosecutors in case of a reoccupation of the national territory.[39]

16.2.2 1940–1944

During the Second World War, the staffing policy of the occupiers was more ambitious. The Germans not only aimed at appointing Flemish magistrates and

---

[37]In the *Etappengebiet*, the situation was different; the strike was not so extended. In the summer of 1918 it was the Germans themselves who prohibited the Belgian magistrates from continuing their functions.

[38]Concerning the magistrates' strike: M. Bost and A. François, "La grève de la magistrature belge (février -novembre 1918). Un haut fait de la résistance nationale à l'épreuve des archives judiciaires", in D. Heirbaut, X. Rousseaux and A. Wijffels (eds), *Histoire du Droit et de la Justice, une nouvelle génération de recherches*, Louvain-la-Neuve, Presses universitaires de Louvain, 2010, pp. 19–43.

[39]Documents of the *Commission permanente de la mobilisation de la Nation*, CEGESOMA, Archives Raoul Hayoit de Termicourt concernant le travail des institutions belges pendant l'occupation, no. 2.

especially those favourable to the New Order, but also sought to break the resistance of Belgian magistrates. The German authority acted indirectly through the successive secretaries general of the Ministry of Justice. Indeed, the appointment of magistrates was a prerogative of the secretary general of Justice. The solution that Servais recommended, that is to say delegating this competence to the general procurators' offices, was not applied.[40]

The heads of judicial bodies nevertheless continued to play an important role. The secretary general asked for their opinion and respected it in many cases. Besides, the judiciary applied the techniques of delegating, substituting and automatically extending mandates that had been implemented during the first occupation as widely as possible in order to avoid the new occupier's control.

The German administration managed to control the carried out appointments through the *Gruppe Justiz* though and regularly interfered in the process by exerting various levels of pressure on the secretary general of Justice according to the time and context. As far as judicial appointments were concerned, German intentions were not homogeneous in nature. Similarly to the civil administration that was pushed by activists into interfering in the appointments of Belgian magistrates in 1917, the heads of the military administration were influenced by the interests of the Belgian New Order organisations. Different measures were taken by the Germans, yielding to the demands of collaborationist parties for greater control of the appointments. This intrusion policy gradually increased.

The first German measure was the decree of 4 April 1941 which laid down that the appointment of the heads of judicial bodies first required the approval of the *Militärverwaltung*.[41] According to German sources, this decree was allegedly used in most cases to remove applicants deemed as opposed to the Germans and to favour Flemish applicants. Indeed, from the perspective of the military administration, "Flemish claims were justified insofar as the Flemish were under-represented in the magistracy in comparison with the share of the total population they corresponded to. In particular, leading positions were almost exclusively held by Walloons, even in Flemish areas."[42]

New Order organisations, especially the *Vlaams Nationaal Verbond* (*VNV*) and the *Rexists*, were dissatisfied with the restriction to leading positions under German tutelage and put pressure on the *Militärverwaltung* in order to obtain more control and a more *political* and significant change in the composition of the

[40]The archives do not explain why the solution suggested by Servais did not come into effect in May 1940. However, this option disappeared when the general delegation of ministerial competences to secretary generals was ratified at the beginning of the occupation. The Germans aimed at having only one contact person per department.

[41]Bundesarchiv-Militärarchiv, Freiburg, RW 36/397, p. 10. On 19 May 1941, a complementary German decree was made public specifying that the potential substitutes of the chief prosecutors are also concerned by the decree of 4 April 1941, but not those who replaced the principal judges.

[42]Bundesarchiv-Militärarchiv, Freiburg, RW 36/397, p. 11. We notice that in the language of the military administration, an amalgamation was frequently made of "Walloons" and "French-speaking Belgians".

magistracy, considering that "appointments are a perfect field of battle on which the resistance of the courts can be fought and broken".[43]

In the early period of the occupation, Secretary General Ernst de Bunswyck[44] was concerned about the legality of the decrees he might issue. For the sake of caution, he refrained from proceeding to judicial appointments. To make up for the absence of magistrates or substitutes due to derelictions of duty and mobilisation of the army, especially for courts of justices of the peace and courts of first instance, he used the decrees issued on 22 July 1940 and 20 December 1940, that authorised the temporary appointment of lawyers as substitutes.[45] In spring 1941, after de Bunswyck was forbidden to carry out his duties following a decree on the maximum age of officials (see Sect. 16.3.2 below), he was replaced as secretary general by Gaston Schuind, a judge at the Brussels Court of Appeal. The military administration made him understand he was expected to make up for the under-representation of Flemish magistrates by appointing new officials accordingly. Indeed, as soon as Schuind was in office, a clear increase in appointments can be observed. The caution that had prevailed at the beginning had drawn to an end. Appointments in the magistracy reached a peak at the time of the opening of the legal year 1941.

In summer 1941, following the orders of the military administration, Schuind appointed Selschotter, a lawyer from Veurne (West Flanders), as head of his cabinet.[46] The choice made by the Ministry of Justice to appoint a Flemish legal practitioner to this key position was strategically aimed at appeasing the occupiers. Later on, the New Order organisations complained that appointing Selschotter to the Ministry of Justice was useless as the appointments remained "anti-Flemish and germanophobic".[47] As a matter of fact, the profile that parties such as the VNV looked for in a magistrate, that is to say a politicised, openly Flemish nationalist, germanophile and docile individual, was almost non-existent among the legal practitioners.

The occupiers in turn had to satisfy their allies and occasionally gave into the incessant requests from leading figures of the New Order to support certain applicants and to remove others. Judicial crises in the summer of 1942 and the winter

[43]"De benoemingen in het gerecht onder het beleid van den Heer Schuind" (AGR, Ministère de la Justice, Secrétariat général, Service du personnel de la magistrature, Dossiers des magistrats, 1953–1980, dossier no. 2118).

[44]This secretary general was the head of the cabinet of Minister of Justice Carton de Wiart during the First World War seems strange.

[45]"Art. seems strange 1er de l'arrêté du 20 décembre 1940, modifiant l'arrêté-loi du 6 novembre 1939 relatif au remplacement temporaire des magistrats rappelés sous les armes", quoted in AGR, *Ministère de la Justice, Secrétariat général, Service du personnel de la magistrature, Dossiers des magistrats*, 1953–1980, dossier de Louis Berger, no. 115.

[46]For this purpose, Selschotter had been appointed judge in Brussels immediately before.

[47]"De benoemingen in het gerecht onder het beleid van den Heer Schuind" (AGR, Ministère de la Justice, Secrétariat général, Service du personnel de la magistrature, Dossiers des magistrats, 1953–1980, dossier no. 2118).

of 1942/1943 (see below, Sect. 16.3.2.3) poured oil on the fire and the German authorities considered the appropriateness of widening the tutelage on appointments to *all* magistrate positions.[48] These considerations coincided with the enacting of decree-laws by the secretaries general which would modify the political landscape of Belgium by creating large urban areas. As the occupiers were aware that, in view of the tense background, resistance from the magistracy was predictable (the decree-laws issued by the secretaries general amending the political structure of the country were considered illegal by Belgian judges), the issue of appointments in the magistracy seemed particularly urgent at the time. Concurrently, Secretary General Schuind's appointment policy was subject to more and more criticism in the circles of the New Order.[49]

The claims of the New Order organisations regarding appointments were proving difficult to put into practice, however. The lack of qualifications of the applicants proposed by the collaborationists was an issue and the *Gruppe Justiz* was perfectly aware of this fact.[50] However, to avoid appointments that would offend the New Order organisations and to give the impression that their claims were taken into consideration, the *Militärverwaltung* unofficially requested to be consulted by the secretary general of Justice at the latest two weeks before each magistrate's appointment.[51] This system proved difficult to implement, as the military administration did not have enough staff to investigate the applicants. Therefore, the head of *Gruppe Justiz*, van Randenborgh, clearly stated his disapproval of the extension of the order of 14 April 1941; he considered getting relevant information about the candidates to be complicated and not always reliable. He further objected that if the *Militärverwaltung* gave official permission to candidates, it would undermine the German authority if these magistrates would later have to be discharged. Further, he declared that sufficient good Flemish candidates were not available.[52]

The appointment of a public prosecutor in Hasselt, in particular, caused a shift in Secretary General Schuind's appointment policy. In September 1941, Hasselt Public Prosecutor Massa was relieved of his duties following a campaign against him by a local collaborationist group. According to the tradition the secretary general planned to appoint one Vandevelde, who already filled the post of public prosecutor *ad interim* as a substitute for Massa. The *Gruppe Justiz* also favoured this choice. Yet, the *VNV* vividly expressed its disapproval of Vandevelde who was considered by them to be an opportunist.[53] Ultimately, a substitute public prosecu-

[48]See Ch.-L. Louveaux, "La magistrature dans la tourmente des années 1940–44", in *Revue de droit pénal et de criminologie*, 1981 and idem, "Le moindre mal", in F. Ringelheim (ed.) *Juger*, no. 6/7, Gily, François Collinet, 1994, pp. 28–30.

[49]"De benoemingen in het gerecht onder het beleid van den Heer Schuind" (AGR, Ministère de la Justice, Secrétariat général, Service du personnel de la magistrature, Dossiers des magistrats, 1953–1980, dossier no. 2118).

[50]K. Peters, "L'influence de l'occupant sur les nominations et les destitutions de magistrats", p. 64.

[51]Bundesarchiv-Militärarchiv, Freiburg, RW 36/397, p. 12.

[52]Bundesarchiv-Militärarchiv, RW36/407, p. 48.

[53]Ibid., p. 10.

tor from the tribunal of Antwerp, one Rubens, was appointed. Rubens was accepted by the New Order organisations and German administration gave its approval.[54] In this case, the occupying force interfered significantly in a field of competence that normally came under the secretary general.

In order to avoid this scenario from repeating itself in other prosecution offices, especially in Brussels, Antwerp and Leuven, which had vacant prosecutor positions, Secretary General Schuind refrained from proceeding to new appointments.[55] But this circumvention strategy was rapidly thwarted by the Germans.[56]

In the meantime, the officials at the head of the *Gruppe Justiz* had noted that it was impossible to investigate the political behaviour of the applicants properly within two weeks. The request for preliminary inspection was withdrawn around February 1943. Moreover, the *Gruppe Justiz* realised that magistrates appointed following a proposal from the *VNV* were not necessarily more 'docile'. A clear example of this was that of Antwerp Public Prosecutor Edouard Baers, who had been strongly supported by the *VNV* and took office in February 1942. At the beginning of 1943, the *Militärverwaltung* was utterly surprised to discover that this prosecutor firmly advocated against the Belgian police's collaboration in implementing German measures. As a result, he was removed from office.[57] Baers' behaviour was a great disappointment for the *VNV*.[58]

In spite of the vivid criticism expressed by New Order parties against Gaston Schuind's appointment policy, the *Gruppe Justiz* supported the secretary general for a long time. Van Randenborgh still defended him as the pressure in favour of his dismissal increased at the *Militärverwaltung*.[59] On 17 September 1943, Schuind was dismissed on various grounds. The former administrator of public safety, Robert de Foy, was appointed secretary general *ad interim*, which was quite a surprising choice as de Foy had been arrested by the Germans at the beginning of the occupation due to his involvement in the May 1940 arrests.

---

[54]Bundesarchiv-Militärarchiv, RW 36/384, p. 180.

[55]"De benoemingen in het gerecht onder het beleid van den Heer Schuind" (AGR, Ministère de la Justice, Secrétariat général, Service du personnel de la magistrature, Dossiers des magistrats, 1953–1980, dossier no. 2118).

[56]Cf. "Tätigkeitsbericht des Chefs des Militärverwaltungsstabs", no. 24, April–June 1943 (Bundesarchiv-Militärarchiv, Freiburg, RW 36/193, p. 138).

[57]"Tätigkeitsbericht der Gruppe Justiz für die Zeit vom 15. November 1942 bis 15. Februar 1943", in Bundesarchiv-Militärarchiv, Freiburg, RW 36/382, p. 54. Later, in 1944, Edouard Baers was accused of participation in a secret service. He was imprisoned in Germany until April 1945.

[58]"De benoemingen in het gerecht onder het beleid van den Heer Schuind" (AGR, Ministère de la Justice, Secrétariat général, Service du personnel de la magistrature, Dossiers des magistrats, 1953–1980, dossier no. 2118).

[59]Letter of the *Gruppe Justiz*, addressed to the director of the administrative section of the *Militärverwaltung*, von Craushaar, on 23 March 1943, in Bundesarchiv-Militärarchiv, Freiburg, RW 36/422, p. 2: "His appointment policy in the judiciary, which has often been violently attacked by the *VNV* and *Rex*, has too often been judged unilaterally to his disadvantage. Fourteen out of 26 public prosecutors have been removed from office as a result of our measures. By the way, this caused him several attacks from the Belgian magistracy."

In November 1943, when de Foy took office, the issue of the extension of the 4 April 1941 order to all appointments was debated once again. The initiative came from the *Militärverwaltung*'s administration department head, von Craushaar. When de Foy took office as secretary general, he argued he had more urgent matters to attend to and was able to delay any intervention in the beginning.

For three years, successive secretaries general managed as far as possible to prevent the Germans from completely pulling the strings of magistrate appointments. However, in March 1944, the heads of the *Militärverwaltung* decided it was time to make its approval compulsory for all appointments and issued the order of 16 March to this end.[60] This decision was taken in the context of radicalisation that marked the last months of the occupation in Belgium. The Germans had a critical need for a docile Belgian judicial body. Yet, the latter proved constantly more uncomfortable for the occupiers and the New Order.[61] As a result, it became more and more difficult to get magistrates appointed. The heads of judicial bodies massively resorted to temporary delegation of competences.

Altogether, with at least 250 magistrate files including an appointment decree dating from the 1940 to 1944 occupation period,[62] the situation strongly differs from the records concerning the first occupation.

16.3 A Second Type of Restriction on the Magistracy's Independence: Measures Aimed at Controlling Magistrates

16.3.1 1914–1918

After the First World War, in the context of the negotiation of the Treaty of Versailles, cases of interference with the independence of justice and measures targeting magistrates committed by the occupiers were carefully reported, as they could support Belgian claims for German reparations. On the basis of those post-war lists, two periods can be distinguished: before and after the judicial strike. This event indeed marked the end of the modus vivendi between judicial and occupying powers.

[60]"Tätigkeitsbericht des Chefs des Militärverwaltungsstabs", no. 27, March 1944, in Bundesarchiv-Militärarchiv, Freiburg, RW 36/196, p. 32.

[61]"Niederschrift über eine Besprechung bei Herrn Ch.M.V. über Massnahmen auf dem Gebiet der Justiz …", 7 March 1944 (*Bundesarchiv-Militärarchiv*, Freiburg, RW 36/402, p. 29).

[62]This is a minimal estimation, as research is still ongoing.

16.3.1.1 A Few Figures

From the period following the invasion in 1914 to the magistrates' strike in February 1918,[63] about 90 incidents were mentioned in the post-war reports,[64] involving approximately 60 magistrates. This figure globally covers the occupiers' intrusions in the carrying out of justice and the measures targeting magistrates, from mere intimidation to deportation. It certainly does not represent the reality of the many minor obstacles to the dispensing of justice.

Amongst the 60 identified cases, half the magistrates only had to face pressures or measures of intimidation (verbal threats, convocations and interrogations at the *Kommandantur*). Eleven of them were arrested and either detained without trial or imprisoned following a condemnation (only a few cases). Twenty magistrates were sentenced to prison terms or to pay fines (in most cases). As a rule, detentions without trial only lasted for a few days, ten at most. Condemnations to prison terms were mainly pronounced for clandestine actions (four cases), from a few months of detention for selling prohibited newspapers to prison terms of several years including hard labour for the most severe cases, such as crimes of "treason" (soldier exfiltration, intelligence). One magistrate was detained for several months in a Belgian prison and three magistrates were deported to Germany for actions committed while carrying out their duties. These deportations were not penal sanctions, but arbitrary removal measures. Three magistrates were suspended on disciplinary grounds. No magistrate was executed. A justice of the peace deported in 1916 died of natural causes (as a result of his detention conditions?) a few months later, at the German camp where he was detained for continuing to carry out his duties without signing the statement of loyalty required by the Germans at the beginning of the occupation.

The collective measures taken against the members of the Brussels Court of Appeal in February 1918 and the strike provoked a headlong rush by both groups of actors. Retaliatory measures against strikers fell on the Mons Court (the president spent one month in custody before being tried and acquitted), and all the judicial personnel of Arlon (province of Luxembourg, *Etappengebiet*)—judges, prosecutors, justices of the peace and even deputy judges—were deported to the German camp of Holzminden and detained in very bad conditions until the end of the war.[65] However, these means of intimidation and punishment did not succeed in ending the strike. Over a period of ten months, the magistrates were not remunerated. Some Belgian charities supported them discreetly.

[63] The sentences taken against the magistrates since the strike, a departure from the three preceding years and which marks a leap forward of the protagonists, are not recorded here.

[64] Source: AGR, Commission d'enquête sur Ministère de la Justice. Commission d'enquête sur la violation des règles du droit des gens, des lois et des coutumes de la guerre (archives de la Guerre).

[65] See also the postwar testimony written by the juvenile court judge L. Gofflot: idem, *Souvenirs de Holzminden, 1918*, Renaix: J. Leherte-Courtin, 1918.

16.3.1.2 Categories of Targeted Magistrates/Typology of the Incidents

Though personal behaviours may have played a role, such as in clandestine actions (espionage), it was first and foremost the competence of the magistrates concerned that explained the German intervention. The interest of the occupying force in some competences of justices of the peace was the cause for the intrusions. The reported incidents firstly concerned cases involving rents, secondly arbitrary breaking of seals, enabling the Germans to requisition materials and premises and lastly, for police matters, infringements of municipal regulations (balls, cabarets). The examining judges and the prosecution office staff were also very well represented. In view of their investigation powers and the critical role they played in judicial proceedings, these were two categories of judicial officer that could potentially hinder the actions of the occupying forces. The carrying out of punishments, which was a prerogative of the prosecution office, also was a source of conflicts.

By contrast, other categories of judges were very little concerned by such measures (as long as they did not show patriotic or anti-German views). Unlike justices of the peace, magistrates of courts of first instance rarely faced pressures from the occupier in order to obtain a favourable jurisprudence. In its official reports, the civil administration took pride in respecting the independence of judges "so much that it admitted that courts declared orders from the general governor as illegal".[66] Of course, there were a few attempts to forbid them to take decisions in specific cases but to no avail, as judges refused to yield to *diktats* that jeopardised their independence. High-ranking magistrates, also, whether they were judges or prosecutors, were barely harmed during the three first years of occupation.

Local variation may also be observed. At the local level, the situation was very contrasting. In the jurisdiction of the Ghent Court of Appeal and particularly in areas of military operations (*Operationsgebiet*), the essentially military regime acted far more arbitrarily. Belgian judicial power was also less respected in Ghent, which is statistically shown by a proportionally higher rate of intrusions than for the two other jurisdictions of the Brussels and Liège Courts of Appeal. Even high-ranking magistrates did not seem to be protected by their status. The Chief Public Prosecutor of Ghent, Alexis Callier, for instance, was twice taken hostage and his passport requests for travel in the exercise of his duties were systematically denied. Callier was even condemned in October 1916 to pay a fine of 2000 marks as a disciplinary measure for having forwarded a ruling which the Germans considered subversive from the Court of Cassation to the prosecutors within his jurisdiction. He protested and finally obtained the withdrawal of the sanction. Before the strike, this was the only sanction targeting a high-ranking Belgian magistrate.

Behind the front lines (*Etappengebiet*), the negotiation margin of the judicial authorities seemed thin. The situation was even worse in the area of military operations (*Operationsgebiet*). Several unfair measures were taken against low-ranking

[66] *Verwaltungsbericht des Verwaltungschefs von Sandt*, August 1916–January 1917 (GSaPK, Rep. 89, 32457, 37–38).

magistrates. For instance, the Hooghlede justice of the peace was relieved from his duties for leaving his residence when the area, in the middle of the battle front, had become uninhabitable. In July 1916, the justice of the peace of Termonde was detained for three days for having held a professional meeting with the district judicial officers. Examples of unfair treatment were numerous.

16.3.1.3 Motives for Interventions

Protecting allies

Recurring issues occurred within proceedings—such as when the Germans demanded that some cases be withdrawn from examining judges and transferred—as well in the carrying out of punishments. The occupiers then overrode judicial rulings by freeing prisoners or arbitrarily extending their detention. The most common intrusions in the dispensing of justice concerned the carrying out of punishments, as prisoners were a useful source of manpower which was critically lacking for the occupation forces.

Globally, the independence of Belgian magistrates was at risk when individuals under the protection of the occupation regime were prosecuted by Belgian judicial authorities. These could be collaborators (activists, editors of the censored press, traffickers etc.,), civilians or German companies, or even mere Belgian private individuals the occupiers wanted to buy off. When this was possible, the easiest strategy was to have these people join the German army so that they fell under the jurisdiction of military justice.

Beside official withdrawal of cases, other interventions were disguised. One of the processes for the removal of Belgian magistrates consisted in sanctioning, according to the situation, their 'germanophobic' attitude. The decree of 4 September 1915 was the main judicial tool aimed at protecting the German's allies.[67] All those who tried to harm or dissuade germanophiles with threats were punished and sent in front of German military courts. The decree was extremely vague and could be widely interpreted. A second process consisted in stating that arrests did not have anything to do with the carrying out of judicial functions and that they originated from military motives. The mere statement of military motives pulled the rug out from under the Belgian judicial authorities which were particularly attentive not to interfere in the spheres of other powers.

[67]Decree of the general governor, 4 September 1915, with regard to the repression of the abuses committed to the disadvantage of germanophile persons (C. Huberich and A. Nicol-Speyer, *Législation allemande pour le territoire belge occupé (textes officiels)*, La Haye, vol. IV, 1916, pp. 303–304).

Punishing hostile or disobedient magistrates

Alongside their duties as judicial officials, some magistrates engaged in clandestine activities and dangerously risked their personal security.[68] Jurisprudence too was sometimes a way of expressing patriotic messages. In view of the moral authority they carried, moralising and too openly patriotic views were considered a threat to German authority. The decree of 4 September 1915 issued by the general governor which condemned "germanophobia" and the statement of loyalty that was signed in the early period of the occupation with criminal and disciplinary sanctions compelled magistrates to a strict neutrality. They also had to refrain from expressing hostile comments towards Germans or their followers since former defendants might denounce them to German authorities to take revenge.[69] A few magistrates were sanctioned for their overly patriotic judgments.

The resistance to the occupying force's policy could also consist in failures to respect German proceedings. To schedule an audience at the Belgian hour, while the occupation authorities had imposed the German hour, or to refuse to exempt a married man from his military obligations while a German decree had suspended them for the last two years are examples. More importantly, when the occupiers tried to compel the Belgian tribunals to enforce occupation decrees issued in the penal field, the magistrates would fail to proceed against anyone. This was the case, for example, when a decree stipulated that unemployed persons who refused work proposed by the occupier should be punished. The Belgian prosecution offices also refused the collaboration of Belgian police forces in prosecution measures conducted by the Germans against Belgian offenders.

Another form of resistance, which was as dangerous as the previous one, was to help defendants escape from German judicial authorities. We know that the most important Belgian prosecution office, that of Brussels, had very close ties with the resistance movement (intelligence networks, distribution of underground press). In some cases the prosecution office deliberately purged files requested by the occupying authorities before transferring them. Unfortunately, as magistrates do not like to be associated with illegality, few references exist regarding this kind of wartime resistance practice.

16.3.1.4 Reactions of High Magistracy—Corporate Solidarity Put to the Test

More often than not, the violations of the magistrates' independence and the pressures they potentially had to deal with resulted in reports and protestations that were addressed to German authorities. In the most serious cases, the Court of

[68]The historian Emmanuel Debruyne, who worked through the dossiers of patriotic services (AGR) listed eight magistrates engaged in information services (personal communication).

[69]After the war, the majority of these denouncers were convicted for denunciation or crimes against national security.

Cassation, Belgium's highest-ranking magistracy, was consulted by its prosecution office to contemplate if issuing an official protestation was appropriate.

Within the magistracy, the decisions to support or not to support prosecuted magistrates systematically gave rise to debates. The deliberations of the counsellors of the Court of Cassation showed the limits of the corporate solidarity that was always supposed to be so strong among magistrates. The fate of three magistrates who had been removed from office by the German civil administration led to deliberations in the Court of Cassation. In only one of these case the Court officially protested and demanded that the deported magistrate be sent back to Belgium; it decided not to intervene in the other two cases. This difference in the way the cases were handled may be linked to a deontological conception of the magistrate's action in times of war, which probably did not differ much from the one that was applied in times of peace. The rescued magistrate was a 'model' magistrate. Even in the context of the enemy occupation, he enforced the law impartially. By contrast, the other two magistrates gave their judicial interventions a political character and they lacked moderation in the views they expressed. This recklessness endangered the judicial power as a whole. Neutrality, an *ordinary* virtue of the magistracy, therefore played a strategic role in the context of the occupation.

The 1918 strike, initiated by the Court of Cassation in reaction to the disciplinary measures taken against the Brussels Court of Appeal, broke with the preceding 'wait-and-see' policy. The fact that the occupier for the first time sanctioned high magistrates, probably partially explains this reversal in the attitude of the highest court.

16.3.2 1940–1945

In the second occupation, the magistrates' situation was even more unfavourable. Various methods were used by the Germans to get rid of undesirable individuals, temporarily or definitively. Nevertheless, the opposition of the magistracy against such measures was less confrontational than in 1918.

16.3.2.1 Magistrates Removed from Office Through Orders Issued by the Militärbefehlshaber

A first type of removal measures was taken through German orders. In the case of a removal from office, the military governor ordered the secretary general of Justice to relieve the magistrate of his duties.[70] As for the magistracy, the removals were always justified on grounds of following orders.

---

[70]For this, the secretary general resorted to a royal decree of 30 March 1939. ("Arrêté royal du 30 mars 1939 relatif à la mise en disponibilité des agents de l'État", in *Moniteur belge*, 2 April 1939, p. 2161).

Orders Concerning the Carrying Out of a Public Activity

On 18 July 1940, the military administration promulgated an order preventing members of the former Pierlot government from returning to Belgium.[71] Persons who had held a leading public position and who had fled the country at the time of the invasion were only allowed to take on a new public activity following the military governor's approval. This policy applied to all kinds of public positions, including magistrates. This order, initially concerning those who had fled Belgium, additionally stipulates that the military governor can also prevent other people in leading public positions from carrying out their activities. This would be crucial for the German intrusion into the personnel policy of the magistracy during the following years.[72]

The order of 18 July 1940 had a far wider scope than that of the order on 'germanophobia' issued in September 1915. Thanks to this means of preventing the holder of a public position from carrying out his duties, the Germans acquired extended powers over the Belgian administrative and judicial bodies as a whole. Removals from office were often used by the Germans to exclude individuals who were politically undesirable from Belgian institutions. On 5 August 1940, the categories of positions targeted by the order were specified: for the magistracy, these were the heads of judicial bodies.

On 19 December 1940, an order supplementing that of 18 July was published.[73] By this order, the military administration reserved the power of veto for all appointments of successors to officials removed pursuant to the order of 18 July. A second supplementary order was published two years later.[74] This time, the circle of targeted officials was extended to all public posts and did not only apply to leading positions as was the case before. The second order notably stated that the German order did not impede more stringent disciplinary sanctions. At the same time, an order given to the secretary general of Justice provided that, whereas Belgian law laid down that removed officials were entitled to compensation for the first year following the removal, and a pension afterwards, it was now decided that full compensation would be paid for only three months, so as to foster fear and prevent indocile behaviour.[75]

---

[71]"Ordonnance du 18 juillet 1940 relative à l'exercice d'une activité publique en Belgique", in *Verordnungsblatt*, no. 8, 25 July 1940.

[72]Cf. N. Wouters, *De Führerstaat: overheid en collaboratie in België (1940–1944)*, Tielt, 2006, p. 25.

[73]"Ordonnance du 19 décembre 1940, complétant l'ordonnance relative à l'exercice d'une activité publique en Belgique", in *Verordnungsblatt*, no. 27, 23 December 1940, p. 8.

[74]"Deuxième ordonnance du 20 novembre 1942 complétant l'ordonnance relative à l'exercice d'une fonction publique en Belgique", in *Verordnungsblatt*, no. 90, 28 November 1942, p. 2.

[75]Although, during the preceding years, the military commander held the view that it was better to assure the income of the excluded magistrates, in order to prevent them from being dependent on "illegal organisations". Cf. BA-MA, Freiburg, RW 36/224, p. 53.

These more stringent measures were taken in a context of political radicalisation. The military administration noticed that resistance movements were increasingly recruiting members from among civil servants and other holders of public positions. Amongst other things, it reacted by intensifying the removals from office.[76]

Globally, the *Militärverwaltung* applied the order moderately. The military governor adopted the principle that removals from office were

> only to be applied when the interests of the occupation forces are jeopardised and no other methods [...] can be considered any longer. A removal from office should not lead to a situation where officials serving a disruptive public body, who work efficiently and appropriately carry out their duties according to the law, would be relieved from their duties so as to avoid difficulties, whereas their actions cannot be qualified as obstructive or malicious in nature. In the end, after an official is removed from office, the issue of selecting his successor must be examined.[77]

The order was used to remove about 20–30 magistrates (as a minimal estimation) at various moments during the occupation and for diverse motives, although most of them had not left Belgium in May 1940. The Germans never stated any motives for the removals from office, in order not to give the opportunity to the magistracy and the secretary general of Justice to protest against the violation of the magistracy's independence.[78]

Order Concerning the Replacement of "High-Ranking Officials" by "Younger Officials"

On 7 March 1941, the military administration promulgated an "Order against the aging of high-ranking officials in Belgian public administration".[79] According to this order, all holders of a public position had to retire when they reached the age of 60. The military governor reserved the right to allow exceptions. The public prosecution magistrates fell under the order's scope.

It should be noted that the military administration absolutely did not take magistrates into account when it drew up the order. Its enactment mainly targeted recalcitrant secretaries general. As a matter of fact, the two secretaries general

---

[76]Bundesarchiv-Militärarchiv, Freiburg, RW 36/192, p. 73.

[77]Bundesarchiv-Militärarchiv, Freiburg, RW 36/224, p. 53.

[78]There is an exception. The vice-president of the Ghent Court of First Instance, Karel Reychler, was relieved from his duties on 29 September 1941, for delivering a judgment that was contrary to German interests. The representatives of the *Oberfeldkommandantur* committed a mistake by explaining at length their decision to remove him from office. This enabled the Court of Cassation to prove the illegality of this decision, since it harmed the magistracy's independence and to obtain that Reychler be re-instated. Following that event, the military administration systematically refrained from justifying removals from office.

[79]*Verordnungsblatt*, no. 34, 8 March 1941.

least docile towards the occupying force at that time, that is to say the secretaries general of Justice and Home Affairs, were over 60 years of age. This can be seen mainly as a way to have Gerard Romsée[80] appointed to one of these positions.

The New Order organisations voiced their dissatisfaction regarding the order and especially criticised the fact that judges did not fall under its scope.[81] The military administration was aware that extending the order's scope to judges would lead to the "unhappiness of courts and tribunals, because about a third of judges are over 60 years old and because the issue of recruiting their successors is an especially complex one".[82] The *Militärverwaltung*'s archives show that there was no project to include the judges, as long as their attitude "does not provoke it".[83] In fact, the *Militärverwaltung* rejected the extension of the order's scope for the reason that judges were appointed for life.

However, the order provided the opportunity for the Germans to get rid of a few high-ranking magistrates of the prosecution office.[84] For example, the *VNV* wished an official of the Ghent Court of Appeal's prosecution office to be replaced and the enactment of this order was an opportunity to make it happen.[85] This measure gave rise to vivid criticism against the secretaries general by the exiled government established in London, who did not tolerate the fact that more docile magistrates had been appointed to fill vacant positions pursuant to the order issued on 18 March 1941.[86]

The military administration was pleased that the enactment of the order did not bring about reactions of resistance within the judicial authorities.[87] By reference to the documents of the military administration, it appears that the "age" order applied to 44 magistrates from different prosecutor's offices.[88] In most of these cases exceptions were granted. Indeed, in the archives of the Justice Department of Belgium, we could only detect about ten personal files concerning an occupational ban resulting from the 18 March 1941 order.[89]

---

[80]E. Raskin, *Gerard Romsée. Een ongewone man. Een ongewoon leven*, Anvers, Hadewijch, 1995.

[81]"De benoemingen in het gerecht onder het beleid van den Heer Schuind", (AGR, Ministère de la Justice, Secrétariat général, Service du personnel de la magistrature, Dossiers des magistrats, 1953–1980, dossier no. 2118).

[82]Bundesarchiv-Militärarchiv, Freiburg, RW 36/185, p. 52.

[83]"Tätigkeitsbericht des Chefs des Militärverwaltungsstabes", n° 15, mars 1941", p. 76.

[84]Bundesarchiv-Militärarchiv, Freiburg, RW 36/382, p. 33.

[85]Ibid., p. 39.

[86]Bundesarchiv-Militärarchiv, Freiburg, RW 36/400, p. 12.

[87]Bundesarchiv-Militärarchiv, Freiburg, RW 36/382, p. 33.

[88]Bundesarchiv-Militärarchiv, Freiburg, RW 36/384, pp. 46 and 76, and particularly: "Tätigkeitsbericht der Gruppe Justiz für den Monat März 1941", in Bundesarchiv-Militärarchiv, Freiburg, RW 36/382, p. 26. The reason given here for this massive number of exceptions is that appropriate candidates were not available.

[89]This count is approximate, as research is still ongoing.

16.3.2.2 Arrests of Magistrates

In addition to removals from office, other measures of control were taken against the magistrates. In most cases, they were imprisoned for political motives (resistance to the occupiers of various forms).

Arrests of magistrates seem to have occurred far more often than removals from office. We identified about 50 cases of political prisoners among the magistrates' personal files. If we add to this the 20–30 magistrates who were temporarily arrested and kept as hostages, this shows that arrests were indeed the most frequently applied measure of control over the course of the second occupation. In fact, many magistrates experienced both arrest and removal from office under the occupation. While arresting a magistrate was a way to punish him individually, it also served as a deterrent for the magistracy as a whole. In most cases, the magistrates were arrested for taking part in a clandestine resistance movement (effectively or supposedly). Most of the arrested magistrates were incarcerated in Belgium, but some were sent to concentration camps in Germany. A few magistrates died during their detention.[90] The military administration did not provide any information on the detained magistrates. Families, colleagues and the secretary general of Justice were deliberately left uninformed.

As for the hostage-taking, it is important to note that magistrates were part of a specific hostage "category", that is to say *protection hostages*. In order to protect military supplies, trains etc., the Germans used these hostages taken from among the local officials, in order to deter resistance activists from attacking the trains. It is to be noted that magistrates selected as hostages were often those who adopted a disruptive (yet legal) attitude in the carrying out of their duties. They were suspected of "judicial sabotage" and were intentionally selected in order to intimidate them.

16.3.2.3 Reactions of the Magistracy

After the Second World War, criticisms arose—mostly from the political left—against the magistracy's attitude under the occupation. Cowardice by making too many compliant compromises with the military administration and by showing too little fighting spirit to protect those considered *subversive* by the Nazi regime was the most frequent accusation. And it is true that the behaviour of the magistracy as a professional group was far from being in constant opposition to German measures, even though, individually and clandestinely, many magistrates took part in resistance movements and intelligence services.

Like during the main part of the occupation in the First World War (until the 1918 strike), there was widespread consensus among the magistracy that it was imperative to maintain judicial power under the occupation. Continuing in

[90]About ten magistrates died during or as a consequence of their detention..

operation, even by means of compromises, would at least prevent the Belgian judiciary from being replaced by representatives of the New Order or by German justice, as had been the case in 1918. For the legal system and the population, this was thought to be the least evil of the potential solutions.

It is evident that the magistracy as a professional group and high moral authority in occupied territory failed in protecting or trying to defend social groups that were persecuted by the occupying regime. There would have been the possibility much more frequently to invoke Article 46 of the Hague Convention, which limits the occupier's legislative power by stipulating that the honour and the rights of families, the right to life and private property of individuals, and religious beliefs and practices must be respected.[91] Probably the worst case of non-intervention of magistrates is that of the Public Prosecutor of Antwerp, Édouard Baers, who did nothing to stop the massive raids committed by Antwerp police agents against the Jewish population of his judicial district in August and September 1942.[92]

Nevertheless, research into the archives of the military administration[93] makes it very clear that the Belgian judiciary and its resistance in numerous fields sometimes became a real spanner in the works of the occupier. Examples are the judicial crises of 1942–1943.[94] These crises are situated in the context of opposition to the constitutionality of various pieces of legislation published by secretary generals. The institution of an agricultural corporation and special courts in this domain were considered illegal by judges and were the main issue in the first crisis. The constitutionality of secretary generals' legislation was again examined and found illegal when the centralisation of numerous smaller municipalities into large agglomerations (Antwerp, Ghent, La Louvière, Charleroi, Liège and Brussels) was decided. This second crisis even led to a partial strike of the Brussels magistracy in the middle of December 1942.[95] Both crises ended with compromises. Judicial resistance can be detected in various cases throughout the whole period of the occupation. This type of resistance is limited to fields of competence and the concrete work of the magistrates.

Other examples of judicial resistance are linked to the interpretation of the Hague Convention and to questions about the prerogatives of Belgian civil and German military justice. One important subject was the resistance of many prosecution offices against the collaboration of Belgian police organs in German measures, like for example, in tracking people who refused to perform forced labour on behalf of the occupier, as well as pursuing cases involving illegal arms, as the risk

---

[91]Cf. Van Goethem, "La convention de La Haye, la collaboration administrative en Belgique et la persécution des Juifs à Anvers, 1940–1942", p. 142f.

[92]Ibid., pp. 149–186.

[93]Bundesarchiv-Militärarchiv Freiburg im Breisgau, RW 36.

[94]E.g.: E. Verhoeyen, *La Belgique occupée, De l'an 40 à la Libération*, Brussels, 1994, pp. 85–88, and Wouters, *De Führerstaat*, pp. 156–160.

[95]Bundesarchiv-Militärarchiv, Freiburg, RW 36/401 and CEGES AA 1941/270. A magistrates strike was probably already planned during the first crisis, but prevented because of discoveries in this context by the *Sipo-SD* in Liège. (Cf. Bundesarchiv-Militärarchiv, RW 36, dossiers 399 and 400).

was high of identifying resistance activists who would then be extradited to the German courts.[96] In all these cases, the magistrates involved took high risks. Some were arrested, some removed from office, some were victims of both measures.

The Court of Cassation, even though it did not intervene in all cases of removal from office or arrest, occasionally voiced protests to the Germans or the secretary general against measures of control. This mostly took place by means of negotiation meetings between the military administration—often represented by the officials of the *Gruppe Justiz*—and the Court of Cassation mostly represented by the Chief Public Prosecutor and the first president. Sometimes, the Court sent protest letters as well. At least, it provided moral support to the victims' families, for example, by sending letters to the wives of imprisoned magistrates. Globally, these signs of solidarity seemed far stronger in cases where a violation of the magistrates' independence could be clearly identified (which explains why the military administration refrained from justifying the measures of control). By contrast, magistrates arrested in consequence of their personal clandestine activities, considered as a personal choice that had nothing—or little—to do with the judicial body, rarely received any support. Here again, the parallels with the attitude of the high magistracy during the previous war are obvious.

16.4 Conclusions

Both of the German occupations, even if they gave rise to frequent violations of the magistracy's independence and unprecedented attempts, mainly during the Second World War, to discipline its members with a large set of measures, had a limited impact on the body's continuity.

Indeed, even if the intrusions and the removal measures obtained by collaborationist parties (mostly) against magistrates were the first direct external threat magistrates had to face since 1830, they only had a temporary effect. The measures taken by the occupying forces in the years 1914–1918 and by the secretaries general under German pressure in the period 1940–1945 were cancelled when the legitimate powers were re-instated.

Even during the second occupation, in which a great many appointments to vacant positions were made, very few of them opened the way to a sociological transformation of the body. Individuals who matched the applicant profiles defined by the Belgian collaborators were very difficult to find, especially because of the conservatism and political neutrality of the magistracy, a body that was not easily influenced by new and extreme ideologies. Even the applicants that best corresponded to the requirements of the New Order parties toed the line after taking office. The body's mindset quickly prevailed upon individual views.

[96]These subjects have been developed by R. Van Doorslaer, "De Belgische politie en magistratuur en het probleem van de ordehandhaving", in E. Verhoeyen et al., *België in de Tweede Wereldoorlog*, Kapellen, 1990, pp. 100–123.

The two experiences of military occupation, in spite of an impressive difference in terms of risks to the independence of the magistracy and different political backgrounds, are similar in many ways. In both cases, the magistracy (or secretaries general) and occupiers showed a relative will to spare their adversaries. As a rule, negotiations and workarounds took precedence over frontal attacks, which were exceptional. In 1914–1918 the Germans in charge of controlling the Belgian judicial authorities were pragmatic and their main objective was to guarantee the judicial system operated properly and to avoid strikes and uprisings. The spectre of the 1918 strike certainly played an important role in the second occupation, even though it was rarely explicitly mentioned. The professional proximity of the *Justizabteilung* staff, then the members of the *Gruppe Justiz*, with the Belgian judiciary (they were legal practitioners or even magistrates themselves) probably favoured some level of understanding. However, other stakeholders within the German administration, pertaining to more politicised groups, demanded a more radical transformation of the occupied country's magistracy. Contradictory objectives influenced German policy and explained the inconsistency of its practices.

Chapter 17
Prosopography, History and Legal Anthropology: Two Comments on the Belgian Case

Jean-Claude Farcy and Derk Venema

17.1 Prosopographical Databases and the History of the Judiciary

Jean-Claude Farcy

The chapters presented in this book undeniably testify to the extent, the scope and the interest of the "Prosopographie des magistrats belges 1795–1960" ("Belgian Magistrates") database for research work. The project aims at collecting all the available information on magistrates—recruitment, career, intellectual and political path, social relations—relating to their bonds with the jurisdictions in which they served, while taking care to indicate the archival source for all information. The scope of the database, which was first restricted to the ordinary magistracy in the period from 1830 to 1914, has expanded chronologically. At a later stage, colonial and military magistracies were added. The scope might even be extended in the future to judicial practices, disputes handled and individuals subject to trial—should available sources allow it!

The chapter written by Aurore François and Françoise Muller effectively demonstrates the issues related to such a project (especially the missing information and doubts concerning its reliability) and provides a good idea of the rigorous way problems have been solved. Obviously, the software application which requires each unit of information to be entered consistently has helped historians to

J.-C. Farcy (✉)
CNRS Retired Researcher, Grenoble, France
e-mail: jean-claude.farcy@wanadoo.fr

D. Venema
Radboud University, Nijmegen, The Netherlands
e-mail: D.Venema@jur.ru.nl

A. Hondeghem et al. (eds.), *Modernisation of the Criminal Justice Chain and the Judicial System*, Ius Gentium: Comparative Perspectives on Law and Justice 50, DOI 10.1007/978-3-319-25802-7_17

overcome the restrictions of traditional prosopography, for which it proved difficult to overcome the biographical prism. Instead of relying on supporting documentation and sample files, the researchers have shifted to a well-structured database aiming at providing an exhaustive selected corpus and including the information necessary for historians to put their hypotheses to the test (Claire Lemercier, Emmanuelle Picard).[1] Yet, the scope of the application of the "Belgian Magistrates" database is far wider since it provides the researcher with all the information available in the sources on magistrates and their jurisdictions. The database will be a complete biographical directory and an amazing research tool for historians who will be able rigorously to select a study corpus or test their hypotheses by querying and crossing several fields. In view of the time spent analysing sources for a thesis or a research project (which is also a Sisyphean ordeal, as every researcher starts from scratch the work done by the previous one), the advantages offered by such an application are invaluable. Even if the notion of productivity is not necessarily relevant in the field of historical research, it is nonetheless a determining factor.

The "Belgian Magistrates" database is a tool that historians who carry out research on the French judicial system would dream of having at their disposal. Of course, prosopography has not been neglected in France, far from it. The pioneer in the field was Jean-Pierre Royer who, at the turn of the 1980s when he analysed the extensive series of magistrates' personal files (Archives nationales, BB/6 II), selected 850 of them "from each letter of the alphabet in order to build up a representative sample through a balanced appearance of each category" to provide a portrait of judges in the nineteenth century.[2] Several scholars followed in his footsteps with theses at the local level, for instance, on the magistracy in the French city of Angers,[3] or on lawyers in Nantes.[4] The work that we have carried out at national level cannot be compared with the extensive content of the "Belgian Magistrates" database, even if it also uses the relational database tool. We had long been familiar with this type of software—many specific research studies we perform in the fields of criminality or judicial practice are based on databases of judgments, statements of offence, prosecution office records, etc. The starting point for the "Annuaire rétrospectif de la magistrature XIXe-XXe siècles" (Retrospective directory of the magistracy, nineteenth and twentieth centuries[5]), however, was a research question related to the career paths of the magistracy's staff: information

[1]"Quelle approche prosopographique?" http://halshs.archives-ouvertes.fr/docs/00/59/00/81/PDF/prosopographie_Lemercier_Picard.pdf.

[2]J.-P. Royer, R. Martinage and P. Lecocq, *Juges et notables au XIXe siècle*, Paris, PUF, 1982, p. 8.

[3]V. Bernaudeau, *La justice en question. Histoire de la magistrature angevine au XIXe siècle*, Rennes, Presses universitaires de Rennes, 2007, 349 p.

[4]S. Defois, *Les avocats nantais au XXe siècle. Socio-histoire d'une profession*, Rennes, Presses universitaires de Rennes, 2007, 397 p.

[5]Available at http://tristan.u-bourgogne.fr:8080/.

that was not systematically written down in sources, or for which doubtful round numbers were used. We therefore had the idea to calculate this figure from the *Annuaires de la magistrature* (Directories magistracy), the published collection of which proved very incomplete (as it only started in the 1880s, with interruptions).[6] In order to complete it, we have used the collection of career sheets (available from the middle of the nineteenth century), the personal appointment records of the different jurisdictions (specific series for courts, tribunals and justices of the peace), as well as the *Almanachs nationaux* (National almanacs) and, should these sources be incomplete or for verification purposes, the appointment orders and decrees. The *Matricule de la magistrature* (record of magistrates) provides a comprehensive overview of judicial staff. It was first published in 1827, hence this date is the starting point for our database. Our *Annuaire rétrospectif* stops in 1987. Indeed, paper files were replaced by a computer database at the Ministry of Justice for staff management, to which researchers are not allowed access.

The purpose of the "Annuaire rétrospectif de la magistrature XIXe-XXe siècles" is to provide exhaustive information on the judicial career paths of the magistracy. Therefore, the information is identical to that provided in the printed *Annuaires* (directories), except that we offer a complete overview of the judicial career path (except for the most recent generations in office after 1987). Each career step is documented by the appointment date in the position, the end date being considered as a start date in a new position or a removal (dismissal, retirement, death). Information entry, although it was limited, has raised identical issues to those mentioned for Belgium, especially the lack of reliability for positions in the colonies. The latter correspond to the main blindspot in our database, that is to say, the gap between the appointment date and the actual date when the official took office, which is even worse for periods where positions were filled in *ad interim*.

The "Annuaire rétrospectif de la magistrature XIXe-XXe siècles" database can be interrogated in various ways, for instance, to consult the career sheet of a given magistrate, to reconstruct the complete directory for a specific date or to follow the appointed staff for a specific category of jurisdiction. Therefore, it is first and foremost a research tool that makes it possible to select a sample of magistrates for an in-depth study from the personal files available in the archives and sources we have mentioned.

We have to admit that this online directory has mainly drawn the attention of genealogists, eagerly looking for any nominative file. Except for Benoît Garnot, who used it to calculate several indicators which provide details on judges' careers,[7] it seems historians have not so far shown much enthusiasm for the "Annuaire rétrospectif de la magistrature XIXe-XXe siècles". This raises the issue of the possibilities of exploitation of the database and its limits. In view of the

[6]Published first by the periodical *La France judiciaire* then by the *Association amicale de la magistrature* and, for the most recent, by the Ministry of Justice.

[7]B. Garnot, *Histoire des juges en France de l'Ancien régime à nos jours*, Paris, Nouveau monde éditions, 2014, 396 p.

large amount of information stored in the "Belgian Magistrates" database, it offers a wide array of possibilities for analysis. The chapters provide the first indications for these possibilities. For instance, Emmanuel Berger was able, through the specific case of the magistrates of the Directory, to present the general issue of the magistrate's distance/proximity to the people under his jurisdiction by crossing data related to the magistrate's origin (residence, place of birth) and the location within a jurisdiction, as well as the more particular issue of the role of French magistrates in Belgium. Likewise, Laurence Montel, Enika Ngongo, Bérengère Piret and Pascaline le Polain have used the database in order to provide details on the recruitment (nationality) of colonial magistrates and produce overviews of their career paths, including their return to the metropolis. Yet, the importance given to Antoine Sohier's biography demonstrates that a classic biography based on richer sources, especially in the case of an exceptional career, may be more helpful than the database alone, since it is difficult to get a good grasp of colonial reality by using the software alone. Mélanie Bost and Kirsten Peters's chapter on magistrates and occupying authorities during the two world wars benefits from the information on magistrates' career paths in these periods in order to assess the importance of "sanctions" and their typology, which targeted a part of the Belgian judicial staff. In the cases studied in these three chapters, the database provides undeniable grounds for the conclusions. It makes it possible to take stock accurately of the studied phenomena and to confirm or not the way they are interpreted. Its use consolidates the status of proof (cases indicated as "examples" or a priori "representative" are excluded) in history.

However, a database cannot provide more information than it contains. Except for the exceptional case of the "Belgian Magistrates" database, which is a meta (mega?) source, and given the restricted possibilities of launching an equivalent programme in France, a database intentionally restricts its scope to the studied topic and the research hypotheses that exist in the beginning or are formulated in the analysis stage or as the research progresses.[8] As for the "Annuaire rétrospectif de la magistrature française", in spite of the relatively scant information (restricted to the career), we have been able to reject or confirm some of the interpretative hypotheses that are generally accepted based on qualitative documentation (essentially legal practitioners' books and administrative reports). The research report delivered with the database to the contracting institution (the *Mission Droit et Justice* (Law and Justice Research Mission) of the French Ministry of Justice)[9] provides the results of the first statistical analyses of the database on staff career paths, the average age of recruitment for a position and of taking office, the geographical origin (place of

[8]It is at this level that the flexibility of relational databases, allowing the restructuring of data along the way, the addition of tables, etc., is the most significantly appreciated.

[9]"Les carrières des magistrats (XIXe-XXe siècles), Annuaire rétrospectif de la magistrature", Dijon, Centre Georges Chevrier, June 2009, 211 p. This is an unpublished report; only the study of the examining judge was included in a book, co-authored with J.-J. Clère, devoted to the history of the examining judge (J.-J. Clère and J.-C. Farcy (dir.), *Le Juge d'instruction. Approches historiques*, Dijon, Editions Universitaires de Dijon, 2010, 320 p).

birth criterion) and magistrates' mobility in the considered period. For the latter, it has been possible to observe that, especially in the nineteenth century, attaining a position in the prosecution office was a factor that facilitated promotion to higher-ranking positions at a later career stage, or even accelerated the magistrate's promotion, but not in all cases. We have also proposed three more in-depth analyses on the *juges auditeurs* (trainee judges who attended hearings to "listen" to the debates) in the Restoration, justices of the peace and examining judges, respectively.

The first analysis shows that even if the institution of the legal adviser's office was initially conceived as a judicial noviciate, its importance grew during the Restoration, which was more concerned with making up for the lack of magistrates by drawing on the inexpensive resources provided by unpaid young law graduates than appointing "commissioner judges" in order to achieve the desired majority for political rulings (which is the conventional wisdom). The second research studies how the justice of the peace (*juges de paix*) gradually deviated from the model of the paternalistic judge, a local official rooted in his home region, to a professionalised model. It highlights the important role played by the purges that affected this local magistracy when shifts in regime took place. For example, 45 % of the justices of the peace left the magistracy during the July 1830 revolution. The third research project aimed at verifying the hypothesis—suggested by well-known cases like the *Outreau* case in France—, that the position of examining judge (*juge d'instruction*) and its heavy workload was entrusted to young and inexperienced magistrates. Searching the database for the age of appointment to this position enabled us to confirm the hypothesis for the last decades analysed, whereas in the nineteenth century the position of examining judge was rather entrusted to relatively old and experienced magistrates. Later on, we used the data collected in the "Annuaire rétrospectif" to mitigate the portrayal of the colonial magistrates: even if these were relatively mobile (but did not constantly travel from one assignment location to the other, as is often stated), they did not go to the colony to take up the same position from which they were removed in the metropolis (punishment by transfer). In fact, we have been able to confirm that, except for the period when courts were being established, this magistracy was relatively autonomous and the magistrates started serving in the colonies and stayed in Africa for most of their careers.[10]

Based on these analyses and the chapters related to the "Belgian Magistrates" database, we conclude that prosopographical databases are of major interest for research work.[11] As resources enabling a significant saving of time, they provide

[10]"Quelques données statistiques sur la magistrature coloniale", *Clio@Thémis*, no. 4, http://www.cliothemis.com/Quelques-donnees-statistiques-sur.

[11]After the "Annuaire rétrospectif de la magistrature XIXe-XXe siècles", we have continued with the prosopographical method (combining research instruments and relatively poor information) with the study of the victims of political repression during the working-class insurgency in June 1848 and just after the *putsch* of Louis Napoleon Bonaparte in December 1851. See the online databases on the website of Flora Tristan from the Université de Bourgogne (http://tristan.u-bourgogne.fr/CGC/prodscientifique/bases_donnees.html). Work of the same nature on the Communards is ongoing.

undeniable value to the conclusions put forward in the analysis, which are far more reliable than those drawn from a classic manual examination and interpretation of sources. Lastly, the material and human means necessary to achieve such databases have to be dealt with. The Belgian software application and the French "Annuaire rétrospectif de la magistrature XIXe-XXe siècles" program have little in common. In this respect, it is worth considering the usefulness of encouraging archivists to generalise the creation of name indexes, which would then simplify the design of databases created by historians.

17.2 Judiciaries and Foreign Rule. Legal Anthropological Reflections on Three Belgian Cases

Derk Venema

The common denominator in the three different types of government in these case studies—annexation, colonialism, occupation—is *foreign rule*: Belgium under French and German rule, and King Leopold and Belgium as foreign rulers of Congo. After introducing the concept of foreign rule, I will offer an anthropological perspective on certain aspects of judicial (group) behaviour that might otherwise be left aside as irrational[12] or overlooked as falling outside regular prosopographical research. This is the perspective of purity and contamination, in connection with (evolutionary) group dynamics. It provides an essential background for assessing the sociological and symbolic importance of the judiciary in a constellation of foreign rule.

17.2.1 The Sociological Concept of Foreign Rule

The phenomenon of foreign rule can generally be characterised by 'a "Self," most often in the form of a weaker group that is dominated and/or governed by an "Other," stronger entity.'[13] It is from this constellation of a ruled 'we' as opposed to a ruling 'they' that terms like collaboration, patriotism, nationalism, treason, and resistance derive their meaning. This is not to say, of course, that these categories are always clear-cut or universally agreed upon in any given instance. Minimally, some kind of important *perceived difference in nature* between rulers and ruled is required for the concept of foreign rule to be applicable. The different guises of foreign rule discussed here—annexation, occupation, colonialism—share

[12] Z. Mach, *Symbols, Conflict, and Identity. Essays in Political Anthropology*, Albany, State University of New York Press, 1993, p. 7.

[13] K. Brüggenmann, "Foreign Rule and Collaboration in the Baltic Countries, 1860–1920. New Directions in Research", in *Journal of Baltic Studies* 2006, 37:2, pp. 155–162, at 155.

another common feature: the threat of direct, unchecked violence.[14] An institution that offers an alternative to this threat, is the judiciary. In judicial application of the law, the use of force is rationalised, formalised, legitimised and justified. Especially in the long run, it is more efficient to exercise power by more or less *legitimate* threats of *legal* force or *sanctions*, such as criminal proceedings before a court of law as in any domestic democratic regime, than by one-sided repression and arbitrary violence.[15] This makes courts of law pivotal instruments in the power schemes of foreign regimes that aim at retaining power for some time.

In the cases concerned here, the judiciary appears on both sides of the divide between 'Self' and 'Other' from the perspective of the ruled people in question. In the Congo Free State, the Belgian-international judiciary was clearly part of the 'Other', the ruling elite, with little or no affiliation with the local population. It was, in the terminology of organisational sociologist Lammers,[16] a completely foreign 'loyal elite,' meaning '[regime] auxiliaries legitimized from above.' Under the German occupations of Belgium during the World Wars, on the other hand, the Belgian courts were 'native elites', a term denoting cooperating institutions 'legitimized from below,' because they were perceived by the Belgians as part of the 'Self,' at least for as long as they did not compromise their loyalty to the Belgian people too much. The French period shows a mixed image because of the fact that the judiciary was composed of native as well as foreign French judges.

The political concepts 'foreign (rule),' 'Self,' 'Other,' 'native elite,' and 'loyal elite' are all related to the concept of the *legitimacy* of regimes, government bodies, and individual politicians and civil servants. According to Max Weber, there are three ideal-types of political legitimacy: legitimacy based on tradition, on charisma and on legal-rational procedures.[17] Two additional ideal-types are legitimacy based on shared values and norms (overlapping with tradition), and legitimacy based on pragmatism.[18]

Courts have a crucial role in supporting—or undermining—a regime's legitimacy, because they have the choice to either apply or refuse to apply its laws. In this role, their own legitimacy is also at stake. The position of the courts can be especially precarious when they are a 'native elite' facing a very unpopular foreign ruler, or when they are a very unpopular foreign elite themselves. An important

[14]C.J. Lammers, *Vreemde overheersing. Bezetten en bezetting in sociologisch perspectief*, Amsterdam, Bert Bakker, 2005, pp. 11 20. Apparently, this threat of violence is meant as a stronger form of the threat of sanctions used by any government to ensure obedience to the law.

[15]M. Conway and P. Romijn, *The War for Legitimacy in Politics and Culture 1936–1946*, Oxford, Berg, 2008, pp. 1–4. Cf. N. Luhmann, *Legitimation durch Verfahren*, Neuwied am Rhein, Luchterhand, 1969 and Lammers *Vreemde overheersing*, p. 323.

[16]C.J. Lammers, "Occupation Regimes Alike and Unlike: British, Dutch and French Patterns of Inter-Organisational Control of Foreign Territories", in *Organisation Studies,* 2003, 24(9), pp. 1379–1403.

[17]M. Weber, *Wirtschaft und Gesellschaft*, Tübingen, Mohr, 1922, p. 124 & Teil 1, Kapitel 3.

[18]M. Hechter, "Alien Rule and Its Discontents', *American Behavioral Scientist* (53) 2009-3, pp. 289–310, at 298; Lammers, *Vreemde overheersing*, p. 66; Conway & Romijn, *The War for Legitimacy*, pp. 8–11.

reason for this precariousness is that the Self/Other distinction is about identities of persons and groups. This has its roots in the *condition humaine*. Life is a constant trade-off between our two most basic needs, which are material existence and identity: *that* we are and *who* we are. Of both, governments can be important suppliers. They aim at guaranteeing safety and subsistence, which may in itself already be an important precondition for perceived legitimacy. In addition, they provide something to identify with ideologically or culturally, or to oppose one's identity to, which everyone does to a greater or lesser extent. Personal or group identities, however, are not unchangeable, and neither is identification with, or dissociation from, their government. And in the end, all 'normal' indigenous as well as alien regimes are only temporary phases of stability within an eternal—*longue durée*—global process of expanding and migrating populations, changing borders, and alternating regimes—from democratic elections to enemy annexation.[19]

Although periods of foreign rule are part and parcel of long term global developments, they are considered the exception in relation to the 'normal' and desired state of affairs. The presupposed 'normal' situation for any country is government by the 'Self' as in 'self-government' in a representative democratic nation state with rule of law. When the people, or 'nation', is represented in the government, it is called a nation-state. Nationalist movements claim the right to self-rule as a natural and inalienable human right.[20] Indeed, the right to self-determination has been heralded since at least the first social contract theories up to contemporary human rights charters,[21] and its general acceptance is reflected in the period of decolonisation of the 20th century. Consequently, the situation in which 'the rulers of the political unit belong to a nation [= a people, DV] other than that of the majority of the ruled', i.e. foreign or alien rule, is a particularly sensitive 'violation of the nationalist principle.'[22] I will now discuss the problems the judiciary might face in such a constellation in terms of purity, contamination, and dirty hands.

17.2.2 Purity and Contamination

In the flux of changing governments, we treasure our impermanent cultural identities, consisting of semi-settled ways of doing things, as well as many social categorisations of people, actions, things, and events. Distinguishing and categorising

[19]On this process of continuous change: D. Day, *Conquest. How Societies Overwhelm Others*, Oxford, Oxford University Press, 2008, Introduction.

[20]L. Tivey, "Introduction", in: L. Tivey (ed.), *The Nation State*, Oxford, Martin Robertson, 1981, pp. 1–12; cf. Mach, *Symbols, Conflict, and Identity*, pp. 102–103.

[21]Article 1, Sect. 2 of the United Nations Charter 1945; Article 1, International Covenant on Civil and Political Rights 1966.

[22]E. Gellner, *Nations and Nationalism*, Oxford, Blackwell, 1983, p. 1; cf. Mach, *Symbols, Conflict, and Identity*, pp. 102–103.

is a fundamental characteristic of thinking and perceiving: everything we see and recognise, we distinguish from other things. If we could not make more or less clear distinctions, we would be 'lost in a chaos of fleeting impressions.'[23] This not only a precondition for survival (*that* we are), but it also provides an identity (*who* we are). In anthropology, someone's cultural identity, consisting of 'the cluster of preconceptions that a culture possesses regarding man's position between nature and the religious sphere, in various social connections, between birth and death, and in the order of being in general,' is called a 'cosmology.'[24]

It is well known that the most used way of expressing the categories and distinctions included in a society's cosmology, which is language, can be learnt only in interaction within a group. As groups, ranging from several dozens of individuals to whole countries, we build our meaningful life-world, our cosmology, with these distinct meanings which define the group's identity. The role of the group as supplier of meaning in our lives fortifies the individual's identification with and loyalty to the group.[25] Group identities emerge from interactions within and between groups, in an ever ongoing process, marking off identities against each 'Other.'[26] This is not a rational activity, rather a pre-rational mode of perception.[27] In guarding the boundaries between the social categories in our culture we try to keep our cultural identity safe and stable. Many symbols and rituals fulfil this task, of which legal rituals, such as court proceedings, are an important example, in guarding many detailed normative distinctions concerning what counts as legal or illegal, guilty or innocent, liable or non-liable.[28] Taking all this into account, it is not surprising that making and maintaining distinctions between 'us' and 'them', or 'friend' and 'enemy', has been identified as the most fundamental function of politics.[29]

This background explains that transgression of social category boundaries or ambiguity or uncertainty as to the category of a certain person, thing, or event may

---

[23]Th. Oudemans & A. Lardinois, *Tragic Ambiguity. Anthropology, Philosophy and Sophocles' Antigone*, Leiden, E.J. Brill, 1987, p. 28; Cf. M. Douglas, "Introduction to Grid/Group Analysis", in M. Douglas (ed.), *Essays in the Sociology of Perception*, London, Routledge & Kegan Paul, 1982, pp. 1–8, at 1.

[24]Oudemans and Lardinois, *Tragic Ambiguity*, p. 1.

[25]R. Brown, *Group Processes. Dynamics within and between groups*, Second Edition, Malden, Blackwell Publisheres, 2000, pp. 132–133, with references to the work of Leon Festinger.

[26]D. Venema, "Transitional Shortcuts to Justice and National Identity", in *Ratio Juris* (24), 2011-1, pp. 88–108, at 93–94, 96–98; Mach, *Symbols, Conflict, and Identity*, Chap. 1.

[27]Mach, *Symbols, Conflict, and Identity*, pp. 7, 103.

[28]Chapter 4 of Lawrence Rosen's *Law as Culture. An Invitation*, Princeton, Princeton University Press, 2006, makes this explicit in its title: 'Law as Cosmology.' See also R. Girard, *Violence and the Sacred*, Baltimore: Johns Hopkins University Press 1979, 22–27, 298–299; cf. Mach, *Symbols, Conflict, and Identity*, Chap. 3 (esp. p. 163), p. 266.

[29]C. Schmitt, *Der Begriff des Politischen*, Berlin, Duncker and Humblot, 2002 (1st ed. 1932); Cf. C. Mouffe, *The Democratic Paradox*, London, Verso, 2000, Chap. 2; Chantal Mouffe, *On the Political*, London, Routledge, 2005, pp. 24–25; 119–120.

be a cause for concern. This concern will be graver when categories are involved that are more fundamental to the group's identity or sense of meaningfulness. Transgression or leakage from one category to another, or the mixing of categories, is called 'pollution.' It endangers not only the purity of the categories, but also social order in general.[30]

The concept of pollution and the related concepts of contamination, purity, taboo, danger, and moral or social hygiene have been primarily developed in anthropology.[31] As Mary Douglas points out in her famous study *Purity and Danger*, these terms describe ways of thinking and behaving not only present in ancient or primitive societies, but also in modern ones.[32] An important aspect of pollution is that it is contagious, which is independent of questions of causal responsibility. This means that contamination occurs irrespective of intentional or causal links between the contaminated individual(s) and the actions of the contaminating individual(s).[33] For example, a judge who remains in office under an enemy occupier, is often considered to be contaminated with the enemy's negative image and therefore held co-responsible for the bad consequences of that occupier's policies, as happened to the Dutch Hoge Raad (Supreme Court) under the Nazi German occupation.[34]

Two phrases often used in contemporary contexts of political conflict are 'dirty hands'[35] and the 'lesser evil.' The latter term amounts to a rationalisation of dirty hands by claiming that doing nothing (and keeping clean hands) would have had, all considering, worse effects for the community as a whole.[36] 'Dirty hands' quite explicitly uses the same imagery as pollution and contamination. The 'lesser evil' fits in perfectly as well, because 'evil' is the most radical term to denote the 'Other,' with whom one does not wish to associate or be associated. Committing the lesser evil supposedly leaves a lesser or better washable stain than some alternative action. Interestingly, and leading us back to the cases of foreign rule at hand, the 'lesser evil' is exactly how Belgian 'accommodating' politics under German Nazi occupation has always been understood by the politicians at the time

[30]Oudemans and Lardinois, *Tragic Ambiguity*, p. 52.

[31]Key texts are M. Douglas, *Purity and Danger. An Analysis of the Concepts of Pollution and Taboo*, London, ARK Paperbacks, 1984 [1966]; P. Ricoeur, "La Symbolique du mal, in *Finitude et culpabilité*, Paris, Aubier, 1960; Oudemans and Lardinois, *Tragic Ambiguity*, esp. Sec. 3.1, Chap. 4 and Sect. 8.2.

[32]Douglas, *Purity and Danger*, pp. 39–40, 128, 138.

[33]Douglas, *Purity and Danger*, Chap. 6, esp. p. 99, 113; Ricoeur, *La Symbolique du mal*, esp. the first chapter.

[34]D. Venema, *Rechters in oorlogstijd. De confrontatie van de Nederlandse rechterlijke macht met nationaal-socialisme en bezetting*, Den Haag: Boom Juridische uitgevers 2007, pp. 163–164, 174–175; Venema, "The Judge, the Occupier", p. 223.

[35]M. Walzer, "Political Action: The Problem of Dirty Hands", in *Philosophy & Public Affairs*, Vol. 2, No. 2 Winter, 1973, pp. 160–180.

[36]Cf. M. Ignatieff, *The Lesser Evil, Political Ethics in an Age of Terror*, Princeton University Press, 2005.

as well as by later historians.[37] But first, I will use some examples from Emmanuel Berger's contribution on the Belgian judiciary under French rule to illustrate this anthropological approach and develop it further.

17.2.3 The French Period

Numerous appointments of French judges, prosecutors, and commissioners in key positions in the courts became possible because, first, many Belgian judges resigned in protest when the first French judges were assigned to their posts, and subsequently other Belgian jurists refused to fill any of the vacancies. These are clear examples of maintaining what might be termed 'socio-moral hygiene': avoiding contamination with the oppressor's policies by not joining the 'polluted' judiciary. In other words, many legal professionals did not wish to 'get their hands dirty' or 'their fingers burnt.' This aversion is the more understandable when we recall that these polluted courts were pivotal institutions in guarding and reaffirming the local cosmology or cultural identity. Such an infiltration by officials of a foreign 'loyal elite' evidently created direct tensions between the 'Self' and the 'Other.' By making a court's identity ambiguous, this pollution with foreign elements is contagious: it may contaminate any jurist participating in the polluted court, or even any civilian appealing to it, and thus obscure their identities and stain their reputations as well.[38] The Belgian courts were contaminated with 'Frenchness' by the presence of French officials. Consequently, Belgian jurists were less willing to participate in the judiciary, because of the risk of becoming personally contaminated.

Belgian judges had to keep both the French regime and the Belgian people satisfied in a position later termed the predicament of the 'wartime mayor': either remain in office to do good for the people, while risking contamination with the oppressor's policies, or leave office to keep clean hands, while running the risk of being replaced by a loyal collaborator.[39] Clearly, this embodies a dilemma

[37]Conway & Romijn, *The War for Legitimacy*, p. 77; See also, for example: Mark van den Wijngaert a.o., *België tijdens de Tweede Wereldoorlog*, Antwerpen, Standaard Uitgeverij, chap. 2, titled: 'Bestuur en politiek. Het minste kwaad' ('Administration and politics. The lesser evil').

[38]Cf. Oudemans and Lardinois, *Tragic Ambiguity*, pp. 52–53.

[39]P. Romijn, "Ambitions and dilemmas of local authorities in the German-occupied Netherlands, 1940–1945", in H. van Goethem, B. De Wever en N. Wouters (eds.) *Local Government in Occupied Europe*, Antwerp, University Press, 2006, pp. 33–66; D. Venema, "The Judge, the Occupier, his Laws, and their Validity: Judicial Review by the Supreme Courts of Occupied Belgium, Norway, and the Netherlands 1940–1945 in the Context of their Professional Conduct and the Consequences for their Public Image", in M. de Koster and D. Heirbaut (Eds.), *Justice in Wartime and Revolutions, Europe, 1795–1950*, Brussels, Algemeen Rijksarchief, 2012, pp. 203–223. Cf. Lammers, 'Occupation Regimes Alike and Unlike', p. 1383. See also: J. Elster, *Closing the Books, Transitional Justice in Historical Perspective*, Cambridge, Cambridge University Press, 2004, p. 144–150.

between rational calculation of material consequences and pre-rational perceptions of pollution and contamination.

The threat of contamination probably also motivated French concerns about the degree to which the French commissioners were allowed to integrate into the local population: just enough to learn local customs, without being compromised, lest their loyalty should shift from the rulers to the ruled. Too much contamination with 'Belgianness' would change them from members of the loyal elite into members of the native elite.

This worry is expressed in yet another example. To keep the new revolutionary laws free from compromise and distortion, the French revolutionaries desired, in the spirit of Montesquieu, a strict division between the legislative power and the judiciary. The Belgian judges were supposed to be mere automata or 'bouches de la loi': they were not supposed to have any discretion at all to interpret the French laws or to show leniency. In other words: the application of the French laws was not to be contaminated by any Belgian interpretations. The purpose of this 'monopolisation of symbolic life' (also encompassing things like censorship) was to gain legitimacy by not having to compete publicly with rival ideologies.[40] The opposition between the Belgian 'Self' and the French 'Other' came to a clash when a Belgian court decided to exercise discretion nonetheless. As Berger explains, this court acquitted a priest of refusing to make the enforced 'declaration of submission,' after it declared the relevant law unconstitutional. Judicial review of an oppressor's legislation has often been as much a concern for oppressors as an instrument for oppressed peoples to defend the national identity against contamination with a foreign regime's laws.[41]

17.2.4 The German Occupations

During the two German occupations, the judiciary again decided not to apply certain ordinances and to review others. The judiciary also exhibited other anti-contamination behaviour in these periods, such as resisting the appointments of Flemish activists (*flamingants*) who tried to make use of the situation to push the Flemish nationalist agenda. In Bost and Peters' account of the judicial sentiment, these appointments would 'plague' the judicial body, which clearly evokes the language of pollution and contamination. The German occupying forces themselves also tried to make use of the strong feelings of group identity when they ordered the secretaries-general to issue certain sensitive ordinances instead of issuing them themselves, because they knew the Belgian people would probably accept them more readily when they came from their 'own' native elite.

[40] Mach, *Symbols, Conflict, and Identity*, pp. 107–109.

[41] Venema, "The Judge, the Occupier".

Expression and defence of a cultural identity might under foreign rule harm that identity. This is apparent from the way the Court of Cassation dealt with the removal by the occupier of three magistrates. The Court intervened, but only on behalf of the one magistrate who had never exhibited any political activism in his judicial decisions. One the one hand, the Court did something extraordinary and precarious: it questioned the occupier's policy, but on the other hand, it showed its loyal intentions in only intervening on behalf of a judge who would not question the occupier's policies. In this case, the Court acted in two opposite, but complementary ways which shows the 'limits of corporate solidarity': it tried to keep the judiciary intact, but sacrificed elements from it that endangered that objective by being too explicitly activist in their judicial role. As Bost and Peters put it very appropriately: political neutrality, which is an '*ordinary* virtue' for normal situations, can play a 'strategic role' in exceptional circumstances.

Often, there are 'mediators' between an occupying regime and the local elites.[42] These mediators constitute a boundary which allows 'foreignness' to pass through, but only in adapted or diluted form to make it more easily acceptable for the nation, and to prevent a too harmful contamination. Bost and Peters describe the secretary general of the Justice department as such an intermediary during the Second World War.

17.2.5 The Colonial Judiciary

Montel et al. offer an example of an anti-pollution attitude of judges towards other judges: the Belgian metropolitan judiciary refused to recognise judges who had served in the Congo Free State as equals when these colonial judges wished to pursue their careers in Belgium. The colonial judges were apparently polluted with strange and un-Belgian experiences. But when circumstances had changed after the first World War, an element from the colonial judiciary was adopted: single judge hearings. It would be interesting to know whether there was any resistance to this innovation motivated by the fact that it came from the Congo.

The great heterogeneity and the large turnover of staff in the Congo Free State judiciary (in stark contrast with metropolitan Belgium), combined with the small amount of training, the youth of the judges, and the constant relocations, were very probable causes of a lack of group identity, expressed in an equal lack of *esprit de corps*. Where there is hardly any common identity, resistance to change and sensitivity to pollution and contamination can be expected to be smaller. This would explain that strong judicial heterogeneity in Congo allowed for much greater adaptability, which is an evolutionary mechanism: when many different variants of judicial behaviour are allowed to emerge, this might sooner yield better working strategies than in an environment of strong central supervision where

[42] Conway & Romijn, *The War for Legitimacy*, p. 77.

every change of practise needs a preceding legal foundation. Further research might point out how this affected the development of the relation between the judiciary and the indigenous population, as it might shed some light on the perceived legitimacy of the colonial courts and the effects of their decisions.

17.2.6 The Prosopographical Method and Evolution

Interesting from this point of view, are the different positions of the judiciary in the case studies: in Congo, they were a multinational group of Europeans, not including any Congo natives; in the French period, they were a mix of French and Belgians; and under the German occupying forces, the judiciary consisted solely of Belgians, although some Belgian collaborationists were appointed. The different compositions and different degrees of 'purity' may have their effects on the possible group dynamics. Where there is no strong common identity, as presumably in the Congo, there may be less loyalty, and more selfish behaviour, which diminishes stability. This may be a self-reinforcing loop. Firmly established judiciaries, on the other hand, can more easily overcome temporary attacks on their identity, as during the German occupations. Group dynamics, therefore, could provide an explanation for stability, additional to political loyalty and legal competence (cf. Berger).

The combination of 'group biography' and 'network analysis' in the prosopographical research (Montel et al.), might benefit from Mary Douglas' group/grid theory. 'Group' designates constraints on behaviour originating from a social group: group pressure, feelings of loyalty and identity, whereas 'grid' means individual network relations and the rules governing them.[43] In these terms, the relative power of group dynamical processes (involving perceptions of identity and pollution etc.), can be measured against group-neutral network relations and rules.

Cooperation within groups is an evolutionarily highly adaptive trait, and with it a preference evolved for (cooperation with) group members to (cooperation with) members of other groups.[44] It is likely that the need for a positive personal self-image, assisted by identifying with the own group as 'better' than other groups, co-evolved with the benefits of in-group cooperation.[45] This employs our afore-

[43]M. Douglas, *Natural Symbols*, London: Barrie and Rockliff: The Cresset Press 1970; M. Douglas, *Cultural Bias*, London, Royal Anthropological Institute, 1978 (reprinted in M. Douglas, *In the Active Voice*, London, Routledge and Kegan Paul, 1982); J.J. Spickard, "A Guide to Mary Douglas's Three Versions of Grid/Group Theory", in *Sociological Analysis* (50), 1989-2, pp. 151–170.

[44]W.D. Hamilton, "The Genetical Evolution of Social Behavior" (I & II), *Journal of Theoretical Biology* (7) 1964-1, pp. 1–16, 17–52; R.L. Trivers, "The Evolution of Reciprocal Altruism", in *Quarterly Review of Biology*, 1971, 35–57; A. Olsson, J.P. Ebert, M.R. Banaji, & E.A. Phelps, "The role of social groups in the persistence of learned fear", in *Science*, 2005-309, 785–787.

[45]Brown, *Group Processes*, Chap. 8, linking anthropological concepts around identity preservation with evolutionary explanations.

mentioned fundamental capacity to make distinctions and our basic need to hold on to fundamental cultural distinctions between good and bad things, people, and behaviour, in order to cope with an uncertain world. All this must have evolutionarily favoured 'moral hygienic' patterns of thought and action compared to group-indifferent attitudes.[46] This innate psychological tendency is, however, relative to the circumstances and highly manipulable.[47]

Human evolution produced behavioural dispositions that are more fundamental to the behaviour of individuals in groups than their conscious, rational, and seemingly autonomous decisions.[48] This nicely fits with the statistical approach of prosopography. For example, the prosopographical use of 'intellectual links' besides merely 'concrete links' (François and Muller) will enable researchers to trace the evolution of ideas in the judiciary independently from personal ties and interactions between judges as well as abstracted from their conscious decisions.

The judiciary is called a state 'organ' or a 'body', which are biological terms. This is not unappropriate. In admitting carefully selected new cells, through a protective porous membrane of rules, this body kept its sense of identity, while at the same time adapting to changing circumstances. One of the lessons from evolutionary biology is that boundaries are never absolute, but that they are relative, changeable and porous. This is also the case with social groups or bodies like the judiciary. As yet, the database seems to have some limitations in accommodating this aspect, as for example it does not include the non-Belgian judges in the Congo, and separates historical periods by strict boundaries, making it harder to assess the level of continuity between them.

Comparisons with other judiciaries would be very interesting, for example with the French, Dutch and Norwegian judiciaries under Nazi occupation: is there a clear prosopographical explanation possible for the differences in protesting style and capability?[49] Or with the prosopography of the judiciary in other colonies, such as the Netherlands Indies, especially the transition from VOC rule to Dutch colonial rule. Or, of course, with the French period in the northern Netherlands.

The key aspects of the judiciary's development that can now be extensively studied with the aid of the database, seem to be professionalisation (from well-respected to well-trained lawyers?), composition (from traditional to intellectual elite?), and its position in the system (from implementation to review of government policies?). Group dynamics, perceptions of identity and its pollution, and the influence of periods of foreign rule may well prove important factors in the historical trajectory of the Belgian judiciary.

---

[46]Cf. D.S. Wilson, *Darwin's Cathedral. Evolution, Religion, and the Nature of Society*, Chicago, The University of Chicago Press, 2003, esp. pp. 20–37.

[47]H.E. Hale, "Explaining Ethnicity", in *Comparative Political Studies*, (37) 2004-4, pp. 458–485.

[48]See, for example, Van Vugt, M., & Kameda, T. "Evolution and groups", in J.M. Levine (Ed.), *Group processes*, New York, Psychology Press, 2012.

[49]Cf. Venema, "The Judge, the Occupier".